THE ILLUSTRATED
ENCYCLOPEDIA OF
HERBS

THE ILLUSTRATED ENCYCLOPEDIA OF
HERBS

THEIR MEDICINAL AND CULINARY USES

EDITED BY
SARAH BUNNEY

FROM A TEXT BY
JIŘÍ STODOLA AND JAN VOLÁK

ILLUSTRATED BY
FRANTIŠEK SEVERA

CHANCELLOR
PRESS

PUBLISHER'S NOTE

This book contains information on a wide range of plants that are, or can be used in the treatment of human disorders. It is primarily intended to be read as a source of interesting information and not as a practical guide to self-medication. To anyone who is tempted to use any of the information in a practical way we should like to point out that several of the plants are poisonous, some extremely so, and some which are beneficial in small doses can be harmful if taken to excess or for long periods. The full effect of many others is incompletely known as they have never been fully investigated. For these reasons many plants should not be used for self-treatment without first consulting a qualified medical or herbal practitioner. We should like to stress that we regard the use of *any* plant or derivative as being entirely at the reader's own risk and we hereby disclaim all legal responsibility for any harmful or unwanted effects that might arise from such use.

Edited by Sarah Bunney
from a text by Jiří Stodola and Jan Volák
Translated by Ivan Kuthan and Olga Kuthanová
Graphic design by František Prokeš
Colour illustrations by František Severa
Line drawings by František Severa

English edition first published 1984 by Octopus Books Ltd under the title *The Illustrated Book of Herbs*

This 1992 edition published by
Chancellor Press
Michelin House
81 Fulham Road
London SW3 6RB

© 1984 Aventinum, Prague

ISBN 1 85152 135 6

Printed in Czechoslovakia by Neografia, Martin
3/13/07/51-05

Contents

Preface

Although far fewer plant-based remedies are used by doctors today than 100 years ago, this does not mean that medicinal herbs and drugs made from them have been totally abandoned by the medical profession. With the great increase in the number of synthetic medicines made by the pharmaceutical industry during the past decades it is easy to forget that plants still provide the raw material for the preparation of medicines that cannot be produced synthetically at all or, if they can be, the cost of manufacturing them remains prohibitive. Such essential medicines include those extracted from Ergot Fungus (ergometrine and ergotamine), foxgloves (digitoxin and digoxin) and Opium Poppy (morphine and its derivatives). We must also not forget the important antibiotics prepared from *Penicillium* and other moulds. Many other herbs more familiarly known in the kitchen or sweetbox than in the medicine cupboard, such as Anise, Caraway, Fennel and Liquorice, also still have a useful place in medicine as flavourings for drugs and as treatments for minor complaints. Furthermore, many herbs used for medicinal purposes also continue to have an important part to play in the tobacco, brewing, wine and perfume industries and, increasingly, in cosmetic manufacture.

What, though, has happened to the tried and trusted herbal remedies of old? The days have gone when doctors knew about medicinal plants and prescribed herbal preparations as a matter of course. Fortunately for us today, however, the accumulated traditional knowledge of past centuries has not been forgotten because it has been preserved in the writings and practice of herbalists. Plant preparations also feature prominently in homeopathic medicine, which has a more recent history.

It is true that there was a low point earlier in this century in interest in natural substances; synthetics were thought to be the answer to almost everything. The swing away from the natural world and medicinal herbs, however, seems to have been halted. To everybody's benefit the healing properties of herbs are at last being scientifically investigated. This research is going on in two main directions. One is the examination by modern chemical and physico-chemical techniques of the active constituents of well-known plants used in medicine and as home remedies, and the testing of their therapeutic effects by means of clinical trials. This research will ultimately provide a much-needed scientific basis for the comparison of herbal and synthetic remedies. Another important research topic is the search for new drugs among known plants or in new plant species waiting to be discovered in unexplored parts of the world, such as tropical forests. It is unfortunately already too late for us to learn about some potentially useful plants because of the destruction of so many tropical forests in Africa, Asia and America, but there still remain thousands of new species for scientists to investigate. The collection of folklore from indigenous peoples about the healing properties of plants is another very useful line of research that national governments and international bodies such as the World Health Organization are now actively encouraging.

There is much mystique surrounding herbal plants. This is a pity. Although many herbal remedies still in use today undoubtedly have beneficial actions and have an important part to play in modern medicine, they are not the panaceas they are sometimes claimed to be. Medicinal plants will never replace all synthetic products — nor the surgeon's scalpel. Because they are 'natural' substances it should not be assumed that medicinal herbs are completely safe and free from side-effects. Like any foreign chemicals introduced into the body many normally harmless medicines can be poisonous if taken to excess in strong doses or over a long period of time. They may react adversely with other medicines or foods that are being taken or aggravate a pre-existing condition. The precise pharmacological effect of most herbal remedies is still not known. For this reason it is inadvisable for pregnant women to take any herbal preparation internally (except for the mildest of herbal teas), especially during the early stages of pregnancy. Professional advice should be sought too before children are dosed with herbal medicines. Many of the well-known potent herbal remedies of old are now considered far too dangerous for herbalists — or even doctors — to prescribe. Such plants should *never* be used for home treatment.

This book is not intended as a practical manual. Rather it is a reference source on a wide range of some 250 medicinal herbs, some of which have been used for centuries — even thousands of years — for curing ills of various kinds and have provided foods and flavourings as well. Inevitably the described plants include a number that are poisonous (marked ☠ in the plates section), some extremely so (marked with ☠ ☠). There are, however, many other herbs that are much safer to use, though we strongly advise the seeking of professional guidance before any is taken for a specific complaint. Several of the plants will already be familiar as culinary herbs.

Accompanying each plate is a short botanical description and notes on the British distribution, the derivation of the names, any pertinent historical use, the part used in medicine, the principal chemical constituents and their main effects, how the plant is used in conventional medicine or in herbalism today, and edible parts. Cautionary notes on use have been added where necessary. The plants are arranged in alphabetical order of their botanical, not common, names. The recommendations of the *Flora Europaea* are followed in the main and where, for production reasons, there is slight deviation from this modern authority on plant classification, the recommended name is indicated by an equals sign and is indexed. Many of the included herbs have as their specific names *officinalis* or *sativus;* the former epithet indicates that the plant has long been used medicinally; the latter means a cultivated plant. Some plants have a subsidiary scientific name prefixed by the abbreviation 'syn'. These names have been rejected or superseded but are included for reference because they are used in older herb books or botanical field guides. The botanical names – in Latin – are followed by the preferred English common name in bold type, with some of the alternatives. At the top left-hand side of the text page is the name of the family to which the plant belongs. Unfamiliar botanical and medical terms are explained in the two glossaries at the end of the book.

Preceding the plates are background chapters on the history, cultivation, constituents and therapeutic effects of medicinal herbs, and notes on some treatments. For reasons of space these sections deal in only the briefest way with the subjects, but further information will be found in the books mentioned in the reading list at the end of the book. As sensible and modern introductions to herbalism we recommended *Green pharmacy* and *The home herbal* by Barbara Griggs, and *Encyclopaedia of herbs and herbalism* edited by Malcolm Stuart.

History of herbalism

Ancient Egyptian and Mesopotamian medicine

The medicines and medical knowledge of the ancient Egyptians are revealed to us by medical hieratic papyri. The most precious of these is the Edwin Smith Surgical Papyrus from the first half of the 17th century BC – a copy of an older papyrus from 2980–2700 BC. Next oldest are the gynaecological hieratic papyri from Kahun and Gurob and the Ebers Papyrus. Other existing priestly papyri and fragments are prescription manuals copied by medical students.

Magic was still included in some ancient Egyptian prescriptions, which often featured exorcisms against diseases. Some 400 substances were prescribed as medicines, all of which one would probably have found in an Egyptian pharmacy of that time. In a first group of medicines were blood, meat, horns, eggs, milk, honey, urine, faeces, and other substances of animal origin. In a second group were substances of plant origin, such as trees – for example, Carob or Locust Tree (*Ceratonia siliqua*), Cedar (*Cedrus libani*), Date Palm (*Phoenix dactylifera*), Fig Tree (*Ficus carica*), Olive Tree (*Olea europaea*), the palm *Hyphaene coriacea*, Peach Tree (*Prunus persica*), Pomegranate (*Punica granatum*), Storax (*Styrax officinalis*) and Sycamore (*Ficus sycomurus*). Also in this second category were other plants, for example Anise, barley (*Hordeum* spp.), beans (*Phaseolus* spp.), Caraway, Castor-oil Plant, Coriander, Cucumber (*Cucumis sativa*), Dill, Ergot Fungus, Garlic, grapes (*Vitis* spp.), lettuce (*Lactuca* spp.), Lotus (*Nymphaea lotus*), Onion, poppies (*Papaver* spp.), reeds (e.g. *Cyperus edulis*), Sugar Cane (*Saccharum officinarum*), Watermelon (*Colocynthis* spp.) and wheat (*Triticum* spp.). The leaves, flowers, fruits, roots, resin, juice, oil, wood, sawdust, ash and even smoke from plants were used in treatments. Among the minerals used were alabaster, alum, antimony, baked clay, kaolin, lapis lazuli, lead, saltpetre and sea salt. Solid medicines were dispensed in the form of powders, pills, suppositories, lumps and cakes, and, for external application, ointments, mushy pastes and dough.

Three examples of old Egyptian prescriptions are:
For roundworms: Let root of pomegranate stand overnight in water, strain and drink during the day.
For the complexion: Make equal parts of honey, red saltpetre and sea salt into a paste and spread over the skin.
To prevent build-up of urine: Mix wheat, dates, cooked carob and water in the proportions 1 : 2 : 2 : 6, press through a sieve and take over a period of four days.

These prescriptions are still valid. Present-day prescriptions would read somewhat differently but the effect would be the same.

Mesopotamian prescription manuals

We know of the medicinal substances of Babylonian medicine from cuneiform tablets, painstakingly kept records of drugs, the oldest of which dates from as far back as the Sumerians. Medicinal herbs were the principal raw material for medicines (*materia medica*) between the Euphrates and Tigris.

Mardukapal-Iddina II (772–710 BC) of Babylon built a garden where 64 species of medicinal plants were grown, including Apple (*Malus sylvestris*), Asafoetida (*Ferula foetida*), Box, Caraway, Coriander, Cucumber, Dill, Fennel, Garlic, Juniper, Liquorice, Marrow, mustards, Myrrh (*Commiphora myrrh*), Oleander (*Nerium oleander*), Onion, Pomegranate, purslanes (*Portulaca* spp.), roses (*Rosa* spp.) and Saffron. Classed as potent plants were Hemp, Hellebore (*Helleborus niger*), Henbane, Mandrake (*Mandragora officinarum*) and Opium Poppy.

Unlike ancient Egyptian prescriptions, those of the Babylonians gave neither weights nor measures. It seems that there was a tacit understanding among physicians as regards the matter of dosage. Only occasionally does one come across a notation. Thus, for example, the following doses are given for a tea mixture stimulating the flow of bile: 10 shekels of pine resin, 10 shekels of galbanum (a bitter gum resin), mustard and glasswort (*Salicornia* spp.). Also the time

when the medicine was prepared and administered was considered very important. Night and early morning before sunrise were both thought to be propitious. Beverages (decoctions from herbs) and infusions were generally prepared in the evening and taken by the patient in the morning before eating. Medicines were often administered with honey, oil, water, or wine and milk, and, since they were usually unpleasant concoctions, the patient was supposed to gulp them down without tasting them.

According to R. C. Thompson, the Mesopotamian prescription manual includes some 250 plants, 120 mineral substances, and 180 animal and other medicines, some of which have not yet been deciphered. Many, as is evident, were also used by the Egyptians; and both the Egyptian and Mesopotamian *materia medica* were used by the ancient Greeks and Romans, and later also by the Arabs.

India — treasure house of drugs and spices

Ancient Hindu philosophy recognized an eternally repeated cycle of creation and believed that the mysterious forces of nature could be harnessed by means of magic formulae. These have been preserved in priestly collections such as the *Rg Véda*, where we find an apotheosis of medicinal herbs that deifies the herbs and begs them to heal the afflicted.

The principal aim of ancient Hindu medicine was to prolong life, and one of the most important things in medical science was a knowledge of medicinal materials. Drugs were primarily of plant origin and to this day vast numbers of medicinal plants are to be found in the subcontinent.

Ancient tradition says of the plants that:

they should be collected only by a respectable native of the jungle, a man pious and clean, who has duly fasted beforehand. Fresh plants are the most potent. They should be collected only in places difficult of access to man, places with good soil and run-off of water, places without temples or shrines or burying grounds. The herb itself should be firmly rooted, well supplied with water, exposed to the heat of the sun as well as shaded during the course of the day, and facing north.

Herbal medicines prepared by the Hindus were of two kinds: the first cleansed the body and had an emetic or cathartic action, or stimulated the flow of nasal secretions as in the case of the head cold; the second were sedatives. Thus, for example, a hot milk decoction made from the flour of unripe barley seeds and butter was prescribed for fever. Coughs were treated with molasses diluted with water, honey and pepper. Medicines prescribed by mouth were taken with clarified butter, honey or sesame oil. Medicines could also be taken in the form of pills or in powder form with sugar, and were also administered through a hollow tube. The narcotic drug obtained from Hemp was known to the Aryans before the Hindu culture was established. In the *Vágbhat* textbook of medicine, a kind of anaesthetic is mentioned and the so-called Bower manuscript includes an ode to the healing properties of Garlic.

Hindu drugs became known throughout Asia and also found their way into the pharmacopoeias of eastern countries. Europe has India to thank for its spices and many irreplaceable medicines, including Aloe (*Aloe vera*), the resin benzoin, Caraway, Cardamom (*Elettaria cardamomum*), castor oil from the Castor-oil Plant, Clove (*Syzygium aromaticum*), Ginger (*Zingibar officinale*), Hemp, Nutmeg (*Myristica fragrans*), Black Pepper (*Piper nigrum*), Sandalwood (*Santalum album*), sesame oil from Sesame (*Sesamum indicum*) and Sugar Cane.

China and the *Pen-Ts'ao Kang-Mu*

In ancient China, pharmacology (the science dealing with the effect of drugs on living organisms) was the most thoroughly elaborated branch of medicine, next to the popular practice of acupuncture. The compendium entitled *Pen-Ts'ao Kang-Mu,* reputed to be the work of the Emperor Shen-nung (3737−2697 BC), in its final published version of AD 1597 contains a vast number of plant and animal substances used as drugs − far more than the medicinal assortment of all other nations. The Chinese believed that for every ill there was a corresponding natural remedy. And so, over the centuries, they compiled this compendium, which describes many effective medicines as well as uninvestigated or perhaps ineffective substances. One such material is Ginseng root (*Panax pseudoginseng*), whose medicinal effects have not yet been fully investigated although it is used throughout Europe for a wide range of afflictions from infertility and ageing to cancer.

Modern medicine is indebted to the Chinese for many plants and medicines. These include Star Anise (*Illicium verum*), Camphor (*Cinnamomum cam-*

Old Chinese pictures of two plants with similar medicinal properties and fruits of similar shape − Vegetable Marrow (see Pl. 78) and Egg Plant or Aubergine (*Solanum melongena*).

phora) and ephedra or ma-huang (*Ephedra* spp.). The Chinese also introduced into Western medicine Monkshood and the alkaloid isolated from it (aconitine), Pomegranate root, and the minerals arsenic, iron, mercury and sulphur.

The pharmacopoeia *Pen-Ts'ao Kang-Mu* in its final version contains 8,160 prescriptions prepared from 1,871 substances, mostly of plant origin. The medicines were administered in the form of decoctions, mixtures, powders, pills, plasters, suppositories and ointments. Besides the medicinal herbs already mentioned, other efficacious herbal remedies used by the Chinese include many common in Europe, such as Greater Burdock, Caraway, Castor-oil Plant, Daisy, Sweet Flag, gentians, Liquorice, Peach, Pomegranate, Rhubarb, Ribwort Plantain, China Tea (for coughs, colds, headache, diarrhoea) and Walnut. But it is difficult for us to comprehend the use by their physicians of various animal organs such as tiger hairs and whiskers, the tips of antlers, toad slime, rhinoceros horn, snake meat and sea molluscs. They also made wide use of human organs and human body waste.

Opium, the dried latex from the unripe capsules of the Opium Poppy, does not appear in Chinese medicine until after 1000 BC − and then as a drug for treating diarrhoea and dysentery. It was not smoked in any quantity until, in the 16th century, during the reign of the last emperor of the Ming dynasty,

Chinese tin tea box. Ming dynasty, 16th century.

alcoholic beverages were banned and opium was used as a substitute.

Physicians of history

In former times physicians prepared their medicines themselves from material supplied by collectors of roots and dealers in crude drugs. Their number also included charlatans who prepared various 'miraculous' medicines, beautifying agents and love potions, as well as various poisons. Most physicians were, however, seriously interested in medicinal plants and left to posterity drawings and descriptions of plants, including notes as to their effects.

Hippocrates, called the father of clinical medicine even in the Middle Ages, was purportedly born in the year 460 BC on Kos, a Greek island in the Aegean Sea, and died c. 377 BC in the city of Larissa in Thessaly on the Greek mainland. He was one of the Asclepiadae, a group of physicians named after Aesculapius, Greek god of healing and medicine, depicted in most Greek statues holding a staff entwined by a snake.

In ancient Greece the physician learned his art in the same way as any craft — as an apprentice. Hippocrates became the symbol of Greek medicine, medical virtues and moral principles, good judgement, self-denial and sacrifice. Hippocrates' principles — his medical ethics — remain valid to this day, although nearly 2,500 years separate our time from

his. With his extraordinary wisdom, Hippocrates realized how extremely difficult it was, in the working conditions of his day, to determine the causes (aetiology) of a disease and to cure or relieve its effects. He first and foremost viewed medicine philosophically, rather as an art of healing than as a science, and thus, given the conditions of his day, arrived at the conclusion that 'Life is short, the path of art long, a moment ephemeral, experience deceptive, judgement difficult'.

According to Hippocrates, the bodily functions are dependent on the equilibrium of four main principles: earth, water, fire and air. The representatives of these four basic principles in the human organism are the four body fluids or cardinal humours: blood, phlegm, yellow bile and black bile. When these are in harmony a person is healthy; when there are changes, for instance when they occur in excessive amounts or when there is a change in temperature, then a person becomes ill. This theory of body fluids (humoral theory) influenced the further development of medical science and held its own for a very long time. Hippocrates' writings also refer to numerous medicinal plants, including many narcotic drugs of antiquity such as Deadly Nightshade or Belladonna, Henbane, Mandrake and Opium Poppy.

Hippocrates' day also marks the arrival of the belief (in the Middle Ages known as the Doctrine of Signatures), which held that the shape and appearance of drugs and plants indicated the disease they were intended to treat (theory of similarity), that Nature herself indicated the medicinal effect (*natura signa*). Thus, for example, the yellow rhizomes of Rhubarb were used to treat hepatitis, the spotted leaves of Lungwort for lung diseases, the red flowers and fruits of Pomegranate to check bleeding, and the like. This theory survived until medieval times and even later.

The fame and medical successes of Greece's medical profession spread throughout the countries bordering the Mediterranean and the steps of their physicians led mainly to Rome, where many made brilliant careers.

Claudius Galenus or Galen (AD 130−c. 201) was born in Pergamom, Asia Minor. He began as a physician in the school for gladiators in Alexandria and later was personal physician to the Emperor Marcus Aurelius in Rome. He made use of Hippocrates' experience and writings but also pursued his own studies on his travels, publishing the results in eleven books. His works were the foundation of medical science for many centuries, and his classification of plant drugs and the medicines prepared from them into groups was widely followed. He is the founder of galenic pharmacy (the science of preparing medicines) and even to this day remedies prepared from plant and animal material are called galenicals.

Pedanius Dioscorides, of the first century AD and another Greek, served as military physician under the Roman emperor Nero. He collected medicinal plants in many countries around the Mediterranean Sea and described them, with information about their use, in his five-volume treatise *De Materia Medica* published in about AD 78.

This store of knowledge contained in the Greek and Roman texts of the times later served as the foundation of the pharmaceutical practice of the Arabs, who read them in Syrian and Old Persian translations and who came to dominate the Mediterranean world of the seventh century AD. Later, when they brought their learning and expertise to Spain by conquest, their lead in the practice of clinical medicine spread throughout Europe.

Famous Arab physicians

The first Moslem to make extensive use of the translated writings was Abú Bahr Mohammad ibn Zakarijá ar-Rází, known as Rhazes (*c.* AD 865—925), of northern Persia. For a time he was physician and teacher at the hospital in Baghdad and was considered to be an outstanding clinician and excellent diagnostician. He wrote many textbooks on medicinal sub-

Large 16th-century apothecary vessel (*alberello*) from Italy.

stances, first and foremost *Kitáb al-Mansúrí* (*Liber Almansoris*) as well as 24 volumes of medical texts including a vast number of medical prescriptions. The prescription for treating colic, for instance, includes Chamomile, Fennel, Fenugreek and the seeds of Quince.

The greatest Arabian physician was Abú Alí Síná, known as Avicenna (AD 980—1037). He was an exceptionally talented student of all disciplines — he studied logic, geometry, metaphysics, philosophy, medicine, astronomy and the other natural sciences of his day as well as translations of ancient authors. At the age of 17 he became a renowned physician in Bukhara and his fame spread as far as Baghdad. During his seven years as court physician in Isfahan (1014—21), he completed his *Canon of Medicine* (*Canon Medicinae*), a medical treatise in Arabic. The most efficacious medicines of his day, primarily of plant origin, were described by him in the second volume of the *Canon of Medicine,* dealing with pharmacology. In it he describes 811 medicinal substances, drugs as well as minerals, and at the same time explains their effect on the human body. The medicinal plants in his treatise are of Indian, Tibetan, Chinese and oriental origin, though not all have been identified. Besides herbs Avicenna also used mercury. He was acquainted with Camphor, Chamomile, Lavender, Senna (*Cassia angustifolia*) and Rhubarb. He introduced glucose treatment with fruits that had

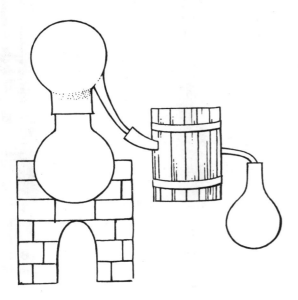

Medieval distillation apparatus used by European and Arab alchemists.

a high concentration of sugar, and likewise used complex medicines. He also used numerous dressings, cuppings and compresses, enemas, massages, and other methods of treatment, including extension of fractured and dislocated limbs. Before his death Avicenna gave away his entire estate and freed his slaves. For six centuries he was known as the 'prince of physicians', and still stands as a representative of progressive medical science and a model for educated people throughout the world.

From the Middle Ages to the present day

In the early Middle Ages the monasteries became the centres of medical learning as the monks copied manuscripts and recorded the medicinal effects of various plants. Of great importance in spreading the cultivation of medicinal herbs and the knowledge and practice of folk medicine was an edict of the Holy Roman Empire issued in AD 812 towards the end of the reign of Charlemagne, ordering towns and monasteries to grow vegetables, medicinal plants, flowers and trees.

In the twelfth century, Hildegarde of Bingen, Germany (1098–1179), prophetess and herbalist, became famous with her two treatises, *Physica* and *Causae et Curae,* which played an important role in the evolution of German names for medicinal herbs (which probably appeared here for the first time along with the Latin names).

In Salerno, Italy, the tenth century saw the establishment of a school of medicine, based on the classic authors of antiquity as well as on Arab medical science, which became the model for later universities. At this school, Arab treatises were translated by the illustrious Constantine of Carthage (1020–87), also known as Constantinius Africanus, who taught there from about the year 1050. Widely acclaimed, also, was the treatise *Antidotarium Salernitanum* (*c.* 1125) by Nicolaus Praepositus. However, the best-known treatise and the one that made the Salerno school famous far and wide was their *Regimen Sanitatis Salernitanum* (Regimen of Health), a comprehensive work on medicinal plants and hygiene.

Plant drugs recommended by the Salerno school were readily available in the Mediterranean region. North of the Alps, however, it was a different matter; there it was necessary to find among the indigenous species of the region substitutes for many imported medicinal plants, or else to cultivate them. In accord-

ance with Charlemagne's edict of 812, this cultivation was carried out mostly in the monasteries, where the first botanical gardens of medicinal plants were established alongside the hospitals of the various monastic orders.

After the decline of the Salerno school, its members, led by Arnoldus of Villa Nova (*c.* 1235–1313), attempted to revive the fame of that institution. That was how the Montpellier school came into being. Although the latter was never of the stature of the Salerno school, it produced several outstanding physicians, among them the famous Guy de Chaulias, the surgeon who treated John of Luxembourg, King of Bohemia, for his blindness.

Main room of a medieval pharmacy (*officina*) as depicted in an old engraving.

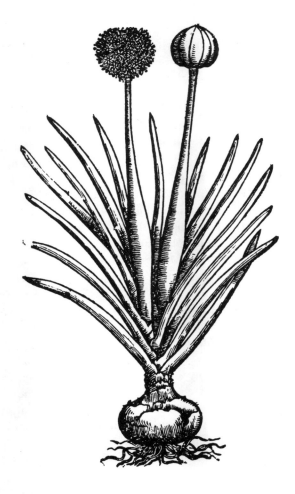
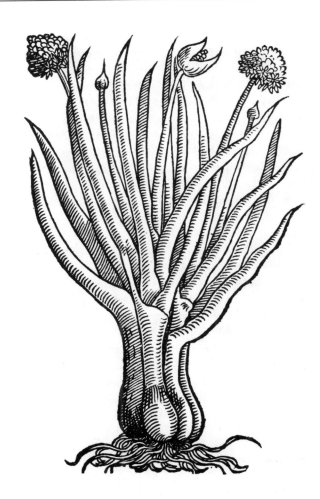

Page from the *Commentarii* by Mattioli or Matthiolus published by Daniel Adam of Veleslavin in Bohemia in 1596.

The evolution of herbal healing from the end of the twelfth century was sporadic. New knowledge accrued slowly, and the old was forgotten. The thinking of scholars of that time was dominated by scholasticism — fruitless learned disputations and philosophizing that intentionally avoided direct observation and impeded progress in the natural sciences. In those days trade in drugs and medicines was via Alexandria, the Levant, Florence and Venice. One who made a name for himself in botany and medical science at that time was the scholar Albertus Magnus (*c.* 1200–1280), Bishop of Regensburg, who wrote six treatises on healing with plants. In the first half of the 14th century, Simon of Genoa and Mattaeus Sylvaticus revised and compared the Arabic and Greek names of plants with their Latin equivalents, thereby facilitating the work of later herbalists.

The spread of knowledge about medicinal plants was given impetus by two revolutionary events — the invention of printing by Gutenberg in 1450 and the discovery of America by Columbus in 1492. The direct result of these events was the appearance of numerous printed herbals and the importation of foreign plants to Europe.

The general populace had long needed a book about healing and the use of plant medicines and the year 1484 saw the publication, in Mainz, of a herbal by an anonymous author entitled *Herbarius Moguntinae Impressus,* which described the drugs sold at that time in pharmacies by means of drawings made from live plants. This herbal was published several more times, in Germany, Holland, Passau, Venice and Vicenza. Its great popularity led to the printing in German of a much larger work, the *German Herbarius* or *Gart der Gesundheit* (Garden of Health) in 1485.

The late 14th and early 15th centuries saw the transition from accounts of merely the medicinal effects of various plants to botanical descriptions; in other words, to the foundation of the scientific study of botany. In 1530 Otto Brunfels, one of the Rhine authors of herbals known as the 'fathers of botany' – *patres botanicae* – published illustrations made from living material of the plants in the vicinity of Strasbourg in his *Herbarum Vivae Eicones.* In 1542 Leonhard Fuchs or Fuchsius, Professor of Medicine at Tübingen, published his *De Historia Stirpium,* with pictures arranged alphabetically according to the Greek names of the plants. In his book *Neu Kreüter Buch* published in 1539, Hieronymus (Jerome) Bock, called Tragus, described herbs, shrubs and trees according to their shape.

In 1583 the Italian Andrea Cesalpino published his great work *De Plantis Libri,* in which he describes the nourishment of plants and their propagation. Credit for knowledge about plant drugs goes to the 'fathers of pharmacognosy' – *patres farmakognosiae* – Valerius Cordus (1515–44) of Erfurt, who wrote many treatises on medicinal plants, in which he also described drugs from the New World; Nicolás Monardes of Seville (*c.* 1493–1578), who, in his treatise *Historia Medicinae,* described Sarsaparilla (*Smilex regelii*) and Sabadilla (*Schoenocaulon officinale*); and the famed

Famed alchemist Leonhart Thurneysser of Thurn (1530–96). Wood engraving from the portrait collection of the Vienna National Library.

French botanist Carolus Clusius (Charles de l'Ecluse) (1526–1609), who wrote dispensatories and antidotaria (an obsolete term for a book dealing with antidotes to poisons), with descriptions of the medicinal effects of drugs and also prescriptions – pharmacopoeial articles of a sort. This period also marked the appearance, in Florence, of the first pharmacopoeia, *Antidotarium Florentinum,* an authoritative work containing a list and description of drugs and medicinal products.

The author of probably the most famous herbal was the Italian physician Pier Andrea Mattioli, also called Petrus Andreas Matthiolus (1500–77), who from 1544 was court physician to Emperor Ferdinand I and later also to Maximilian II. Mattioli's basic work is his commentary in Italian on the treatises of Dioscorides, written in 1544. (The illustrated Latin version was published ten years later.) By 1563, 32,000 copies had been sold – a truly remarkable number for a 16th-century book. Its popularity was confirmed by the number of further editions in Bohemia, Germany and Italy. Matthioli's popular herbal became the classic text on all that was known about native and exotic medicinal plants in the latter half of the 16th century. It marked the transition between the old herbals and later scientific books on plants with a pharmacological evaluation of their effects.

New discoveries, overseas collecting expeditions and printing technology contributed also to the development of pharmaceutical chemistry. The first to apply knowledge of chemistry to medical science was Phillippus Aureolus Paracelsus, born Theophrastus Bombastus von Hohenheim (1493–1541), whose personality and oeuvre went far beyond the bounds of his time. Hippocrates' theory of the four body fluids still prevailed in medicine, as did alchemy, charlatanism, and the exaggerated demand for exotic drugs for which people paid enormous sums. Among other things, Paracelsus rediscovered folk medicine and its basic soundness as he gained knowledge and experience on his travels throughout Europe. It was during his stay in Strasbourg that he compiled his own *Herbarius,* one of his most important works. In his day, the German market was flooded with foreign drugs and Paracelsus wrote that an abundance of medicinal herbs could be found in Germany itself, that every land had its own medicines and physicians as well as its own diseases.

Paracelsus was his own chemist and pharmacist, and his prescriptions were simple and effective. He had no use for the complicated and absurd treatments of that time and concerned himself with the medicinal effects of mineral waters and of native medicinal plants. He was, however, the first to introduce chemistry into therapy — he used numerous compounds of antimony, arsenic, copper, mercury, silver and gold. He entered the annals of history as the great reformer of medicine, expert on the effects of medicinal plants, and founder of iatrochemistry (the theory that all phenomena of life and disease are based on chemical action).

The further development of pharmaceutical chemistry and the recovery of active constituents from drugs was influenced by many notable chemists, physicians and pharmacists of the new era. Andreco Libavius (*c.* 1540—1616) wrote the solid treatise *Alchemia,* which became the first textbook of chemistry. A great chemist of his day was Johann Rudolph Glauber (1604—68), who discovered sodium sulphate — known to this day as Glauber's salt(s) (*sal glauberi*). Robert Boyle (1627—91), of Ireland, a prominent member of the Royal Society, became the founder of experimental and analytical chemistry. Another outstanding chemist and physician was Friedrich Hoffmann (1660—1742), known for his popular drops containing alcohol and ether (*spiritus aetheris*). One of Hoffmann's interests were essential oils.

Chemistry and pharmacy continued to develop concurrently. Baron Jons Jakob Berzelius (1779—1848), a Swedish chemist, discovered the elements selenium and thorium. The French pharmacists Jean-Baptiste Caventou (1795—1877) and Pierre-Joseph Pelletier (1788—1842) isolated the alkaloids quinine, emetine and caffeine; the German pharmacist Friedrich Wilhelm Adam Sertürner (1783—1841) isolated morphine and meconic acid from Opium Poppy; and the Heidelberg pharmacist P. L. Geiger (1785—1836), together with fellow chemist Germain Henri Hess (1802—50), isolated the alkaloids atropine, daturine, hyoscyamine, colchicine, coniine and aconitine.

Pharmacognosy — the science that deals with medicinal products of plant, animal or mineral origin in their crude or unprepared state — became a scientific discipline with the publication of *Handbuch der Pharmakognosie* by Swiss professor Alexander Wilhelm Oswald Tschirch (1856—1939).

Herbalism in Britain

Herbalism existed in the British Isles long before the Romans came — and went, leaving behind their herbs and healers who had learnt through them the classic lore of Hippocrates and Dioscorides. The herbal traditions of the British peoples, however, stretched much farther back in time; it is known, for example, that the Druids were skilled in their use of medicinal plants, which included their seven 'sacred' herbs — Clover, Henbane, Mistletoe, Monkshood, Pasqueflower (*Pulsatilla vulgaris*), Primrose and Vervain. The skills the Druids passed on were such that, in the period after the Romans, the Anglo-Saxons may have been ahead of their continental neighbours in their knowledge of the properties of medicinal plants.

Certainly by the time the first emissaries of Christianity arrived in the sixth century, there was a well-established school of healers operating from Myddfai in Wales, whose members were doctors rather than druidic priests. The monks in their turn spread their accumulated traditions of healing through their network of monasteries and abbeys, which acted as centres of learning and which had libraries containing manuscripts of extracts from the leading Greek and Roman texts on curative herbs. (Later, in the ninth century, translations into the vernacular were made of these by the express command of Alfred, King of Wessex.) The monks had the duty of care for the sick and each monastery would have an infirmary and a physic garden — physic meaning 'pertaining to things natural'. St Bartholomew's Hospital, London, founded in 1123 for the new order of Austin Canons, provided care not only for the sick but for the aged, women in childbirth, the crippled, and war wounded — in fact, anyone in need.

Outside the monasteries, the lady of the manor also cared for the sick of her household and estate with simple herbal remedies. Sometimes she possessed a copy of one of the popular books with descriptions and accounts of the properties of herbs, to which marginal notes and drawings of familiar local plants might be added. With the advent of printing and more translations into the vernacular, the possession of a herbal became less of a rarity and, consequently, a knowledge of herbal remedies and the necessary plants became more commonplace.

William Turner (1520—68), physician and father of English botany, produced *A New Herball* in instalments from 1551. Master-surgeon John Gerard (1545—1612) published *The Herball or Generall Historie of Plantes* in 1597, improving on a translation of a work by Rembert Dodoens and describing the plants and their location in detail. John Parkinson (1567—1650), apothecary to James I, in his *Theatrum Botanicum* (Theatre of Plants) of 1640, examined the

Copper engraving by H. Cock based on a drawing by Breughel showing the strict principles according to which the 'gardens of health' were founded.

uses of almost 4,000 species at a time when English physicians were turning to toxic metals as well as drastic physical measures in their fight against disease, mainly for the use of the privileged classes. The herbal *The English Physitian* (1652) by Nicholas Culpeper (1616–1654) was a popular counterblast to this dangerous 'new' medicine. Culpeper's subtitle, 'An astrolo-physical discourse of the vulgar herbs of this nation being a compleat method of physick, whereby a man may preserve his body in health; or cure himself, being sick for three pence charge, with such things onely as grow in England, they being most fit for English bodies', explains why this herbal had such great appeal among the general population, where the herbal remedy still prevailed, and in numerous enlarged editions came to form a major part of the stock-in-trade of the apothecary.

Discounting the astrological connotations and the Doctrine of Signatures — the theory that a similarity to the symptoms of the disease it was meant to cure was 'signed' upon the relevant herb — then prevalent (though they were gradually being supplanted by more scientific experimentation and study), there still lingered the belief that nature had provided in every plant the antidote to a particular disorder, if only the connexion could be discovered. It was probably this hope for potential remedies that led to the foundation of botanic and physic gardens at the universities of Europe. Oxford's garden dates from 1621 to 1632,

and Edinburgh's Royal Botanic Garden traces its history back to the physic garden created in 1699 in the King's Garden established at Holyrood in 1670.

Another famous herb garden, created for the Society of Apothecaries of London in 1673 and still in existence, is the Chelsea Physic Garden, which has as its aims: general education; scientific instruction and research in botany, including vegetable physiology; and instruction in technical pharmacology as far as the culture of medicinal plants is concerned. It cultivates a wide range of modern and historical medicinal and culinary plants, and has a large section laid out in a system of botanical family beds designed to show a possible evolutionary sequence.

Another link, John Evelyn (1620–1706), author and authority on landscape gardening, knew the Chelsea Physic Garden well and wrote of the plants he saw. His *Acetaria, a Discourse of Sallets* (1699) encouraged people to make use of herbs in their diet, but the attitude of the College of Physicians and organized medicine at this time was one of contempt for traditional herbal remedies — blood-letting, purging, prescriptions containing heavy metals, and a range of novel and expensive plant materials from the New World were the preferred treatments of the day.

The Compleat Herbal of Physical Plants (1694) by John Pechey (1655–1716) marked the end of the 17th century. The 18th century, with a large increase in urban population, saw the development of organic chemistry and use of better laboratory techniques leading to the isolation of the active constituents of medicines. Druggists stocked the highly toxic chemicals which their customers expected miracles from — in spite of John Wesley's (1703—91) crusading efforts and pamphlets aimed at 'the natural way of curing most diseases', which his *Primitive Physick* advocated.

By the 19th century, for the educated, botanic medicine had become a drawing-room discussion curiosity and only country people and certain industrialized factions in the north were left, in the main, relying on herbal remedies as were those disciples of the various enthusiasts for 'botanic medicine' who crossed over from the United States to lecture in Britain.

Orthodox medicine advanced very little in Victorian times and was still much given to prescribing antimony, arsenic, mercury, and other toxic substances. Strong opposition was shown to the healing art of homeopathy — that substances which are poisonous in their natural state can be used to cure, but to cure only that which they can cause, and that the use of minute doses is a necessary corollary of this principle — first expounded by Christian Samuel Hahnemann (1755—1843), a German with an international reputation as physician, scholar and chemist. However, homoeopathy has many adherents today; and its 'law of similars' has a close parallel in the use of vaccines in immunology.

In this century, hand in hand with great medical advances, there has been a marked renewal of interest in therapeutically useful plants, and a desire to establish herbalism on a scientifically documented level. The publication of the *British Herbal Pharmacopoeia* (Parts 1—3, 1976—81) by the British Herbal Medical Association is a landmark in the history of the subject and marks a more scientific approach to studies and uses of medicinal plants. Training of herbalists in Britain is in the hands of the National Institute of Medical Herbalists based in Tunbridge Wells. It conducts a four-year course in herbal medicine by correspondence or full-time study. After passing the final examinations herbal practitioners can apply to become a member — later a fellow — of the institute and are then allowed to use the initials MNIMH or FNIMH after their names.

Ways of obtaining medicinal herbs

The easiest — and surest — way of obtaining good-quality medicinal herbs or parts of them is to buy them from a qualified herbalist, a retail chemist or from a reputable specialist supplier, either over the counter or by mail order. Commercial growers collect herbs in the right conditions at the correct time of year and day, and they dry and store them in the best possible way. Buying herbs also takes away the worry about identifying the plant correctly. Unfortunately there are occasional cases of adulteration of herbs bought from trade sources. It is therefore important to choose only recommended suppliers. Herbs bought in this way are ready for use in the ways suggested later in this book, but beginners should always get professional advice before diagnosing and treating themselves. Most tea substitutes are, however, normally harmless.

Identification should usually not be a problem if the herbs have been grown in a private garden. The important medicinal or aromatic properties of the herb may, however, be lost if the herb is not collected, dried and stored in the correct way (see later).

Several of the medicinal herbs described in the pictorial part of this book are not native to the British Isles and either can never be found in the wild or are only rare escapes from cultivation. Among native British plants there are also several that are extremely poisonous and should never be collected by amateurs (see page 34). There are also several good reasons for not collecting even harmless, common wild herbs.

For one thing, identification can be tricky and it is all too easy for the inexperienced person to mistake one species for another closely related one. The wrong species may be harmless but have no medicinal action or it may have an unintended effect, or be highly dangerous. Because one part of a plant is edible (say the berries of a woodland species), it does not necessarily follow that the other parts are too. It is also extremely important not to pick a part of another species with the herb being collected. This book provides only the briefest botanical descriptions of plants in the illustrated part; **these are insufficient for identification purposes,** and other guides will need to be consulted. If wild herbs *are* collected expert advice should always be sought if there is any doubt about the identifying signs or about other aspects of herb collecting.

Another important reason for *not* collecting wild herbs in Britain is that nowadays there are few places, except in the remotest parts, which have not been in contact with chemical sprays and pollution. This means that herbs should never be collected from or near agricultural land, along roadsides and paths, near factories or sewage works, or from anywhere where the plants may have been exposed to chemicals, fertilizers, traffic fumes or industrial activity.

Even in localities free from such contamination there are now legal restrictions on what can be collected. In Britain under the Wildlife and Countryside Act 1981 it is illegal for anyone, without permission of the owner or occupier of a piece of land, to uproot *any* wild plant. This law means that roots and rhizomes of wild plants cannot be freely collected anywhere except on your own property. Furthermore, although none of the plants in this book is one of the 62 very rare British species now specially protected by law, some, such as Mezereon and Breckland (Wild) Thyme, are very uncommon in the wild and should never be collected in their natural habitats.

For all these reasons the collection of wild medicinal herbs is not recommended. Instead, herbs should be grown or bought as required. In gardens the right selection of herbs can provide not only a source of refreshing beverages and remedies for simple ailments, but a variety of foods and flavourings and also decoration both in the garden and indoors. Some ideas about which herbs to grow and basic guidelines about cultivating them in gardens, window-boxes and balconies are given in the next section.

Cultivation of medicinal and culinary herbs

The large herb and physic gardens of the past have practically disappeared from Britain and production of medicinal and culinary herbs on a commercial scale tends to be a specialized, small undertaking by contract, usually within easy reach of the factory concerned. The pharmaceutical and food manufacturers rely chiefly on imported dried supplies of herbs, often grown by peasant cultivators or collected from the wild. However, commercial cultivation of garden mints, Parsley, Sage and thymes has not diminished in Britain and these herbs find a ready market.

If a medicinal plant grows easily and in good numbers in the wild and it produces a good yield of active constituents, or takes several years to mature, in some countries it is still practicable to collect it from the wild. Nowadays, though, many medicinal plants have to be grown commercially. This happens when the wild plant has become rare or only grows in inaccessible places, when the yield of active constituents needs to be improved by breeding and pest control, or when there is government control over certain dangerous plants (Hemp, Opium Poppy), which then have to be grown under licence. Controlled cultivation also makes it easier to harvest and process the plants for use. Many countries therefore cultivate certain medicinal plants on a large scale, for their own use and for export to countries such as Britain, which, for climatic or other reasons, cannot grow them in useful quantities.

Although many medicinal and culinary herbs are now available in dried — and occasionally fresh — form from commercial suppliers, the private individual can get much pleasure from growing a selection of herbs in a small garden, a window-box or trough, or a series of pot containers. A few kitchen herbs can even be grown indoors. In a large garden, a model of an Elizabethan herb garden, laid out in decorative form with intertwining, ribbon-like hedges of low-growing clipped perennial herbs, can make a most attractive feature.

A list of plants that can be grown fairly easily by the enthusiastic amateur is given below. These herbs have been chosen for their relative 'safeness' and because of their moderate soil and climatic requirements. Common Nettle is not included in the list because most gardeners should have easy access to this weed, providing the plants have not been sprayed or are not near the roadside. Some Eastern spice herbs are also not included; they are best bought for use (in sealed containers) because the fruits rarely mature in Britain; others, such as Anise and Cumin, need a good summer in order to produce a crop.

Agrimony (*Agrimonia eupatoria*)
Angelica, Garden (*Angelica archangelica*)
Balm, Lemon (*Melissa officinalis*)
*Basil (*Ocimum basilicum*)
Bistort, Common (*Polygonum bistorta*)
Borage (*Borago officinalis*)
Burdock, Greater (*Arctium lappa*)
Burnet, Salad (*Sanguisorba minor*)
Catmint (*Nepeta cataria*)
Chamomile, Roman (*Chamaemelum nobile*)
Clover, Red (*Trifolium pratense*)
Coltsfoot (*Tussilago farfara*)
Comfrey, Common (*Symphytum officinale*)
Cowslip (*Primula veris*)
Dandelion (*Taraxacum officinale*)
Dill (*Anethum graveolens*)
Elecampane (*Inula helenium*)
Eyebright (*Euphrasia officinalis*)
*Fennel (*Foeniculum vulgare*)
Feverfew (*Chrysanthemum parthenium*)
Garlic (*Allium sativum*)
Goldenrod (*Solidago virgaurea*)
Hop (*Humulus lupulus*)
Horehound, White (*Marrubium vulgare*)
Lavender, Garden (*Lavandula angustifolia*)
Marigold, Pot (*Calendula officinalis*)
*Marjoram, Sweet (*Origanum majorana*)
Marshmallow (*Althaea officinalis*)
Mayweed, Scented (Wild Chamomile) (*Chamomilla recutita*)
Mullein, Large-flowered (*Verbascum densiflorum*)
Nasturtium (*Tropaeolum majus*)

Parsely (*Petroselinum crispum*)
Peppermint (*Mentha × piperita*)
Raspberry (*Rubus idaeus*)
Sage (*Salvia officinalis*)
St John's Wort, Perforate (*Hypericum perforatum*)
Tarragon (*Artemisia dracunculus*)
Thyme, Garden (*Thymus vulgaris*)
Valerian, Common (*Valeriana officinalis*)
Violet, Sweet (*Viola odorata*)
Yarrow (*Achillea millefolium*)

* For best results start the seeds of these herbs indoors.

Laying out and tending of a herb garden

From the practical point of view, a herb garden is best laid out on a slightly sloping site, bounded on its rear side by a bank, fence or wall, and facing south or west. Flagstones, paving slabs or a series of paths, make for an easy access and cultivation and for freedom from disease. The portion to be allocated to mints must have below-ground defences of tile, slate or stone to curb the spread of encroaching runners into neighbouring areas, or they can be grown in a separated bed or in earthenware containers with drainage. Care should be taken to plant the tallest herbs, such as Garden Angelica, Elecampane, Fennel, Goldenrod and mulleins, at the rear of the plot and the low-growing ones, such as dwarf forms of Eyebright, Nasturtium, and Sweet Violet, to the front.

First, since the site will be a permanent one, the ground must be deeply dug and fertilized with well-rotted organic material and a scattering of bone-meal. A soil pH that is close to neutral (7) should be aimed at. If the ground is heavy, sharp sand and weathered ash should be incorporated as good drainage is essential for most of the plants that will be cultivated, although Common Comfrey, Elecampane, Marshmallov and various mints are examples of species for which a good supply of moisture is preferable.

Generally, on heavy wet soils the leaves of herbs tend to be less aromatic, and, if drainage cannot be improved satisfactorily on a poor site, for instance by laying pipes or a percolation layer of rubble or pebbles at a depth of about 1 foot (30 cm), then a raised above-ground bed can be made, enclosed in a container or held within retaining walls of brick, stone or timber.

Perennial and biennial herbs will need a top

dressing each spring of good loam, a mulch of moist compost or peat round the plants in the early summer, and general tidying up and cutting down of dead growth at the end of the autumn. Regular fertilization will not be needed, and overwatering should be avoided. Pruning and/or picking should be a routine task, but insect-eaten and blighted or faded herbs should not be harvested.

Perennials should be lifted and the young, outer portions replanted about every four years; or they may be propagated by stem cuttings taken in spring or early summer. Root cuttings, taken in the autumn, and layering are other means of propagation. Biennials and annuals will perpetuate themselves by seeding around the parent plant, if given enough space, or they can be raised from seed in the usual way in a nursery bed or in seed trays.

Winter protection will be needed for certain half-hardy subjects such as Rosemary and Southernwood — bracken, leaves or straw pinned down with wire netting against the activities of blackbirds and gale-force winds are useful here. In northern Britain and in very severe frosts, such plants may have to be dug up and be brought indoors if they are to be saved. If they have been grown in tubs and are under cover already, the tubs themselves may need to have some extra outer covering as these are particularly vulnerable to frost. For those plants remaining outside, a winter mulch, put on after the ground has frozen, will guard against root damage in premature thaws.

Where space is limited, herbs can be grown in a window-box, or in pots on a window-sill or sheltered balcony in good light. The usual rules for such plantings should be followed but it is especially important to ensure that the drainage is adequate and that the soil is no more than barely moist. Natural fertilizers, rather than water-soluble chemicals, should be used, with the soil in the pots (which should contain some pieces of charcoal) being renewed once a year. Most of these suggestions also apply to indoor growing and to the cool greenhouse kept at a minimum night temperature of 50 °F (10 °C), remembering that sunlight is essential and rainwater beneficial.

Herbicides and insecticides should not be used for controlling weeds, plant diseases and parasites because of harmful residues which might remain. Hand weeding and hoeing will obviate the need for the former, and plants can be protected against the latter to some extent by scattering powdered charcoal, or crushed Basil or aromatic herbs mixed with wood ash around them — not forgetting the well-tried method of spraying with soapy water. Plants affected with rust should be dug up and burnt at the end of the season, and young Sage should be watched for signs of mildew and any infected leaves should be removed and burnt. Garlic, which should be moved to a fresh site each year, may act as an insect repellent — not always desirable, for instance near Basil, which requires insect pollination.

Collection, drying and storage of home-grown medicinal and culinary herbs

The collection of a leaf, flower cluster or some other plant part is followed by metabolic changes in the part removed. The cells begin to die as soon as their supply of water and nutrients ceases. If the separated parts are not immediately spread out in a thin layer to dry they begin to spoil from overheating and from condensation of moisture in the case of large quantities of material. The enzymes in the cells that

previously stimulated the formation of active constituents begin to break down these substances. As decomposition proceeds the chemical composition of the plant parts changes. Incorrect drying increases this effect and the herb then has a poor medicinal action.

The drying of medicinal herbs should therefore take place generally as soon as possible after harvesting, and it is important to collect the required part of the plant when it has reached its optimum point of growth — for leaves, this is just before flowering; for flowers, just before full bloom; for roots and rhizomes, when the aerial parts are beginning to wither and die. Bark should be gathered in spring or autumn. It may be best collected in damp weather because then it peels off easily from the wood. Other parts should, however, be gathered on a dry day, when they are not wet with dew or rain, as this causes decomposition and mould to grow during storage. The best collecting time is usually in the early afternoon, but some herbs need collecting early in the morning when the concentration of the active constituents is at its highest. Commercial growers of medicinal herbs have to be particularly careful about choosing the right time. In the garden care should be taken to ensure that medicinal herbs are not sprayed accidentally with chemical herbicides and insecticides.

Drying is a process by which water is gradually removed from the plant parts. Often it is necessary to wash roots and other underground parts briefly with cold water before drying to remove soil particles. Bark may also need washing. Any unwanted material should be discarded as this increases bulk and could cause adulteration. As a rule medicinal herbs are never dried in direct sunlight for they lose their potency and coloration. In the case of herbs containing essential oils the potency is reduced by as much as one third.

Leaves, stems and flowers must be dried until they become fragile and even the tougher parts break easily when bent. Drying time varies from a few days to several weeks, depending on the species and part being dried. Plants that have been dried for too long crumble into powder and the concentration of active constituents declines. On the other hand, if the plant parts are insufficiently dried there is always the danger that they will become mouldy or begin to ferment, and will spoil.

In Britain herbs will usually need to be dried by artificial heat because normal outdoor temperatures are unlikely to be sufficient. They can be dried in a temperature of about 90 °F (32 °C) for the first 24 hours, after which the temperature can be reduced. Thick underground parts and bark may need a higher temperature (up to 120 °F or 50 °C) to start with. When a large quantity of herbs is being dried it is best to spread the plant parts on wooden, slatted fruit-box trays, which can then be stacked one on top of the other when necessary and where it is relatively easy to turn the plant material as required to ensure proper access of air. The drying room should have plenty of circulating air, have a high ceiling and ideally be darkened. If necessary, because of the fineness of the material, the plant parts should be spread on clean white lining paper; never newspaper.

Plants can also be tied in bunches and strung up to dry, stem upwards, in flowing air, on lines across the drying room, but the bunches should be small enough to dry evenly and right through. Smaller amounts can be dried on a rack above a boiler as long as they are out of direct sunlight (put perhaps in open brown-paper bags), or in a warm attic off the floor, or even in a large warm airing cupboard. Drying herbs in the oven is not a good idea because water and oils in the herb evaporate too quickly that way. Each species of herb should be dried separately so that there is no chance of a mix-up. Some strong-smelling herbs (for example, Lovage and Sweet Flag) must be dried well away from other herbs. After the plant material has been dried careful attention should be paid to storage and to labelling.

Dried herbs are stored according to the character of their active constituents. They must always be stored in dark, dry, dust-free conditions, preferably in tightly stoppered glass containers, only temporarily in paper bags or boxes (large amounts in cloth sacks) protected from light and moisture. They should never be put into plastic containers or tins. Most herbs need replacing by a fresh supply after one year. Plants containing essential oils must be stored with great care loosely in brown-glass jars. The top parts of these herbs should not be cut either before or after drying so that the essential oils do not evaporate.

Some dried herbs are hygroscopic — they absorb moisture from the air. This can be sufficient to reactivate enzymes, which can cause chemical changes to occur. Such herbs should not be stored for too long. They include mullein flowers (their yellow colour turns brown if they absorb moisture), roots of Parsley and Garden Angelica, and Marshmallow. Some herbs actually improve in quality with storage (Great Yellow Gentian) or they may become safe to use only after at least a year (bark of Alder Buckthorn). Stored herbs should be frequently checked for signs of moisture, mould or insect attack and be discarded if necessary. Storage jars should always be clearly labelled with the name and part of the herb, the date collected and the date bottled. Further information about preparing, drying and storage of herbs for use is given in the text that follows, describing the various plant parts. A few more details are given in the text accompanying each colour plate of individual species in the pictorial section. Information not given in this book for reasons of space can usually be obtained from the many specialized herb books now available on the market.

Roots, rhizomes and bark

Roots and rhizomes are usually collected during the dormant period when they contain the greatest amount of active constituents; they may also be collected in early spring. In the case of perennials they are gathered in the second and third year of growth; in the case of annuals in the autumn of their first year. (In Britain, remember, it is illegal to dig up without permission any wild plants on land that does not belong to you.) Care should be taken not to bruise or cut the underground part while lifting it. Loose earth can be removed by washing under a strong jet of water. Roots and rhizomes should not be scrubbed with a brush as this may cause the loss of precious constituents — the epidermal (surface) cells of Common Valerian, for example, contain essential oil. All green parts should be removed before drying. Bark is best collected from young trunks or branches — preferably felled ones — when it should peel readily from the wood, especially in damp weather.

The turnip-like root of Mandrake (*Mandragora officinarum*) resembles the human body in shape. Mandrake contains poisonous tropane alkaloids with narcotic properties and was used in the Middle Ages for its magical as well as medicinal powers. It was believed to protect the owner from demons and to bring good luck; however, it had to be gathered only beneath gallows and in the company of a black dog, otherwise it had no effect!

The top parts of Common Centaury (see Pl. 52) contain efficacious bitter substances.

Thick tough roots and rhizomes may need to be cut in half lengthways and then into small pieces when fresh in order to dry properly. While drying they should be turned occasionally, and dried until they are fragile and break easily. Temperatures for these parts — and bark — can be up to 120 °F (50 °C) or maximum 140 °F (60 °C). During storage they should be checked for insect infestation. Some roots and rhizomes are peeled before drying (for example, Great Yellow Gentian, Liquorice and Marshmallow).

Flowering stems (aerial parts)

The aerial parts — or 'herb' — should be cut off with a sharp gardening knife or secateurs. They should never be broken off for this could damage the plant tissues and cells. The roots should be left in the ground to be harvested later or to make new growth. Only plants that are young and fresh should be gathered, in the case of tall plants only the top growth. Prostrate creeping plants such as Garden Thyme should be washed in water to remove soil particles.

Leaves

Leaves should be gathered before the flowering period, when they contain the greatest amount of active constituents. Some should be left on the plant to enable the process of photosynthesis to be maintained. The leaves should be young, juicy and healthy, without spots, which are often a sign of a viral disease, also free of insect pests and not faded or yellow. Care should be taken not to crush or bruise the leaves; they should not be stuffed or packed tightly in baskets or bags when being collected. The leaves of Black Currant, Marshmallow, Ribwort Plantain and Wild Strawberry readily begin to sweat in such condtitions. Leaves should be dried in thin layers so that they do not require frequent turning. They should not be in direct light or in temperatures above about 90 °F (32 °C), particularly in the case of leaves containing an essential oil.

Flowers

The best time to collect flowers is at midday, when they are first fully open, and in dry weather. Morning is not a good time and damp weather is likewise unsuitable. Flowers are usually picked by hand carefully, without touching the petals. Damaged or wilted flowers should be avoided. Because they readily begin to sweat they should be transported in a basket, never in plastic bags. Only the parts of some flowers are dried, such as the petals of Common Poppy, occasionally just the ray-florets of Pot Marigold, and the stigmas and styles of Maize. When dried correctly flowers should retain their original coloration. After a time, however, they may begin to turn brown or their scent changes, in which case they should be replaced by a fresh supply.

Fruits and seeds

Seeds are collected when fully ripe and fruits such as berries when just ripe, before they get soft. The whole flowerhead on its stalk is cut and hung over a tray to catch the seeds. Berries can be forked off their stalks when half dry. Fleshy fruits will need frequent turning during drying.

Freezing

Kitchen herbs can be frozen either in aluminium foil, cut up in water in ice trays or in plastic bags. This method is not suitable for herbs wanted for therapeutic purposes, but for cooking, freezing is better and can be more convenient than drying.

Active constituents of medicinal herbs

Medicinal plants prepared as herbal remedies contain numerous chemical substances, some of which affect the human body. These 'active' constituents (or 'principles' as they are sometimes called), their structure and location in the plant, the chemical changes and processes that take place during the plant's life cycle and during the preparation and storage of the plant material are the sciences of plant chemistry (phytochemistry) and pharmacognosy. Closely allied to these subjects is pharmacology, which deals with the physiological effect of these medicinally active substances on the body, takes note of the mechanism and rapidity of this effect, the absorption and elimination of the substances and their uses in treating various diseases.

The active constituents of plants are of two kinds: (1) Products of primary metabolism, chiefly carbohydrates (for example, sugars and starch), amino acids and fatty (fixed) oils, which are substances produced by light-absorbing (photosynthetic) processes in plants. (2) Products of secondary metabolism (processes resulting in the production of chemicals from the primary metabolites). These latter products may often seem useless to the plant but may in some cases be therapeutically very effective in the human body. They include essential (volatile) oils, glycosides, terpenoids and important alkaline substances called alkaloids, such as morphine from Opium Poppy and ergotamine from Ergot Fungus. The value of these substances to plants is largely a matter of conjecture.

Medicinally active constituents usually occur in plants in groups of closely related compounds together with other substances, and the various constituents in each group may potentiate each other's effect in the healing process. This synergistic action of plant compounds is considered by herbalists to be a great advantage in treatments with medicinal plants (phytotherapy). An example is opium, the dried juice (latex) of the unripe capsules of Opium Poppy, which contains several important alkaloids as well as other chemical substances. The physiological effect of the individual alkaloids is quite different from that of the combined group of drugs represented by opium; each has a specific, characteristic and different pharmacological effect in the body. The same is true of the cardiac glycosides from foxgloves. Even if a medicinal plant contains only one active constituent, some herbalists still believe that this vegetable substance has a more beneficial effect on the body and causes fewer harmful side-effects than the same chemical compound produced synthetically.

There are several modern methods of analysing the chemical constituents of medicinally active substances, among them thin-layer chromatography, paper chromatography, gas chromatography and high-performance liquid chromatography. Details of such methods are given in textbooks of analytical chemistry and in many pharmacopoeias or other official national drug compendia.

Many of the active constituents of medicinal plants are highly complex compounds and the precise chemical nature of some of them is still largely unknown. Others have been isolated, purified and crystallized and even synthesized from simpler substances. It is known that the constituents of a particular plant species can vary from one individual plant to another according to the part of the plant and to the time of year, time of day and the weather conditions when the material is collected. Most countries thus control the quality of certain plant drugs, especially the most potent ones, by issuing qualitative and quantitative standards the plant or extract from it must pass before it can be used in 'official' medicinal preparations.

The active constituents of plant drugs belong to several different chemical groups, among them alkaloids, glycosides, saponins, bitter compounds, tannins, essential or volatile oils, terpenes, resins, fatty or fixed oils, mucilages, pectins, mineral compounds, organic acids, vitamins and carotenoids.

Alkaloids

Alkaloids are a diverse group of basic compounds with alkaline properties and generally a marked physiological effect on the nervous and circulatory systems. They are often of complex structure, typically with heterocyclic rings containing nitrogen. They generally have a bitter flavour and most are poisonous to varying degrees. They show varied pharmacological effects: for example, they can act as analgesics, local anaesthetics, tranquillizers, vasoconstrictors, antispasmodics and hallucinatory agents.

Several thousand alkaloids are known, the most familiar medically being atropine, caffeine, codeine, coniine, morphine, nicotine and strychnine. Their function in plants remains unexplained. They could, for example, be by-products of metabolism; or their bitter taste may repel insects and other plants. Many more alkaloids remain to be discovered, especially in tropical plants, which tend to contain more alkaloids than plants growing in temperate regions.

Some alkaloids are liquid, some amorphous, but most are crystalline. They are insoluble in water, but soluble in organic solvents such as ethanol, ether and chloroform. Isolated alkaloids may have a more potent action than the plant material from which they have been extracted. Several isolated alkaloids — or their synthetic derivatives — have a great therapeutic value in medicine but because of their toxicity they must be used only by qualified medical personnel.

Plant families rich in alkaloids include the Solanaceae (nightshades), Leguminosae (peas), Papaveraceae (poppies), Apocynaceae (periwinkles), Rubiaceae (bedstraws), Liliaceae (lilies) and Amaryllidaceae (daffodils). Alkaloids are completely absent from some other families, for example Rosaceae (roses).

Alkaloids are divided into several groups according to their chemical composition and the amino acids from which they mainly derive. This book includes plants containing alkaloids derived from the following amino acids:

1. Phenylalanine: for example, *isoquinoline alkaloids,* such as morphine, codeine and papaverine (Opium Poppy) and colchicine (Meadow Saffron).

2. Tryptophan: for example, *indole alkaloids,* such as ergometrine, ergotamine and ergotoxin (Ergot Fungus).

3. Ornithine: for example, *tropane alkaloids,* such as scopolamine and atropine (Deadly Nightshade or Belladonna).

Some alkaloids are not derived from amino acids. For example, some of the *pyridine* and *piperidine alkaloids,* such as ricinine (Castor-oil Plant), trigonelline (Fenugreek) and the extremely toxic coniine

(Hemlock); the *steroidal alkaloids,* such as veratrine (False Helleborine) and dulcine (Bittersweet); and the *diterpene alkaloids* of Monkshood, such as aconitine.

Glycosides

Glycosides are products of secondary metabolism in plants. When hydrolysed (split by the action of water, acids or enzymes) they separate into two parts — one of several sugars (for example, glucose or fructose), called the glycone component, and the nonsugar (aglycone) component. Each glycoside is usually associated with an enzyme, but this occurs in different cells elsewhere in the plant. Crushing or ingesting the plant part breaks up the cells, the enzyme is brought into contact with the glycoside, hydrolysis occurs and the aglycone is activated. As a rule, the sugars have no therapeutic effect, but they increase the solubility of the glycoside and its absorption in the body and they can facilitate its transport to a specific organ. The therapeutically active constituent is the aglycone, which can selectively effect a particular organ in the body. Glycosides include some of the most effective plant drugs and some of the plants containing them are among the most toxic known.

Glycosides are classified according to the chemical composition of the aglycone part. Among the most important in modern medicine are the cardiac glycosides, which occur, for example, in the families Ranunculaceae (buttercups), Liliaceae (lilies), Asclepiadaceae (milkweeds), Scrophulariaceae (figworts), and Apocynaceae (periwinkles). So far several hundred have been isolated.

1. *Cardiac glycosides.* These glycosides affect the contraction of the heart muscles and are used to correct arrhythmias in the heartbeat (they are cardioactive substances). They are divided into two groups: *cardenolides* (in, for example, foxgloves and Lily-of-the-Valley) and *bufadienolides* (in, for example, Christmas Rose).

2. *Mustard glycosides* (*glucosinolates*). These glycosides contain bonded sulphur and are characteristic of mustards and other members of the Cruciferae (cabbage) family. They occur in plants together with the enzyme myrosinase. When the enzyme is activated — when, for example, mustard seeds are ground — it breaks down the glycoside into its sugar component (glucose) and its aglycone (an allyl isothiocyanate). The liberated isothiocyanates, called mustard oils, are antiseptic due to the activity of the sulphur compounds. Mustard glycosides are found in the seeds of Black Mustard, White Mustard and Nasturtium, and in Horseradish root.

3. *Cyanogenic glycosides.* In these glycosides the aglycone is a cyanohydrin compound bonded to sugar. Upon hydrolysis in the presence of an enzyme (say in the saliva of the mouth), poisonous hydrogen cyanide (prussic acid) is liberated, in trace or larger amounts. Cyanogenic glycosides have antispasmodic, purgative and sedative actions of varying potency. They are especially characteristic of some members of the families Rosaceae (roses), Leguminosae (peas), Caprifoliaceae (honeysuckles) and Linaceae (flaxes). For example, seeds of Bitter Almond, flowers of Blackthorn (Sloe) and Elder, and leaves of Dwarf (Sour) Cherry and Bird Cherry.

4. *Phenolic glycosides.* These glycosides have a wide range of chemical structures. They are divided into four main goups:

(a) *Simple phenolic glycosides.* These compounds contain a simple phenol. They have a characteristic effect and are usually aromatic. They include salicylic derivatives in, for example, willow bark, in Meadowsweet and poplar buds, and arbutin and methylarbutin in the leaves of Bearberry, Bilberry and Heather.

(b) *Coumarin glycosides.* These compounds are phenylpropane derivatives. They have a characteristic sweet smell of new-mown hay, which is most pronounced when the plants have been dried and is characteristically found in, for example, melilots and Woodruff. There are several different kinds of coumarin glycosides.

The *hydroxycoumarins* are found, for example, in Ash and Horse Chestnut. Aesculin, which occurs in Horse Chestnut bark, strengthens the walls of the capillaries (like the flavonoid rutin — see below). Another coumarin in Horse Chestnut, aesculoside, adsorbs ultraviolet radiation and is used in sunscreen preparations.

The *furanocoumarins* are found in several members of the Umbelliferae (carrot) family, including Garden Angelica and Masterwort. Some furanocoumarins are poisonous and some are phototoxic (they heighten the sunburn response to ultraviolet light).

(c) *Anthraquinone glycosides.* These glycosides are generally pigmented phenolic compounds, which break down readily to lose their sugar molecules; if ingested many of them exert a laxative action within 6 to 8 hours. All of them are aromatic. Such substances are found in the rhizomes of Rhubarb and Madder and in Alder Buckthorn bark.

(d) *Flavonoid glycosides.* These aromatic phenolic compounds – formed from flavones and related substances – are widely distributed as water-soluble pigments in the cell sap of higher plants. Not all flavones are associated with glycosides; some occur freely in the plant, while others are associated with tannins (see later). They and their derivatives are usually yellow (the latin word *flavus* = yellow). Flavonoid glycosides occur in abundance in the Compositae (daisy) and Rutaceae (rue) families.

The *anthocyanins* are a group of flavonoid glycosides largely responsible for the yellow, red and blue colours of flowers. Among medicinal herbs they are particularly found in such plants as Cornflower, Common Mallow, Peony and Sweet Violet.

Some flavonoid glycosides are called *bioflavonoids*. When their therapeutic activity was discovered they were called vitamin P substances, but this term is no longer used. They are usually yellow and cause, for example, the colour of dried Liquorice root. Rutin, from Rue, buckwheats and Japanese Pagoda Tree, is one of the most important therapeutically because, like the coumarin aesculin, it affects the strength and permeability of the capillary walls and is used to treat hypertension and various heart disorders. The flavonoids of hawthorns are also strong cardiotonics and hypotensives. A flavonoid-containing plant that is currently receiving much attention on the Continent is Milk Thistle. It is used to treat liver disorders.

5. *Saponins.* These glycosides occur in many plants and are often associated with cardiac glycosides. They consist of a triterpene aglycone (called a sapogenin) and a sugar portion (glucose or galactose). The chemical composition of some saponins is very similar to that of sex hormones and some saponin-containing plants are the source of substances used in the manufacture of contraceptive pills.

A physiological characteristic of saponins is the ability to reduce the surface tension of water. They produce a soapy foam in water (the name saponin is derived from the Latin word *sapo* = soap) and are excellent emulsifiers. Saponins also typically destroy the membranes of red blood cells, so liberating haemoglobin into the surrounding fluid (this process is called haemolysis). This activity varies considerably

from one saponin-containing plant to another. Plants in which it is strong are highly toxic and they cannot be taken internally; those in which it is weaker are safer to use. Saponins also have an irritant effect on the mucous membranes of the respiratory and digestive tracts. They thus may be used as expectorants or as laxatives (mullein flowers and roots of Liquorice and Soapwort). Many saponin-containing plants are also diuretic and have an antiseptic action in the urinary tract (flowering stems of Smooth Rupturewort, leaves of Silver Birch, root of Restharrow). Since saponins aid the absorption of various substances they are effective constituents of tea mixtures.

Bitter compounds

These compounds, which herbalists also call bitter principles, have diverse chemical compositions but they have in common a strong bitter taste, they irritate the taste buds in the mouth and in so doing they stimulate the appetite and the flow of digestive juices. Some bitter plants activate the secretion and flow of bile (choleretics and cholagogues), while others increase urine production (diuretics). Pharmacologically bitter compounds are terpenoid substances and may, in some cases, be derived from azulene or they may be glycosidic. They are found in many members of the Compositae (daisy) and Gentianaceae (gentian) families (for example, Common Centaury, Great Yellow Gentian, Blessed Thistle and Wormwood). In herbalism bitter compounds are widely used in tea mixtures as appetizers.

Tannins

Tannins are complex colourless polyphenolic compounds with one characteristic in common – the ability to coagulate proteins, heavy metals and alkaloids (but only as long as they are fresh enough to dissolve in water). There are two groups of tannins – hydrolysable tannins, which are esters of gallic acid and also glycosides of these esters, and condensed tannins, which are polymers derived from various flavonoids.

Tannins have astringent and antiseptic properties. They are used in medicine chiefly because they precipitate proteins in mucous membranes and other body tissues, causing a thin layer of coagulation to form. This precipitated matter deprives bacteria of nutrition aiding the rapid healing of wounds and inflamed mucosa. Tannin action also reduces sensitivity and relieves pain. (This ability of tannins to precipitate proteins has long been utilized for curing and preserving (tanning) of animal hides, hence the name tannin.) In medicine tannin-containing plants are particularly used for such ailments as diarrhoea, bronchitis, slow-healing wounds, mouth infections and haemorrhoids. They are also used in some cases of alkaloid poisoning. The dose always needs to be given with care because if tannins are taken in excess they can be harmful.

Tannins are found in abundance in Ericaceae (heath), Rosaceae (rose), Salicaceae (willow) and Betulaceae (birch) families. They are common in leaves, vascular tissue, bark, unripe fruits, galls and seed coats (for example, oak galls and oak bark, leaves of Blackberry and Raspberry, leaves and fruit of Bilberry, flowering stems of Agrimony, root of Great Burnet and Tormentil, and seed coat of Walnut).

Essential (volatile) oils, terpenes and resins

Essential oils, which are also called volatile oils, are liquid components of plant cells. They are volatile (they vaporize when heated), soluble in alcohol and other organic solvents, are colourless when fresh, usually aromatic and, unlike fatty or fixed oils (see later), they do not leave a permanent mark on paper. Chemically their principal constituents are complex mixtures of terpenoid substances. Many plants containing essential oils are well known because of their fragrant smell and they are commercially cultivated for the food and perfumery industries.

Essential oils accumulate in certain tissues, in specialized cells or in intercellular spaces. They are usually contained within the plant in globules, which can be observed microscopically. They may occur in only one part of a plant (rose petals) or in morphologically related parts (flower and fruit). If they occur anywhere else in the plant they may be of different chemical composition and of less quality. Using the correct part of the plant is as important in medicine as it is in perfumery. The concentration of essential oils in plants is highest in constant warm weather and this is the best collecting time.

Essential oils are used in medicine in several different ways. The plant part containing them may be used in crude form — in, for example, an infusion — or the essential oil may be obtained from the fresh or dried herb by steam or water distillation or extraction in alcohol and used on its own. Some of the isolated components of essential oils (for example, menthol from mints and thymol from thymes) also have important medicinal properties and many are included in proprietary medicines. Essential oils have varied physiological effects and are used in the appropriate way in medicine. For example, some are used mainly as aromatic spices and flavouring agents (Anise), although they may act as digestive tonics (stomachics) as well (Caraway). Others have antiseptic (Garlic), carminative (Fennel), expectorant (thymes), rubefacient and antirheumatic (Garden Lavender), anthelmintic (Tansy) and anti-inflammatory (Pot Marigold) properties. If taken in excess, however, some essential oils can irritate the lower abdomen and cause more general poisoning (Wormwood).

All essential oils, and the plant parts containing them, must always be stored in airtight containers in a dark place. Exposed to air and light they rapidly oxidize, polymerize, become resinous, less aromatic and less effective. Many plants containing them are best known as culinary herbs (for example, Basil, Caraway, Coriander, Dill, Fennel, Sweet Marjoram and Garden Thyme). Plants rich in essential oils with a medicinal action belong mainly to the families Compositae (daisies), Labiatae (mints), Rutaceae (rues), Umbelliferae (carrots), Iridaceae (irises) and Pinaceae (pines).

Terpenes can occur as companions to various other substances in plants; Ribwort Plantain has a particularly high concentration of them. One particular type of terpene, which occurs in several medicinal plants including Bogbean, Great Yellow Gentian, Valerian and Woodruff, is the iridoid group. *Iridoids* are unstable terpene esters with a five-membered ring in their molecule. Some of them occur naturally as glycosides.

Often associated with essential oils in many trees and shrubs, especially conifers, are **resins.** Some resins are derivatives of phenols; others terpenoid derivatives. They occur either as solids which soften and melt when heated, or dissolved in essential oils forming **balsams.** Like essential oils they are produced by special plant cells and are secreted into cavities or, in conifers (for example, pines), into resin ducts.

Fatty (fixed) oils

Fatty oils of plant origin are mixtures of triglycerides, which are insoluble in water but dissolve in organic solvents. They are not volatile, hence the term 'fixed'. Many plant or vegetable oils contain substantial amounts of unsaturated fatty acids and are liquid at room temperature but congeal and become cloudy at cooler temperatures. Examples of fatty oils with a medicinal application are almond oil, maize (corn) oil, linseed oil (from Flax), soybean oil and castor oil. Castor oil has a specific purgative action. Fatty oils are used not only in medicinal preparations but also in industry and in food and cosmetic products.

Mucilages and pectins

Plant mucilages are amorphous mixtures of polysaccharides that dissolve in water to form extremely viscous colloid systems. In cold water they swell and form a slimy gel; in warm water they dissolve into colloid solutions that gel when cooled. Most are formed by the plant cell walls.

Mucilages are therapeutically useful because they reduce mechanical and chemical irritations. When they pass through the respiratory and digestive tracts they form a thin protective coat over the mucous membranes and prevent irritants from reaching inflamed surfaces. Mucilages are thus used to treat infections of the chest, throat and intestinal tract. In small doses they decrease intestinal peristalsis and have an antidiarrhoeal effect. In large doses, however, they become laxative. Applied in poultices mucilages also alleviate the pain of bruised tissues and soften the skin. They are not absorbed by the body tissues so their effect is always restricted to the area of application. In the pharmaceutical industry some are used as emulsifiers.

Mucilage-containing plants are used either on their own or in tea mixtures. Among the most useful for medicinal purposes are Coltsfoot (leaves and flowers), Fenugreek, Flax (seeds), Iceland Moss, Common Mallow (flowers and leaves) and Marshmallow (leaves and roots).

Pectins are classed as plant mucilages because they are also polysaccharides and form gels in the same way. They are used in the treatment of diarrhoea and in fruit diets. Pectins are found in many whole fruits, less so in fruit and vegetable juices. Plants containing them include Blackberry, Carrot, Black Currant and Quince.

Mineral compounds

Medicinal plants contain varying amounts of mineral substances, but they are rarely prescribed to replace minerals that have been lost from the body. Silicic acid is especially characteristic of horsetails and grasses, and some members of the Labiatae (mint) and Boraginaceae (borage) families (for example, hemp-nettles and Common Gromwell). Common Gromwell also contains abundant calcium salts, and nettles and Watercress iron. Potassium salts are found in Dandelion, Kidney Bean and nettles, and in some fruits. Plants rich in potassium may be useful in low-sodium diets.

Organic acids

There are many different types of organic acids and some of them are mentioned in other sections. For example, the nutritive ascorbic acid (vitamin C) is included under vitamins, the astringent gallic acid (in oaks) under tannins, and the anti-inflammatory and analgesic salicylic acid under phenolic glycosides. One acid is potentially dangerous. This is oxalic acid, which is found in the free state or as calcium or potassium salts in, for example, the leaves of Wood Sorrel and Rhubarb. It is an irritant and in large doses is toxic.

Vitamins

Few plants contain sufficient amounts of any vitamin for them to be medically prescribed when there is a deficiency, but any vitamin-rich herb is an excellent addition to the diet, especially during the winter months.

As examples, Carrot, Dandelion and Watercress are sources of carotenes (see below), which are precursors of vitamin A; many cereals, including Common Oat, are good sources of vitamin B complex; vitamin C is abundant in fruits such as Black Currant, Red Pepper and Sea Buckthorn, and in the leaves of Dandelion, nettles, Parsley and Watercress; vitamins D and E are found in Watercress; and nettles are a source of vitamin K. The vitamin content is always greatest in fresh, uncooked plant parts.

Carotenoids

Carotenoids are yellow or red pigments found in all photosynthesizing plants. With anthocyanins they contribute to autumn foliage shades when chlorophyll is lost. There are two types of carotenoids: the *carotenes* and *xanthophylls*. Carotenes are hydrocarbons (tetraterpenes), which are converted to vitamin A in the body. Xanthophylls are oxygenated derivatives of carotenes; they have no provitamin A activity.

A guide to the therapeutic effects of medicinal herbs

The active constituents of a medicinal plant determine its effect on the human body. Herbal remedies, like other medical treatments, can be broadly grouped according to their use. A medicinal herb does not always have just one effect — sometimes it has a broad therapeutic range (spectrum); in other words a single plant, such as Marshmallow or Yarrow, can be used to treat several disorders. It is also the case that combinations of different herbs, all with the same action, can potentiate a medicinal effect; herbal mixtures are often used for this purpose.

The following groups include herbal remedies for both internal and external use. Only a selection of the plants described in the main illustrated part are included in the groupings. Many of the listed herbs can be self-administered with care, but this is not recommended for the inexperienced without professional advice. **Those plants prefixed by an asterisk can be poisonous, some extremely so, or are harmful in strong doses or if taken over a long period of time;** cautionary remarks about these herbs are given in the text accompanying the plates. A special note about poisonous plants is also included later in this section (page 34).

Analgesics (Anodynes)

Substances that relieve pain. Herbs with this property include: Balm, Elder, Feverfew, *Monkshood, Common Oat, *Opium Poppy, Rosemary, Common Valerian, White Willow, Woodruff.

Anthelmintics (Vermifuges)

Substances that cause the death and elimination of intestinal worms. Herbs with this property include: Burning Bush, Carrot, Garlic, *Male Fern, *Forking Larkspur, Vegetable Marrow, *Mugwort, Onion, Polypody, *Tansy, Breckland(Wild) Thyme, Garden Thyme, *American Wormseed, *Wormwood.

Antiasthmatics

Substances that relieve or prevent spasmodic contractions of the airways and are used in the treatment of asthmas. Herbs with this property include: Balm,

Coltsfoot, Elecampane, *Deadly Nightshade, Round-leaved Sundew, *Thornapple, Common Valerian.

Antidiarrhoeals

Substances that combat diarrhoea. Herbs with this property include: Wood Avens, Common Bistort, Bilberry, Blackberry, Great Burnet, Catmint, Cowberry, Black Currant, Daisy, Small-leaved Lime, Canadian Fleabane, Creeping Jenny, Knotgrass, Lady's Mantle, Peppermint, Pedunculate Oak, Common Oat, Quince, Herb Robert, Cabbage Rose, *Sage, Silverweed, Wild Strawberry, Tormentil, Waterpepper.

Antidiaphoretics (Anhydrotics)

Substances that check excessive perspiration. Herbs with this property include: Common Horsetail, Pedunculate Oak, Sessile Oak, *Sage, Common Valerian, Walnut.

Antirheumatics

Substances that relieve rheumatism. Herbs with this property include: Ash, Aspen, Silver Birch, Borage, Cowberry, Common Couch, Black Currant, *Juniper, Meadowsweet, Black Mustard, Common (Stinging) Nettle, White Poplar, *Rosemary, Sweet Violet, White Willow.

Antisclerotics

Substances that reduce the amount of fat in the blood and help prevent hardening (sclerosis) of the arteries. Herbs with this property include: Cardoon, Garlic, *Hawthorn, *Mistletoe, *Japanese Pagoda Tree, Round-leaved Sundew.

Antitussives

Substances that relieve or prevent coughing. Herbs with this property usually contain mucilages that swell in water and which, because they take up water (that is they are hydrophilic), moisten the area around the throat opening and counteract inflammation. Herbs with antitussive action include: Anise, Coltsfoot, Liquorice, Lungwort, Common Mallow, Marshmal-

Early spring brings with it the yellow flowers of Coltsfoot (see Pl. 240). The leaves are particularly used to treat coughs.

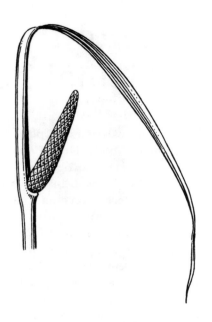

Sweet Flag (see Pl. 4) contains primarily bitter substances and an essential oil.

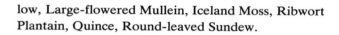

low, Large-flowered Mullein, Iceland Moss, Ribwort Plantain, Quince, Round-leaved Sundew.

Aromatics

Substances that have a fragrant smell, and usually a pleasant taste. They are used to give flavour and aroma to medicinal preparations; they are also mildly antiseptic. Herbs with this property include: Anise, Caraway, Chamomile, Coriander, Fennel, Garden Lavender, Liquorice, Cabbage Rose, *Rosemary, *Sage.

Astringents

Substances that tighten the skin, constrict blood vessels, thereby reducing blood flow, and decrease mucous secretions. Herbs with this property include: Agrimony, Bilberry, Blackberry, Greater Burdock, Great Burnet, Common Comfrey, Daisy, *Hepatica, Hyssop, Lady's Mantle, Lungwort, Marjoram, Motherwort, Pedunculate Oak, Sessile Oak, Smooth Rupturewort, *Sage, Perforate St John's Wort, Silverweed, Heath Speedwell, Wild Strawberry, Tormentil, Walnut, Waterpepper, White Willow, Rosebay Willowherb.

Bitters (Appetizers)

Bitter-tasting substances that stimulate the appetite by affecting the secretion of digestive juices. Herbs with this property include: Garden Angelica, Bogbean, Caraway, Common Centaury, Elecampane, Sweet Flag, Great Yellow Gentian, Wall Germander, White Horehound, Iceland Moss, *Mugwort, Peppermint, *Blessed Thistle, *Wormwood, Yarrow.

The leaves and isolated constituents of Foxglove (Pl. 89) are irreplaceable cardiac medicines.

Cardiacs

Substances that affect heart action. Secondarily they promote the elimination of water from the body. They include the toxic cardiac glycosides and should be used only **under strict medical supervision;** many of them are highly dangerous. Herbs with cardiac action include: *Foxglove, *Large Yellow Foxglove, *Woolly Foxglove, *Hawthorn, *Midland Hawthorn, *False Helleborine, *Hedge Hyssop, *Lily-of-the-Valley, *Yellow Pheasant's Eye, *Rosemary.

Carminatives

Substances that relieve flatulence and griping pains in the stomach and bowel. Herbs with this property include: Garden Angelica, Anise, Balm, Caraway, Chamomile, Dill, Fennel, Hyssop, Garden Lavender, Lovage, Scented Mayweed (Wild Chamomile), *Ribbed Melilot, Peppermint, *Sage, Common Valerian.

Choleretics and Cholagogues

Substances that either stimulate the production of bile in the liver (choleretic) or stimulate the release of bile from the gall bladder and bile ducts into the duodenum (cholagogue). **Any serious disorder of the liver, gall bladder and bile ducts, and gallstones needs professional medical attention.** Herbs with choleretic or cholagogic action include: Agrimony, *Barberry, Cardoon, *Greater Celandine, Common Centaury, Dandelion, Elecampane, Great Yellow Gentian, *Hepatica, White Horehound, Pot Marigold, Marjoram, Peppermint, Water Mint, Garden Radish, Raspberry, Rosemary, *Blessed Thistle, Milk Thistle, Common Toadflax, *Wormwood.

Diaphoretics (Sudorifics)

Substances that induce or increase perspiration. Herbs with this property include: Greater Burdock, Butterbur, Catmint, Black Currant, Elder, Large-leaved Lime, Small-leaved Lime, Scented Mayweed (Wild Chamomile), Meadowsweet, Large-flowered Mullein, Orange Mullein, Wild Pansy (Heartsease), Yarrow.

Diuretics

Substances that stimulate the elimination of water from the body by increasing the production and the flow of urine. Diuretics are also used to treat disorders of the urinary tract, where they have an antiseptic action, and kidney stones and uroliths. **Any serious kidney or bladder disorder and oedemas caused by heart disorders need professional medical attention.**

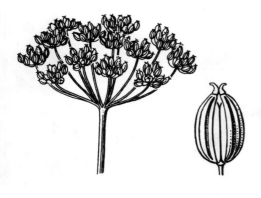

The dried sweet fruits of Fennel (see Pl. 97) are a component of medicinal teas and are also widely used for flavouring.

Large-flowered Mullein (see Pl. 247) bears yellow flowers which are used in tea mixtures, especially for chest colds.

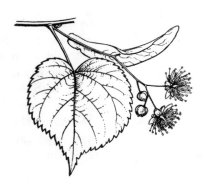

The leaves of Bearberry (see Pl. 22) are used for treating urinary disorders.

The blossoms of Small-leaved Lime (see Pl. 234) are an excellent remedy for colds and chills.

Herbs with diuretic action include: Kidney Bean, *Bearberry, Lady's Bedstraw, Bilberry, Silver Birch, Blackthorn, Greater Burdock, Common Couch, Dandelion, White Deadnettle, Elder, Goldenrod, Heather, Downy Hempnettle, Herb Robert, Common Horsetail, *Juniper, Knotgrass, Lovage, Madder, Meadowsweet, Stagshorn Moss, Nasturtium, Common (Stinging) Nettle, Parsley, Spiny Restharrow, Smooth Rupturewort, Perforate St John's Wort, *Shepherd's Purse, Silverweed, Wild Strawberry.

Expectorants

Substances that promote the formation and expulsion of phlegm from the airways. They have an irritant effect on the mucous membranes, they relieve spasms of the bronchioles and have a mild antiseptic action. Expectorants are mainly used in the treatment of throat and chest disorders. Herbs with expectorant action include: Anise, Coltsfoot, Cowslip, Elecampane, Fennel, Downy Hempnettle, White Horehound, Hollyhock, Hyssop, Iceland Moss, Lungwort, Common Mallow, Marjoram, Marshmallow, Large-flowered Mullein, Orange Mullein, Peppermint, Ribwort Plantain, *Sage, Round-leaved Sundew, Breckland (Wild) Thyme, Garden Thyme.

Galactagogues

Substances that stimulate milk production. Herbs with this property include: Anise, Basil, Caraway, Black Cumin, Dill, Fennel, Fenugreek, Goat's Rue.

Gynaecologics

Substances that affect the female reproductive tract. Some relieve muscular spasms in the lower pelvic region and so alleviate menstrual pain. Others have a direct or indirect effect on the uterus and are used to check heavy menstrual bleeding or menstrual irregularities. Some supposedly induce menstruation (*emmenagogues*). Professional medical advice should always be sought for serious menstrual problems. Herbs with gynaecological effects include: Burning Bush, Black Cumin, Chamomile, White Deadnettle, Canadian Fleabane, Madder, Lady's Mantle, Motherwort, Parsely, *Rue, Perforate St John's Wort, *Shepherd's Purse, Silverweed, Waterpepper, Yarrow.

Ergot Fungus (see Pl. 64) is artifically cultivated on Rye for the pharmaceutical industry. The alkaloids it contains are used to make many important medicines.

Haemostatics (Styptics)

Substances that control bleeding by contracting the tissues or blood vessels. Herbs with this property include: Wood Avens, Common Comfrey, Canadian Fleabane, Common Horsetail, Lady's Mantle, Sanicle, Perforate St John's Wort, *Shepherd's Purse, Waterpepper.

Hypertensives

Substances that increase blood pressure. Like cardiacs, these are dangerous unless professionally prescribed. Herbs with this property include: *Broom, *Shepherd's Purse.

Hypnotics (Soporifics)

Substances that induce sleep. Herbs with this property include: Balm, Chamomile, White Deadnettle, Dill, Hop, Motherwort, Common Valerian, Vervain, Woodruff.

Hypoglycaemics

Substances that reduce the level of blood sugar. **For diabetics they can be dangerous unless professsionally prescribed.** Herbs with this property include: Kidney Bean, Bilberry, Bogbean, Greater Burdock, Chicory, Cowberry, Fenugreek, Common (Stinging) Nettle, Goat's Rue.

Hypotensives

Substances that reduce blood pressure. The potent ones are dangerous unless professionally prescribed. They are used in combination with a suitable diet and other medicines. Herbs with this property include: Garlic, *Hawthorn, *Midland Hawthorn, Hop, *Mistletoe, Onion, *Rue.

Laxatives (Aperients or Aperitives)

Substances that loosen the bowels and ease constipation. *Cathartics* and *purgatives* have a stronger, quicker action and can be dangerous. Herbs with laxative action include: Ash, *Barberry, *Alder Buckthorn, Dandelion, Elder, Fennel, Flax (Linseed), *Common Fumitory, Liquorice, Common Mallow, Ribwort Plantain, Polypody, *Rhubarb, Dog Rose, Rowan, *Soapwort, Common Toadflax, Yarrow.

Stomachics

Substances that alleviate stomach disorders and are digestive tonics. Herbs with this property include: Garden Angelica, Wood Avens, Balm, Blackberry, Bogbean, *Greater Celandine, Common Centaury, Chicory, Coriander, Dandelion, Yellow Gentian, Wall Germander, Hop, Ground Ivy, Sweet Marjoram, Marshmallow, Dwarf Milkwort, Iceland Moss, *Mugwort, Peppermint, Perforate St John's Wort, Heath Speedwell, Wild Strawberry, *Blessed Thistle, Garden Thyme, *Wormwood, Yarrow.

Sedatives and Tranquillizers

Substances that soothe and calm the nerves, relieving anxiety and strain. Herbs with this property include: Balm, Catmint, Chamomile, Heather, Hop, Garden Lavender, Large-leaved Lime, Small-leaved Lime, *Wild Lettuce, Motherwort, Common Oat, Peppermint, Common Valerian, White Willow.

Hawthorn (see Pl. 76) is still prescribed for high blood pressure.

Common Valerian (see Pl. 245) has a mainly sedative action.

Scented Mayweed or Wild or German Chamomile (see Pl. 55) is a popular and widely used medicinal herb.

Deadly Nightshade (see Pl. 33) is an extremely poisonous plant.

Vulneraries

Substances that counteract inflammation and promote the healing of wounds and skin disorders. Herbs with this property include: Greater Burdock, Chamomile, Common Comfrey, Small-leaved Elm, Common Horsetail, Lady's Mantle, Pot Marigold, Marshmallow, Scented Mayweed (Wild Chamomile), *Ribbed Melilot, Ribwort Plantain, Perforate St John's Wort, Sanicle, Silverweed, Kidney Vetch, Yarrow.

Plant poisons

Poisons, whether of inorganic, synthetic or plant origin, and their effects are the subject of the science of toxicology. The term poison or *toxin* is applied to any plant or plant part that might be harmful either taken internally or applied externally. In the pictorial section of this book poisonous plants are indicated by the symbol  ; if extremely toxic, a double symbol is shown. Appropriate warnings are included where necessary. **These herbal remedies should never be self-administered.**

Some herbs are not poisonous if used externally, but are so internally. Some other plants are normally harmless but they may become toxic if preparations from them are taken to excess in strong doses or for a long period of time. Wormwood is one such plant and cautionary notes about this and other potentially harmful herbs are given on the relevant pages in the plates section. Although it is certainly the case that many herbs have beneficial actions when used sensibly it has to be said that there is insufficient knowledge about the long-term effects in the body of the constituents of even commonplace medicinal plants.

Unlike synthetic drugs very few herbal remedies have been clinically tested in a scientific way for both their good and possible harmful properties. It is therefore inadvisable for pregnant women to take *any* herbal remedy other than very mild herbal teas (for example, Chamomile) and those prescribed by a qualified medical or herbal practitioner. Some herbal remedies should not be taken if there is a pre-existing kidney, liver or heart disorder, or if an individual is diabetic. For example, Juniper should not be taken by individuals with inflamed kidneys and Rhubarb not by those with urinary disorders and kidney stones and uroliths. **Professional advice should always be sought if there is any doubt about the toxicity of a plant or about the interactions of herbal remedies with other medications that are already being taken.** Advice should also be sought if there is any doubt about the safety of a herbal remedy for a child.

Some highly toxic plants yield such valuable medicines (alkaloids and glycosides mostly) that they are cultivated commercially for the pharmaceutical industry (for example, Ergot Fungus, foxgloves, Deadly Nightshade and Opium Poppy). The collection and preparation of these plants are closely supervised and the resulting medicines are prescribed with great care by qualified medical personnel. A selection of extremely poisonous medicinal plants has been included for reference in this book. **These herbs should never be collected and prepared for use in the home:**

Aconitum napellus (Monkshood)
Adonis vernalis (Yellow Pheasant's Eye)
Arum maculatum (Lords-and-Ladies)
Atropa belladonna (Deadly Nightshade)

Bryonia alba (Black-berried Bryony)
Buxus sempervirens (Box)
Cannabis sativa (Hemp)
Cicuta virosa (Cowbane)
Claviceps purpurea (Ergot Fungus)
Clematis recta (Erect Clematis)
Colchicum autumnale (Meadow Saffron)
Conium maculatum (Hemlock)
Convallaria majalis (Lily-of-the-Valley)
Coronilla varia (Crown Vetch)
Corydalis cava (Bulbous Corydalis)
Daphne mezereum (Mezereon)
Datura stramonium (Thornapple)
Delphinium consolida (= *Consolida regalis*) (Forking
    Larkspur)
Digitalis grandiflora (Large Yellow Foxglove)
Digitalis lanata (Woolly Foxglove)
Digitalis purpurea (Foxglove)
Dryopteris filix-mas (Male Fern)
Gratiola officinalis (Hedge Hyssop)
Hedera helix (Ivy)
Helleborus niger (Christmas Rose)
Hyoscyamus niger (Henbane)
Laburnum anagyroides (Laburnum)
Lactuca virosa (Wild Lettuce)
Papaver bracteatum (Iranian Poppy)
Papaver somniferum (Opium Poppy)
Ricinus communis (Castor-oil Plant)

Robinia pseudoacacia (False Acacia)
Sedum acre (Biting Stonecrop)
Solanum dulcamara (Bittersweet)
Taxus baccata (Yew)
Veratrum album (False Helleborine)
Vinca major (Lesser Periwinkle)

A curious aspect of poisonous plants is that the concentration of toxic substances in them is not constant; it varies according to such factors as the locality, the time of year, the time of day, the temperature and whether it is wet or dry, sunny or overcast. For commercial cultivation greater yields of the medicinally active substances are obtained by breeding varieties with a constant, high concentration of the desired substances or by special preparation techniques. Sometimes the poisons occur only in certain parts of the plant – the leaves, fruits or rootstock. For example, the flowers of Forking Larkspur are not poisonous, but the other parts of the plant, especially the seeds, are very toxic. The familiar Potato (*Solanum tuberosum*) tuber is normally quite harmless, as long as it is not green (when green it is poisonous), but the flowers and young leaves are toxic.

If plant poisoning is suspected, medical attention should be sought immediately.

Preparation of medicinal herbs for use

Medicines made from crude material of plant or animal origin (for example, extracts, tinctures, tablets and ointments) are called **galenicals** in pharmacy and are distinct from the isolated constituents (for example, glycosides and alkaloids). Galenicals are named after the Greek physician Galen, who was one of the earliest to prepare medicines from plants and other natural substances. Some of his 'galenic' remedies are still used today.

The modern pharmacy, of course, stocks chiefly commercial products – tablets, capsules, ointments, liquid medicines and such like – made from synthetic substances and sold under various trade names. However, some prescriptions are still made up by pharmacists from crude plant material and an increasing number of herbal preparations, particularly for cosmetic uses, are being manufactured for sale in chemist and health-food shops. Some herbal remedies are also obtainable direct from specialist manufacturers. Herbal practitioners prepare and sell herbal preparations, often blended mixtures, themselves. Not all herbs are freely available for sale in Britain. Under the Medicines Act of 1968 herbal preparations cannot claim to be remedies for cancer, diabetes and other serious disorders, and certain dangerous herbs can be prescribed only by qualified medical practitioners. For example, herbalists are not allowed to prescribe medicines containing Ergot Fungus, foxgloves, Male Fern, False Helleborine, Opium Poppy, American Wormseed and several other toxic plants. Another group of plants can be supplied by herbalists but only within limited dosages. These plants include

Greater Celandine, Hemlock, Henbane, Lily-of-the-Valley, Deadly Nightshade, Monkshood, Meadow Saffron and Thornapple. Several hundred other herbs can, however, be freely supplied by a herbalist or purchased without a prescription in a medicinal preparation from a chemist, a specialized store or from a manufacturer (reputable suppliers should always be used if herbs are bought in this way). If bought herbal remedies have a product licence (PL) number on them it means that the product is what it says it is. It is a guarantee that the medicine has been manufactured under licence from the Department of Health and that all stages of its preparation have been strictly controlled. Imported unlicensed herbal remedies with dubious contents should *never* be bought.

So-called official galenical preparations — those included in pharmacopoeias and national formularies and dispensed by pharmacists — are always prepared only from plants and plant extracts of prescribed quality and by special standardized pharmaceutical methods. Included in the *British Pharmacopoeia,* for example, are descriptions of the respective medicines and the official, established standards for the production, testing and storage of the preparation. There are also regulations concerning the amount of extract or active agent in the finished product, which may be in tablet, capsule or liquid form, so that the formulation is the same in each batch of the medicines. These standards ensure that a specific dosage of an official plant drug will produce a constant therapeutic effect in most patients.

At the beginning of the 20th century more than 90 per cent of the medicines listed in the *British Pharmacopoeia* were derived directly from plants. Since then the number of herbs used in medical practice has steadily declined. Today perhaps only 25 per cent of the drugs prescribed in Britain are based on plants — whether in the form of unprocessed or crude material, crude extracts or purified isolated constituents from plants (but if drugs from microorganisms are included the percentage is much higher, perhaps 45 per cent). The downward decline in the number of official plant preparations available has probably halted. It has been realized that there are no effective and cheap synthetic alternatives to many plant-based drugs. In some Continental countries the pharmacopoeias still contain a relatively high proportion of official herbal preparations and medical practitioners prescribe them as a matter of course. On the Continent, too, doctors will sometimes prescribe

herbal teas and tea mixtures, which is not the case in Britain. It is encouraging that the World Health Organization is now taking a special interest in traditional medicine. With the help of WHO and other international bodies many Third World countries are actively sponsoring research on medicinal plants in their countries and herbalists are being integrated into official health systems.

Purchased herbal remedies, such as tablets, extracts, ointments and powders, must be stored at home in suitable wrappers or containers, they must be kept clean and be clearly labelled with the contents and the date the medicine was prepared or purchased. They are best kept in a cool, dry, dark place, in hot weather even in the refrigerator. The efficacy of the active constituents in these preparations — and in unprepared dried herbs — is relatively stable, but the medicines should not be stored for longer than about a year as they will slowly deteriorate in time, especially those containing essential oils and saponins, and lose their potency.

Different rules apply to simple, home-prepared remedies such as teas and aromatic waters. These should be prepared when and as required and never stored, although they will remain fresh for up to 12 hours if covered and kept in the refrigerator.

If there are children at home, all medicines should be stored out of their reach and **under lock and key.** It is recommended that medicines for internal use (marked with a white label with black inscription) are kept separate from those for external use (marked with a white label with red inscription and preferably in a ribbed bottle) to prevent any possibility of a mix-up.

Herbal preparations are applied in various forms, externally and internally. The form a medicinal preparation takes usually depends on the structure of the plant or its constituents. Some processing methods are elaborate and need expensive equipment and specialized knowledge (for example, for the preparation of tablets, capsules, injections and alcohol extracts). Such methods are usually carried out by pharmaceutical manufacturers. Several methods are, however, suitable for use by the amateur at home, the simplest being maceration, infusion and decoction (pp. 37–38), which are the bases of herbal teas (tisanes) and tea mixtures. These methods involve steeping the herb in hot or cold water or in alcohol for varying lengths of time to extract the soluble constituents; the preparation may then be evaporated to thicken it. Herbal vinegars (p. 40), wines (p. 40) and

Ornamented balance scales from the early 20th century.

oils (p. 40), aromatic waters (p. 40), medicinal syrups (p. 40), pressed juices (p. 40), poultices (p. 41) and compresses (p. 41) can also be prepared at home, although a selection of some of these preparations is available commercially.

Before any remedy can be prepared the fresh or dried herb has to be cut, crushed or ground (rhizomes and roots are usually cut up and shredded before drying). In the home a pestle and mortar are useful for grinding fruits and seeds. For preparing remedies that require heating, heatproof glass, earthenware or porcelain containers should be used, never metal ones unless they are well and faultlessly enamelled (metal reacts with tannins).

Macerations

The maceration method of preparation is used for mucilaginous seeds or for those plants with active constituents (such as essential oils) that might be adversely affected by heat. The plant material is steeped in water, alcohol (ethanol), spirits or white wine at a room temperature (15−20 °C). Normally the proportions are 1 part herb to 20 parts liquid − a typical quantity would be 5 grams and 100 ml. The length of time the herb is steeped depends on its properties and the steeping liquid. If water is used the steeping time should not be long, otherwise the preparation begins to ferment or become mouldy. Mucilaginous material (Fenugreek, Flax, Marshmallow) is macerated for about 30 minutes; aromatic and bitter substances for 2−12 hours. Herbalists will advise the necessary time when they prescribe a treatment. Before use the mixture can be warmed and strained. Alcohol-based macerations keep longer than aqueous ones. The alcohol used for macerating should always be obtained from a chemist or other pharmaceutical supplier.

Digestion is a method of extracting constituents from hard plant parts or from plants with constituents that do not readily dissolve. The herb is steeped in water, as for macerations, but at a higher temperature (35−40 °C) for a minimum of 30 minutes with occasional shaking.

Infusions

The infusion method is used for extracting active constituents from a herb by steeping it in hot water. It is a quick and common method of making herbal teas (much like making a pot of ordinary tea) and is applied mainly to the soft parts of plants − the leaves, flowers, stems and seeds. It is a good method for aromatic herbs containing essential oils (Chamomile, Peppermint), which would lose up to 60 per cent of their effectiveness if boiled. The infusion is prepared by pouring the required amount of boiling water onto the herb or herb mixture in a warmed cup or larger nonmetallic container, then covering it with a tight-fitting lid (to prevent the volatile oils from escaping). The liquid is then allowed to stand (infuse) for 5−15 minutes with occasional stirring. After the mixture has been strained through muslin, a filter paper or a fine nonmetallic sieve it is usually taken immediately. If infusions are frequently made, it may save time to buy a herbal infuser with a built-in strainer.

The usual proportions are one to three teaspoons (about 2−5 grams) of dried herb to each teacupful (about 150 ml) of liquid. The precise quantities vary according to the plant and the part being used. The quantity of herb is usually trebled for fresh material. For a day's dosage (two or three cups) 1 oz (30 grams) or two to three tablespoons of dried herb are used per pint (560 ml) of water. After the first dose from the larger quantity the remainder should be covered and stored in the refrigerator for use the same day. It can be gently reheated, without boiling, in a nonmetallic pan. **For any but the mildest of teas (Peppermint, Chamomile) it is wise to get professional advice before**

preparing and taking infusions because some quite harmless herbs can be poisonous in strong doses or if taken over a long period of time. In the case of toxic plants, the amounts of the herb and of water and the dosage must always be prescribed by a qualified herbalist or medical practitioner.

Decoctions

The decoction method is for extracting active constituents from a herb by boiling it in water. It is applied mainly to hard plant parts — wood, bark, stems, roots, hard fruits and some seeds — for which a simple infusion would not be sufficient. It is not suitable for plants that contain essential oils. Furthermore, other constituents, such as mucilage, enzymes and glycosides, are affected by heat and decoctions have therefore a limited application. Decoctions also tend to be more potent than infusions and in many cases they should be used internally only under medical supervision.

To prepare a decoction water at room temperature is poured over the cut-up herb in a nonmetallic container and this is then brought slowly to the boil and simmered gently for the necessary time, usually 15–20 minutes. Woody parts may need boiling for as long as 1 hour, water being added as needed to replace that lost by evaporation. The decoction is usually strained while still hot and water is added to it to bring it up to the required volume. The usual proportions are one to three teaspoons of the dried herb to one cup (150 ml) of water, or 1 oz (30 grams) of the herb to 1³/₄ pt (1 litre) of water. The decoction from the tubers of various orchids (salep) is not strained. Decoctions should always be used as soon as possible, and always within one day. For some plants with hard and soft parts, a mixture of maceration and decoction is used.

Extracts

An extract is obtained by steeping a herb in water, alcohol, ether or a combination of these liquids and then concentrating the preparation by evaporating it. The method is mostly used commercially for the preparation of various galenicals.

Fluid or *liquid extracts* have the consistency of a thick liquid. They are the most concentrated of herbal medicines. *Thin* or *soft extracts* have the consistency of thick honey. *Thick* or *solid extracts* are not liquid at room temperature; they contain at least 80 per cent of dry matter. *Dry extracts* are so

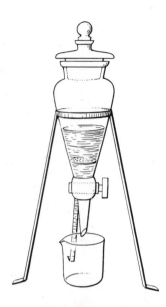

A percolator, used to make extracts from plants in small quantities.

completely evaporated that they are like a powder; they contain 5 per cent water at the most.

Aqueous extracts. These are prepared either by maceration or by infusion or by a combination of both processes. The herb is usually first steeped in water. Then the liquid is strained off and simmered very gently for a long time in a nonmetallic container with constant stirring until most of the water has evaporated and the extract has the required consistency. In industry evaporation is performed in a vacuum vessel.

Alcohol extracts. These are prepared either by steeping the herb in alcohol and then evaporating the liquid in a vacuum vessel or by percolation. In the percolation method alcohol is passed through the herb until all the soluble constituents have been extracted.

Tinctures

A tincture is prepared by prolonged steeping of a fresh or dried herb in a solvent, which is usually alcohol or alcohol and water. As their name indicates (it comes from the Latin word *tingere* = to wet or dye), these solutions are variously coloured by the herb involved. The alcohol is effective at drawing out the active constituents and the solution is much stronger and keeps longer than a maceration.

Tinctures are prepared from either one herb or a mixture of herbs. They are usually made from unprocessed plant material but they may also be prepared from dry extracts. Instructions for their preparation are given in pharmacopoeias. Quantities vary according to the herb but generally the proportions are 1 part of crushed plant material to 5 parts of 60 per cent alcohol. For small amounts this is about 5 grams to 25 ml alcohol. The prepared herb is soaked in the alcohol in a stoppered glass vessel for 3−7 days, the precise time depending on the herb. It is kept in a cool, dark, dry place and occasionally stirred or shaken. The liquid is then poured off and also pressed out of the soaked plant material and topped up to the required volume with alcohol, or alcohol and water. The solution is then left to stand undisturbed until it is clear − for a minimum of 12 hours − after which it is filtered.

Many tinctures are prescribed for internal use in so many drops, so much of a teaspoon or so many teaspoons and often for external use − to paint on the gums or as a gargle. They are much used in homeopathic medicine.

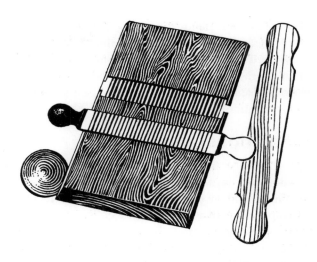

A pill-making board used for making pills by hand. The two metal moulds are pressed together to shape the dough-like mixture into a given number of balls of equal size.

Powders

Some dried herbs are best processed as powders. They are finely cut or crushed and then ground down to the required degree of fineness. They are used on their own or in mixtures both internally and externally. Tisanes prepared from fine powders do not need straining.

Pills

Pills are small balls of a medicinal substance. Besides the main active constituent, which can be either the crude plant material or a plant extract, pills include various auxiliary substances, usually of plant origin (such as Liquorice juice, powdered Marshmallow root and yeast extract). Pills must be of a uniform size, firm and thoroughly dry. To keep them from sticking together they are sometimes sprinkled with sugar, powdered Liquorice root or the spores of Stagshorn Moss. Their preparation is laborious because they have to be rolled by hand on a special board from a dough-like mixture. Pills used to be dispensed more often than they now are. They have largely been replaced by tablets, which are mechanically made, can be stored for longer and can be more accurately formulated.

Tablets

Tablets are small, flat pieces of compressed powdered medicinal material of various shapes and sizes. They are made of one substance or a mixture, and are prepared in tens of thousands by the pharmaceutical industry. Because of their shape they dissolve more quickly in the stomach than pills do and for this reason they may be coated with various substances to slow up their breakdown so that they pass through to the intestines before being absorbed. Nowadays the isolated active constituents from a plant tend to be made into tablets rather than the powdered crude material. Their preparation from toxic alkaloids and glycerides is strictly controlled, and such medicines are obtainable only by prescription.

Capsules

Capsules are soluble cases, usually made of gelatine, enclosing a dose of a medicine such as an oil or even a dose of dried herb. They are usually without odour and taste and are easily swallowed.

Injections

Injections are sterile solutions prepared from pure isolated natural substances or synthetic chemicals. They are contained in ampoules (small sealed glass or plastic capsules containing one dose) ready for injection (by medical personnel only) with a syringe into the skin (intracutaneously), below the skin (subcutaneously), into a muscle (intramuscularly) or into a vein (intravenously). It is one method of administration of potent plant medicines such as atropine, morphine, digitoxin and ergotamine, which can be prescribed only by medical practitioners. Occasionally plant extracts are also given by injection to treat various diseases. Injections are also used to diagnose and treat allergies such as hay fever.

Inhalations

Essential oils, finely dispersed solutions and fine powders are used as inhalants. They are breathed in for the treatment of respiratory disorders. They are best applied with an instrument called a nebulizer, which produces a fine spray of the substance for inhalation. In the home hot infusions can be used for steam inhalation. Inhalation of smoke produced by herbal cigarettes can be an effective treatment for asthma and herbal snuffs also have a place in phytotherapy.

Herbal vinegars

Herbal vinegars are prepared by steeping about 1 tablespoon (10 grams) of fresh or dried herbs in 7 fl. oz (200 ml) of wine or cider vinegar and alcohol or vinegar and water. This mixture should be left for at least 24 hours and then strained into bottles.

Herbal wines

Herbal wines are prepared by steeping fresh or dried herbs in a good white wine. The proportions are the same as for vinegars.

Herbal oils

Herbal oils are prepared by steeping about 1/4 oz (5 grams) of fresh or dried herbs in 4 fl. oz (100 ml) of a pure vegetable (fatty) oil (such as almond oil or olive oil) for several weeks in a warm, dry, sunny place and then straining. They are used when ointments and compresses are not suitable. They should always be stored in brown-glass containers. These oils should not be confused with the much more potent essential oils.

Aromatic waters

Aromatic waters are aqueous solutions, usually saturated, of essential oils to which alcohol is usually added. They are freshly prepared as required, a month's supply at the most because they do not keep as long as herbal vinegars. They are used externally and internally.

Medicinal syrups

To prepare medicinal syrups liquid plant extracts are added to sugar solutions. They are used internally, particularly as antitussives and expectorants for children.

Pressed juices

Fresh plant parts are crushed and pressed by hand or mechanically. They can be rich in vitamins and minerals. Juices do not keep well so they need freshly preparing unless preservatives are added.

Liniments

Liniments are oily, liquid, sometimes almost gel-like preparations that become runny when rubbed on or into the skin. They are solutions, suspensions or emulsions of medicinal substances in a suitable medium. Camphor and soap liniment is a preparation of green soap, camphor, rosemary oil, alcohol and purified water used as a rubefacient.

Spirits

Spirits are solutions of essential oils in alcohol, such as spirits of lavender and spirits of rosemary. They are used externally or as flavouring agents or internally.

Suppositories and pessaries

Suppositories are solid pieces of medicated substances (usually cocoa butter), conical, ovoid or cylindrical in shape, which are inserted into the rectum or vagina where they melt. The medicine acts locally or is transported to other sites. Vaginal suppositories are usually called pessaries.

Ointments (Salves)

Ointments are fatty substances, usually containing medicaments, which readily spread at room temperature and are softened on contact with the body. They are soothing and healing when applied to the skin or mucous membranes. The ointment base can be pure lard, but is usually petroleum jelly, lanolin, oil or a synthetic substance. *Pastes* are of thicker consistency and cosmetic *creams* are fine ointments of varied consistency, often with more than 10 per cent water.

Medicated plasters and soaps

Plasters are pasty medicinal preparations spread on cloth and applied to the skin. They are softened by the body temperature, they adhere to the skin and do not melt. Besides medicinal substances (for example, mustard), plasters may include lanolin or resin. Medicated soaps often contain substances of plant origin, such as birch tar and essential oils.

Poultices

Poultices are preparations of a hot, moist, pasty medicinal substance spread between layers of muslin, gauze or towels and applied to the skin. They are removed when cool and they can sometimes be reheated a few times.

Compresses

Compresses are pads of lint or gauze dipped in a cold or hot medicinal solution, such as an infusion or decoction, and applied to the skin. Their temperature should not exceed 60 °C. They are usually covered with a piece of flannel and bandaged in place. Cleaned, bruised fresh leaves or roots held in place by a bandage make the simplest compresses.

Herbal baths

Baths involve the total immersion of the body or the immersion of just the limbs, hands or feet in water to which various plant substances have been added. Usually an infusion or decoction is used plus a few tablespoons of sea salt. For a normal bath at home about 1³/₄ pints (1 litre) of the herbal solution is sufficient. Another bath method is to mix a herb or herbs with oatmeal and sew them into a muslin bag, which is then hung from the hotwater tap.

Treatments with medicinal herbs

Teas, tea mixtures

Several herbs with very mild therapeutic actions, such as Chamomile, limes and Peppermint, make pleasant, wholesome and refreshing or soothing beverages for drinking hot or cold instead of ordinary tea. Unlike ordinary tea and coffee they contain no caffeine and are thus especially suitable for persons with delicate constitutions. Unless taken to excess these teas are harmless and complement the normal diet. A selection of such teas for making at home is given on page 42. These herbs do not have to be freshly picked, although growing them adds extra pleasure to their use. Many of them are easily obtainable in dried, sometimes fresh, form from herbal suppliers or herbal practitioners, who will also advise on the best way of using them effectively. Health-food stores and a growing number of retail chemists also stock the commonest herbs. If they are not obtainable locally they can be purchased by mail order from commercial suppliers.

Before taking any herbal tea regularly for a specific therapeutic purpose, however, particularly if there is any doubt about its action or about the disorder being treated, it is wise to seek the advice of a professional herbalist. Side-effects can be caused by the overuse of some quite common herbs, such as Wormwood, which is often recommended for appetite loss and indigestion. A trained herbalist will take a medical history, ask about diet and lifestyle and will recommend the most appropriate treatment and dosage. It is well worth seeking such advice. Careful note should always be taken about the recommended dosage and any guidance about treatment.

A single herb may be the preferred treatment, but combined teas or tea mixtures are more usually recommended. These mixtures are complicated to formulate because the chemical and botanical compatibility of the plants has to be known so that the right herbs are used in the correct proportions. The choice of herbs to use in recipes is thus best left to the experts. Every combined tea recipe includes several constituents:

1. The basic remedy that determines the general effect; there may be up to three or more ingredients in it.
2. The adjuvant that complements or enhances the basic remedy.
3. Substances that determine the final flavour, aroma, texture and appearance of the mixture. They include colour additives such as the blue flowers of

Cornflower and the orange-yellow flowers of Pot Marigold, a sweetener such as honey, and a taste-enhancer such as Liquorice.

These tea mixtures (without the sweetener) are usually prescribed by a herbalist or are bought over the counter already mixed and ready for use. The basic methods of preparing teas are given on pages 37−38 and in the next section on tea substitutes, but quantities vary according to the herb and the disorder being treated. Teas should never be steeped for too long, otherwise the delicate flavour of some herbs will be lost. Many may need sweetening − with honey, not sugar − but some should be drunk unsweetened. A slice or two of lemon or a little lemon juice may help to bring out the flavour. Therapeutic teas are usually taken three times a day: in the morning about 15 minutes before breakfast; in the afternoon around 5 p.m.; and in the evening before going to bed.

Some substitutes for ordinary tea

Many herbs make deliciously flavoured teas which can be drunk warm or chilled during the day in place of Indian or China Tea or are soothing beverages in the evening or before going to bed. Among the many tea substitutes are: Balm (leaves), Chamomile (flowers), Cowslip (flowers), Elder (flowers), Fennel (seeds), Hop (female cones), limes (flowers), nettles (leaves),

The flowers and fruits of Elder (see Pl. 211) are used medicinally.

Peppermint (leaves), roses (petals and hips), thymes (flowering stems) and Wild Strawberry (leaves).

The basic method follows that for ordinary tea:

1. Warm a china or glass teapot or jug.
2. Put 1 heaped teaspoon (dried) or 3 teaspoons (fresh crushed) herb for each cup in the pot or jug.
3. Pour in sufficient boiling water. Cover, if using a jug.
4. Leave to stand for 4−5 minutes.
5. Strain into a cup and sweeten (with honey) and flavour if desired.

For iced tea follow the same method; after straining the tea, cover and leave to cool in the fridge. It should be drunk within 12 hours. A tea from seeds is made by adding 1 tablespoon of bruised seeds to a pint (560 ml) of boiling water in an earthenware, heatproof glass or enamelled pan and simmering for 5 minutes. After straining drink this tea warm.

Fruit and vegetable juices

Many fruits, such as bilberries, blackberries, black currants, raspberries, rosehips, rowanberries and strawberries, can be pressed for their juices, as can many common vegetables (for example, Carrot). Dried fruits and non-pulpy fresh fruits should be soaked in water before pressing. Juices can be drunk undiluted or diluted with water, with or without a sweetener. They are best prepared only as needed, although it is possible to store them if a preservative such as citric acid or tartaric acid is added. Commercially prepared juices should be kept in the refrigerator and used as recommended. In winter time these can serve as a substitute for fresh fruit.

Elderberry juice
Wash 5^1/$_2$ lb (2.5 kg) of elderberries (with stalks), put them in an earthenware, heatproof glass or enamelled pan and add 3^1/$_2$ pt (2 l) of boiling water plus ^{3}/$_4$ oz (20 g) citric acid; steep for 24 hours. Then put the mixture through a nylon sieve. Add a cinnamon or vanilla stick for flavour and boil the juice for 15 minutes without sugar. Then add 1^3/$_4$ lb (800 g) sugar per 1^3/$_4$ pt (1 l) juice and boil for another 10 minutes. Pour the juice while still warm into warmed sterilized bottles, and stopper tightly with a cork. Coat the top of the bottle with candle wax or cover with cellophane and tie with string until needed. The bottles should be stored in a cool, dark place. This juice will keep for 6 months unopened, but should be drunk within 3 days once opened.

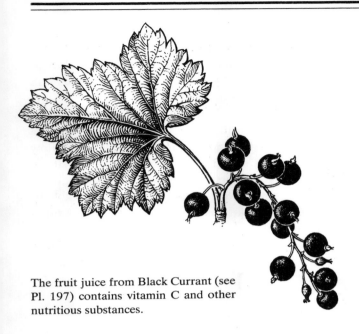

The fruit juice from Black Currant (see Pl. 197) contains vitamin C and other nutritious substances.

Cooked blackcurrant juice

Wash 5¹/₂ lb (2.5 kg) of fresh blackcurrants in a colander. Then put them in an earthenware, glass or enamelled basin, add 3¹/₂ pt (2 l) of boiling water and ³/₄ oz (20 g) citric or tartaric acid. Let stand undisturbed for 24 hours. Then strain through a nylon sieve. Do not press the pulp. Combine the strained juice with sugar (2¹/₄ lb or 1 kg for every 1³/₄ pt or 1 l juice), stirring occasionally to dissolve the sugar. Pour the juice into sterilized bottles, and stopper tightly with a cork. Coat the top of the bottle with candle wax or cover with cellophane and tie with string until needed. The bottles should be stored in a cool, dark place. This juice keeps for 6 months unopened but should be drunk within 3 days once opened.

These juices can be taken in a daily dose of 1 tablespoon on their own or made into a cup of tea with boiling water. Blackberries, cherries, bilberries, raspberries and strawberries can be prepared in the same way.

Herbal baths

The method of preparing herbal baths is given on page 41. Immersion is usually for 10—30 minutes.

Herbs used for baths are basically of two kinds: those containing essential oils (for example, Chamomile, Juniper, Lovage, Peppermint, Rosemary and Garden Thyme), which have refreshing or soothing properties; and those containing tannins (for example, oaks, Sage and Walnut), which have astringent properties. A Rosemary bath is invigorating and should be taken in the morning; one containing Lavender is relaxing and is best taken at night.

Herbal cosmetics

Unlike many synthetic preparations, herbal cosmetics do not usually cause allergic reactions, although it should be said that some individuals are allergic to certain plants (for example, primulas such as Cowslip and Primrose). An increasing number of cosmetics are now being made commercially entirely from natural ingredients and are being sold by specialist herbalist and health-food shops and by retail chemists. Many herbal cosmetics are also easy to make at home. They are cheaper than bought products, just as beneficial and, of course, do not contain chemical preservatives. Recipes for making them feature in many herb and beauty books. It should be remembered, however, that home-made cosmetics and some bought herbal preparations do not keep as well as synthetic products.

It need hardly be mentioned that the condition of the skin, hair, eyes, nails and body reflects one's general health. If a person is not eating the correct foods, and not getting sufficient fresh air and exercise, good sleep and relaxation, then cosmetics can do little to improve the appearance. The first condition for effective cosmetic treatment is therefore plenty of sleep and exercise and an appropriate, balanced and wholesome diet. Fruit and vegetables should be taken daily; hot, spicy foods, sugar, tea, coffee and alcohol should be taken in moderation or avoided altogether and there should, of course, be no smoking. Herbal baths and teas can help the appearance with their soothing or refreshing and tonic properties.

Substances that cleanse, nourish and tighten the skin and make it fresher, lighter and smoother include azulenes (found in some essential oils), mucilage, some tannins and vitamins. Azulenes, which lighten the skin, occur particularly in Chamomile and Scented Mayweed (Wild Chamomile). Tannins and mucilage in, for example, Wild Pansy (Heartsease), have astringent, softening and slight bleaching and antiseptic effects. The restorative effect of vitamins becomes evident on application of a face mask made of crushed fruits or vegetables. Wrinkles are held at bay by essential oils, especially from Garden Lavender and Rosemary. Swollen eyelids and pouches under the eyes can be treated with alternate warm and cold compresses of a decoction from Sage. The azulenes in Chamomile have a similar effect. A decoction from Chamomile combined with milk in equal parts soothes reddened or irritated skin and the mucous membranes. The process of healing and the formation of new tissue is speeded up by allantoin, which is found in Common Comfrey and is best applied in an ointment.

Freckles and other pigmented patches on the skin can be treated with preparations rich in vitamins A and C (juices from fruit and vegetables). Vitamin C checks the formation of brown pigment and vitamin

A is nourishing and promotes the formation of new tissue. Herbs rich in antiseptic substances such as azulenes and tannins are used to treat various skin infections and nail disorders.

Several herbs are beneficial to the hair. Shampoos for treating dandruff, falling hair and oily hair include infusions and decoctions from Ash and White Willow (they contain salicylic acid), Soapwort (a natural cleanser), Rosemary, Common Nettle and Sweet Flag. Rosemary, Sage and Walnut suit dark hair; Greater Burdock, Chamomile and Sweet Flag highlight fair hair.

Arrangement of medicinal herbs by plant family

The number in brackets after each species is the number of the plate in which that species is depicted and described in the following pages.

CLAVICIPITACEAE
Claviceps purpurea (64)

PARMELIACEAE
Cetraria islandica (53)

Flowering plants and ferns
APOCYNACEAE
(Dogbane family)
Vinca minor (251)

ARACEAE
(Arum family)
Acorus calamus (4)
Arum maculatum (30)

ARALIACEAE
(Ivy family)
Hedera helix (113)

ARISTOLOCHIACEAE
(Birthwort family)
Aristolochia clematitis (23)
Asarum europaeum (31)

ASCLEPIADACEAE
(Milkweed family)
Vincetoxicum hirundinaria (252)

BERBERIDACEAE
(Barberry family)
Berberis vulgaris (37)

BETULACEAE
(Birch family)
Alnus glutinosa (13)
Betula pendula (38)
Corylus avellana (74)

BORAGINACEAE
(Borage family)
Anchusa officinalis (15)
Borago officinalis (39)
Lithospermum officinale (135)
Pulmonaria officinalis (189)
Symphytum officinale (228)

BUXACEAE
(Box family)
Buxus sempervirens (42)

CANNABACEAE
(Hemp family)
Cannabis sativa (46)
Humulus lupulus (119)

CAPRIFOLIACEAE
(Honeysuckle family)
Sambucus ebulis (210)
Sambucus nigra (211)
Sambucus racemosa (212)

CARYOPHYLLACEAE
(Pink family)
Herniaria glabra (117)
Saponaria officinalis (215)

CHENOPODIACEAE
(Goosefoot family)
Chenopodium ambrosioides (58)

COMPOSITAE/
ASTERACEAE (Daisy family)
Achillea millefolium (1)
Achillea ptarmica (2)
Antennaria dioica (18)
Arctium lappa (20)
Arctium tomentosum (21)
Arnica montana (25)
Artemisia abrotanum (26)
Artemisia absinthium (27)
Artemisia dracunculus (28)
Artemisia vulgaris (29)
Bellis perennis (36)
Calendula officinalis (43)
Carlina acaulis (49)
Centaurea cyanus (51)
Chamaemelon nobile (54)
Chamomilla suaveolens (56)
Chrysanthemum cinerarifolium (59)
Chrysanthemum parthenium (= *Tanacetum parthenium*) (60)
Chrysanthemum vulgare (= *Tanacetum vulgare*) (61)
Cichorium intybus (62)
Cnicus benedictus (66)
Conyza canadensis (70)
Cynara cardunculus (80)
Helianthus annuus (114)
Inula helenium (123)
Lactuca virosa (128)
Petasites hybridus (162)
Silybum marianum (221)
Solidago virgaurea (224)
Taraxacum officinale (229)
Tussilago farfara (240)

CONVOLVULACEAE
(Bindweed family)
Calystegia sepium (45)

CRASSULACEAE
(Stonecrop family)
Sedum acre (219)
Sempervivum tectorum (220)

CRUCIFERAE/
BRASSICACEAE
(Cabbage family)
Armoracia rusticana (24)
Brassica nigra (40)
Capsella bursa-pastoris (47)
Nasturtium officinale (147)
Raphanus sativus (193)
Sinapis alba (222)

CUCURBITACEAE
(Gourd family)
Bryonia alba (41)
Cucurbita pepo (48)

CUPRESSACEAE
(Cypress family)
Juniperus communis (126)

DROSERACEAE
(Sundew family)
Drosera rotundifolia (90)

ELAEAGNACEAE
(Oleaster family)
Hippophae rhamnoides (118)

EQUISETACEAE
(Horsetail family)
Equisetum arvense (93)

ERICACEAE
(Heath family)
Arctostaphylos uva-ursi (22)
Calluna vulgaris (44)
Vaccinium myrtillus (243)
Vaccinium vitis-idaea (244)

EUPHORBIACEAE
(Spurge family)
Ricinus communis (198)

FAGACEAE
(Beech family)
Quercus petraea (190)
Quercus robur (191)

FUMARIACEAE
(Fumitory family)
Corydalis cava (73)

GENTIANACEAE
(Gentian family)
Centaurium erythraea (52)
Gentiana lutea (106)

GERANIACEAE
(Geranium family)
Geranium robertianum (107)

GRAMINEAE
(Grass family)
Agropyron repens
  (= *Elymus repens*) (8)
Avena sativa (34)
Zea mays (256)

GUTTIFERAE/
HYPERICACEAE
(St John's Wort family)
Hypericum perforatum (121)

HIPPOCASTANACEAE
(Horse Chestnut family)
Aesculus hippocastanum (6)

IRIDACEAE
(Iris family)
Crocus sativus (77)
Iris germanica (124)

JUGLANDACEAE
(Walnut family)
Juglans regia (125)

LABIATAE/LAMIACEAE
(Mint family)
Ballota nigra (35)
Galeopsis segetum (102)
Glechoma hederacea (109)
Hyssopus officinalis (122)
Lamium album (129)
Lavandula angustifolia (130)
Leonurus cardiaca (131)
Lycopus europaeus (137)
Marrubium vulgare (141)
Melissa officinalis (143)
Mentha aquatica (144)
Mentha × piperita (145)
Nepeta cataria (148)
Ocimum basilicum (152)
Origanum majorana (155)
Origanum vulgare (156)
Prunella vulgaris (184)
Rosmarinus officinalis (202)
Salvia officinalis (208)
Salvia sclarea (209)
Satureja hortensis (216)
Stachys officinalis (227)
Teucrium chamaedrys (231)

Thymus serpyllum (232)
Thymus vulgaris (233)

LEGUMINOSAE/FABACEAE
(Pea family)
Anthyllis vulneraria (19)
Coronilla varia (72)
Cytisus scoparius (81)
Galega officinalis (101)
Genista tinctoria (105)
Glycine max (110)
Glycyrrhiza glabra (111)
Laburnum anagyroides (127)
Melilotus officinalis (142)
Ononis spinosa (153)
Phaseolus vulgaris (165)
Robinia pseudoacacia (199)
Sophora japonica (225)
Trifolium pratense (236)
Trifolium repens (237)
Trigonella foenum-graecum
  (238)

LENTIBULARIACEAE
(Butterwort family)
Pinguicula vulgaris (169)

LILIACEAE
(Lily family)
Allium cepa (11)
Allium sativum (12)
Colchicum autumnale (67)
Convallaria majalis (69)
Polygonatum odoratum (173)
Veratrum album (246)

LINACEAE
(Flax family)
Linum usitatissimum (134)

LORANTHACEAE
(Mistletoe family)
Viscum album (255)

LYCOPODIACEAE
(Clubmoss family)
Lycopodium clavatum (136)

MALVACEAE
(Mallow family)
Alcea rosea (9)
Althaea officinalis (14)
Malva sylvestris (139, 140)

MENYANTHACEAE
(Bogbean family)
Menyanthes trifoliata (146)

NYMPHAEACEAE
(Waterlily family)
Nymphaea alba (151)

OLEACEAE
(Olive family)
Fraxinus excelsior (99)

ONAGRACEAE
(Willowherb family)
Epilobium angustifolium (92)

ORCHIDACEAE
(Orchid family)
Orchis morio (154)

OXALIDACEAE
(Wood Sorrel family)
Oxalis acetosella (157)

PAEONIACEAE
(Peony family)
Paeonia officinalis (158)

PAPAVERACEAE
(Poppy family)
Chelidonium majus (57)
Fumaria officinalis (100)
Papaver bracteatum (159)
Papaver rhoeas (160)
Papaver somniferum (161)

PINACEAE
(Pine family)
Pinus sylvestris (170)

PLANTAGINACEAE
(Plantain family)
Plantago lanceolata (171)

POLYGALACEAE
(Milkwort family)
Polygala amara (172)

POLYGONACEAE
(Dock family)
Fagopyrum tataricum (95)
Polygonum aviculare (174)
Polygonum bistorta (175)
Polygonum hydropiper (176)
Polygonum lapathifolium (177)
Rheum palmatum (196)

POLYPODIACEAE
(Polypody family)
Polypodium vulgare (178)

PRIMULACEAE
(Primrose family)
Lysimachia nummularia (138)
Primula veris (183)

RANUNCULACEAE
(Buttercup family)
Aconitum napellus (3)

Adonis vernalis (5)
Clematis recta (65)
Delphinium consolida
  (= *Consolida regalis*) (85)
Helleborus niger (115)
Hepatica nobilis (116)
Nigella sativa (149)
Ranunculus ficaria (192)

RHAMNACEAE
(Buckthorn family)
Rhamnus cathartica (194)
Rhamnus frangula (195)

ROSACEAE
(Rose family)
Agrimonia eupatoria (7)
Alchemilla xanthochlora (10)
Crataegus laevigata (75)
Crataegus monogyna (76)
Cydonia oblonga (79)
Filipendula ulmaria (96)
Fragaria vesca (98)
Geum urbanum (108)
Potentilla anserina (181)
Potentilla erecta (182)
Prunus cerasus (185)
Prunus dulcis (186)
Prunus padus (187)
Prunus spinosa (188)
Rosa canina (200)
Rosa centifolia (201)
Rubus fruticosus (204)
Rubus idaeus (205)
Sanguisorba officinalis (213)
Sorbus aucuparia (226)

RUBIACEAE
(Bedstraw family)
Galium odoratum (103)
Galium verum (104)
Rubia tinctorum (203)

RUTACEAE
(Rue family)
Dictamnus albus (86)
Ruta graveolens (206)

SALICACEAE
(Willow family)
Digitalis grandiflora (87)
Digitalis lanata (88)
Digitalis purpurea (89)
Euphrasia officinalis (94)
Gratiola officinalis (112)
Linaria vulgaris (133)
Scrophularia nodosa (218)
Verbascum densiflorum (247)
Verbascum phlomoides (248)
Veronica officinalis (250)

SOLANACEAE
(Nightshade family)
Atropa belladonna (33)
Capsicum annuum (48)
Datura stramonium (83)
Hyoscyamus niger (120)
Physalis alkekengi (166)
Solanum dulcamara (223)

TAXACEAE (Yew family)
Taxus baccata (230)

THYMELAEACEAE
(Daphne family)
Daphne mezereum (82)

TILIACEAE
(Lime family)
Tilia cordata (234)
Tilia platyphyllos (235)

TROPAEOLACEAE
(Nasturtium family)
Tropaeolum majus (239)

ULMACEAE (Elm family)
Ulmus minor (241)

UMBELLIFERAE/
APIACEAE (Carrot family)
Anethum graveolens (16)
Angelica archangelica (17)
Astrantia major (32)
Carum carvi (50)
Cicuta virosa (63)
Conium maculatum (68)
Coriandrum sativum (71)
Daucus carota (83)
Foeniculum vulgare (97)
Levisticum officinale (132)
Petroselinum crispum (163)
Peucedanum ostruthium (164)
Pimpinella saxifraga (168)
Sanicula europaea (214)

URTICACEAE
(Nettle family)
Urtica dioica (242)

VALERIANACEAE
(Valerian family)
Valeriana officinalis (245)

VERBENACEAE
(Vervain family)
Verbena officinalis (249)

VIOLACEAE (Violet family)
Viola odorata (253)
Viola tricolor (254)

Plates

Yarrow, Milfoil

A perennial herb with a creeping rhizome and erect, furrowed and downy stems. The dark-green basal and stem leaves are lanceolate and finely divided (two or three times pinnate). The small flowerheads are clustered in dense, flat corymbs. The ray-florets are white or occasionally pinkish; the disc-florets whitish. The fruit, an achene, is strongly compressed and slightly winged. All parts of the plant have a characteristic strong smell.

Yarrow is common throughout Europe and Asia in hedgerows and fields and on dry banks and roadsides. It is native to the British Isles. The plant's healing properties were known to the ancient Greeks who named Yarrow *Achillea* after Achilles, the legendary heroic warrior. The specific name *millefolium* (= 'a thousand leaf') refers to the plant's many feathery leaves. The common name Yarrow is derived from the Anglo-Saxon word *gearwe*, but the meaning of this is not known.

The non-woody parts of the flowering stems, sometimes only the flowers, free of stalks, are used medicinally. The principal constituent is an essential oil with azulenes that turn blue after distillation. The plant also contains the alkaloids achilleine and stychydrine, tannins and bitter compounds. These constituents give Yarrow antiseptic, stomachic, antispasmodic, astringent and diaphoretic properties and it has a variety of uses both internally and externally. For example, herbalists use an infusion for digestive upsets, diarrhoea, flatulence, menstrual disorders, colds and fevers. Externally a decoction is used to treat slow-healing wounds, skin rashes and eczema, chapped skin and as a gargle and bath preparation. **Yarrow should always be taken in moderation and never for long periods** because it may cause skin irritation.

The fresh leaves — and the flowers — also have many cosmetic uses. The taste is slightly bitter and peppery and young leaves, chopped up, give 'bite' to a mixed salad.

Flowerhead

Flowering time: June to August

Sneezewort

A perennial herb with a woody, creeping rhizome and erect, angled, leafy stems, which are hairy at the top but not at the base. The greyish leaves are linear to lanceolate and finely serrate. The few flowerheads are clustered in loose corymbs. The ray-florets are white; the disc-florets greenish white. The fruit, an achene, is slightly winged.

Sneezewort is a common species throughout most of Europe, including the British Isles, in damp grassland on acid or heavy soils. The specific name *ptarmica* comes from the Greek word *ptarmos* (= sneezing). In the common name 'wort' is an old word for a plant, usually one used medicinally. Sneezewort has been cultivated for its medicinal properties and for garden decoration since at least the 16th century. In the past it was recommended for toothache and for 'cleansing the head'. It is no longer a common herbal remedy in Britain, but it is still widely grown, usually in double forms, in gardens.

The rhizomes, sometimes also the flowers and flowering stems, are used medicinally. The principal constituent is an essential oil that is very effective in treating fatigue, loss of appetite and urinary disorders. Sneezewort also curbs flatulence, regulates bowel movements and alleviates rheumatic and dental pain. The herb is usually taken in the form of an infusion, but chewing the fresh rhizome is also effective. The dried and powdered leaves are sometimes used as a sneezing powder.

Flowering time: July to August

Monkshood, Aconite

A perennial herb with a tuberous root and a tall, glabrous, erect stem with alternate, palmately divided leaves. The violet or blue flowers, with helmet-shaped hoods, are arranged in long terminal spikes. The fruit is a follicle. **All parts of the plant are deadly poisonous;** it is probably the most dangerous of all British plants.

Monkshood grows throughout the temperate regions of Europe on shady stream banks and in deciduous woods. In the British Isles it is fairly rare; it is native to south-west England, but elsewhere it is probably a garden escape. It is cultivated for the pharmaceutical industry in Britain in small quantities, but most supplies are imported from other countries. There have been several explanations for the derivation of the generic name, *Aconitum,* by which the plant was known in ancient times. One theory is that the name comes from the Greek word *akon* (= dart) because the juice from the plant was used for poisoning arrows. The specific name, *napellus,* means 'little turnip', a reference to the shape of the root. The curious helmet-shape of the upper petals gives Monkshood one of its common names.

The young tubers are used medicinally, but because the plant is so poisonous they should never be collected in the wild. Any contact with the living plant – even the smell of it – is highly dangerous. The tubers contain up to 1.5 per cent of alkaloids – the poisonous aconitine, napelline and nenzylaconitine – and also sugars, starch and resin. Aconitine is one of the most potent nerve poisons in the plant kingdom and it is contained in proprietary analgesic medicines to alleviate pain both internally and externally. These drugs can be prescribed only by qualified medical practitioners. Tinctures of Monkshood are frequently used in homeopathy. **In no circumstances should Monkshood ever be prepared and used for self-medication.** Only 10 grams of the root is a fatal dose.

Tuberous root

Flowering time: May to June

Sweet Flag, Calamus

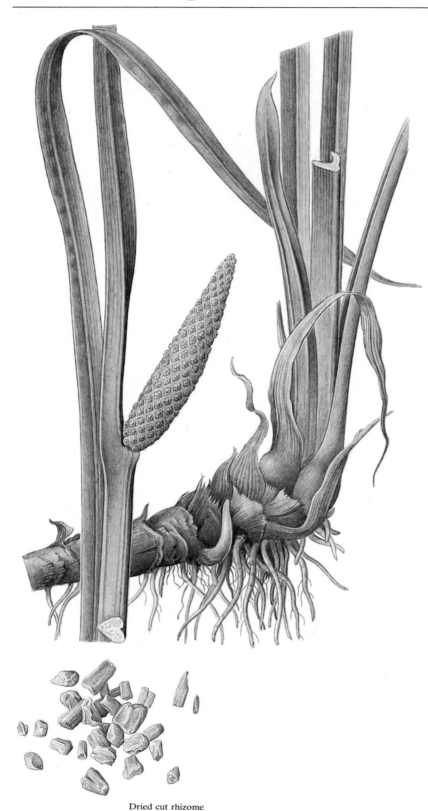

Dried cut rhizome

A perennial herb with a thick branched rhizome. The leaves are narrow, sword-shaped with an undulate edge, and smell of tangerines when crushed. Growing at an angle from the leafless, three-sided flowering stem (scape) is a long cylindrical spadix bearing yellow-green flowers. Plants growing in Europe are sterile, but in its native India Sweet Flag bears fruits (berries).

In the 16th century Sweet Flag was brought from southern Asia to the botanical garden in Vienna from where it was introduced to other botanical gardens. It has also since become established in the wild all over the Continent. In the British Isles Sweet Flag grows locally beside shallow water, mostly in England; it is rare in Scotland, Wales and Ireland. The plant was named Sweet Flag because the leaves resemble those of Yellow Flag (*Iris pseudacorus*), but botanically it is not related to the irises. The generic name, *Acorus,* is derived from the Greek name of the plant used by Dioscorides, who may have been alluding to the belief that the plant cures eye trouble (the Greek word *kore* = pupil of the eye). Another old practice is referred to by the specific name: Sweet Flag was strewn on floors instead of rushes, hence *calamus* (from the Greek word *kalamos* = a reed). The plant remains a popular herbal remedy.

The rhizomes are used medicinally. When dried they are strongly aromatic and brittle. The constituents include up to 4 per cent of an essential oil with asarone as its chief component, sesquiterpenes, the bitter compounds acorin and acoretin, and tannins. Sweet Flag is used in herbalism as a stomachic and carminative. It is also added to bath preparations to alleviate nervous exhaustion. The essential oil is extracted and combined with other substances in stomachic powders, teas and drops. It is also used in perfumery.

Flowering time: June to July

Yellow Pheasant's Eye, Spring Adonis

A perennial herb with a stout, dark rhizome, which bears an erect, glabrous stem with sessile, finely divided (two or three times pinnate) feathery leaves and a large, terminal, solitary, shiny, golden-yellow flower. There may be up to 20 elliptic petals. This species flowers in early spring and the blossoms open fully only on sunny days. The fruit is an achene. **All parts of the plant are extremely poisonous.**

Yellow Pheasant's Eye grows wild on lime-rich soils in southeastern and central Europe, Asia and America. In many countries it has been overcollected and it is now a protected species. It is not native to the British Isles, but is occasionally grown in gardens. The related annual species – Summer Pheasant's Eye (*A. aestivalis*), Autumn Pheasant's Eye (*A. autumnalis*) and Pheasant's Eye (*A. annua*)–are also poisonous. *A. annua* is the only one of the three species that grows wild in Britain; it is a rare, naturalized weed of cornfields in a few southern counties of England and sometimes in Scotland. All these plants are named after Adonis, a beautiful youth loved by Venus. According to a Greek legend, Venus transformed him into this flower after he had been killed by a wild boar. The species are also called pheasant's eyes because the flowers of some of them have a striking dark centre.

In ancient times Yellow Pheasant's Eye was used to treat venereal diseases and later heart disorders. On the Continent the dried flowering stems, without the hard bottom parts, are still used medicinally. The most important constituents are the cardiac glycosides called cardenolides. These substances stimulate the heart, but they work faster than digitalin (from *Digitalis* leaves) and they do not accumulate in the body. They are used by the medical profession as heart stimulants and as sedatives. **No species of pheasant's eye should ever be collected and used for self-medication.**

Flower of *A. aestivalis*

Flowering time: April to May

Horse Chestnut

Seed

Fruit

A tall, deciduous tree with grey-brown, scaly bark and spreading branches. The large, sticky, brown buds open into large palmate leaves with five to seven leaflets. The flowers are yellowish white and are clustered in dense, erect panicles. The fruit is a green, spiny capsule with one or two nut-like shiny brown seeds — the well-known horse chestnuts or 'conkers'. Children have been poisoned, though not fatally, after eating the green outer casing of the fruit and they should be warned about this.

Horse Chestnut is native to southeastern Europe and seems to have been introduced into England around 1550. The tree's generic name, *Aesculus,* comes from the Latin word *esca* (= food). The name was given originally to a type of oak, the acorns of which were ground to make a flour. How it came to be transferred to Horse Chestnut is not known. There is also confusion about the origin of the tree's specific and common names. *Hippocastanum* is a Latin translation of Horse Chestnut, and this name could be derived from a Turkish custom of feeding chestnuts to horses ailing from respiratory diseases. At one time the plant was used to treat malaria.

The fully ripe chestnuts, sometimes the bark, are used medicinally. The constituents include up to 28 per cent of saponins (of which aescin is the most important), the coumarin glycosides aesculin, aesculoside and fraxin, and tannins. Horse Chestnut has astringent, antipyretic and antithrombic properties. In some countries it is included in proprietary medicines used to treat cardiovascular diseases. It is also used for varicose veins, respiratory infections and severe diarrhoea. A tincture of fresh chestnuts is used in homeopathy. **All internal use of Horse Chestnut should be medically supervised.** Externally Horse Chestnut is used to treat cuts and grazes, frostbite, ringworm and haemorrhoids. A coumarin component (aesculoside) is included in some sunscreen preparations.

Flowering time: May to June

Agrimony

A perennial herb with a short rhizome and erect, hairy, usually unbranched stem. The basal leaves are arranged in a rosette and they and the alternate sessile stem leaves are pinnate, serrate and hairy. The small, star-shaped yellow flowers grow in a long, scanty terminal spike. The fruit is an achene enclosed within a cup-shaped receptacle (hypanthium), which is grooved and edged with a ring of hooked bristles. These hooks catch onto fur or clothing and the seeds thus become dispersed.

Agrimony is a common and widespread grassland plant throughout Europe, including most of the British Isles; it is rare in north Scotland. It occurs in field margins, woodland clearings, on hedgebanks and road verges. The generic name, *Agrimonia*, may come from the Greek *agremone*, a word given to plants that supposedly healed cataracts of the eye. The specific name, *eupatoria*, probably refers to Mithradates Eupator, King of Pontus, who resisted the Roman incursions into Asia Minor in the first century BC and who introduced many herbal remedies. Agrimony was used in the old days to treat catarrh, bleeding, skin diseases, tuberculosis, even as a charm to ward-off snakes. It is still a popular medicinal plant.

The flowering stems and leaves are used medicinally. The dried herb has a pleasant, slightly bitter smell and taste and its constituents include tannins, silicic acid, bitter compounds, an essential oil and vitamins. It has astringent, carminative and anti-inflammatory properties and is used primarily to treat gastritis and enteritis. It also stimulates gastric secretions and alleviates liver, bladder and kidney disorders, especially kidney stones. In herbal medicine it is usually administered in the form of a decoction. Externally Agrimony is used as a gargle for sore throat, in compresses for skin rashes and cuts, and in bath preparations. All parts of the plant yield a good yellow dye.

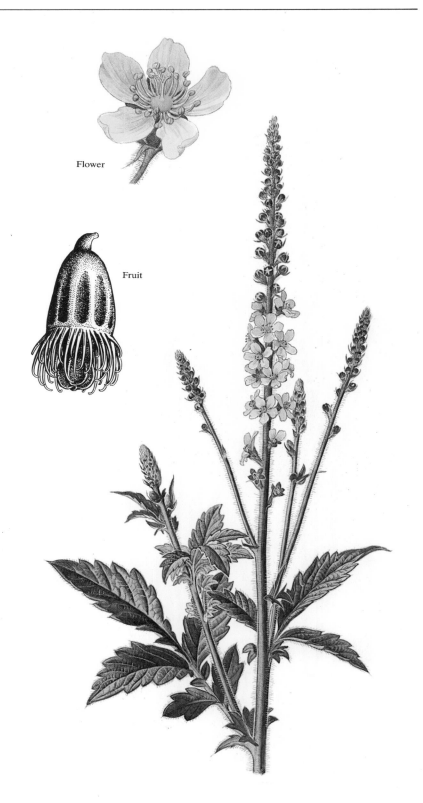

Flower

Fruit

Flowering time: June to September

Common Couch, Couch Grass, Twitch

A perennial grass with a long, white, jointed, creeping rhizome bearing both sterile and fertile hollow, jointed stems (culms). The linear leaves have sheaths that encircle the culms. The flowers are arranged in flat spikelets in a long, stiff, loose terminal spike. The fruit is a one-seeded grain.

Common Couch is a common and troublesome weed of cultivated and waste ground throughout Europe including the British Isles, and most other parts of the world. The former generic name, *Agropyron,* is derived from the Greek words *agros* (= field) and *pyros* (= wheat, grain). The common name—and its variant Quitch — is said to come from the Anglo-Saxon word *cwice* (perhaps meaning quick) on account of the plant's fast spreading habit. Common Couch has long been — and is still — used as a harmless remedy for urinary ailments. The roasted herb was once used as a substitute for coffee and as a raw material for making beer and spirits.

The rhizomes are used medicinally. When dry they have a pleasant aroma and sweetish taste. The constituents include saponins, sugars (triticin, inositol and mannitol), the phenolic glycoside avenein, mucilage and the hydrocarbon agropyrene, which has an antiseptic action. The plant is mildly diuretic and herbalists include it in tea mixtures to treat disorders of the bladder and urinary tract, uroliths and kidney inflammations. Common Couch is also recommended for gout and rheumatism.

Flowering time: June to September

Hollyhock

A biennial or perennial herb with tall, erect, leafy stems. The leaves are alternate and palmate with blunt, dentate lobes. The large showy flowers are white, pink, red or almost black and grow from the leaf axils. They are arranged in a spike-like cluster and open in succession. Double forms occur. The disc-shaped fruit (a schizocarp) separates into one-seeded nutlets (mericarps) when ripe. All parts of the plant are coarsely hairy.

Hollyhock is native to central Europe and China. Cultivated strains are grown in the Balkans as field crops for the pharmaceutical industry. In the British Isles Hollyhock is widely grown in gardens; it can sometimes be found growing in the wild on waste ground as a garden escape. The generic names *Alcea* and *Althaea* come from the Greek word *althein* (= to heal), a reference to the healing properties of this and related species of mallow, among them Marshmallow (*Althaea officinalis*) (Pl. 14) and Common Mallow (*Malva sylvestris*) (Pl. 139 and 140). The actions of Hollyhock and Marshmallow are very similar and both plants have a long history of medicinal use. The derivation of the common name, Hollyhock, is obscure. It is an old name and probably comes from 'holy' plus the Anglo-Saxon word *hoc* for mallow.

The flowers of dark, sometimes also double, forms are used medicinally. All parts of the plant must be free of mallow rust (*Puccinia malvacearum*). The constituents include abundant mucilage, the pigment anthocyanin and tannins. Hollyhock has excellent emollient and demulcent properties, which make it a useful treatment for inflammation of the mucous membranes, cough, asthma, chronic gastritis and enteritis, and for constipation. In herbalism it is usually administered in the form of an infusion. Hollyhock is also used in soothing herbal compresses and in bath preparations for skin disorders and cuts and bruises. The fresh leaves have similar beneficial effects. The dark pigment is used to colour medicines and foodstuffs.

Flower

Seed

Flowering time: July to September

Lady's Mantle

Flower

A perennial herb with a short rhizome bearing ascending or sprawling stems and a rosette of basal leaves that have dentate lobes and are circular or reniform in outline. The small, greenish-yellow flowers are arranged in dense clusters in a compound terminal cyme. The sepals are in two rings of four; there are no petals. The fruit is an achene. All parts of the plant are softly hairy.

Alchemilla xanthochlora occurs throughout Europe in meadows, pastures and woodland clearings. It grows all over the British Isles in lowland areas, but is less common in southeastern England and southern Ireland. It is one of an aggregate of species, collectively called *Alchemilla vulgaris* and Lady's Mantle, which differ in small ways but all have the same medicinal properties. The aggregate species is often cultivated. The drops of dew or rain water that collect in the centre of the leaves were used by medieval alchemists who believed them to have medicinal and magical powers. The plant's generic name, *Alchemilla* (from the Arabic word *alkimiya*), derives from this custom. Traditionally Lady's Mantle has been used for healing wounds and curing women's ailments and it was long ago dedicated to the Virgin Mary, the lobes of the leaves being supposed to resemble the edges of a mantle.

The flowering stems, including the basal leaves, are used medicinally. The constituents include tannins, essential oils, saponins, bitter compounds and salicylic acid. Lady's Mantle is mildly astringent, diuretic and anti-inflammatory and herbalists prescribe it for digestive disorders such as gastritis and enteritis, flatulence and diarrhoea. It also relaxes muscular spasms and regulates the menstrual cycle, particularly during the menopause. Externally Lady's Mantle is used in bath preparations for wounds, bruises and skin disorders, and it is a valuable herbal cosmetic.

Flowering time: June to September

Onion

A perennial herb with an edible brown, scaly bulb bearing hollow, tubular leaves and an erect stem that is thickened at the base and terminated by an umbel of greenish-white flowers. The fruit is a capsule with black seeds. Onion is almost odourless when intact, but if cut it produces a distinctive smell and releases a tear-producing substance. The stronger the smell the stronger the healing constituents.

It is believed that Onion originally grew wild in Asia but no wild form of the plant as we know it today survives. Even several thousand years ago Onion was being cultivated as a vegetable and medicinal plant in Mesopotamia, India and Egypt. It was probably introduced to Europe by the Romans. Nowadays Onion is one of the commonest vegetables and is cultivated in many forms and varieties. The colour of the bulb may be whitish, brownish, purplish or red depending on the variety and the size of the bulb. The generic name, *Allium,* is the Latin for Garlic (*A. sativum*), a related species (Pl. 12). The name Onion seems to be derived from the Latin word *unio* (= one large pearl).

The fresh bulb is used medicinally. The most important constituents are organic sulphur-containing compounds, which are excellent antiseptics. Onion also contains essential oils, sugars, vitamins and minerals. Besides its germicidal action, Onion has expectorant, diuretic, stomachic, choleretic, anthelmintic, hypotensive and hypoglycaemic properties. It is a popular remedy for treating infections of the respiratory passages (especially coughs, bronchitis and the common cold) and of the digestive system. Crushed fresh Onion can be applied to insect bites and boils. The bulb loses its effectiveness when dried.

Bulbil

Longitudinal section of bulb

Flowering time: June to July

Garlic

Bulb

A perennial herb with a bulb divided into segments (cloves), basal linear leaves and an erect stem terminated by an umbel with numerous small bulbils between the purplish-white flowers. The flower cluster is enclosed by a sheath (spathe) of papery bracts. The fruit is a capsule with black seeds, but the seeds do not ripen in cultivated plants.

Originally from India or Central Asia, Garlic has long been cultivated as an important vegetable, seasoning and medicinal herb. It was probably introduced into Britain by the Romans. It is cultivated commercially only on a very small scale in Britain; most supplies are imported. Breeding and selection have yielded countless varieties, which are propagated vegetatively by planting the cloves in rows in prepared soil. Garlic's name is derived from the Anglo-Saxon word *garleac*, from *gar* (= a spear) and *leac* (= a leek), supposedly meaning 'a leek with cloves like spearheads'.

The bulb is used medicinally, either fresh, dried or otherwise processed. It contains essential oils and the sulphuric compound alliin, which breaks down — when the cell tissue is disrupted by cutting — into the pungent allicin and diallyldisulphides. Iodine is another important constituent. Garlic has a wide variety of uses and is a common herbal remedy. Like Onion it is an important antiseptic; it also has hypotensive, weak anthelmintic, choleretic and expectorant properties. It is used to treat intestinal infections, hypertension and arteriosclerosis, and it aids digestion by stimulating bile secretions. Externally Garlic can be applied to insect bites, boils and unbroken chilblains, but **it may cause an allergic rash if used for too long.** It should be used sparingly in cooking. Chewing a leaf of basil (*Ocimum*), mint (*Mentha*), parsley (*Petroselinum*) or thyme (*Thymus*) helps to cleanse the breath after eating Garlic.

Flowering time: July to September

Alder

A deciduous shrub or medium-sized tree with darkish-brown, fissured bark and glabrous twigs with yellow lenticels (wart-like structures) on the bark. The leaves are broadly rounded or sometimes notched at the tip, often doubly serrate, bright-green on both sides and very sticky (viscid) in the spring. Alder is mon-oecious; the flowers are borne on the old wood and appear before the leaves ar-ranged in catkins. The long, dangling male catkins have purplish scales and yellow flowers; the short female catkins are nearly globular, reddish-purple in early spring but they become brown and woody after the seeds have been released form-ing cones or 'berries'. The fruit is a winged achene.

Alder is native to Europe, Asia and Africa. It grows in wet woods and by lakes and streams. It is common throughout most of the British Isles. The wood is light and easily worked when seasoned. The common name, Alder, supposedly comes from the Anglo-Saxon word *alor* or *aler,* which in turn may derive from an old German word *elo* or *elawer* (reddish yellow), a reference perhaps to the colour of the fresh-cut wood.

Grey Alder (*A. incana*) is similar to Alder but it has smooth greyish bark, its leaves are pointed and are greyish green above and pale below. It is not native to the British Isles but it has become naturalized in some places. Green Alder (*A. viridis*) is more of a shrub than a tree. Its leaves have a pointed tip, cordate base and are green on both sides. It grows in mountainous areas on the Continent. All species of alder have similar medicinal properties and are popular remedies.

The sticky young leaves and the bark, best of all from felled trees, are used medicinally. The constituents include tan-nins and anthraquinones which give Alder an astringent action and a bitter taste. It is used to treat enteritis, severe diarrhoea, fever, colds and rheumatic pain. External-ly a decoction of Alder is used as a gargle for tonsillitis and as a mouth wash. The fresh crushed leaves soothe chapped skin.

Flowering time: March to April.

Catkins:

female

male

Marshmallow

Segment of fruit (mericarp)

Root

A perennial herb with a yellow, branched root, tall, erect, leafy stems and large alternate, lobed and irregularly toothed leaves. The stems and the leaves are velvety. The white or pinkish flowers, which are attractive to bees, are arranged in irregular racemes in the leaf axils. The disc-shaped schizocarpic fruit (a capsule) splits into one-seeded nutlets (mericarps). The fruits are popularly called 'cheeses' because of their rounded form.

Marshmallow has a widespread distribution from western Europe to Siberia. In the British Isles, where it is native, it is locally common in salt marshes and on banks near the sea. It has long been cultivated for culinary, medicinal and ornamental purposes. The familiar soft sweet, marshmallow, was originally flavoured with Marshmallow root. In the common name 'mallow' is a corruption of the Latin name *malva* for this and related plants in the Malvaceae family (see also Pl. 139). Both *malva* and Malvaceae probably come from the Greek word *malakos* (= soft), a reference to the softening and healing properties of these herbs. Marshmallow remains a popular herbal remedy for a variety of ailments and is cultivated commercially in some countries, but not in Britain.

The whole plant has a medicinal action. It must be free of rust. Marshmallow is one of the most important mucilaginous medicinal herbs because it contains a high percentage of mucilage (flowers up to 20 per cent, roots up to 30 per cent) and it is included in proprietary medicines and herbal preparations as an emollient, demulcent, antitussive and expectorant. Among its other constituents are sugar, starch, an amino acid (asparagine) and pectin. Marshmallow is used internally for bronchitis and asthma and for stomach and intestinal disorders. It also makes soothing gargles and compresses and poultices for external use. It has many cosmetic uses too. The roots can be boiled and eaten as a vegetable.

Flowering time: August to September

Alkanet

A biennial or perennial herb with a black taproot, which bears a basal rosette of narrow, lanceolate leaves the first year and, in the following years, an erect stem with sessile, lanceolate leaves. The red, later blue, funnel-shaped flowers are arranged in several axillary and terminal, coiled cymes. All parts of the plant are softly hairy. The fruit separates into four one-seeded ovoid nutlets (mericarps) with protuberances on the surface. Like Borage (*Borago officinalis*) (Pl. 39), which is a member of the same family, Boraginaceae, Alkanet is an important source of food for bees.

Alkanet is native to the warmer regions of Europe where it grows on sunny banks and waste ground. In the British Isles it occurs occasionally in waste places as a garden escape. The generic name, *Anchusa,* is said to derive from the Greek word *aghousa* (= a paint) because the root of a related species, *A. tinctoria,* was once used as a source of a red dye. The common name is also connected with dyeing. It is a corruption of the Arabic word *al-hinna'* for Henna (*Lawsonia inermis*), the shrub still used as a source of a reddish-brown dye for hair. Alkanet was once a popular remedy for heart and urinary disorders, but is now seldom used by herbalists.

The flowering stems, sometimes also the roots and flowers, are used medicinally. The constituents include silicic acid, the alkaloids cynoglossine and consolidine, mucilage and pigments (anthocyanins). These substances give Alkanet an expectorant action and it is thus used in herbal medicine to treat coughs, bronchitis and other chest and throat infections. The tender young leaves are a rich source of vitamin C and they can be eaten raw in salads or cooked like spinach. The plant's rough surface may, however, irritate the skin.

Segment of fruit (mericarp)

Root

Flowering time: May to September

Dill

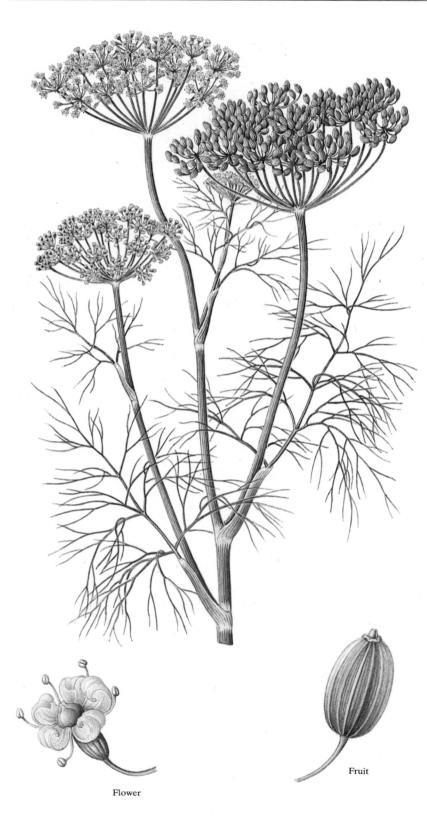

Flower

Fruit

An annual herb with bluish-green, hollow, furrowed, branched stems and alternate, multipinnate, feathery leaves. The yellowish flowers lack sepals and are arranged in compound terminal umbels. The brown fruit, a double achene, is laterally compressed, elliptical and prominently ribbed. All parts of the plant are aromatic, the fruits more so than the leaves. Dill is very similar to Fennel (*Foeniculum vulgare*) (Pl. 97) but is distinguished by its annual habit, hollow stem and flattened, lens-shaped seeds.

Dill is native to the eastern Mediterranean region and western Asia, but it has long been cultivated elsewhere. It was once an important medicinal herb for treating coughs and headaches and an ingredient of ointments. It is still widely used by herbalists but is chiefly known as a vegetable and seasoning herb. It is grown commercially in Britain only on a small scale but seeds imported from other countries are processed for their oil by British firms. The generic name, *Anethum,* is derived from the Greek word *anethon* for a related aromatic herb Anise (*Pimpinella anisum*) (Pl. 167). The common name, Dill, comes from the old Norse word *dylla* (probably meaning 'to soothe').

The fruits, sometimes the flowering stems, are used medicinally. Among the constituents are an essential oil (dill seed oil) with carvone and limonene as its main components, fatty oil, proteins, tannins and mucilage. Dill is a good carminative, stomachic and tranquillizer. It is also a galactagogue — it promotes milk flow in nursing mothers. Dill is safe for children and dill — or gripe — water, which is made from the fruits, is given to babies for hiccups, to relieve colic and to induce sleep. The essential oil obtained by distillation is used in the pharmaceutical industry, in the manufacture of liqueurs and in cosmetic preparations. Besides its use in the kitchen Dill is also extensively used as a flavouring agent by the food industry, especially on the Continent.

Flowering time: July to September

Garden Angelica

A biennial herb of robust habit with a dark turnip-like rhizome and stout roots, which bear, in the first year, a basal rosette of leaves and, in the second year, a tall, much-branched, furrowed, hollow, leafy, green stem. The large leaves are alternate, serrate and finely divided (two or three times pinnate), and have inflated sheathing petioles. The greenish flowers are arranged in compound terminal umbels. The fruit, a double achene, is oval, flattened with thin wings at the edges, and ribbed. All parts of the plant are aromatic. It is an excellent source of food for bees.

Garden Angelica is widely distributed throughout Europe and Asia, especially in more northerly regions and at higher altitudes. It is a common garden plant and is cultivated commercially in several countries for medicinal and perfumery purposes and for the leaf stalks, which are preserved in sugar and used in confectionery or as a flavouring for herbal liqueurs. Garden Angelica is not native to the British Isles but it has become naturalized on river banks and waste ground and can be locally abundant. Wild Angelica (*A. sylvestris*), which is a native British plant, is much commoner. Its leaf stalks can also be candied. These plants used to be called *herba angelica* (angel's plant) because they were thought to have heavenly powers against diseases. The Latin word *angelica* came originally from the Greek *angelos* (= a messenger).

The roots and fruits are used medicinally. They contain an essential oil with phellandrene and limonene as the main components, also coumarin glycosides, organic acids, bitter compounds, tannins and sugars. These constituents give Garden Angelica tonic, carminative, stomachic and antispasmodic actions. It is used internally in particular for loss of appetite, flatulence and bronchial catarrh. Externally it is used in bath preparations for exhaustion and rheumatic pain, and in gargles. The distilled oil (angelica seed oil) is used in perfumery.

Flower   Fruit

Rhizome with roots

Flowering time: July to August

Mountain Everlasting, Cat's-foot

Female flowerhead

A perennial carpeting herb that spreads by means of stolons that root at the nodes. The basal leaves are spathulate and arranged mainly in a rosette; the appressed stem leaves are lanceolate to linear and white-felted on the underside. The flowers are arranged in terminal umbels. The plant is dioecious: the female flowerheads have rose-pink or white, sepal-like woolly bracts and long, narrow tubular florets; the smaller male flowerheads have broad, usually white bracts resembling ray-florets and spreading tubular florets. Some sterile hermaphrodite florets may occur in the male flowerheads. The fruit, an achene, is crowned with a white pappus that helps its dispersal by wind.

Mountain Everlasting is widespread on heaths, mountain slopes and dry pastures throughout central and northern Europe. It is native to the British Isles; it is common in northern parts but is now very rare in southern England. It is a popular rock garden plant and edging for borders. Dried plants are used for winter decorations. The plant's generic name, *Antennaria,* comes from the Latin word *antenna* (= a feeler) and supposedly refers to the resemblance of the seed parachute to insect antennae. The alternative common name of Cat's-foot comes from the downy appearance and feel of the plant. At one time Mountain Everlasting was used to treat dysentery and tuberculosis.

The flowerheads are used medicinally. The coloured flowers have a stronger action than the white ones and they are separated from the others before drying. The dried herb has a pleasant aroma and a bitter taste. The constituents include essential oils, tannins, bitter compounds and organic pigments which give Mountain Everlasting antidiarrhoeal, mild diuretic, expectorant and choleretic properties. In herbal medicine it is used for gastrointestinal infections, bilious conditions and bronchitis. It is also an ingredient of tea mixtures.

Flowering time: June to July

Kidney Vetch

A perennial herb with a taproot and a semiprostrate or erect stem. The alternate leaves are odd-pinnate, with the terminal leaflet much larger than the others. The basal leaves are arranged in a rosette and may be undivided. The usually yellow flowers are clustered in one or two dense terminal cymes. The calyx is woolly; the petals are larger than the calyx and claw-shaped. The fruit, a one-seeded pod, is semicircular, flattened and criss-cross patterned; the seed is kidney-shaped. Apart from the fruit all parts of the plant are softly hairy.

Kidney Vetch is common throughout Europe in dry grassy places on lime-rich and sandy soils, particularly near the sea. It occurs throughout the British Isles. It is also grown for fodder either on its own or mixed with other grassland plants. The generic name, *Anthyllis,* is derived from the Greek words *anthos* (= a flower) and *ioulos* (= down); the specific name, *vulneraria,* from the Latin *vulnus* (= a wound), refers to the traditional use of the plant for healing wounds. The plant was also used against kidney troubles, hence the common name (the flowers look like kidneys and by association they were held to be a good kidney remedy). The word 'vetch' is a corruption of the Latin name *vicia* for beans.

The flowers are used medicinally but old ones are not dried because they turn brown and disintegrate. The constituents include tannins, saponins, mucilage, sugars and organic pigments (flavonoids), and these give the plant astringent, antiseptic and laxative actions. An infusion is used in herbalism as a general tonic; externally a decoction is used in compresses or bath preparations for treating inflamed wounds, ulcers and eczema, and in gargles and mouth washes. It can be used as a substitute for ordinary tea mixed with the leaves of Wild Strawberry (*Fragaria vesca*) (Pl. 98), and Raspberry (*Rubus idaeus*) (Pl. 205) and the flowers of Blackthorn (*Prunus spinosa*) (Pl. 188).

Flower

Flowering time: May to July

Greater Burdock

Floret

Root

Dried cut root

A biennial herb with a brown, spindle-shaped taproot, which bears, in the first year, a basal rosette of ovate to cordate leaves and, in the second year, a tall, angled stem with alternate leaves. The globose flowerheads, with numerous hook-tipped, green involucral bracts and purple tubular disc-florets only, are arranged in terminal corymbose clusters. When mature the flowerheads form spiny balls (burs), which are dispersed by sticking to the bodies of animals or to clothing. The fruit, an achene, has a pappus of short, rough hairs.

Greater Burdock is found throughout Europe commonly near buildings, in waste places, waysides and thickets on heavy soils. In the British Isles it mostly occurs in lowland parts of southern England, in the Midlands and Wales. The generic name, *Arctium,* from the Greek word *arktos* (= bear), alludes to the thistle-like fruit heads, as do the specific name *lappa* and the common name Burdock. Greater Burdock has had many medicinal uses in the past. It is still regarded by herbalists as one of the best blood purifiers. In some countries it is grown commercially for its roots. The related Woolly Burdock (*A. tomentosum*) (Pl. 21) and Lesser Burdock (*A. minus*) have similar medicinal properties.

The roots of one-year or overwintering plants, collected before flowering, are used medicinally. The constituents include a starch (inulin, 27 to 45 per cent), traces of an essential oil, mucilage, tannins and resin, and these give Greater Burdock diuretic, antiseptic, diaphoretic, hypoglycaemic and choleretic properties. It is used in herbal medicine on its own or in tea mixtures for influenza and rheumatic pain. A decoction is used externally for bathing wounds, ulcers and eczema and the oil extract continues its traditional use (though the effect is not proven) as a stimulant of hair growth.

Flowering time: July to September

Woolly Burdock

A biennial herb with a spindle-shaped taproot and branched, furrowed stem. The leaves are ovate to cordate, stalked and white woolly below, the large basal ones forming a rosette. The globose purple flowerheads, which are covered by a 'web' of dense cobweb-like hairs, are clustered in terminal corymbs. The rings of hooked involucral bracts turn the flowerhead into a bur when it is mature. The fruit, an achene, has a pappus of short, rough hairs.

Woolly Burdock grows throughout most of Europe by roadsides and on waste ground. It is not native to the British Isles but it is occasionally found as a casual in woods and scrub. Like Greater Burdock (*A. lappa*) (Pl. 20), this species has had many medicinal uses in the past. The young stalks also used to be eaten raw or cooked. The specific name *tomentosum* means woolly or downy. In the common name the suffix 'dock' refers to the large leaves, which are like those of docks (*Rumex*).

The roots of one-year or overwintering plants, collected before flowering, are used medicinally. The pharmacological investigation of burdocks is not yet complete, but the chemical composition of Woolly Burdock seems to be the same as Greater Burdock's — both contain a large amount of inulin. The presence of inulin — a polysaccharide composed of units of fructose — gives burdocks hypoglycaemic properties. Woolly Burdock is mostly used in herbalism to treat skin diseases and as a hair oil. Sometimes the fresh leaves, fresh root or just the juice from the root are used — they promote bile secretion, urine flow and sweating.

Flowerhead:

A. tomentosum　　*A. lappa*

Flowering time: July to September

Bearberry, Uva-ursi

Leaf (from left to right):

A. uva-ursi (underside)

Vaccinium myrtillus

Vaccinium vitis-idaea

A low evergreen shrub with long, rooting branches that form a dense mat. The branches have many small, oval, entire, leathery leaves that are dark green on the upper surface, paler and distinctly net-veined below (see line drawing), and broadest at the tip. Bearberry leaves can easily be distinguished from those of Bilberry (*Vaccinium myrtillus*) (Pl. 243) and Cowberry (*Vaccinium vitis-idaea*) (Pl. 244): Bilberry's leaves are oval, bright green and finely serrate; Cowberry's are oval, broadest in the middle, entire and the margins are rolled inwards (see fig.) The small white or pink-tipped flowers are arranged in short dense racemes. The edible fruit is a shiny-red, globose drupe with five seeds inside.

Bearberry grows in acid soil on moors, screes and mountain scrub in northern parts of Britain and in northern and western parts of Ireland. It is more common in the Scottish Highlands than elsewhere. It is also found throughout most of Europe. In some countries, however, it has become very rare and is now protected. Bears are said to enjoy the fruit of some bearberry species, hence the common name and the generic name (from the Greek words *arktos* = a bear and *staphyle* = grapes). Bearberry has long been used as a medicinal plant, especially for kidney and bladder problems and today some of its constituents are included in proprietary medicines.

The leaves are used medicinally. Among the constituents are up to 12 per cent glycosides (arbutin and methylarbutin), tannins and organic acids. An infusion of Bearberry is used in herbal medicine as an antiseptic and diuretic for gravel and uroliths and for infections of the urinary tract and kidneys, but *only if the urine is alkaline.* **Bearberry should be taken internally only under the supervision of a qualified medical or herbal practitioner.** If used for long periods it may cause constipation, nausea or more serious side-effects.

Flowering time: May to June

Birthwort

A perennial herb with a long, creeping rhizome and tall, erect, leafy, unbranched stem with alternate, pale-green, ovate to cordate, entire leaves. The dull-yellow trumpet-shaped flowers have swollen bases and grow from the axils of the upper leaves. The fruit is a pear-shaped capsule. All parts of the plant have a disagreeable smell and are **poisonous.**

Birthwort is found in the warmer parts of Europe and Asia in thin woods and at the edges of fields and old vineyards and near houses. It was long ago introduced into Britain as a medicinal plant and subsequently became naturalized. It is now extremely rare in the wild, but it survives in a few places near buildings in England and Wales. The generic name, *Aristolochia,* is derived from the Greek words *aristos* (= best) and *locheia* (= parturition or childbirth) and refers to the traditional use of the plant by mid-wives to ease labour, hence also the common name. Birthwort was also once used as a cure for snakebite. The con-stituents are contained in some propriet-ary medicines, but the plant is nowadays rarely used by herbalists.

The flowering stems are used medici-nally. Among the constituents are aris-tolochic acid, an essential oil, tannins, flavonoid pigments and the alkaloid aris-tolochine. Birthwort has antispasmodic and analgesic properties and it is pre-scribed by medical practitioners for vascu-lar diseases and thrombosis and to pro-mote menstrual flow. **It should be taken internally only under strict medical super-vision.** Aristolochic acid is cytotoxic and in sufficient doses it can cause haemor-rhage, miscarriage in pregnant women, permanent damage to the liver and kid-neys, and even cardiac and respiratory failure. Birthwort is also anti-inflamma-tory and a decoction has been used externally to treat wounds, ulcers, eczema and other skin complaints; there are, however, many safer remedies and its use in these ways is not recommended.

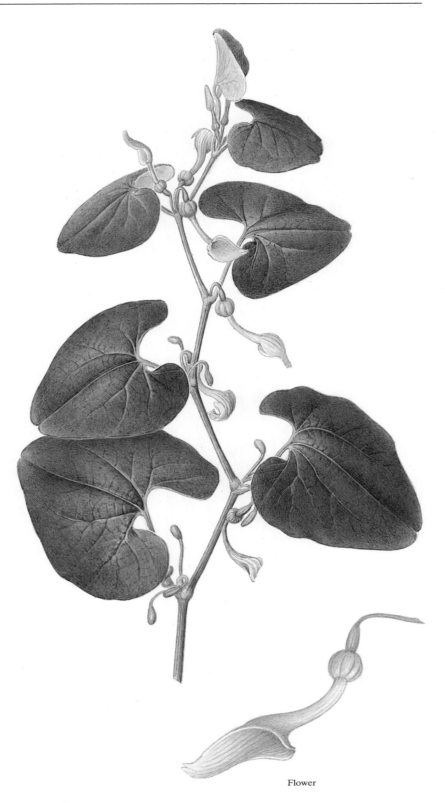

Flower

Flowering time: June to September

Horseradish

Flower

Rootstock

A perennial herb with a thick rootstock and long, cylindrical fleshy roots and an erect, branched stem. The large basal leaves are oblong and long-stalked, with undulate and serrate margins; the stem leaves are smaller and narrower, short-stalked or sessile, and toothed or entire. The numerous white flowers are arranged in a compound terminal panicle. The fruit is an oval silicula, which rarely ripens in Britain.

Horseradish is native to southeastern Europe but it was introduced to other European countries in medieval times. In Britain it is often naturalized on waste ground and by streams; it is much rarer in Ireland. It is widely cultivated for the condiment prepared from the roots; cuttings are planted in light, well-drained soil where they grow to full size during summer and are then lifted either in the autumn or the following spring. The roots can be preserved during winter by storing them in sand. The generic name, *Armoracia,* was used by Pliny who recommended the plant for its medicinal properties. The common name, Horseradish, means a coarse or strong radish, the prefix 'horse' often being used in plant names to denote a large, strong or coarse kind.

The fresh root is usually used for medicinal and culinary purposes, but dried or bottled root is also effective. Among the constituents are an essential oil with mustard glycosides, enzymes and vitamin C. Served as a condiment with cooked meat Horseradish stimulates digestion. It also has diuretic, antiseptic, rubefacient, mild laxative and expectorant actions. It is contained in a few proprietary medicines for influenza and infections of the urinary tract. Rheumatic pain can be relieved by Horseradish poultices. **Frequent application to the same spot, however, may irritate the skin** and cause a rash. Large internal doses may also irritate the digestive tract.

Flowering time: May to August

Arnica, Mountain Tobacco

A perennial herb with a creeping rhizome bearing an erect, branched, slightly hairy, glandular stem. The basal leaves, which are arranged in a rosette, are ovate, downy and crowded near the stem base; the smaller and fewer stem leaves are ovate to lanceolate, opposite and sessile. There are one to three terminal, bright-yellow, daisy-like flowerheads. The ligulate ray-florets are female and irregularly turned back. The fruit — a black, downy, cylindrical achene — has a pappus with one row of rough hairs. All parts of the plant are aromatic.

Arnica is found in grassy places in hills and mountains in Europe and North America but it is becoming rare in the wild and in many countries it is now protected. It is not native to the British Isles but is often grown in gardens. The generic name *Arnica* is thought to be derived from the Greek word *arnikos* (= lamb's skin), an allusion to the texture of the leaves. In countries where Arnica is indigenous it has long been a popular herbal remedy.

All parts of the plant are of medicinal value, but the flowerheads, and sometimes the rhizomes, are mostly used. Only the ray- and disc-florets — without the involucre and receptacle — are processed. Among the constituents of the florets are traces of an essential oil, organic pigments (carotenoids), the bitter compound arnicin, the saponin arnidendiol, arnisterol and the flavonoid glyosides isoquercetin and astragalol. The rhizomes contain tannins, up to 6.3 per cent of an essential oil and resin. Arnica has tonic, anti-inflammatory and vasodilating properties but it is also a severe irritant of the internal organs and is now rarely prescribed for internal use. **It should be taken internally only under strict medical supervision.** Externally a diluted infusion or decoction is used for bathing superficial wounds, bruises and sprains and as a component of mouthwashes and gargles. **Repeated external use can cause skin irritation.** In homeopathy a tincture is used for trauma.

Ray-floret

Flowering time: July

Southernwood, Lad's Love, Old Man

Top of stem

A perennial, compact, woody subshrub thickly covered with finely divided (up to three times pinnate) greyish-green leaves. The tiny yellow flowerheads grow in slender racemes in the axils of the upper leaves. Ray-florets are absent. The fruit is a cylindrical and slightly flattened achene, without a pappus.

Native to Asia, Southernwood has spread through cultivation to Europe and the Americas. It is a popular and easily grown garden plant but it rarely flowers and sets seed in the British Isles and other northern parts of Europe. In the Mediterranean countries it is grown as a field crop for its bitter ingredients. All parts of the plant have a pleasant lemony fragrance and in the old days this was put to good use in the home to freshen the air. The scent repels bees and other insects and dried leaves in muslin bags will keep away clothes moths. The plant can also be used in flower decorations. This species, and others in the *Artemisia* group, are named after Artemis or Diana, the goddess of the hunt and the moon, who watched over women and children. The herb used to be taken to encourage menstruation and it also had a reputation as an aphrodisiac. One of the alternative common names of *A. abrotanum*, Lad's Love, is said to refer to the old habit of including a spray of the plant in bouquets given by country lads to their sweethearts.

The flowering stems are used medicinally. The constituents include a large amount of an essential oil (absinthol), also bitter compounds, tannins and alkaloids. Southernwood has tonic, stomachic, diuretic, anthelmintic and diaphoretic properties. Internally it is used in herbal medicine as an infusion; externally a decoction is used as a bath preparation, as a hair rinse to rinse the scalp or as a compress to treat frostbite and cuts and grazes.

Flowering time: August to September

Wormwood

A perennial herb of tufted habit with tall, erect, furrowed and angled stems, usually woody at the base, and alternate, silvery-green, finely divided (two or three times pinnate) leaves. The hemispherical, yellow, rayless, drooping flowerheads are arranged in long racemose panicles. The fruit is a cylindrical, slightly flattened achene, with no pappus. All parts of the plant are covered with a silvery-white down.

Wormwood grows all over Europe in dry waste places, such as roadsides. It is native to the British Isles but is generally uncommon. It is a very old herbal remedy and is frequently grown in herb gardens. The common name, Wormwood (from the Anglo-Saxon word *wermod*), and the word for the aperitif Vermouth, which used to be flavoured with the herb, have the same linguistic origin.

The flowering stems are used medicinally. The constituents include an essential oil with thujone and thujole, a bitter compound (absinthin), organic acids and tannins. The herb has a very bitter taste. It has tonic, stomachic, choleretic, carminative, antiseptic and anthelmintic properties. It was once used for many disorders but nowadays it is mostly used, on its own or in tea mixtures, for various digestive upsets. **Taken over a long period, however, Wormwood becomes habit-forming and will eventually cause serious brain damage. It is thus advisable to take Wormwood internally only under the supervision of a qualified medical or herbal practitioner.** The neurotoxic agents are thought to be thujone and thujole. The use of Wormwood in alcoholic beverages is now prohibited by law. Externally a decoction is used as a gargle and in compresses for bruises. The essential oil recovered from the fresh plant is used in homeopathic tinctures.

Dried flowering stems

Flowering time: July to August

Tarragon

Flowerheads

A perennial herb with a rhizome, erect leafy stems and alternate, green, entire, linear to lanceolate leaves. The small, yellow, globose, rayless flowerheads are arranged in long, loose terminal panicles. The fruit is a cylindrical achene without a pappus. All parts of the plant are aromatic.

Tarragon has a wide distribution, which extends from eastern Europe through Siberia, Mongolia and China to North America. It is now cultivated in several different varieties as a culinary herb. In Europe it flowers but rarely fruits so it is propagated by dividing the rhizome or by cuttings. It is grown commercially only on a small scale in Britain. The common name is perhaps derived through Arabic and Latin from the Greek word *drakon* (= dragon) − the plant was supposed to cure the bites and stings of venomous animals and dogs. The specific name, *dracunculus,* means 'little dragon-like'. This may refer to the healing properties or to the resemblance of the rhizome and roots to coiled snakes.

Although Tarragon is mainly used for flavouring food, the flowering stems are occasionally used for medicinal purposes. The constituents include an essential oil with estragole and phelandrine, bitter compounds and tannins. Tarragon is used in an infusion, as a powder or tincture to stimulate the appetite, to aid digestion and as a general tonic. The distilled essential oil is used in the manufacture of some toilet preparations.

Tarragon is widely used in the food and canning industries. For home cooking no garden should be without it. Tarragon vinegar is easily prepared by steeping fresh leaves just before flowering in a good, white wine vinegar for two or three weeks, then straining the product into small bottles. Separate leaves can be used in salads, sauces, stews and pickles.

Flowering time: July

Mugwort

A perennial herb of tufted habit with a reddish, furrowed, angled, sparsely hairy stem. The alternate, pinnately lobed leaves are dark green, usually hairless above and white-woolly beneath. The stem leaves are pinnate or bipinnate, nearly sessile and clasp the stem. The small, oval, yellowish flowerheads are arranged in dense leafy panicles that are nearly straight and grow from the leaf axils in the upper part of the branched stem. The fruit is a cylindrical achene without a pappus. All parts of the plant are slightly aromatic.

Mugwort is a widespread weed of gardens, waste places, waysides and hedgerows throughout the British Isles. It is one of the oldest known medicinal plants and it was also believed to have magical powers. The origin of the common name is confused. It may be derived from the Anglo-Saxon words *mycg* (= a midge) and *wyrt* (= a herb) and perhaps refers to the plant's small flowers or to the traditional use of bunches of the plant for catching insects. Or the plant may be named 'mugwort' because it was once used for flavouring beer before the introduction of hops.

The flowering stems are used medicinally. The main constituents are an essential oil, with cineole and thujone, tannins and bitter compounds. Like other species of *Artemisia* Mugwort is used as a general tonic, as an appetizer and stomachic and as a seasoning, but its action is not as strong. It is a traditional treatment for nervous disorders, insomnia and gynaecological complaints. The essential oil extracted from the fresh leaves is used in preparations as an expectorant, diuretic and anthelmintic. Because Mugwort contains the neurotoxic substance thujone **care should always be taken over the dosage and duration of treatment.**

In cooking Mugwort is a useful condiment for roast meat, especially pork and mutton and fat poultry such as goose and duck. It is an effective moth repellent.

Leaf

Flowering time: August to September

Lords-and-Ladies, Cuckoopint

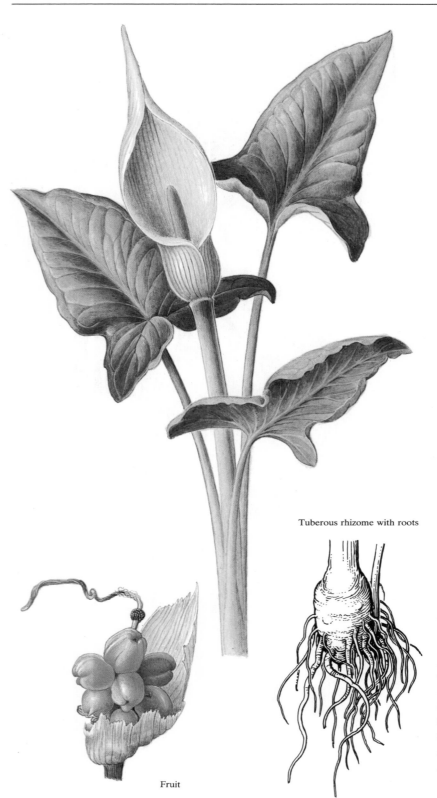

Tuberous rhizome with roots

Fruit

A perennial herb with a tuberous rhizome and basal, long-stalked sagittate leaves, sometimes spotted brown or black. The flowering stem bears a pale yellow-green, trumpet-shaped spathe, edged and sometimes spotted with purple, which encloses the inflorescence — a purplish, cylindrical flowerhead called a spadix. The flowers are all unisexual; those in the lower part of the spadix are female, those in the middle are sterile, and those at the top are male. The spadix has a strong unpleasant smell which attracts insects to the plant. They crawl down inside the spathe and pollinate the flowers. **All parts of the plant are poisonous, especially the scarlet berries which can be fatal if eaten by children.**

Lords-and-Ladies is found throughout Europe in damp woods and in shady copses and hedgerows, particularly on lime-rich soils. It is common in England and Wales but less so in Scotland and Ireland. Through the ages many of the common names of this plant have had a sexual connotation. The generic name, *Arum,* is a corruption of the Greek word *aron* and may originally have been an Egyptian name. The rhizome is rich in starch and it used to be baked and eaten. Preparations from the baked and powdered rhizome were known as Portland arrowroot and Portland sago. However, although the rhizome can be rendered harmless if well cooked, it is best not to eat it. In the past Lords-and-Ladies also had many medicinal uses — for example, in medieval times the rhizome was used in powder mixtures with other herbs to aid digestion — but it is now regarded as too toxic for use as an internal herbal medicine.

The rhizome contains the toxic glycoside aronin, also saponins, starch and calcium oxalate, which gives the plant its sharp burning taste. It is diuretic and strongly purgative. **Lords-and-Ladies should never be collected and used for self-medication.** Symptoms of poisoning are severe vomiting, abdominal cramps and diarrhoea.

Flowering time: April to May

Asarabacca

An evergreen perennial herb of low, creeping habit with a branched rhizome and short hairy stems with whitish or brownish scale leaves at the base. The leaves are glossy, dark green, long-stalked and reniform. The solitary short-stalked, brownish-red flowers are borne terminally and are bell-shaped, three-lobed and downy. The fruit is a globose capsule with flat seeds inside. All parts of the plant have a camphor-like smell and are **poisonous.**

Asarabacca has a scattered distribution in Europe in woods and thickets. In many countries it is now a protected species. In the British Isles it may be native in a few places, though not in Ireland, and is generally extremely rare. It is, however, grown in gardens. Asarabacca was used in ancient Greece to treat kidney complaints and in wine-making and in later times as a purgative and emetic. Because of its harmful effects, however, it is now rarely used in medicine. The common name Asarabacca is a combination of the Greek and Lydian names (*asaron* and *bakkar*) for the plant.

The rhizome and the leaves have medicinal actions. The principal constituents are an essential oil from which asarone (known as Asarabacca camphor) is crystallized, also starch, resin and flavonoids. The dried herb has a bitter taste. It is a strong emetic, diuretic and purgative. A pinch of the powdered herb in snuff mixtures induces sneezing and a copious flow of mucus. **It is dangerous to use Asarabacca internally except under strict medical supervision:** strong doses can cause haemorrhaging and, in pregnant women, miscarriage.

Longitudinal section of flower

Flowering time: March to May

Great Masterwort, Astrantia, Mountain Sanicle

Rhizome with roots

A perennial herb with a black, woody rhizome and an erect, slightly branched stem. The basal leaves, arranged in a rosette, are long-stalked, shiny dark green, palmately lobed and coarsely toothed. The stem leaves are similar but smaller. The white, pinkish or greenish flowers are clustered in simple rounded umbels, which are surrounded by a conspicuous white or reddish whorl of petal-like involucral bracts. The fruit is an oblong achene with a comb-like keel. Although the plant is aromatic it is also **poisonous.**

Great Masterwort has a scattered distribution in Europe in Alpine meadows and open woods. It is not native to the British Isles but it has become naturalized in a few grassy places. It is extremely rare to find it in the wild but it is grown in gardens. The common name is derived from the Greek words *astron* (= a star) and *anti* (= like), and refers to the appearance of the flower clusters. The plant is now only rarely used in herbal medicine.

The rhizomes and flowering stems have medicinal action. Their main constituent is an essential oil that acts as a stomachic. In herbal medicine the dried herb is used in an infusion or as a powder to promote the flow of digestive juices and thus stimulate the appetite. Great Masterwort is also included in diuretic tea mixtures.

Flowering time: June to August

Deadly Nightshade, Belladonna

A perennial herb with a large, turnip-like root and spreading, branched stems. The large, soft, oval leaves are alternate or opposite where a flower arises. The stalked, bell-shaped, reddish-brown flowers grow singly from the leaf axils. The fruit is a black, glossy, conspicuous berry cupped by the spreading sepals. **All parts of the plant are extremely poisonous;** just two or three berries can kill a child who has mistaken them for cherries or bilberries.

Deadly Nightshade is found throughout Europe in hedges, woods and thickets and in waste places, especially on lime-rich soils. In the British Isles it is sometimes found growing wild in England and Wales; elsewhere it has been introduced. It is grown as a field crop for the pharmaceutical industry in several countries, but only on a small scale in Britain. In Greek mythology Atropos is one of the three Fates who severs the thread of life; the Greek word *atropos* means unchangeable or irrevocable. It is said that fashionable Italian women used the juice of Deadly Nightshade berries to dilate the pupils of their eyes and it is this practice that gave the plant its specific name, *belladonna,* meaning 'a fair lady' in Italian. (It is actually dangerous to use the juice in this way because doing so can cause glaucoma.)

The dried leaves and root are used medicinally. They include various potent alkaloids, such as hyoscyamine, atropine, belladonnine and scopolamine. These substances particularly affect the parasympathetic nervous system and are used together or in isolated form in proprietary and homeopathic medicines prescribed by medical practitioners as antispasmodics, sedatives and analgesics and as antidotes to various poisons. Atropine is used in ophthalmology. **Deadly Nightshade is highly dangerous and it should never be collected and used for self-medication.** Even a small dose can be fatal.

Fruit

Root

Flowering time: May to August

Common Oat, Oats

Grain of *A. sativa*

An annual herb grown as an important cereal crop. The hollow, jointed stems (culms) bear terminal, panicle-like flowerheads. The leaves are long and narrow with a sheath clasping the stem and a large ligule (a strap of tissue at the base of the leaf). Each part (spikelet) of the drooping flowerhead contains two or three florets enclosed by two chaff-like bracts (glumes). The lower bract (lemma) usually does not have an awn — a bristle-like projection — unlike the Wild Oat (*A. fatua*), which does. The small hard fruit is the familiar grain.

Common Oat is native to eastern Europe but it has been cultivated since Classical times and is now grown throughout the world except in the tropics. It is cultivated most in northern countries. Wild Oat is also not indigenous to the British Isles but it and Common Oat can sometimes be found growing wild as weeds of arable fields and waste ground. The name Oat is derived from an Anglo-Saxon word *ate,* of unknown origin.

The grains and sometimes the dry stalks (straw) are used medicinally. The grains contain valuable proteins, sugars, fat, starch, vitamin B complex, pigments (carotenes) and various minerals, among them iron, calcium and potassium salts. Rolled oats can be made into nourishing soups and porridge for convalescents and they also control diarrhoea. Oat tea stimulates the appetite, soothes throat and chest pains and is a nerve tonic in cases of mental fatigue, anxiety and insomnia. Externally fine oatmeal can be used as a cleansing and soothing poultice or bath preparation. The straw can also be used as a bath preparation to treat rheumatic pains and sciatica and it is a skin tonic.

Flowering time: July

Black Horehound

A perennial herb with a short, stout rhizome and with erect or ascending, branched, square and leafy stems. The leaves are opposite, stalked, wrinkled and coarsely crenate-serrate. All parts of the plant are hairy and have a strong, disagreeable smell and taste. The pinkish-purple, sometimes white flowers are arranged in numerous whorls in the upper leaf axils. The corolla has two lips; the upper one is hooded, the lower one has prominent white markings on it. The calyx is funnel-shaped with five thick veins and five broad spreading teeth which are curved back in the fruit. The fruit consists of four smooth, one-seeded nutlets. Like all members of the labiate (mint) family Black Horehound is attractive to bees.

Black Horehound is found on roadsides, hedgebanks and in waste places throughout most of Europe. It is common in England and Wales but it has a more local distribution in Scotland and Ireland. The plant's unpleasant smell protects it for the most part from being eaten by farm animals, and this property may be referred to in the generic name, *Ballota*. The plant was originally called *ballote* by the ancient Greeks and it has been suggested that this word comes from the Greek *ballo* (= to reject, cast or throw). The origin of the common name is obscure. It may come from the Anglo-Saxon words *har* (= hoar, hairly) and *hune* (the plant's name). Black Horehound has long been used as a herbal medicine for treating eye and ear disorders and it was thought to be an antidote for bites from mad dogs. It is now little used by herbalists.

The top parts of the flowering stems are used medicinally. The main constituents are tannins, essential oils, organic acids and pectin. In herbal medicine Black Horehound is used internally in an infusion or powder as a general sedative or diaphoretic. It is also applied externally as a compress to alleviate rheumatic pain.

Flower

Flowering time: June onwards

Daisy

Flowerheads of ornamental varieties

A perennial herb of grassland and weed of lawns. The basal rosette of spathulate, bluntly serrate leaves stands up well to competition from other plants, including grasses, and from spring onwards Daisy successively produces several generations of flowers. The solitary flowerheads have white to pinkish, ligulate ray-florets and yellow, tubular disc-florets that close in the evening. Bees find the flowers very attractive. All parts of the plant are sparsely hairy. The fruit is an oval, downy achene without a pappus.

Daisy is very common in the wild and in gardens throughout the British Isles. The generic name, *Bellis,* is said to come from the Latin word *bella* (= beautiful) or from a dryad called Belidis. The common name, Daisy, is derived from the Anglo-Saxon name *daeges eage* (= day's eye), a reference to the plant's resemblance to a 'small sun' as it opens and folds mornings and evenings. The plant was once a popular treatment for wounds and chest ailments and is still included in many modern herbal handbooks.

The flowerheads are used medicinally. The main constituents are saponins, an essential oil, tannins, mucilage, flavones and a bitter compound, all of which give Daisy astringent and expectorant properties. It has a beneficial effect on gastritis, enteritis and diarrhoea, and infections of the upper respiratory tract. In herbal medicine it is usually used as an infusion. Daisy also makes an attractive addition to tea mixtures. Externally it is used in compresses and bath preparations to treat skin disorders, wounds and bruises. A decoction from the fresh leaves is used for the same purposes.

Young fresh leaves can be eaten raw in salads or added to soups.

Flowering time: April to October

Barberry

☠

A deciduous shrub with obovate, spiny serrate, short-stalked leaves borne in clusters on short, furrowed yellowish twigs in the axils of three spines. The small yellow flowers are arranged in drooping racemes. The stamens are sensitive — they spring inwards if touched near the base. The fruits are oblong, bright-red, sharply acid berries which ripen in the autumn. **All parts of the plant, except for the berries, are poisonous.**

Barberry is found throughout Europe as far as the Caucasus in hedges and bushy places, especially where there is plenty of sun. In the British Isles it has a widespread but local distribution. It is introduced in Ireland and perhaps in many other British localities. As an ornamental shrub it is common in gardens. The common name Barberry is a corruption of the Latin word *berberis* for the plant, and in its turn *berberis* may be derived from the Arabic name for the fruit. Barberry's medicinal properties have long been known. It was used to lower fever and to treat stomach, heart and liver complaints. The bark and stems yield a yellow dye.

The bark and fruit are used medicinally. The bark contains alkaloids, in particular berberine, and also tannins, resin and organic pigments. **Berberine is very toxic and Barberry bark should be used only under strict medical supervision.** Despite what many herbal books say, it is not a safe remedy for self-medication. It is occasionally prescribed for disorders of the kidney, liver and gallbladder and as a stomachic and antipyretic. A tincture is used in homeopathy. In mild doses the bark has laxative, diuretic and choleretic actions; in larger doses it causes stupor, vomiting, diarrhoea and even respiratory failure. The ripe berries are, however, harmless and can be eaten fresh, dried or tinned. They are rich in vitamin C, sugars and pectin and they make refreshing herbal teas. They relieve biliousness and are laxative. The pressed juice can be made into a jelly.

Fruit

Flowering time: May to June

Silver Birch

Fruit

A tall, deciduous tree with pendulous brown branches and a trunk with smooth silver-white bark above and blackish fissured bark towards the base. The branches have small, resinous wart-like structures (lenticels) on their surface. The leaves are alternate, long-stalked, pointed oval and doubly serrate and are sticky at first. Silver Birch is monoecious: the purple-brown male flowers are arranged in drooping catkins; the green female catkins are small and erect but hang when mature. The fruit is a winged achene.

Silver Birch is common and widespread in Europe and Asia where it grows in woods, scrub and heaths, preferring sandy or gravelly soils. It is found throughout the British Isles. In northern countries Silver Birch was held to have sacred powers against evil spirits and witchcraft and there are many place names embodying the name of the Birch or its Scottish or northern English equivalent 'birk'. The Anglo-Saxon name for the tree was *beorc* or *birce,* and it was probably derived from a word for 'white' or 'shining'. Birch leaves have long been used to treat disorders of the urinary system and rheumatism.

The young leaves are used medicinally. When dried they are aromatic and have a bitter taste. Among the constituents are saponins, tannins, traces of an essential oil, resin and bitter compounds. These substances give Silver Birch mild diuretic and disinfectant properties, but they do not irritate the kidneys. For this reason Silver Birch leaves are a basic ingredient of herbal tea mixtures used for urinary infections and for kidney stones. The herb is also diaphoretic, particularly in combination with flowers of lime (*Tilia*) and it eases rheumatic pain. Externally the leaves make invigorating bath preparations. Dry distillation of fresh birch wood yields birch tar, which is used in soothing ointments for skin ailments.

Flowering time: April to May

Borage

An annual herb with a taproot and a branched stem bearing many alternate, pointed ovate and sessile leaves with undulate margins. The basal leaves are stalked and are arranged in a rosette. The bright-blue, star-shaped flowers are clustered in loose, terminal, monochasial cymes. The prominent black anthers form a cone in the centre of the flower. The fruit consists of four brownish-black, rough nutlets (mericarps). All parts of the plant are roughly hairy. The leaves and flowers have a smell and taste of fresh cucumbers.

Borage is indigenous to the Mediterranean region from where it has spread to other parts of Europe. It has long been grown in gardens as a medicinal herb and because it is an excellent source of nectar for bees. In the British Isles Borage has become established as a garden escape on waste ground, usually near buildings, but generally it is uncommon in the wild. The origin of Borage's name is obscure. It may be derived from an old word meaning rough-hairy, and this then gave rise to the French name *bourrache* for the plant. There may also be a connection with the Arabic words *'abu 'arak* (literally 'father of sweat') because of its ancient use as a diaphoretic.

The flowering stems, sometimes just the flowers and leaves on their own, are used medicinally. The constituents include tannins, saponins, mucilage, silicic acid and minerals. Borage has anti-inflammatory, mild diuretic, diaphoretic and demulcent properties; it is also a good general tonic. In herbal medicine it is used in infusions for urinary infections, colds, bronchitis and rheumatic conditions. Externally it is used in compresses for skin rashes.

Young fresh Borage leaves have a high concentration of vitamin C and are a tasty addition to salads. The fresh flowers can be candied and used for decoration. They also make an attractive addition to a wine and fruit cup.

Segment of fruit (mericarp)

Flowering time: June onwards

Black Mustard

Seed

An annual herb with a slender taproot and an erect branched stem. The leaves are alternate and stalked; the upper ones smooth, lanceolate and entire, the large lower ones bristly, lyrate and pinnately divided with a large terminal lobe. The bright-yellow flowers are prominently veined and are arranged in a raceme that increases in length as the flowers fade in succession. In the related White Mustard (*Sinapis alba*) (Pl. 222) the sepals spread out horizontally below the yellow petals. The fruit of Black Mustard is a narrow, beaked siliqua with globular black seeds.

Black Mustard is native to Europe and Asia but it has been cultivated as a condiment and for medicinal purposes for 2,000 years or more. It is probably native to the British Isles; it is locally common on cliffs and stream banks and, where it is a relic of cultivation, on roadsides and waste ground. It is a member of the cabbage family and its generic name, *Brassica,* means cabbage in Latin. The common name Mustard is thought to derive through the French word *moustarde* from the Latin words *mustum* (= must, a newly pressed grape juice) and *ardens* (= fiery) because originally the condiment was made by adding must to crushed mustard seeds.

The seeds are used medicinally. Their constituents include glycoside-bonded oil of mustard (up to 35 per cent), the enzyme myrosinase, an alkaloid (sinapine), mucilage and protein. These substances give Black Mustard rubefacient and irritant properties and it is used medicinally to improve the blood supply to the skin and to the lungs, pleura and kidneys. Plasters and poultices made from mustard powder ease rheumatic and arthritic pain, muscular spasms, strained muscles and congested lungs; bath preparations have the same effect. **All Black Mustard preparations irritate the skin.**

Flowering time: May onwards

Black-berried Bryony

☠ ☠

A perennial tendril-climbing herb with a branched, turnip-like root and a long, brittle and roughly hairy stem that can reach a length of 5 metres. The stalked leaves are palmately lobed, like those of Ivy (*Hedera helix*) (Pl. 113), and roughly hairy. The tendrils are spirally coiled and arise at the side of the leaf axils. The small, monoecious, yellow-green flowers are arranged in loose terminal racemes; the male flowers are long-stalked, the female ones almost sessile. The fruit is a black berry.

Black-berried Bryony is native to southern Europe but it has become naturalized elsewhere on waste ground. It does not grow wild in the British Isles. However, the related White or Red Bryony (*B. dioica*) is native to Britain (but not Ireland). It is locally common in hedgerows, copses and scrub in England and Wales but it thins out northwards and westwards. *B. dioica* differs from *B. alba* in being dioecious and having red berries. **Both these species are extremely poisonous** − the sap may cause itching and painful blisters and only about a dozen berries might prove fatal for a child. They were once used medically and in veterinary practice as purgatives, but nowadays are mostly used only in homeopathic preparations. The names *Bryonia* and bryony come from the Greek word *bruein* (= 'to grow vigorously'). The common name of *B. dioica* and the specific name of *B. alba* (*alba* = white) refer to the colour of the roots, which distinguishes these species from the unrelated Black Bryony (*Tamus communis*), which has black roots and is also poisonous.

The roots of Black-berried Bryony contain several glycosides, tannins, an alkaloid (bryonicine) and resin. Together, these substances have strong purgative, diuretic, emetic, anti-inflammatory and antirheumatic actions. Tinctures of the fresh root are used in homeopathy for fevers, rheumatism, constipation and other disorders. **Neither Black-berried Bryony nor White Bryony should ever be collected and used for self-medication.**

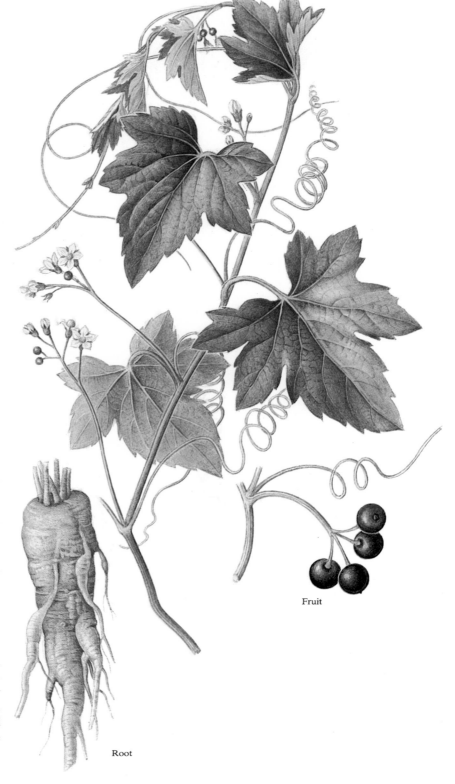

Fruit

Root

Flowering time: June to August

Box

An evergreen shrub or small tree with green twigs bearing many opposite, almost sessile, dark-green, entire, ovate leaves with smooth, shiny leathery surfaces. Early in spring small clusters of whitish-green unisexual flowers, which consist of a terminal female flower surrounded by several male flowers, grow from the upper leaf axils. The fruit is an ovoid capsule. **All parts of the plant, especially the leaves and seeds, are poisonous.** Box leaves are sometimes confused with those of Bearberry (*Arctostaphylos uva-ursi*) (Pl. 22), but they can be easily distinguished by their notched apex.

Box grows wild in central and western Europe in woods and shrub on lime-rich soils. It is rarely found in the wild in Britain, except on the North and South Downs in southern England, but it is frequently grown as an ornamental plant in parks and gardens. The common name Box comes from the Latin word *buxus,* which in turn is derived from the Greek word *puxos* for the tree. At first boxes were made only from the wood of this species. The wood is very hard, close-grained and heavy. It does not warp and is an ideal wood for, besides boxes of all sorts, engraving plates, carvings, and musical and navigational instruments. Box was once used as a substitute for quinine in the treatment of malaria.

The leaves contain various alkaloids (for example, buxine), an essential oil and tannins, which give Box purgative, diaphoretic and antipyretic properties. **It is dangerous if taken internally and it should never be collected and used for self-medication.** In homeopathy a tincture prepared from fresh leaves is prescribed for fever, rheumatism and urinary tract infections. Symptoms of poisoning are vomiting, abdominal pain and bloody diarrhoea.

Flowering time: March to May

Pot Marigold

An annual herb grown in gardens since the Middle Ages for its bright-orange or yellow single or double flowers, which are decorative from summer until autumn. The basal leaves are spathulate and stalked, the stem leaves lanceolate, alternate and sessile. All parts of the plant are roughly hairy. The terminal and solitary flowerheads have sterile, tubular disc-florets and fertile, ligulate, spreading ray-florets. The fruit is a rough, curved achene.

Pot Marigold is native to southern Europe but it is easily grown in the British Isles and it often escapes on to waste ground. The botanical name *Calendula,* a diminutive of the Latin word *Calendae* (= first day of the month) meaning 'little clock', refers to the plant's habit of flowering all year round in the wild. The double forms with bright-orange flowers have the highest concentration of active ingredients and these varieties are grown for medicinal purposes on the Continent. The plant is still used in herbal medicine but not as often as it once was. The flowers have been used as a colouring agent.

Either the whole flowerheads or just the ray-florets are used medicinally. Among the constituents are an essential oil, pigments (carotenoids), bitter compounds, saponins, flavonoid glycosides, mucilage and resin. These give Pot Marigold vulnerary, anti-inflammatory, choleretic and antispasmodic properties. It is not often used internally nowadays, but extracts, tinctures and ointments are sometimes used externally to heal stubborn wounds, bed sores, persistent ulcers, varicose veins, bruises, gum inflammations and skin rashes. It is an excellent mouth wash after tooth extraction. Pot Marigold is probably more often used in complexion creams and lotions for cleansing, softening and soothing the skin. In the pharmaceutical industry the bright-orange pigments in the flowers are used to make medicinal preparations more attractive.

Flowerhead

Fruit

Flowering time: June to September

Heather, Ling

Flower

A short, straggly evergreen shrub with densely leafy carpeting stems that root at the nodes and ascend at the tips. The short leaves are needle-like and arranged in opposite rows. The small, pale pinkish-purple flowers are clustered in dense terminal spikes. Under each flower there is a green, calyx-like involucre. The sepals are longer than the petals but of the same colour and texture. The fruit is a globular capsule enclosed in the persistent calyx and corolla.

Heather is common and widespread throughout Europe; it grows on barren acidic soils on heaths, poor grassland, bogs and moors, where it often forms spreading masses (heather moors). It is found throughout most of the British Isles. The generic name, *Calluna*, is derived from the Greek word *kalluno* (= to sweep) after the use of bundles of twigs of heather as brushes and brooms. Some of the related species of heaths, for example Cross-leaved Heath (*Erica tetralix*), have also been used as herbal medicines. Cross-leaved Heath grows wild in Britain in bogs, on wet heaths and moors. It can be distinguished from *Calluna vulgaris* because its leaves are in whorls of four, its flowers are pink and flask-shaped and tightly clustered at the tops of the twigs and the hairy sepals are much shorter than the petals. There are numerous garden varieties of heaths and heathers and wherever they grow they attract bees.

The flowers alone or the flowering stems are used medicinally. The constituents include the flavonoid glycosides quercitrin and myricitrin, tannins, silicic acid and resin. These give Heather anti-inflammatory, diuretic and mild sedative properties. It is used in combination with other herbal preparations to treat diarrhoea, rheumatic pain, colds and coughs, urinary infections, and it is also effective against kidney diseases and enlarged prostate gland.

Flowering time: August to September

Hedge Bindweed, Bellbine

A perennial climbing herb with fleshy, creeping rhizome and bluntly angled stems up to 3 metres long that twine anticlockwise and branch at the tips. The large leaves are triangular ovate to sagittate, dark green above and pale green below. The large white, rarely pinkish, funnel-shaped flowers grow singly on long stalks in the leaf axils. The five sepals are partially hidden by two large, sepal-like bracts, which give the plant its name. *Calystegia* is derived from two Greek words, *kalyx* (= a cup) and *stege* (= a covering). The fruit is a globose capsule with dark-brown seeds. The flowers produce great quantities of pollen and so are attractive to bees.

Hedge Bindweed grows in hedges, fens, damp thickets and waste places. It is also a troublesome weed in gardens. It is widespread in the British Isles but is less common in the north.

The flowering stems have medicinal action but are nowadays rarely used as a herbal remedy. The constituents include tannins, the glycoside jalapin and mucilage. These give Hedge Bindweed purgative, choleretic and mild diuretic properties. The purgative action is unpredictable and therefore potentially dangerous. **Hedge Bindweed should thus not be used for self-medication.**

Flowering time: July to September

Hemp

Seed

An annual herb with an erect, hairy stem and palmately divided, long-stalked leaves with serrate edges. The plant is dioecious: the male flowers are arranged in panicles and produce large quantities of pollen; the female flowers grow in leafy spikes in the leaf axils and are pollinated by wind. The fruit is a shiny, greyish-green achene ('hemp seed').

Hemp is native to Central Asia and India but is now widely grown in other warm parts of the world for its tough fibres and drying oil as well as for its medicinal and narcotic properties. Indian Hemp (*C. sativa* var. *indica*), which is cultivated on a large scale in the Far East, India and Mexico, has the greatest concentration of active substances. Hemp was probably first cultivated in ancient China about 5,000 years ago and was brought to Europe for growing in the early 16th century. The restrictions on growing and using Hemp for medical purposes vary from country to country. **In the United Kingdom it is illegal to grow, possess or sell Hemp without a government permit.** Occasionally seeds germinate on waste ground but the plant usually grows unrecognized. The common name. Hemp, comes from the Anglo-Saxon word *henep* for the plant.

The leaves and flowering stems of the female plant that contain the dark resin cannabinone are the medicinally active parts. They are dried to yield the drug known as hashish, cannabis, bhang or marijuana, which is smoked, drunk or chewed for hallucinogenic effects. Hemp also has several medicinal uses, but it is less widely used by medical practitioners than it once was. The main constituents are tetrahydrocannabinol, cannabinol and cannabidiol. These give Hemp sedative, analgesic and antispasmodic properties and it has been used in medicines for insomnia, depression, neuralgia, migraine, asthma and as a local anaesthetic in dentistry. Nowadays a promising application of Hemp is as an anti-emetic in cancer therapy.

Flowering time: August onwards

Shepherd's Purse

An annual or biennial herb with entire or pinnately lobed basal leaves arranged in a rosette; the small, lanceolate stem leaves are clasping and sagittate at the base. The inconspicuous small white flowers are arranged in terminal racemes. The fruit is a triangular-obcordate silicula and it is this that gave the plant its name as it looks like an old-fashioned leather purse. The generic name, *Capsella,* has a similar meaning.

Shepherd's Purse is a persistent and common weed of waste ground, fields and gardens throughout the world, including the British Isles. It was traditionally used to check haemorrhage in childbirth and bleeding from open wounds. In many countries the leaves are eaten as a vegetable.

The flowering stems are used medicinally. They should always be free of a parasitic fungus, *Cystopus candidus,* which produces a white coating on the plant. The constituents include the amines choline and acetylcholine, an alkaloid (bursine), a flavonoid glycoside (diosmin), organic acids and tannins. These substances give Shepherd's Purse astringent, haemostatic, vasoconstricting and diuretic properties. It is used to check gastric, uterine and pulmonary bleeding, to treat gastritis and enteritis, and urinary and kidney disorders. It affects the smooth muscles in the uterus and it is thought to assist contraction of the womb during childbirth. Any internal use of Shepherd's Purse should be in moderation and preferably supervised by a qualified medical or herbal practitioner; **large doses are poisonous.** Externally Shepherd's Purse is used in compresses to bathe wounds, eczema and other skin disorders.

Fruit

Flowering period: throughout the year

Red Pepper, Green Pepper, Capsicum

Fruit of mild, sweet variety eaten as a vegetable

Fruit of hot variety used as a condiment

An annual herb cultivated as a vegetable or condiment. It has an erect, branched stem and shining, oval, dark-green leaves. The white, short-stalked flowers grow from the leaf axils. They are soon followed by the elongated fruits (berries) which are red, yellow or green and contain many seeds on thin, fleshy inner partitions.

Red Pepper is native to the tropical and subtropical regions of America. The American Indians long ago began cultivating it and it was introduced to Europe by the Spaniards in the 16th century. The useful part of the plant is the fruit. The berries of a mild variety, Sweet Pepper (*C. annuum* var. *grossum*), are green at first, but become red or yellow when ripe. Stripped of their seeds these are eaten raw in salads or cooked as a vegetable; they are an excellent source of vitamin C. The dried red berries of this variety when powdered produce the spice known as paprika. Chilli powder is a very hot spice obtained from ground berries of another variety, *C. annuum* var. *acuminatum*. The generic name, *Capsicum,* may come from the Greek word *kapto* (= I bite), a reference to the hot pungency of the fruit and seed; or it may be derived from the Latin word *capsa* (= a case). The name pepper is derived through the Anglo-Saxon, Latin and Greek words from the Sanskrit *pippali.*

The varieties with long, pungent red fruits are preferred for medicinal preparations of Capsicum. The grinding of the dried fruits is always done with care because the powder is a strong irritant of the skin and mucosa. The constituents include the irritant capsaicin, the oily capsicin, organic pigments (carotenoids), vitamins B_1, B_2, C and E, and fats. Red Pepper is mainly applied externally in the form of extracts, tinctures, ointments and plasters to improve the flow of blood to the skin and mucosa, and to treat rheumatism, sciatica and pleurisy. Occasionally it is used internally in small doses as a stomachic; **in large doses Red Pepper powder can cause gastroenteritis.**

Flowering time: June to September

Stemless Carline Thistle

A perennial herb with a long taproot and a stem so short that the conspicuous flowerhead appears to rest in the centre of the rosette of pinnately divided and spiny basal leaves. The flowerheads lack ray-florets but the rays of spreading silvery-white, sepal-like involucral bracts look like them. The tubular florets are yellow or reddish and packed tightly together in the centre of the disc. The fruit is an oblong, downy achene with a pappus of one row of hairs.

Stemless Carline Thistle grows on grassy, sunny mountainsides in south and central Europe, but not in the British Isles except as a garden ornamental. In some countries it has become endangered by overcollecting and it is now protected. The generic name, *Carlina*, is thought to come from *carolina* after Charlemagne, the eighth-century king to whom the plant was divinely revealed as a cure for plague. The specific epithet, *acaulis*, means stemless. This thistle has camphor-like properties and in ancient times it was used to treat skin rashes and to expel tapeworms; later in the Middle Ages it was used to treat plague. The dried flowerheads are used as a hygrometer — the bracts close at the approach of rain — and in floral decorations.

The roots are used medicinally. Their constituents include inulin (up to 50 per cent), an essential oil with carlinoxide, resin and bitter compounds. These substances give Stemless Carline Thistle diuretic, diaphoretic, stomachic, laxative, antiseptic and anthelmintic properties. In herbal medicine it is used in the form of an infusion to treat stomach and liver disorders, oedema and urine retention. **Large doses are purgative and emetic.** Decoctions are applied externally to bathe skin disorders, fungal infections and wounds and are used as an antiseptic gargle.

In countries where the plant grows wild the fleshy receptacle is sometimes eaten as a vegetable.

Longitudinal section of flowerhead

Flowering time: June

Caraway

Flower

Fruit

A biennial or perennial herb with a spindle-like taproot, finely divided (two or three times pinnate) feathery leaves and erect, branched, furrowed stems terminated by compound umbels of white or rose-tinted, deeply notched flowers. The fruit is an oblong, ribbed achene with two crescent-shaped seeds. All parts of the plant are aromatic.

Caraway grows throughout Europe and Asia in grassy, sunny places, especially in mountains up to 2,000 metres. It is probably not native to the British Isles, but it is locally established in meadows in Scotland, especially in the extreme north. Elsewhere it is usually a casual on waste ground. It may have been introduced in the 16th century. It is widely cultivated for its seeds on the Continent. In Britain most supplies of Caraway are imported. The plant was known in ancient times as a culinary herb and as a remedy for indigestion. It was also believed to promote milk flow in nursing mothers.

The fruits are used medicinally. Their constituents include an essential oil (3−5 per cent) with carvone and limonene, proteins, starch, sugar, tannins and fatty oil. These substances give Caraway stomachic, antispasmodic, carminative, galactagogic, antiseptic and anthelmintic properties. The dried fruits are used in powdered form, chewed whole or they are crushed and made into an infusion. They are safe for children. The distilled essential oil (caraway oil) is also an effective treatment but large doses are harmful to the liver and kidneys.

Caraway (fruits or oil) is widely used in flavouring food products such as bread, meat, cheese, pickles and sauces. It is also an ingredient of some alcholic beverages such as Kümmel and gin. The fleshy root can be eaten as a vegetable and the young leaves added to salads and soups.

Flowering time: June to July

Cornflower, Bluebottle

An annual herb with an erect, branched, wiry stem and alternate, greyish, downy, linear-lanceolate leaves. The solitary terminal flowerheads, borne on long stalks, have large bright-blue tubular florets. The fruit is a flattened silverish achene with a short pappus of rough hairs. Bees find the flowers very attractive.

Native to the Mediterranean region, Cornflower has spread with the cultivation of corn to other parts of the world. It was once a common weed of cornfields and waste ground but in recent years the use of herbicides has kept its growth in check. In Britain it is becoming rarer in the wild, but many varieties are cultivated as garden plants. The generic name, *Centaurea,* was supposedly given to the plant because, according to a Greek legend, Cornflower healed a wound in the foot of Chiron who was one of the centaurs. The specific epithet, *cyanus,* means blue. Cornflower has long been regarded as an excellent eyewash for tired and weak eyes. A blue ink used to be made from the expressed juice of the petals.

The florets are used medicinally. They contain organic pigments (anthocyanins) – principally centaurin or cyanidin – a glycoside (cichoriin), saponins, mucilage and tannins. These substances give Cornflower weak diuretic, astringent and tonic properties. In herbal medicine it is used as an infusion on its own or added to tea mixtures for digestive and gastric disorders. The flowers give teas and potpourris a pleasing colour. Externally Cornflower is used in bath preparations or compresses to treat wounds and skin ulcers. It is also an ingredient of hair tonics and is used as an eye wash. The isolated blue pigment is used in the pharmaceutical industry to colour certain medicines and in cosmetic preparations.

Fruit

Dried herb

Flowering time: June to August

Common Centaury

Flower

An annual (in Britain) or biennial herb with a basal rosette of prominently veined oval leaves and an erect stem which branches at the top. The stem leaves are shorter, narrower, opposite and sessile. The bright rose-red, funnel-shaped flowers are arranged in flat-topped cymes. The corolla tube is much longer than the calyx. The anthers twist after shedding pollen. The fruit is a capsule with a persistent corolla.

Common Centaury grows throughout Europe. It is widespread and locally common in poor, dry grassy places in England, Wales and Ireland; in Scotland it is rarer. It is cultivated commercially for the pharmaceutical industry in central Europe. Like *Centaurea* (Pl. 51), the generic name of this species, *Centaurium,* originates from the Greek myth about Chiron, the centaur. The specific epithet, *erythraea,* means 'red' and refers to the colour of the flowers. Common Centaury has similar bitter properties to Great Yellow Gentian (*Gentiana lutea*) (Pl. 106), and has the same valuable medicinal uses. It was greatly valued as a medicinal herb in classical and medieval times and an alternative common name, Feverwort, refers to the plant's reputation as a cure for fever. It remains a popular herbal remedy.

The flowering stems are used medicinally. The main components are the glycosidic bitter compounds gentiopicrin and erythrocentaurin. The other constituents include traces of an essential oil and tannins. The bitter substances stimulate salivary and gastric secretions and Common Centaury is a popular digestive tonic and stomachic. In herbal medicine it is used in the form of an infusion for loss of appetite, digestive disorders and biliary conditions. A tincture prepared from the fresh plant is used in homeopathy for the same ailments. Common Centaury is also increasingly being used in making bitter herbal wines and liqueurs.

Flowering time: June to October

Iceland Moss

A shrub-like lichen (not a moss) with an erect, much-branched thallus which forms entangled mats. The lobes of the thallus are brown to olive green, fringed and may be slightly incurved, especially when dry. The thallus may be spotted red at the base; the paler convex lower surface is often spotted white. As it dies off the thallus turns a rust brown.

Iceland Moss grows on poor, acidic soil, generally in the ground layer of pine woods, on trees, rocks and walls, in mountain and moorland regions in central and northern Europe and other northern parts of the world. In the British Isles it grows mainly in the Scottish Highlands. In Arctic regions it provides an important food source for Reindeer. For northern peoples too Iceland Moss has long been a food plant and a traditional medicine. It is still used in folk medicine for its nutritive properties and for treating chest ailments. Another species of lichen, *Evernia prunastri,* has similar medicinal properties. It is found in Britain growing mainly on trees in unpolluted areas, but it may also be found on fence posts and on rocks in wet places. Its flattened forking branches are very distinctive.

The thallus is used medicinally. It is effective when fully grown but still green. The main constituents are abundant mucilage with lichenin and isolichenin, bitter organic acids, carbohydrates, traces of iodine and vitamin A. The mucilage has expectorant and antitussive properties and Iceland Moss is thus beneficial for coughs, hoarseness, whooping cough, tuberculosis and bronchial asthma. The bitter compounds stimulate the appetite and gastric secretions. Iceland Moss is contained in some proprietary medicines.

Iceland Moss can be ground and made into flour for baking bread and cakes. When gently boiled and cooled it makes a nutritious jelly.

Evernia prunastri

Chamomile, Roman Chamomile

Flowerhead

A perennial herb with a short, much-branched creeping rhizome, low-growing, creeping or ascending hairy stems and alternate, finely divided (two or three times pinnate) leaves with inrolled margins. The terminal solitary flowerheads have conical, solid receptacles and either white, ligulate ray-florets and yellow, tubular disc-florets or, in the case of cultivated double forms, only ligulate florets (these are most in demand for medicinal purposes). The receptacle bears chaffy scales between the florets. The flowerheads are ringed by green bracts with white papery tips. The fruit is a laterally flattened achene.

Chamomile grows wild in southern parts of the British Isles where it has a local distribution in pastures and other grassy places on sandy soils. It was once widely cultivated for medicinal purposes and for lawns and is sometimes found elsewhere in Britain as a garden escape. It is now commercially grown on the Continent but only on a small scale in Britain. The flowers smell of apples and its generic name, *Chamaemelum,* which is derived from the Greek word *khamaimelon,* means 'earth apple'. The medicinal properties of Chamomile were known to the ancient Egyptians who dedicated the herb to their gods. The plant remains a favourite herbal remedy, especially in the form of Chamomile tea.

The flowerheads are used medicinally. Their constituents include an essential oil with azulene that turns blue on distillation, bitter compounds, flavonoid glycosides and choline. They have anti-inflammatory, antiseptic, antispasmodic, mild sedative, stomachic and diaphoretic properties. In herbal medicine an infusion is used for fever, dyspepsia, nausea, painful menstruation and insomnia. Used externally as a strong infusion Chamomile is also effective in treating ulcers, eczema and wounds. It has many cosmetic uses, a popular one being as a brightener of fair hair. Distillation of the fresh flowering stems yields the essential oil, which is used by the pharmaceutical industry.

Flowering time: June to September

Scented Mayweed, Wild or German Chamomile

An annual herb with an erect, much-branched, glabrous stem with sparse, finely divided (two or three times pinnate) leaves. The solitary, terminal flowerheads have hollow, conical receptacles, white ligulate ray-florets and yellow tubular, five-lobed disc-florets. The ray-florets are spreading at first, later they are bent downwards baring the receptacle. The fruit is an ovoid ribbed achene. All parts of the plant are aromatic. This species is often confused with Chamomile (*Chamaemelum nobile*) (Pl. 54) but botanically it is not a 'true' chamomile and Scented Mayweed is now the preferred name. It can be distinguished from Chamomile by its hollow, not solid receptacle, which lacks chaffy scales between the florets.

Scented Mayweed grows throughout Europe. In England and Wales it is locally common on arable land, waste ground and roadsides; in Scotland it is rarer. It is also a common garden plant. It is cultivated commercially for the pharmaceutical industry in central Europe and elsewhere. The former generic name, *Matricaria,* comes from the Latin word *matrix* (= womb) or *mater* (= mother) on account of the ancient reputation of the herb as a treatment for female ailments.

The flowerheads are used medicinally. Their constituents include up to 1 per cent of an essential oil with azulene (chamazulene) that turns blue on distillation, and bisabolol and farnesene; also flavonoid and coumarin glycosides, mucilage and fatty acids. These substances give Scented Mayweed anti-inflammatory, antiseptic, carminative, diaphoretic, sedative and antispasmodic properties. It is one of the most widely used herbal medicines, particularly for children's ailments. It is also a common treatment for teething problems in homeopathic medicine. In herbal medicine an infusion is used for colds and influenza, indigestion, diarrhoea, urinary infections, insomnia and 'nerves'. Externally it is used in compresses and bath preparations and in eye and mouth washes.

Flowering time: May to June

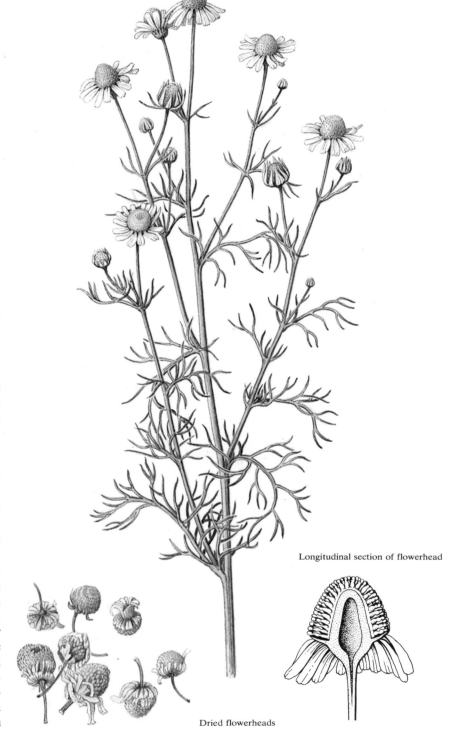

Longitudinal section of flowerhead

Dried flowerheads

Pineappleweed, Rayless Mayweed

An annual herb with an erect, much-branched glabrous stem and many finely divided (two or three times pinnate) alternate leaves. The solitary terminal flowerheads have hollow, conical receptacles and greenish-yellow, four-lobed tubular disc-florets. Unlike Scented Mayweed (*Chamomilla recutita*) (Pl. 55), it has no ray-florets. The bracts encircling the flowerheads have white papery tips. The fruit is a ribbed achene. All parts of the plant are strongly aromatic but less pleasantly so than Scented Mayweed.

Pineappleweed is probably a native of north-east Asia but long ago it became established in North America from where, in the 19th century, it was introduced to Europe. It spread rapidly and it is an increasingly common weed of waysides, tracks and trampled gateways. It is found throughout the British Isles. In cooler regions where Scented Mayweed does not grow it serves as an excellent substitute for the latter. The common name, Pineappleweed, may refer to the plant's rounded flowerhead or to the strong pineapple or apple scent. The specific name, *suaveolens,* means 'sweet-smelling'.

The flowerheads are used medicinally. The constituents include an essential oil (but there is less than in Scented Mayweed or Chamomile, *Chamaemelum nobile*), tannins, glycosides and a bitter compound. Pineappleweed has the same uses as Scented Mayweed except that it is not anti-inflammatory. It is now rarely used in herbal medicine but an infusion is effective for influenza and digestive disorders and it is anthelmintic. Externally it can be used as a mouth rinse and gargle and in treatments for skin disorders.

Longitudinal section of flowerhead

Flowering time: June to July

Greater Celandine

A perennial herb with a taproot and erect, brittle, branched leafy stem. The leaves, which are paler on the underside, are alternate and almost pinnate, with the terminal leaflet three-lobed. The terminal bright-yellow flowers are arranged in loose umbels. The fruit is a thin green capsule which splits from the bottom upwards. The seeds are black with a white appendage. The stem and leaves exude an orange sap (latex) when fresh and broken. This milky juice stains the hands and burns the skin and eyes.

Greater Celandine, which is not related to Lesser Celandine (*Ranunculus ficaria*) (Pl. 192), is probably native to the British Isles. It is common on banks, hedgebanks and walls, often near houses. It has a more local distribution in Scotland and Ireland. The generic name, *Chelidonium,* comes from the Greek word *khelidon* (= a swallow) supposedly because the plant's flowering period coincides with the arrival and departure of swallows.

The flowering stems are used medicinally. The constituents include up to 4 per cent of alkaloids (including chelidonine, chelerythrine, sanguisorbine and berberine) bound to chelidonic and other acids; also traces of an essential oil, saponins and carotenoid pigments. Greater Celandine has antispasmodic, mild sedative and antiseptic properties and it is used in medical practice to alleviate stomach, gallbladder and intestinal pains. It is also a vasodilator and hypertensive. A tincture is used in homeopathy and in folk medicine the ointment prepared from Greater Celandine is used to treat chronic eczemas. The alkaloid chelidonine affects cell division (as does colchicine) and Greater Celandine is one of many plants being investigated for potential anti-cancer properties. Strong doses of Greater Celandine cause severe gastro-enteritis, violent coughing and breathing difficulties. **All internal use should thus be under strict medical supervision. The use of fresh juice to remove warts is also dangerous.**

Fruit   Seed

Flowering time: May to August

American Wormseed, Mexican Tea

Leaves:

Ch. ambrosioides

Ch. album

An annual herb with a branched, reddish, leafy stem. The alternate leaves are oblong to lanceolate and coarsely toothed. The numerous, small, yellowish-green flowers are crowded together in small globose clusters in the leaf axils on the lateral stems. The fruit is an achene. All parts of the plant have a pleasant fragrance, hence the specific name, *ambrosioides*. The generic name, *Chenopodium*, is derived from the Greek word *khen* (= goose) and *pous* (= foot) and refers to the shape of the leaves.

In the 17th century American Wormseed was brought from the tropical regions of America to Europe, where it became acclimatized and in some places naturalized, but not in the British Isles. In South America the leaves have been used in place of ordinary tea, but the principal use of the plant has long been to expel intestinal worms. The cultivated variety (*C. ambrosioides* var. *anthelmintium*) is grown on a large scale as an anthelmintic. Two closely related plants, Fat Hen or White Goosefoot (*Ch. album*) and Common Orache or Iron-root (*Atriplex patula*), are edible and are good substitutes for spinach. Both are common in the British Isles on cultivated and waste ground. The species of orache grown as a vegetable is *Atriplex hortensis*.

The flowering stems of American Wormseed are used medicinally. The constituents include an essential oil with ascaridole as the main component, saponins, tannins and bitter compounds. An infusion prepared from American Wormseed has anthelmintic, antispasmodic, stomachic and tonic properties. It has also been recommended for asthma, nervous disorders and for menstrual disorders. Nowadays, however, the main use of the plant is as a source of the essential oil (chenopodium oil), which is obtained by distillation from the fresh plants and is used particularly against roundworm and hookworm. **American Wormseed and the oil from it are poisonous in large doses and they should be used only under strict medical supervision.**

Flowering time: June to September

Dalmatian Pyrethrum, Pyrethrum Flower

A perennial herb with slender erect stems and many alternate, finely divided leaves that are felted on the underside. The solitary terminal flowerheads have long, white, ligulate ray-florets and yellow, tubular disc-florets. The fruit is a ribbed achene. All parts of the plant are strongly aromatic.

A native of Dalmatia, Pyrethrum is now cultivated in many parts of the world as an ornamental plant and for the effective natural insecticide prepared from the dried flowerheads. The generic name *Chrysanthemum* comes from the Greek words *skhrusos* (= gold) and *anthemon* (= flower); the specific epithet, *cinerariifolium,* refers to the ash-coloured down on the leaves; and the common name Pyrethrum is derived from the Greek word *pur* (= fire), an allusion to the hot taste of the root.

The flowerheads have the active ingredients pyrethrins and cinerins, plus an essential oil and glycosides. Pyrethrins and cinerins are contact insecticides used externally to kill insects and other pests living on the skin of man and animals as well as those that are harmful to plants. These substances are important insecticides because they are non-toxic to mammals and they do not accumulate in the environment or in the bodies of animals. They act by paralysing the nervous system of insects and the animals do not become resistent to them. The actions of pyrethrins and similar substances are still the subject of research. Pyrethrum is not used medicinally.

Fruit

Flowering time: July to August

Feverfew

Flowerheads

Dried flowering stems

A perennial herb with an erect, branched, downy and leafy stem and many alternate, yellowish, pinnate to bipinnate leaves, which are sometimes downy. The terminal flowerheads with short, broad, white ligulate ray-florets and yellow, tubular disc-florets are arranged in loose corymbs. It is distinguished from Chamomile (*Chamaemelum nobilis*) (Pl. 54) in having a flat, not conical receptacle, an upright stem and less finely divided leaves. The fruit is a ribbed achene without a pappus. All parts of the plant are strongly aromatic.

Probably native to south-east Europe, Asia Minor and the Caucasus, Feverfew has spread via the Mediterranean region to many other parts of the world. It is now naturalized over most of Europe, including the British Isles. It grows on walls, waste ground, in hedgerows and other disturbed places and is also a common garden plant, especially in double forms. The common name, Feverfew, is a corruption of the Latin word *febrifugia*, a reference to the plant's former use as a fever-reducing medicine or 'febrifuge'.

The flowerheads, sometimes also the flowering stems, are used medicinally. The dried herb has a penetrating aroma and must always be stored well away from other herbs. It contains an essential oil with camphor (so-called chamomile camphor), bitter compounds, tannins and mucilage. Herbalists use an infusion as a stomachic, mild sedative, disinfectant, antispasmodic and mild anthelmintic. Feverfew is also receiving increasing attention from the medical profession as a safe herbal treatment for migraine. In Britain a clinical trial is in progress and scientists have isolated new substances from the plant, which seem to oppose the actions of prostaglandins. Prostaglandins are naturally occurring substances in the body that may play a part in causing migraine. Externally a strong infusion of Feverfew soothes swellings and open wounds and is a mouth rinse after tooth extraction.

Flowering time: July to August

Tansy

A perennial herb with an erect, angled, almost hairless stem, usually reddish and branched at the top. The alternate dark-green leaves are pinnately lobed and toothed. The terminal, rayless, button-like flowerheads, which are made up of short, tubular, bright-yellow florets, are arranged in dense flat-topped corymbs. The fruit is a greenish-white, ribbed achene.

Tansy grows wild in Europe and Asia in waste places, roadsides, hedgerows and other grassy places and it is also grown in gardens. It is common throughout the British Isles. All parts of the plant, particularly when dried, smell like camphor and Tansy was once widely used as an insect repellent and to rid man and animals of internal parasites. Tansy was also popular as a flavouring and colouring, and Tansy cakes or tansies were eaten at Easter time. The names *Tanacetum* and Tansy are both thought to derive from the Greek word *athanatos* (= immortality) because the plant was believed to have powers of prolonging life – or because it is very persistent once it has been planted.

The flowerheads and leaves are used medicinally. They should always be stored well away from other herbs. The principal constituent is an essential oil (0.2–0.6 per cent) with the poisonous thujone. The other constituents include bitter compounds (tanacetins), tannins and organic acids. Tansy has a variety of medicinal uses but it is now mainly used as an anthelmintic – but there are safer remedies. An infusion or powder has been used for this purpose. The essential oil obtained by distilling the fresh flowering stems is used in homeopathy for worms and as an emmenagogue. **Tansy should be used internally only under strict medical supervision;** large doses are powerful irritants and may also cause kidney and brain damage. Externally Tansy is applied to swellings, bruises and varicose veins.

Tubular floret

Flowering time: July to September

Chicory, Wild Succory

Root

A perennial herb with a long taproot and a stiffly erect, branched, angled and furrowed stem. The leaves in the basal rosette are stalked, deeply pinnately toothed and hairy beneath; the stem leaves are sessile and lanceolate. The flowerheads, arranged in clusters of two or three, grow from the upper leaf axils. The bright-blue florets are all ligulate. The fruit is an achene. All parts of the plant are glandular.

Chicory grows throughout Europe in fields, hedgerows and on roadsides. It is locally common especially on lime-rich soils in England and Wales; it is rare, and probably introduced in Scotland and Ireland. Chicory was an important medicinal herb and vegetable and salad plant in ancient Egyptian, Greek and Roman times; since the 17th century dried, roasted and ground roots have been used as a coffee substitute or adulterant. Varieties of Chicory are widely grown for the roots and for the blanched heads (chicons), which are produced by forcing the roots in darkness and warmth. They are a popular salad ingredient. The related Endive (*C. endiva*) is also grown for salads. The generic name, *Cichorium,* is said to be of Egyptian origin (perhaps from *kehsher*). The common names Chicory and probably Succory derive from it. The specific name, *intybus,* comes from the Arabic word *hendibeh* for the plant and this source also gave Endive its name.

The roots of wild plants are used medicinally. The dried root has a pungent and bitter taste. The constituents include the bitter compounds lactucin and intybin, inulin (up to 58 per cent), tannins, sugars and vitamins. These substances give Chicory aperitif, stomachic, tonic, hypoglycaemic, mild diuretic and laxative properties. In herbal medicine a decoction is used for liver disorders, gallstones and kidney stones, and for inflammations of the urinary tract.

Flowering time: July to October

Cowbane, Water Hemlock

A perennial herb with a hollow, rigid, furrowed stem, which is tuberous and horizontally chambered at the base. The basal leaves are long-stalked, bi- or tripinnate with lanceolate, sharply serrate segments; the stem leaves have sheath-like stalks clasping the stem. The small white flowers are arranged in a compound umbel. The fruit is a curved, ribbed, double achene. **All parts of the plant, especially the roostock, are extremely poisonous.** It is fatal to cattle, hence the name.

Cowbane grows throughout northern and central Europe in shallow water, marshes and ditches and similar moist localities. Its stems are sometimes partly floating. It is native to the British Isles, but it has a very local distribution in most parts. Cowbane's aquatic habit and hollow stem distinguish this species from harmless members of the umbellifer (parsely or carrot) family. Nevertheless, Cowbane can still be easily mistken for celery because the tuber is of the same shape, has a sweet taste and smells like parsely.

The rhizomes contain poisonous acetylenic compounds and an essential oil that has a narcotic effect but is not toxic. These substances affect the central nervous system and Cowbane was once used for treating various brain disorders and spasms of the smooth muscles. Nowadays it is usually regarded as far too toxic for internal use. **Cowbane should never be collected and used for self-medication.** The poison acts quickly on the nervous system causing salivation, vomiting, abdominal cramps, widely dilated pupils, delirium and violent convulsions. Death occurs due to paralysis and respiratory failure.

Flower

Longitudinal section of rhizome with roots

Flowering time: July to August

Ergot Fungus

Sporophores on a sclerotium

Sclerotia

A spore-bearing parasitic fungus which chiefly grows on the ears (spikes) of Rye (*Secale cereale*). Wind carries the spores to the flowering host plant. There they grow into a mycelium, a web of minute tubular threads (hyphae) that penetrate the ovaries of Rye. Small spores (conidia) are formed at the tip of specialized hyphae. At the same time the mycelium secretes a clear sweet fluid attractive to insects on the surface of the rye grains or seeds and the infection is transmitted to other flowers. The grains attacked by the fungus atrophy as the fungal threads grow and intertwine until they form a hard, black, club-shaped mass (sclerotium). When the grain is harvested the sclerotia fall to the ground where in early spring they germinate to produce new, stalked sporeheads (sporophores) and the cycle of infection starts again.

The name Ergot is derived from the old French word *argot* (= a cock's spur), a reference to the appearance of the fungus. Flour made from Rye infected with Ergot has been the cause of episodes of mass poisoning (ergotism) in the past. Symptoms were convulsions and hallucinations along with burning pains and gangrene in the hands and feet. In the Middle Ages the disease was known as St Anthony's Fire. Ergot is an irreplaceable raw material for many important medicines. Nowadays it is obtained by artificial cultivation on Rye and also by cultivation of the mycelia in fermentation vats. There are strict regulations in Britain for keeping the fungus out of the country and it is now uncommon in cereal crops.

Ergot contains more than a dozen potent alkaloids, most of them derivatives of lysergic acid, among them ergometrine, ergocitrine, ergocornine, ergotamine and ergotoxin. Ergometrine is the most important of these substances. It is extracted and used in pharmaceutical preparations principally to assist women in childbirth and in the treatment of migraine. Ergotamine is also used to treat migraine. **These medicines are available only on prescription.**

Erect Clematis, Upright Virgin's Bower

A perennial with a hollow, erect (not climbing or twining) stem, hairy in the upper part. The basal leaves are entire; the stem leaves are opposite and pinnate. The numerous fragrant, white flowers with conspicuous yellow anthers are arranged in dichasiums which grow from leaf axils. The fruit is an achene with a persistent, long, feathery style (plume). **All parts of the plant are poisonous.**

A native of central, eastern and southern Europe, but not the British Isles, Erect Clematis grows in woodland margins, thickets, hedgerows and dry bushy slopes, chiefly in warmer regions. It is grown in gardens. The generic name, *Clematis,* is derived from the Greek word *klema* (= vine branch) because many species in the genus are climbing plants. The specific epithet, *recta,* means 'upright'. Erect Clematis was once a popular herb for treating venereal diseases, gout, rheumatism and bone diseases but it is now rarely used medicinally.

The flowering stems have medicinally active constituents, among them glycosides, saponins and other, so far unidentified, substances. In homeopathy tinctures of the fresh plant are used to alleviate rheumatic pains, migraine and headache, and to treat varicose veins, slow-healing wounds and skin ulcers. The fresh leaves may cause stubborn eczemas and irritate the eyes. The toxicity of the plant is slightly lessened by drying. If eaten the plant can cause enteritis, severe abdominal cramps and diarrhoea. For these reasons **Erect Clematis should never be collected and used for self-medication.**

Fruit

Flowering time: June to July

Blessed Thistle

Longitudinal section of flowerhead

Fruit

An annual herb with a branched, spreading stem. The many alternate stem leaves are toothed or pinnately lobed and spiny and have prominent white veins on the underside. The solitary, terminal yellow flowerheads are enveloped by the upper leaves, the involucral bracts ending in downward curving, long, brown bristles. The fruit is a ribbed, yellow-brown achene with a long yellow pappus. All parts of the plant are hairy.

Native to the Mediterranean region and neighbouring parts of Asia, Blessed Thistle has been used in Europe since at least the 16th century for treating lung diseases and as a tonic and aperitif. Nowadays the plant is grown commercially for the pharmaceutical industry in some European countries. It is sometimes found as a casual in the British Isles in sunny waste places. Blessed Thistle is said to have acquired its names from its reputation as a cure-all, even for plague.

The flowering stems and the leaves are used medicinally. The herb gets its bitter taste from the bitter compound cnicin. It also contains traces of an essential oil, tannins, abundant mucilage and minerals. Blessed Thistle has diaphoretic, choleretic, carminative, tonic and antiseptic properties. It is contained in several proprietary medicines and a tincture is used in homeopathy. In herbal medicine small amounts of Blessed Thistle are used to treat digestive disorders and lack of appetite, and to promote the flow of gastric secretions and bile. **Large doses irritate the mouth, digestive tract and kidneys and may cause vomiting and diarrhoea.** Internal use of Blessed Thistle should therefore be professionally supervised. The herb should never be taken during pregnancy.

Blessed Thistle is also used to make bitter liqueurs and was once used in beer making. The tender young shoots can be eaten like artichokes and the leaves can be added to salads.

Flowering time: June to July

Meadow Saffron, Autumn Crocus

A perennial herb with an underground, brown, scaly corm which bears solitary, long, violet and tubular crocus-like flowers in the autumn. (It differs from crocuses in having six — not three — stamens.) The orange anthers give the plant one of its common names. After pollination the seeds remain in the ovary until spring when several large, fleshy, bright glossy-green, oblong to lanceolate leaves appear, arranged in a rosette with the fruit — a capsule — in the centre. The small brown seeds are pitted. **All parts of the plant are extremely poisonous.**

Meadow Saffron grows throughout Europe, in some parts in large numbers in damp meadows and pastures. In the British Isles it is rare except in western England, East Anglia and Yorkshire and in woods in the Cotswolds where it remains locally common. The generic name, *Colchicum,* is derived from Colchis, an ancient country in Asia Minor.

The corms and seeds are used medicinally. Besides the poisonous alkaloid colchicine, which is found in all parts of the plant, the seeds contain other alkaloids, large amounts of fat, tannins and sugars. Colchicine is extracted and used in preparations prescibed by medical practitioners mainly for acute attacks of gout and rheumatism. Tinctures of Meadow Saffron are used in homeopathy for the same complaints. Demecolcine, a derivative of colchicine, was for a time used in the treatment of chronic leukaemia. **Meadow Saffron is a dangerous plant and it should never be collected and used for self-medication.** If the seeds or flowers are eaten, the outcome is often fatal. Symptoms of poisoning include salivation, vomiting, diarrhoea and abdominal cramps. Convulsions, general paralysis and respiratory failure may follow. The plant is also toxic to animals, particularly when they are fed dry fodder. The alkaloids even pass into milk and can accumulate to reach a toxic level. Colchicine inhibits the division of certain cells and this property has been used to produce new plant varieties.

Fruit

Corm

Seed

Flowering time: August to September

Hemlock

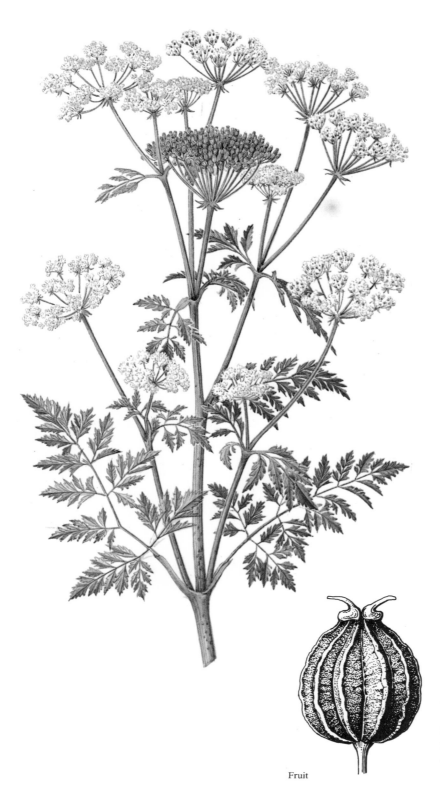

Fruit

A biennial herb with a tall, hairless, furrowed, branched and hollow stem, its lower part smooth and purple spotted. The smooth, alternate, finely divided (two to four times pinnate) leaves are coarsely toothed, dark green above and grey green below. The petioles are long and sheath the stem at the base. The small white flowers with unnotched petals are arranged in terminal compound umbels. The fruit is a roundish double achene with wavy ribs. **All parts of the plant, especially the green, almost ripe seeds, are deadly poisonous** and have a fetid smell. This marked smell (of mice) and the presence of purple blotches on the stems and petioles and the form of the fruit distinguish Hemlock from many other members of the umbellifer family.

Hemlock grows wild in damp places, open woods and near water throughout most of the British Isles. The plant's generic name, *Conium,* comes from the Greek word *koneion,* which may in turn be derived from *konos* (= a cone), but the reason for this connection is not clear. The specific epithet, *maculatum,* means 'spotted' and refers to the stalks. The origin of the common name is unknown. The poisonous effects of Hemlock were known to the ancient Greeks who used it for executions. For example, Socrates was put to death in 399 BC by being given Hemlock juice to drink. Greek and Arabic physicians considered Hemlock an effective treatment for tumours, pains in the joints and for skin infections. The plant is little used today in medicine.

The fruits are the most medicinally active parts. The main constituents are poisonous alkaloids, principally coniine, and essential oils and organic acids. A tincture of Hemlock is still used by qualified practitioners in homeopathy. The isolated pure coniine is also contained in a few proprietary ointments and suppositories to relieve severe pain. **Hemlock is a highly dangerous plant and it should never be collected and used for self-medication.** Even a small dose can be fatal.

Flowering time: June to August

Lily-of-the-Valley

☠ ☠

A perennial herb with a tangle of underground rhizomes which, in spring, bear stalked, broadly elliptic leaves, two on each stem, and later a scape with a one-sided raceme of drooping white, sweet-scented, bell-shaped flowers. The fruit is a bright-red, globose berry. **All parts of the plant are extremely poisonous** and children should be warned not to eat the attractive berries.

Lily-of-the-Valley grows throughout Europe in the undergrowth of shady woods, in thickets and hedgerows, mostly on lime-rich soils. It grows wild locally in England and Wales and in Scotland, but it is becoming rarer. It is not native to Ireland. The plant has long been grown in gardens. The common and generic names refer to the plant's usual habitat. Lily-of-the-Valley has a long history of medical use for heart conditions. The leaves yield a yellow dye and at one time the dried ground roots were an ingredient of snuff.

The flowering stems, but more often the leaves, are used medicinally. They contain poisonous cardiac glycosides, among them convallotoxin, convallatoxol and convalloside, and also saponins, essential oils and organic acids. The individual glycosides are isolated and included in proprietary medicines prescribed for various heart conditions. The glycosides are considered as effective and safer than digitalin from foxgloves (*Digitalis* spp.) for regulating heart action. Tinctures of Lily-of-the-Valley are also used in homeopathy. Contrary to the advice in some popular herbal books, **Lily-of-the-Valley should never be collected and used for self-medication.** It is a dangerous plant and should be used only under strict medical supervision. Some components have purgative and emetic actions. The berries may cause paralysis and respiratory failure and a doctor's help should be sought immediately if a child eats them.

The aromatic extracts from the flowers are used in the cosmetic and perfumery industries.

Fruit

Flowering time: May to June

Canadian Fleabane

Flowerhead

An annual herb with an erect, glabrous or slightly hairy stem, which is much branched near the top. The leaves are slightly hairy and linear to lanceolate. The numerous small bell-shaped flowerheads are arranged in long terminal panicles; the small ray-florets are whitish, the disc-florets pale yellow. The fruit is a yellow downy achene.

Canadian Fleabane is a native of North America but it was introduced into Europe in the 17th century and it has become a troublesome weed of field and garden, the small light seeds being easily dispersed by wind. In the British Isles it is locally common in dry waste places and on cultivated ground throughout most of England and Wales, but it is rare in the north. Canadian Fleabane is related to plants that were supposed to drive away fleas, hence the common name. The seeds were also thought to look like fleas. The former generic name, *Erigeron,* comes from the Greek words *eri* (= early) and *geron* (= aged person) and refers to the 'worn-out' appearance of some of the species in the genus, even when still in flower. The plant was introduced into medical practice in the 18th century. It was regarded as a useful remedy for diarrhoea, dropsy and many kidney disorders. It is still used in herbalism.

The flowering stems are used medicinally. Their constituents include an essential oil with limonene and terpineol as its main components, tannins and choline. These substances give Canadian Fleabane astringent, diuretic and haemostatic actions. Herbalists prescribe an infusion or decoction for severe diarrhoea, gravel and kidney disorders, and for throat infections. A tincture is used in homeopathy for these complaints and for haemorrhoids and painful menstruation. The essential oil (oil of erigeron) obtained by distillation of fresh plant material has been used to expel intestinal parasites.

Flowering time: August to October

Coriander

An annual herb with an erect, furrowed, solid, branched stem. The alternate leaves are pinnate or bipinnate, the lower ones with broader leaflets than the upper ones which are finely divided. The white or pink flowers, with outer petals longer than the inner ones, are arranged in compound umbels. The fruit is an ovoid, ribbed, red-brown double achene. All parts of the plant smell strongly of bed bugs. However, the fruits lose their disagreeable scent when they ripen and become pleasantly spicy and aromatic.

Coriander is native to the eastern Mediterranean region and India but it has been cultivated and used as a medicinal and culinary herb for at least 3,000 years. It is grown on a small scale in Britain but most supplies of the herb are imported. The plant can sometimes be found growing wild in waste places in Britain as a garden escape. There is uncertainty about the generic name, *Coriandrum*; it may be derived from the Greek word *koris* (= a bug), a reference perhaps to the plant's smell and the appearance of the fruits.

The fruits contain up to 1 per cent of an essential oil with a linalool (coriandrol) as its main component, plus fatty oil, proteins, tannins, pectin, sugars and vitamin C. The dried fruits are used by themselves or in tea mixtures, primarily as an aperitif, as a digestive tonic and a carminative. Coriander also has a sedative effect. The essential oil (coriander oil), obtained by distillation from the fruits, is used to make a water solution for windy colic with much the same effect as that made from Caraway (*Carum carvi*) (Pl. 50). It is also used in many compound preparations and to disguise the taste of other medicines. The fruits — or the oil on its own — are included in ointments for painful rheumatic joints and muscles.

Coriander is an important culinary herb. The fruits and the fresh leaves are widely used for flavouring food and the root can be cooked and eaten as a vegetable.

Fruit

Flowering time: June

Crown Vetch

Fruit   Seed

A perennial herb with a deep root and a straggling, branched, ascending stem. The alternate leaves are odd-pinnate with no tendril. The white, purple or pink flowers are arranged in a solitary rounded umbel at the end of a long stalk, which is longer than the leaves and grows from the leaf axils. The flowers appear in succession almost all summer long. The fruit is a four-angled erect, slender, jointed pod with a terminal beak. **The plant is extremely poisonous** and cattle avoid it. Children should be warned not to pick the flowers for posies.

Crown Vetch is native to central and southern Europe, but it has been introduced to the British Isles and it is now well naturalized in several scattered localities. It grows in grassy places, on roadsides and in hedgerows, mostly on lime-rich soils. The generic name, *Coronilla,* is a diminutive of the Latin word *corona* (= a crown) and refers to the arrangement of the flowers. In the common name 'vetch' is a corruption of the Latin word *vicia* for bean plants.

The flowering stems have been used medicinally but nowadays the plant is generally regarded as too toxic for use as a herbal remedy. The constituents include the poisonous water-soluble glycoside coronillin, tannins, bitter compounds, organic salts and vitamin C. Coronillin has an action very similar to that of digitalin from foxgloves (*Digitalis* spp.) in that it regulates heart action. **Crown Vetch is a dangerous plant and it should never be collected und used for self-medication.** Symptoms of poisoning are pallor, diarrhoea, rectching, muscular spasms and eventually coma and death.

Flowering time: May to August

Bulbous Corydalis, Bird in the Bush

A perennial herb with a large, hollow, globose, underground tuber with wiry roots. The stem is erect and bears two biternate lobed leaves, bluish green below and light green above. The irregularly shaped violet or white flowers are arranged in a solitary terminal raceme. The upper petal is drawn out into a long, apically curved spur. The fruit is a capsule. **All parts of the plant are extremely poisonous.**

Bulbous Corydalis is found throughout Europe and neighbouring parts of Asia. It grows in open woods and hedgerows, where it is conspicuous in spring with its early flowers and greyish stems. It is attractive to bees. Bulbous Corydalis is also grown as a garden plant and although it is not native to the British Isles it is occasionally found in the wild as a garden escape. The generic name, *Corydalis,* comes from the Greek word *korudallis* (= crested lark), and refers to the appearance of the flowers. The specific epithet, *cava,* means 'hollow'. Bulbous Corydalis has been used as a vermifuge in the past. Nowadays it is not used in herbal medicine but the isolated constituents still have a place in conventional medicine.

The tubers are used medicinally. When dried they have a strong aroma and bitter taste. They contain alkaloids, the most important being corydaline and bulbocapnine. Bulbocapnine has antispasmodic, sedative and hallucinogenic properties. It lowers the blood pressure and inhibits the contractions of striated muscles. In some countries it is used in preparations to treat Parkinson's disease and other serious neurological disorders, vertigo and muscular tremors. Bulbocapnine is also beneficial before and after treatment with anaesthetics. Large doses of the drug can cause severe headache and other side effects. **Bulbous Corydalis is a dangerous plant and it should never be collected and used for self-medication.**

Flowers

Underground tuber with wiry roots

Flowering time: February to May

Hazel

Fruit

A tall shrub, rarely a small tree, with smooth, reddish-brown peeling bark. The leaves are entire, oval to rounded, doubly serrate and hairy. The plant is monoecious: the male flowers are clustered in pendulous catkins; the female flowers are in erect, short, bud-like spikes with protruding red styles. The flowers appear early in spring before the leaves and produce large quantities of pollen. The fruit is a hard, brown, rounded nut (cobnut) enclosed by the irregularly lobed green involucre.

Hazel is common in woods, scrub and hedges throughout Europe, including the British Isles. There are also many cultivated varieties. The generic name, *Corylus,* is said to come from the Greek word *korys* (= a helmet), an allusion to the shape of the fruit. The common name, which is a corruption of the Anglo-Saxon word *haesel,* may have the same meaning. Hazel is seldom used in conventional medicine and only little used in herbalism. Mostly the plant is grown for its nutritious nuts and the oil from them. Hazel rods are used to make hurdles, wattles, hedging and baskets.

The leaves, bark and fruits have medicinal actions. The main constituents of the leaves are essential oils, glycosides and sugars; those of the bark chiefly tannins and organic acids. These substances give the leaves diuretic properties and they have been used in tea mixtures. They have also been used for treating varicose veins and circulatory disorders. Externally they have been used in bath preparations to treat haemorrhoids and slow-healing wounds. The nuts contain up to 60 per cent fatty oils, plus proteins, sugars and vitamins. They are very nourishing and tasty and are widely used in confectionery and bakery goods. The expressed oil from them is a valuable salad and vegetable oil and it is also used to make soap and cosmetics and as a machine lubricant.

Flowering time: January to April

Midland Hawthorn

A deciduous shrub or small tree with grey thorny twigs. The leaves are alternate, obovate, shallowly lobed, serrate and leathery. The white to pinkish flowers are borne in erect corymbs. The fruit (haw) is a red, barrel-shaped pome with the remnants of the recurved triangular sepals and two or three dry stigmas; it has two or three stones.

Midland Hawthorn grows throughout Europe in woods, less often in hedgerows and scrub. In the British Isles it is locally common in southern and eastern parts of England and in Wales, but it is rare in northern England and Ireland and introduced in Scotland. The generic name, *Crataegus,* is derived from the Greek word *kratos* (= strong), a reference to the hardness of the wood. The common name, hawthorn, is a corruption of the Anglo-Saxon word *hagathorn, haga* meaning 'hedge'. The medicinal properties of Midland Hawthorn were known to the ancient Greeks. The plant is still widely used, especially on the Continent, for the treatment of hypertension.

The flowers (white forms only) have the strongest medicinal action. They are used on their own, or with the leaves; or the leaves are used by themselves. The main constituents of the flowers are the glycoside quercitrin with the sugar component quercetin, also flavones and traces of an essential oil. The leaves contain the flavonoid glycoside vitexin 4-rhamnosid, sterols and catechins. These substances give Midland Hawthorn hypotensive, vasodilating, antisclerotic and sedative properties and the plant is used for various heart and circulatory disorders such as high blood pressure, abnormal heart rate, arteriosclerosis and angina pectoris. Because of its effects on the heart **Midland Hawthorn should be used only under the supervision of a qualified medical or herbal practitioner;** no part is suitable for self-medication. The fruits have the same constituents as those of Hawthorn (*C. monogyna*) (Pl. 76).

Fruit

Flowering time: May to June

Hawthorn

Flowers

A deciduous thorny shrub or small tree with much-branched twigs, which are felted at first, later glabrous. The dark-green leaves are wedge-shaped and deeply lobed with tufts of hair in the vein axils beneath. The leaf lobes are entire or toothed at the tips. The strong-smelling white flowers are arranged in dense corymbs. The fruit (haw) is a red, barrel-shaped pome with the remnants of the appressed sepals and one blackened stigma; it has one stone.

This hawthorn is widely distributed throughout Europe, including the British Isles, where it grows in scrub, woods and hedges. It is commoner than Midland Hawthorn (*C. laevigata*) (Pl. 75) but less tolerant of shade. Cultivated varieties of Hawthorn − mostly pink-flowering and double forms − are grown as ornamental plants in hedges. These do not have the same medicinal properties as the wild plant. The specific epithet, *monogyna*, refers to the single style in this species.

The flowers, leaves and fruits are used medicinally. They have basically the same action as parts of other hawthorn species, particularly Midland Hawthorn. The fruits contain flavonoid glycosides, organic acids, tannins, an essential oil, vitamin C, vitamin B complex and pectins. Like the flowers and the leaves the fruits have hypotensive, antisclerotic, vasodilating and sedative properties and they are used in the form of an infusion or tea mixtures in herbal medicine or in proprietary medicines to treat various heart and circulatory disorders, migraine, menopausal conditions and insomnia. Because of its effects on the heart, **Hawthorn should be used only under the supervision of a qualified medical or herbal practitioner;** no part is suitable for self-medication.

Flowering time: May to June

Saffron

A perennial herb with a scaly under-ground corm and linear leaves with a pale midrib. The short scape is terminated by a large pale-violet, six-lobed, funnel-shaped flower. The yellow style is tipped with three orange stigmas that extend beyond the perianth. (The colour of the style, the three – not six – stigmas, and the shape of the leaves distinguish Saffron from the poisonous Meadow Saffron, *Colchicum autumnale,* Pl. 67.) The fruit is a capsule. Saffron also spreads by means of the cormlets that form on the base of the old corm.

Saffron has been cultivated and highly valued in the Middle East for at least 4,000 years as an aromatic flavouring, perfume, dye, medicine – even as an aphrodisiac. It has been so prized that at times it has been worth almost its own weight in gold. For a time Saffron was grown in England – at Saffron Walden in Essex. The plant is no longer known in the wild and its area of origin remains a mystery. The common name, Saffron, origi-nally came from the Arabic word *za'faran* and refers to the orange-coloured stigmas. Saffron has been a cure-all remedy for a variety of ailments but it is now little used in medicine because of its high cost. Today the total world production is only about 30 tons a year and one ounce (30 g) may cost as much as £50 on the retail market. It is still, however, used to taste and flavour medicines and as a flavouring in many culinary dishes. It is often adul-terated or another spice is substituted for it.

The stigmas are the medicinal parts. Among their constituents are a series of crocine glycosides, a bitter glycoside (picrocrocine) and an essential oil. These give Saffron stomachic, antispasmodic and emmenagogic properties. **It is a pow-erful medicine and not suitable for self-medication:** large doses can cause haemorrhage, vomiting, diarrhoea and vertigo. It was once widely used as an abortifacient.

Style with stigmas   Stigma

Flowering time: September to October

Vegetable Marrow, Pumpkin, Squash

Seed

Cross-section of fruit

Fruit

An annual cultivated herb with a trailing stem up to 5 metres long. The alternate, cordate leaves are very large and hairy. The long-stalked, large, bright-yellow, star-shaped flowers are dioecious: the male flowers are in axillary clusters; the female flowers are solitary. The plant is in flower a long time and is an important source of food for bees. The fruit, a berry, is usually very large and hollow and contains flat, oval, white seeds in the watery fruit flesh.

Vegetable Marrow is native to Central America where it has been cultivated for several thousand years. It is now grown all over the world as a vegetable, for its oil and for fodder. There are many different varieties which produce fruit of all shapes and sizes. The specific name, *pepo,* is the Latin word for pumpkin and comes from the Greek *pepon* (= a large melon) as does the common name Pumpkin (formerly pompon or pumpion). The seeds have long been a safe and popular remedy for intestinal worms.

The seeds contain up to 50 per cent fatty oil, proteins, a glycoside (cucurbitin), resin and substances yet to be identified. They are still used as an anthelmintic, dried, or eaten fresh (chewed or pounded) with the seed coat removed. They have no irritating side effects. A decoction from the dried seeds combined with castor oil can be used for the same purpose. The seeds of the related Cucumber (*Cucumis sativa*) are also anthelmintic. The fruits of Vegetable Marrow contain, besides water, sugars, proteins, a fatty oil, vitamins and minerals. They can be made into compotes and marmalade. The raw fruit juice is slightly diuretic and is sometimes recommended for urinary complaints.

Flowering time: June to September

Quince

A deciduous shrub or small tree with grey, felted shoots. The leaves are alternate, entire, ovate to oblong, glabrous above, white-woolly beneath. The rather large, whitish flowers are short-stalked and solitary and have a pleasant fragrance. The fruit is a large, globose or pear-shaped, felted, aromatic pome with firm flesh and dark-brown, flattened seeds, which are **poisonous**. It is green at first, yellow when ripe.

Quince is probably a native of the Near East and Central Asia but it has been widely introduced elsewhere. It is now cultivated all over the world for its fruit, especially in warmer regions where the fruit is often more juicy. Quince is also used as a stock for pears. The common name, Quince, means 'apple of Cydonia', after the place in Crete where a variety of the tree grew. In ancient times Quince was regarded as a symbol of happiness, fertility and love and was one of the most popular of medicinal plants.

The fruits and the seeds are used medicinally. The fruit pulp contains sugars, pectins, essential oils, tannins and organic acids, including vitamin C. In herbalism an infusion of the dried fruit is used to treat digestive disorders, sore throat, diarrhoea and haemorrhage of the bowel. The seeds contain up to 22 per cent mucilage, a fatty oil, a glycoside (amygdalin) and tannins. They have emollient, expectorant, anti-inflammatory and astringent properties and are used dried, **uncrushed,** in an infusion or decoction to treat cough, gastritis and enteritis. Externally mucilaginous compresses made from soaked curshed seeds can be applied to wounds, ulcers, inflamed joints, chapped skin and eye inflammations. The mucilage from the seeds also makes a gargle for sore throats.

The fresh pulp of Quince fruits makes excellent preserves, jellies and syrups. The fruit is only edible when cooked; the **seeds must not be eaten.**

Longitudinal section of fruit

Seed

Flowering time: May

Cardoon

A perennial herb with a stout, erect, branched stem and numerous spiny lanceolate leaves, which are smooth above and white-felted below. The terminal globose flowerheads with a fleshy receptacle have blue-violet ligulate florets, but no ray-florets. The flowerhead in bud is almost completely enclosed by conspicuous, spiny, green, leathery involucral bracts. The fruit, an achene, has a pappus of branched, feathery hairs.

Cardoon is a native of Mediterranean Europe and was known to the ancient Egyptians, Greeks and Romans. It is still grown as a vegetable in some countries but in the British Isles it is used mainly for floral decorations. It may well be the ancestor of the familiar Globe Artichoke (*C. scolymus*), which is more widely cultivated for the inner tips of the fleshy involucral bracts and thickened receptacle of the flowerheads. The generic name, *Cynara,* comes from the Greek word *kynara* and means a kind of artichoke. The common name, Cardoon, is derived through the French *cardon* from the Latin word *carduus* for a thistle.

The leaves are used medicinally. The constituents include a bitter compound (cynarine), mucilage, tannins, organic acids and vitamin A. These substances give Cardoon strong choleretic and diuretic properties and it is used with success in the treatment of gall bladder and liver disorders, including hepatitis. Cardoon is also hypoglycaemic and antisclerotic. On the Continent extracts of Cardoon are included in proprietary digestive tonics, in aperitifs and in liqueurs. The fresh juice from the leaves can be used externally to treat some skin disorders.

The inner leaf stalks and midribs can be blanched and eaten as a vegetable.

Fruit   Detail of fruit

Flowering time: August to September

Broom, Scoparium

A shrub with erect, green, angled, tough, spineless stems. The numerous small alternate leaves are lanceolate below and trifoliate in the upper parts of the stems. The large yellow flowers grow singly in the upper leaf axils. They produce large quantities of pollen and are attractive to bees. The fruit is an oblong black pod with brown hairs on the margins. It twists open when ripe. **All parts of the plant are poisonous.**

Broom grows on sunny slopes, on heaths and waste ground and in open woods, usually on acid soils. It often forms spreading masses. It occurs throughout temperate Europe, including the British Isles. The medicinal properties of Broom have long been known and there were also many traditions associated with the use of the branches to make brooms (hence the common name). The specific epithet, *scoparius,* also means broom-like; it comes from the Latin word *scopae* (= a besom). Broom was once used as a cure for dropsy but the plant is now only rarely used in medicine.

All parts of the plant have a medicinal value – the flowers, flowering stems, seeds and roots, the flowering stems being used the most. The most important active constituent is the alkaloid sparteine. Other ingredients include a glycoside (scoparin), tannins, essential oils and bitter compounds. The amounts of these substances vary a great deal and Broom is now regarded as too unreliable – and therefore potentially too toxic – for general use. Some of the constituents are, however, isolated and included in proprietary preparations. For example, medicines containing sparteine are sometimes prescribed for heart and circulatory disorders because this substance dilates the blood vessels and raises blood pressure (it is hypertensive). Sparteine also stimulates the smooth muscles of the intestines and the uterus and it is utilized in obstetrics. **Dosage and treatment with any preparation containing Broom must be prescribed by a medical practitioner.**

Fruit

Flowering time: May to June

Mezereon, Spurge Olive

Cultivar with white flowers

A small deciduous shrub with erect greyish twigs. In early spring it bears racemes of fragrant pinkish-mauve flowers in the axils of fallen leaves of the previous year. The alternate, pale-green, lanceolate to oblong leaves appear after flowering is over. The fruit is a bright-red drupe. **All parts of the plant are poisonous; the red berries can be fatal if eaten by a child.**

Mezereon is native to temperate Asia and to most parts of Europe, including the British Isles, but it is now rare and protected in many countries. Until recently it was protected in Britain, but although it is still very rare it is no longer considered to be in danger of extinction. It grows wild in woods and scrub in some parts of England. It is also frequently grown in gardens. The genus is named after Daphne, one of the nymphs of Greek myth who was saved from the attentions of Apollo by being changed into a laurel tree. The specific epithet, *mezereum,* — and the common name — are derived from the Arabic word *mazaryun* used by the Arabian physician Avicenna. In the old days Mezereon was used medicinally to alleviate headache and toothache and in more recent times as a purgative and as a treatment for rheumatic, venereal and scrofulous conditions. It is now rarely if ever used in conventional medicine but it still has a place in homeopathy. It is too toxic for internal use.

The bark is the medicinal part. Its constituents include the acrid poisonous alkaloid mezereine and the glycoside daphnine. These substances have an irritant, rubefacient effect and cause blistering if used for a long period. Daphnine is also hallucinogenic. A tincture is used in homeopathy for various skin disorders. All Mezereon preparations, including ointments and liniments, should be applied only under strict medical supervision. The herb should not be taken internally. **Mezereon is dangerous and it should never be collected and used for self-medication.**

Flowering period: February to April

Thornapple, Jimsonweed, Stramonium

An annual herb with a robust, branched, leafy stem. The alternate leaves are pointed oval with incurving, coarsely toothed margins. The large erect, white or violet-tinted, trumpet-shaped flowers grow singly either in the axils of the branches or at the tips of the stems. The flowers are pleasantly scented, unlike the leaves which have a fetid smell. The fruit is a prickly ovoid capsule with small, black, kidney-shaped pitted seeds. Thornapple is in the nightshade family and **all parts of the plant are extremely poisonous, especially the seeds,** a fatal dose for a child being about 20.

Thornapple is a native of North America but it has been introduced elsewhere. In the British Isles it is an occasional weed of waste ground and rubbish tips, being most commonly seen at the end of hot summers. It was introduced into medical practice in Britain in the 16th century. It and other *Datura* species are grown commercially for the pharmaceutical industry in some countries, but in Britain only on a very small scale. The plant gets its most common English name from its spiny fruits. An alternative name, Jimsonweed, probably refers to the settlement of Jamestown in Virginia, USA. Thornapple is still used in conventional and homeopathic medicine but rarely, if ever, in herbalism on account of its toxicity.

The leaves and seeds are used medicinally. Their constituents include tropane alkaloids (0.4 per cent), principally hyoscyamine, atropine and scopolamine, and traces of an essential oil. These substances give Thornapple antispasmodic and hallucinogenic actions, they inhibit glandular secretions and dilate the airways. In medicine today Thornapple is mostly used in tinctures and proprietary preparations to treat asthma, bronchitis and Parkinson's disease. It is occasionally prescribed in the form of cigarettes. **Thornapple is a dangerous plant; it should never be collected and used for self-medication.** It induces symptoms of poisoning similar to those caused by Deadly Nightshade.

Seed

Flowering time: June to October

Carrot

Flower

Root of *D. carota sylvestris*
(Wild Carrot)

Root of *D. carota sativus*
(Cultivated Carrot)

Fruit

A biennial herb with a spindle-shaped taproot, which is white in the wild sub-species (*sylvestris*) and generally orange-red or yellow in the cultivated form (*sativus*). In the second year the plant produces an angled, branched, hairy, fur-rowed stem bearing alternate, bi- or tri-pinnate, finely divided leaves. The flow-ers, which are arranged in dense terminal compound umbels, are white but a middle one is usually pinkish. The much-divided bracts under the flowerheads are distinc-tive. The fruit, a double achene, is flat-tened and ribbed with bristles and hooked spines on the ribs.

Wild Carrot grows in fields and other grassy places, especially on chalky soils and near the sea, throughout most of the British Isles. The root is tough and ined-ible; that of the cultivated varieties is long, cylindrical and fleshy — the familiar kitch-en carrot. The common name, Carrot, and the specific epithet, *carota,* are derived from the Greek word *karoton* for the wild plant. Carrots were known as a vegetable in ancient Greek and Roman times. The practice of cultivating them was intro-duced to Elizabethan England by Flemish refugees. Their use as a herbal remedy has a long history and they remain a popular treatment.

The fully grown fresh root is used medicinally, finely grated or the juice is strained off and used on its own. The constituents include carotenes (provita-min A) and vitamins B complex and C, the alkaloid daucine, which has a nicotine-like odour, and sugars and pectins. Fresh carrot, particularly the carotene constituent, affects the keenness of sight and the ability to see in dim light. It has anthelmintic, diuretic and stomachic properties. For children it is effective for digestive ailments and tonsil-litis. A carrot diet is said to alleviate pain in cancer patients. Carrot juice can, how-ever, be toxic if taken in excessive amounts as it induces hypervitaminosis A. An infusion of the fruits is sometimes used in tea mixtures as an anthelmintic.

Flowering time: June onwards

Forking Larkspur, Field Larkspur

An annual or biennial herb with a slender taproot and an erect, branched, leafy stem. The leaves are sessile, alternate and palmate with the segments finely divided. The blue flowers have a pronounced upward-curving spur which secretes nectar. They are arranged in a terminal spike. The fruit is a follicle with flattened, black, pitted seeds. **All parts of the plant, except the flowers, are poisonous.** The seeds are especially toxic and the fruits should be removed before the flowerstems are used in floral decorations.

Forking Larkspur is native to the Mediterranean region but it has spread to all parts of the world along with the cultivation of grain. In the British Isles it occurs as a rare casual of cornfields and waste places, especially near to ports. Some large-flowered varieties of larkspur are very decorative; they are also poisonous. The usual garden species is *D. ajacis* (= *Consolida ambigua*). In ancient times the plant was used to heal wounds and the specific epithet, *consolida,* and the preferred generic name, *Consolida,* may refer to this former medicinal use. More likely, however, these names allude to the fused, or consolidated, perianth segments. The name *Delphinium,* from the Greek word *delphinion* (= dolphin-like), was given to the larkspurs because their flowers were held to resemble a dolphin's head. Forking Larkspur, and its close relative Stavesacre (*D. staphisagria*), were once used for a variety of ailments. They are now rarely used except to destroy lice and nits in the hair.

The flowering stems and seeds contain alkaloids, the glycoside delphinine, aconitic acid (not in the flowers) and constituents yet to be identified. These substances give Forking Larkspur diuretic, anthelmintic, insecticidal and purgative properties. It is dangerous to take any preparation from it internally. **Forking Larkspur should never be collected and used for self-medication.** The alkaloids act on the nervous system like those of Monkshood causing general weakness and eventually respiratory failure.

Flower

Flowering time: June to July

Burning Bush, Dittany, Gas Plant

Rhizome with roots

Fruit   Seed

A bushy perennial herb with a whitish, branched rhizome, fibrous roots and erect branched stem. The alternate dark-green leaves are odd-pinnate, the leaflets lanceolate to ovate and finely serrate. The large, pinkish flowers are arranged in terminal racemes. The fruit is a star-shaped capsule with black seeds. All parts of the plant are covered with oil glands that give off a penetrating orange-like scent, especially when rubbed. The vapour this essential oil produces is inflammable, hence the plant's common names Burning Bush and Gas Plant.

Burning Bush is widely distributed from southern Europe to northern China and grows in warm, sunny places on lime-rich soils. In many countries it is a protected species. It is not native to the British Isles but it is grown in gardens for its fragrant leaves and handsome flowers. The generic name, *Dictamnus,* and an alternative common name come from the Greek word *diktamnion,* which is in turn perhaps derived from Dikte, a mountain in Crete where another aromatic plant, Dittany of Crete (*Origanum dictamnus*), also grows. Burning Bush was once widely used as a herbal remedy but it has little application today.

The rhizome is the medicinal part. Its constituents include an essential oil, bitter compounds and the alkaloid dictamine. Dictamine in particular causes contractions of the smooth uterine muscles. Burning Bush also has diuretic, laxative, carminative and anthelmintic actions. In herbalism it is prescribed in the form of an infusion. In homeopathy a tincture prepared from the fresh leaves is prescribed for gynaecological disorders and constipation. **Dictamine is toxic in strong doses.** Burning Bush can also cause allergic skin reactions in hypersensitive individuals.

Flowering time: May to June

Large Yellow Foxglove

A medium-tall hairy perennial herb with a taproot and alternate, lanceolate, serrate leaves, the lowermost ones in a rosette. The leaves further up the erect, unbranched stem are smaller and sessile. The large, bell-shaped, nodding flowers coloured pale ochre netted with brown inside are arranged in a long, terminal one-sided spike. The fruit is a capsule. **All parts of the plant are extremely poisonous.**

Large Yellow Foxglove grows wild in Europe (but not in the British Isles) in woods and in rocky mountain places. It is protected in many countries. It is not grown commercially on a large scale because the needs of the pharmaceutical industry are met by the cultivation of Woolly Foxglove (*D. lanata*) (Pl. 88) and Foxglove (*D. purpurea*) (Pl. 89). Foxgloves may get their name from the belief that their flowers resemble glove-fingers, 'fox' perhaps being a corruption of 'folk's' meaning the 'little folk' or fairies. Or 'glove' may be derived from an Anglo-Saxon word *gliew* for a musical instrument with small bells. The source of the generic name, *Digitalis,* was first the German *fingerhut* (= thimble) and then the Latin *digitus* (= a finger), again a reference to the shape of the flowers.

The leaves are used medicinally. They provide a basic raw material for making cardenolides (purpureaglycosides and lanatosides), which are important medicines for strengthening and regulating the contractions of the heart muscles. They are highly toxic and can be prescribed only by qualified medical practitioners. **This and other foxglove species should never be collected and used for self-medication.**

Leaf

Flowering time: July to August

Woolly Foxglove

Flower

A biennial herb which produces a rosette of basal leaves the first year and in the second year, a tall, erect stem with many sessile, lanceolate leaves. The leaves are smaller, narrower and less woolly than those of the common Foxglove (*D. purpurea*) (Pl. 89). The bell-shaped, brownish-white woolly flowers are arranged in a long, terminal spike. The flowers secrete abundant nectar and so are attractive to bees. The projecting lower lobe of the two-lipped flowers provides an alighting platform for the insects. The fruit is a capsule. **All parts of the plant are extremely poisonous.**

Woolly Foxglove is native to the Balkans and is also grown there as a field crop for the pharmaceutical industry. It has been introduced to other countries, including Britain, for commercial growing. The reason that this foxglove is preferred for commercial cultivation is its resistance to frost and to disease and the high concentration of active constituents in the plant. The seed is sown in spring (if the leaves are to be collected) or in autumn (for the collection of seeds the following year).

The principal constituents of the leaves are the cardiac glycosides lanatosides A, B and C, digitoxin and digoxin. Therapeutically lanatosides are four times as potent as the purpureaglycosides of Foxglove. They, but especially digoxin, are used in medical practice in the form of tinctures, tablets, injections, suppositories and other preparations as cardioactive medicines that stimulate and regulate heart action in cases of arrhythmia, tachycardia (an abnormal increase in the heartbeat) and heart failure. These drugs can be prescribed only by qualified medical practitioners.

Flowering time: July to August

Foxglove

☠ ☠

A biennial herb which produces a rosette of basal leaves the first year and, in the second year, a tall, erect, usually unbranched, hairy stem with only a few broad lanceolate, wrinkled leaves. The flowers are large, bell-shaped and pinkish mauve, occasionally white, with dark-purple spots on a white ground and hairs inside. The fruit is a capsule. The style persists on the top of the fruit after flowering. **All parts of the plant are extremely poisonous.**

Foxglove is common throughout Europe including most parts of the British Isles, in woodland clearings, heaths and on mountains, usually on acid soils. It is also a popular garden plant. For the pharmaceutical industry it is grown commercially as a field crop, but only occasionally in Britain (most British supplies come from abroad). For the origins of Foxglove's names see Pl. 87. Foxglove's action against dropsy, discovered by William Withering in the 1770s, led to the wide use of the plant in medical practice. The importance of this and other foxglove species in medicine has not diminished.

The leaves of Foxglove (known in medicine as digitalis) contain several cardiac glycosides (purpureaglycosides A and B), saponins, organic acids, tannin and mucilage. The glycosides, among them digitoxin and gitoxin, are isolated and used to make important cardiac medicines which are used, like those of other foxgloves, to strengthen and regulate the heart. The leaves and the isolated glycosides are also strong diuretics. They do not act directly on the kidneys but by improving heart function they improve blood circulation to the kidneys, which then function more effectively in flushing out excess fluid from the tissues. The glycosides are dangerous in high doses and they tend to accumulate in the body. Symptoms of poisoning include abdominal pain, irritation of the stomach and bowel, nausea, abnormal heart action and perhaps tremors and convulsions. Death can follow. Digitalis preparations are available only on prescription.

Flowering time: June to August

Part of stem with leaf

Round-leaved Sundew, Common Sundew

A perennial carnivorous herb that grows in acidic soils in wet heaths and boggy moorland and obtains the nitrogenous substances it needs by catching and digesting insects. The leaves are all basal, long-stalked and almost circular and they are covered with sensitive, red, glandular hairs or tentacles that secrete droplets of a sticky fluid at their tips. The sticky drops attract midges and other insects which are held fast on the hairs and then the soft parts are digested. The slender scape arises from the centre of the leaf rosette; it bears a coiled spike of small white flowers. The fruit is a capsule.

Round-leaved Sundew is a protected species in many countries but in the British Isles, although uncommon in the wild, it is not yet rare and can be found in suitable habitats throughout Britain and Ireland. A related species, Great Sundew (*D. anglica*), is also native to the British Isles. It has longer, narrower leaves than Round-leaved Sundew and has a more local distribution in wet peaty bogs, chiefly in Scotland and Ireland. Both species are vulnerable because of the increasing drainage and cultivation of moorland. The generic name, *Drosera,* is derived from the Greek word *drosos* (= dew), a reference to the fly-catching droplets that resemble dew on the leaves. Round-leaved Sundew is still used in herbalism and in homeopathy.

The leaves and flowering stems are used medicinally. The most important constituents are enzymes, glycosides, vitamin C and pigments. These substances give Round-leaved Sundew antispasmodic, sedative, hypoglycaemic and diuretic properties. In herbalism it is prepared as an infusion, in homeopathy as a tincture for treating bronchitis, persistent cough, whooping cough and asthma. It should not be taken by individuals with tuberculosis or low blood pressure.

Flowering time: June to August

Male Fern

A large herbaceous perennial fern with a scaly creeping rhizome bearing stalked, bipinnate leaves (fronds). Young fronds are coiled in a spiral and are covered with brown scales. In summer two rows of green sori (round groups of sporangia) appear on the underside of the fronds. They turn brown as they ripen and produce spores by means of which the fern reproduces and spreads. **All parts of the plant are poisonous.**

Male Fern is common in shaded woods, on rocks and by streams throughout the British Isles. The generic name, *Dryopteris,* comes from the Greek words *drys* (= a tree) and *pteris* (= a fern). The common name is a translation of *filix-mas,* a term used by 16th century herbalists to distinguish this fern from another used then for female complaints. Male Fern has a long tradition as a remedy for expelling worms. It is still occasionally used but nowadays there are much safer anthelmintics.

The rhizome along with the frond bases are used medicinally. The main constituents are an oleoresin, filicin, phloroglucinol compounds (for example, flavaspidic acid), starch and tannins. An ethereal extract is used in both human and veterinary medicine as an anthelmintic, especially against tapeworms. Male Fern preparations are strictly controlled and cannot be obtained from herbal practitioners. It is a dangerous plant; strong doses are very toxic and may lead to permanent blindness, even death. **Male Fern should never be collected and used for self-medication.**

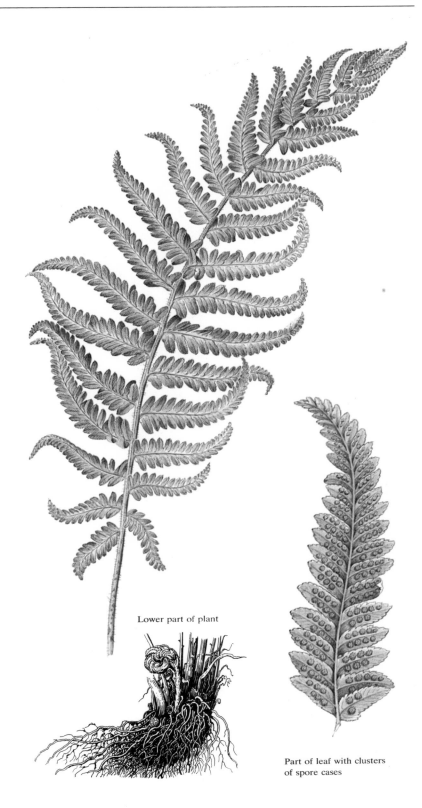

Lower part of plant

Part of leaf with clusters of spore cases

Rosebay Willowherb, <small>Fireweed</small>

Part of stem with ripening fruits

A perennial herb with a creeping rhizome and a tall, erect, usually unbranched leafy stem. The leaves are alternate and lanceolate with entire or slightly toothed and undulate margins. The rose-purple flowers are arranged in a long terminal raceme. The fruit is a long, four-valved capsule with many plumed seeds. The flowers are attractive to bees.

Rosebay Willowherb grows throughout most of Europe in clumps in woodland clearings, on embankments and in waste places. It is a common weed in the British Isles. It thrives on ground that has been cleared by fire, hence one of its alternative common names, Fireweed, and it was one of the first plants to colonize London's bomb sites during the Second World War. In the main common name Willowherb refers to the willow-like form of the leaves. The generic name, *Epilobium*, comes from two Greek words, *epi* (= upon) and *lobos* (= a pod), and refers to the fact that the flowers stand upon the top of the long, thin fruits, which look rather like the flowerstems. The leaves have been used as a tea substitute and are still taken that way in the Soviet Union.

Mainly the leaves are used medicinally. Their constituents include tannins (up to 20 per cent), mucilage, sugars, pectin and vitamin C. These substances give Rosebay Willowherb demulcent, astringent and tranquillizing properties. A decoction or infusion is used to treat headache and migraine. Being rich in vitamin C the tea is recommended as a spring tonic. The rhizomes, which contain fewer tannins and no mucilage, are used in a decoction or chewed fresh for stomach disorders, including diarrhoea. The fresh rhizome, and also the fresh leaves and young shoots, can be eaten as a vegetable.

Flowering time: June to August

Common Horsetail

A perennial, non-flowering herb with black rhizomes bearing two kinds of hollow stems with 6−19 grooves, the first in spring, the second in summer. The fertile spring stems are jointed, without chlorophyll and with a compact terminal cone of sporangia; the sterile summer stems are green with grooved toothed sheaths at the joints, and branch in whorls. The branches are solid. The sheath teeth have black tips.

Common Horsetail is a common and widespread weed of light sandy soil in fields, by roadsides and on waste ground where it is an indication of the presence of underground water. There are several other species of horsetail native to the British Isles but *E. arvense* is the only one now usually collected for medicinal purposes. It is a popular remedy for circulatory and kidney troubles. Marsh Horsetail (*E. palustre*), with 4−8 grooves on its stems, is common and widespread in damp places. The sheath teeth are blackish with narrow whitish margins. Shady Horsetail (*E. pratense*) has a more local distribution in northern England and Scotland. The stem has 8−20 grooves and the sheath teeth are brown with blackish tips.

The green stems are the medicinal parts. They contain silicic acid (more as the plant grows older), traces of the alkaloids nicotine and equisitine, flavonoid glycosides and saponins. These substances give Common Horsetail diuretic, antidiaphoretic, and weak haemostatic properties. It is used in tea mixtures to treat kidney and bladder disorders, arteriosclerosis, and to check internal and external bleeding. It was once used to treat pulmonary diseases such as tuberculosis. It is added to gargles for sore throat and is used in compresses or in bath preparations to treat stubborn wounds, skin rashes and skin ulcers. The stems are abrasive and can be used for polishing and scouring.

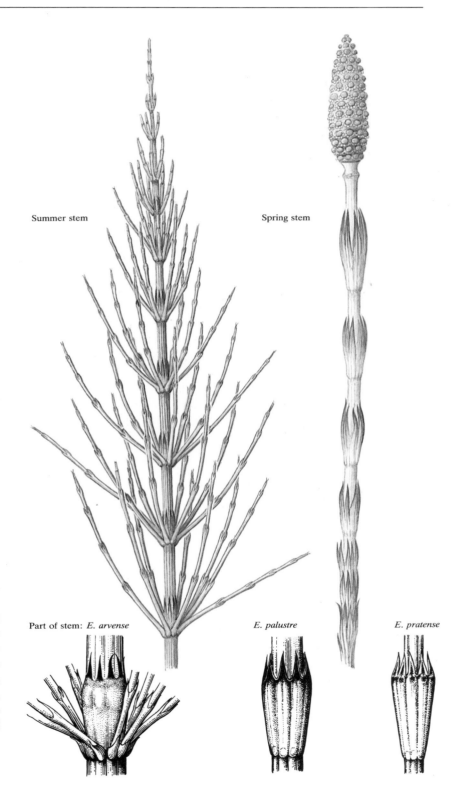

Summer stem

Spring stem

Part of stem: *E. arvense*

E. palustre

E. pratense

Eyebright

Flower

An annual herb with a short, branched, leafy stem. The mainly opposite leaves are small, ovate to lanceolate, toothed and hairy. The solitary flowers, which grow from the leaf axils, are white, yellowish or tinted violet and have two pronounced lips, the lower one longer than the upper lip and three-lobed. There is a bright-orange spot at the entrance to the throat of the flowers. The flowers attract bees and purple 'honey guides' on the lips point the way down the throat. The identification of European species of *Euphrasia* is difficult, even for specialists. Many of them interbreed and for convenience they are grouped in an aggregate species, *E. officinalis.*

Eyebright is relatively common in damp meadows, pastures, heaths and woods throughout the British Isles. It is semiparasitic — it grows successfully only where suckers from the roots can attach themselves to other plants. The plant has long been used to treat eye diseases and the generic name, *Euphrasia,* is derived from the Greek word *euphraino* (= to gladden), probably a reference to the plant's reputed property of preserving eyesight. It remains a popular herbal remedy.

The flowering stems are used medicinally. They contain the iridoid glycoside aucubin, tannins, an essential oil, bitter compounds and pigments. These substances give Eyebright anti-inflammatory properties and it is primarily used as an eyebath and in compresses applied to the eyes. Washing out the eyes with an infusion helps treat inflammation of the conjunctiva, photophobia (an abnormal sensitivity to light) and general tiredness of the eyes. A tincture prepared from fresh plant material is used in homeopathy for the same complaints. Internally Eyebright is used as a stomachic. In the past Eyebright was recommended for headache, hysteria and insomnia as well. Poultices of Eyebright are sometimes used to treat stubborn wounds.

Flowering time: June onwards

Green Buckwheat, Tartary Buckwheat

An annual herb with an erect, green, hollow and branched stem. The alternate sagittate leaves have undulate margins; the upper ones are sessile, the lower ones stalked. The greenish flowers are arranged in racemes in the axils of the uppermost leaves. The fruit is a rough-surfaced, four-sided achene with wavy, toothed margins.

Green Buckwheat is a native of central Asia where it still grows wild; it is also cultivated because it has a short growing period — only 90 days. The seeds are rich in starch and are ground into a tasty flour, which can be used like ordinary flour for making bread and cakes. A closely related species, Buckwheat (*F. esculentum*), was introduced from central Asia to Europe in the Middle Ages. It is widely grown as a source of flour and as fodder for animals. In the British Isles *F. esculentum* is sometimes found as an escape on waste ground. Its stem is usually red, instead of green like Green Buckwheat's, and its fruit is three-sided and smooth. The common name Buckwheat may be a corruption of the Dutch word *boecweite* meaning beech wheat, because the fruit resembles a beechnut. A better explanation might be that the name comes from an old German word *bukweten* (goat's wheat) for a grain that is inferior to true wheat.

The discovery of rutin, a substance that affects the strength and permeability of the capillary walls, was of primary importance for the pharmaceutical use of Green Buckwheat because the flowering stems contain up to 1 per cent of rutin, a flavonoid glycoside. The substance is used in proprietary medicines for treating circulatory disorders. Buckwheat has, however, been supplanted as a major source of rutin by Japanese Pagoda Tree (*Sophora japonica*) (Pl. 225).

Feeding buckwheats to cattle is suitable only if the livestock are not out in the sun. If exposed to sun the animals are subject to fagopyrism, a disease characterized by skin rash, swelling of the head and neck, and spasms.

Flower: *F. esculentum*   *F. tataricum*

Fruit

Flowering time: May to June

Meadowsweet

Flower

A perennial herb with a short, pink rhizome and a tough, erect, branched and leafy stem. The stem leaves are alternate, odd-pinnate, doubly serrate, dark green above and usually white-felted below; the stipules are broadly cordate and conspicuous. The small, creamy-white, fragrant flowers are arranged in a terminal corymb. The flowers have reflexed hairy sepals and numerous long stamens. The fruit, a one-seeded follicle, is spirally twisted. The scent of the leaves is quite different from that of the flowers.

Meadowsweet is common in damp woods and meadows, in fens and by riversides throughout Europe, including the British Isles. The common name, Meadowsweet, is said to be derived from the Anglo-Saxon word *medu* (= mead) because the plant was once used to flavour the drink made from fermented honey. It has been used as a medicinal plant since ancient times and it remains popular as a herbal remedy. It was in the flowerheads that salicylic acid was first discovered in 1839. It was from this substance that aspirin (acetylsalicylic acid) was later synthesized.

The flowers, and sometimes the young leaves and rhizomes, are used medicinally. All parts contain the glycosides gaultherin and spiraein, traces of an alkaloid (heliotropine), tannins, a yellow pigment, vanillin and free salicylic acid, produced by the splitting of gaultherin and citric acid. These substances give the plant antipyretic, weak antispasmodic, astringent and antirheumatic properties. The flowers are used in an infusion to treat influenza, and to alleviate headache and rheumatic and arthritic pain. Meadowsweet is gentler on the stomach than aspirin and it is one of the most effective herbal remedies for gastritis and peptic ulcers. Both the leaves and flowers are also strongly diuretic and are used to treat certain bladder and kidney disorders. The fresh root is used in homeopathic preparations.

Flowering time: June to September

Fennel

A biennial or short-lived perennial herb with an erect, furrowed, blue-green branched stem. The finely divided feathery leaves with thread-like lobes are alternate and have fleshy sheaths at the base. The small yellow flowers are arranged in terminal compound umbels. The fruit is an ovoid, ribbed, double achene, blue green at first turning a greenish brown as it ripens. All parts of the plant smell strongly of aniseed.

Fennel is native to the Mediterranean region and the Caucasus but it has become naturalized in most parts of Europe. In the British Isles it can be found growing wild on sea cliffs, mostly from Wales and Norfolk southwards. It is also found as a casual in waste places inland. It is grown in many varieties in gardens and as a field crop, but it is commercially cultivated only on a small scale in Britain. *Foeniculum* was the name given to this plant by the Romans and is derived from the Latin word *foenum* (= hay), perhaps because the smell of Fennel resembles that of hay. Although Fennel is chiefly known as a culinary herb it also has several medicinal uses; it remains especially popular as a remedy for flatulence. It is widely used by the food industry.

The fruits are used medicinally. The main constituents are an essential oil (up to 6 per cent) with anethole and fenchone, plus fatty oil, proteins, sugars and mucilage. These substances give Fennel antispasmodic, carminative, stomachic, galactagogic, aromatic, and weak diuretic properties. Tea mixtures containing Fennel are used to treat both long-term constipation and diarrhoea, to allay colic pain, to stimulate milk flow in nursing mothers, to treat urinary disorders and coughs and bronchitis. The essential oil, obtained by steam distillation from crushed ripe fruits, is used in tinctures as a gargle and eyewash and in carminative preparations.

The young fresh leaves are excellent for flavouring food, especially fish, and the roots and swollen leaf bases can be eaten as a vegetable.

Flowering time: July to November

Flower

Fruit

Wild Strawberry

Fruit

Dried leaves

A perennial herb with a short rhizome, a rosette of trifoliate basal leaves and long stolons rooting at the nodes. The leaves are long-stalked, bright-green above, white-felted below. The white flowers are arranged in a terminal loose raceme. The fruits are achenes spread over the surface of the fleshy, juicy, usually red receptacle – the familiar tasty strawberry. The sepals usually curve backwards away from the ripe fruit.

Wild Strawberry grows throughout Europe including the British Isles in woods, scrub, grassland and hedgerows, especially on lime-rich soils. The Alpine Strawberry (*F. vesca* var. *semperflorens*) is a form of this species that grows northwards from the Alps. Another species of northern temperate regions, Hautbois Strawberry (*F. moschata*), produces the most aromatic fruit of all strawberries. The familiar Garden Strawberry (*F. ananassa*), originated from a cross between two American species. In this large cultivated form the achenes are sunk in the flesh of the receptacle. The name Strawberry seems to have no connection with the habit of placing straw under the cultivated plants to keep the berries free of dirt and slugs. Instead it is probably derived from the Anglo-Saxon word *streauberige,* and may refer to the tangled appearance of the runners or to the scattering of pips (achenes) on the fruit, 'straw' in this context meaning 'strew'. The leaves of all wild species of strawberry have been, and still are, used in herbalism. Those of Garden Strawberry, however, do not have medicinal action.

The dried leaves have a bitter taste and are aromatic. Among their constituents are tannins, an essential oil with a lemon-scented component, and vitamin C. They give Wild Strawberry astringent, diuretic and tonic properties. An infusion of the leaves and tea mixtures benefit sufferers from anaemia and nervousness. Wild Strawberry is also used for gastrointestinal disorders and kidney and urinary diseases. Fermented leaves serve as a tea substitute.

Flowering time: May to August

Ash

A large deciduous tree with greyish-green bark and terminal black buds from which panicles of small reddish-brown flowers grow in early spring. The flowers produce abundant pollen. The leaves, which appear after the flowers, are odd-pinnate with lanceolate to ovate, finely serrate leaflets. The fruit is a slightly twisted samara (key) with a terminal wing. The keys hang from the twigs in bunches; they are at first green and then brown.

Ash grows throughout the British Isles. It forms woods on lime-rich soils, especially in wetter parts. It is less common on acid soils. It produces a hard, pale wood which is well suited for making tools and furniture. The generic name, *Fraxinus,* is the original Latin word for the tree. The common name, Ash, is a corruption of the Anglo-Saxon word *easc* for the tree, but it has an older origin. The medicinal properties of Ash bark have long been known; it was used to treat fever and as a substitute for quinine obtained from Peruvian Bark (*Cinchona succirubra*) and other *Cinchona* species.

The bark and leaves are used medicinally. The bark contains the coumarin glycoside fraxin, tannins and bitter compounds. The leaves also contain fraxin and tannins and also the sugar alcohol mannite and organic acids. Both parts are mildly laxative and diuretic. An infusion is used in herbalism to regulate bowel movements, to expel intestinal parasites, to reduce fever, to treat kidney and urinary infections, to expel uroliths and to alleviate rheumatic and gouty pains. Externally the leaves are used in compresses or in bath preparations to treat suppurating wounds.

Twig with flowers

Flowering time: April to May

Common Fumitory

Flower

An annual herb with a weak, low-branching, leafy stem. The stalked, alternate, grey-green leaves are several times pinnately divided into flattened lanceolate segments. The small tubular flowers are arranged in long racemes. The petals are pink with dark-red tips, the upper one spurred. The fruit is a rough achene. **All parts of the plant are poisonous.**

Common Fumitory is a common weed of cultivated ground and roadsides all over Europe, including the British Isles, especially on light soils. The generic name, *Fumaria,* and the common name are derived from the Latin words *fumus terrae* (literally meaning 'smoke of the earth') because the plant has an unpleasant smoke-like smell, it irritates the eyes and also because the leaves give the appearance of smoke rising from the ground. Common Fumitory has long been used for medicinal and cosmetic purposes; it is still widely used by herbalists.

The flowering stems are used medicinally. Their constituents include alkaloids (mostly fumarine), tannins and mucilage. They stimulate the appetite and are laxative by increasing the peristaltic action of the smooth muscles of the intestines. They are also diuretic and choleretic. Externally Common Fumitory is a good skin cleanser and it is used in the treatment of certain skin disorders such as eczema. In a mixture with the leaves of Walnut (*Juglans regia*) (Pl. 125) it heals haemorrhoids. Common Fumitory is toxic and large doses can cause severe diarrhoea, muscular spasms, and even respiratory failure. **It should therefore be taken internally only under the supervision of a qualified medical or herbal practitioner.**

Flowering time: May onwards

Goat's Rue, French Lilac

A bushy perennial herb with an erect, angled, hairless stem. The alternate leaves are odd-pinnate with four to twelve pairs of oblong leaflets and large sagittate stipules. The white, pinkish or lilac flowers are arranged in longish erect racemes in the leaf axils. The calyx is bell-shaped with five bristle-like teeth. The fruit is a straight, red-brown smooth pod with many brown seeds.

Goat's Rue is a native of southern and eastern Europe and western Asia. It was supposedly introduced into the British Isles from France as an ornamental garden plant, hence the alternative common name. It has since become widely naturalized on damp and waste ground. The generic name, *Galega,* is derived from the Greek words *gala* (= milk) and *agere* (= to promote) and refers to the herb's traditional reputation as a stimulant of milk flow in nursing mothers and in livestock. Goat's Rue was also once used to banish the plague, to treat fevers and as a remedy for worms. It is still occasionally used in herbalism.

The flowering stems are used medicinally. Their constituents include the alkaloid galegine, flavonoid glycosides, saponins and tannins. These substances give Goat's Rue hypoglycaemic, galactagogic, diuretic and diaphoretic properties. It is mostly used in an infusion for nursing mothers. On the Continent an extract from Goat's Rue is also applied in ointments used to hasten skin healing after plastic surgery.

Seed   Flower

Flowering time: July to September

Downy Hempnettle

Flower: *G. segetum*

G. tetrahit

An annual herb with an erect, branched, square stem. The leaves are opposite, ovate to lanceolate and serrate, and from their axils grow the pale-yellow flowers arranged in apparent whorls. The corolla is two-lipped; the upper lip is helmet-shaped, the lower lip has three spreading lobes. The fruit consists of four one-seeded nutlets. All parts of the plant are softly hairy.

Downy Hempnettle is native to western Europe where it grows on arable land and in waste places. In some countries it is cultivated commercially for the pharmaceutical industry. In the British Isles it is an extremely rare species and should not be collected in the wild. A related species, Common Hempnettle (*G. tetrahit*) is, however, a widespread and common weed in Britain. It grows in woods, fens and wet heaths. The flowers of Common Hempnettle are pinkish purple, less often yellow or white, with a network of dark markings on the lower lip. The generic name of hempnettles, *Galeopsis*, is derived from the Latin word *galea* (= a helmet), a reference to the shape of the flowers. The specific epithet, *segetum,* means 'cornfield'. The leaves of hempnettles are similar to the leaflets of Hemp (*Cannabis sativa*), hence the common name. Botanically and medicinally, however, there is no resemblance between the plants. In the Middle Ages Downy Hempnettle was used to treat wounds, swellings and tuberculosis. It is still used for various internal complaints and skin disorders.

The flowering stems are the medicinal parts. Their constituents include tannins, saponins, a glycoside, traces of an essential oil and silicic acid. These substances give Downy Hempnettle diuretic, astringent, stomachic and expectorant properties. It is used in tea mixtures to treat chest colds, cough, whooping cough, bronchitis, to stimulate the appetite, improve digestion and to treat disorders of the spleen. A tincture is used in homeopathy for the same purposes.

Other species of hempnettle have similar medicinal uses.

Flowering time: July to August

Woodruff, Sweet Woodruff

A perennial carpeting herb with un-branched, hairless, erect, square stems that grow from a tangle of rhizomes and rootlets in early spring. The leaves, in whorls of six to eight, are lanceolate with tiny, forward-pointing prickles on the margins. The small, white, star-shaped flowers are arranged in dichasial cymes. The corolla is funnel-shaped with the tube a little shorter than the free lobes. The fruit is a double achene with hooked, black-tipped bristles. All parts of the plant are pleasantly hay-scented, especially when dried.

Widespread throughout Europe, Woodruff has been collected and culti-vated since the Middle Ages. It has been − and is still − used in European coun-tries to flavour wine (May cups) and it was put amongst linen to keep away moths. It grows throughout most of the British Isles in woods, especially on damp, lime-rich soils where it can be locally common. The vernacular name, Woodruff, is derived from the Anglo-Saxon word *wudurofe,* from *wudu* (= wood) and *rofe* of unknown origin, but it may mean 'root', a reference to the plant's creeping habit.

The flowering stems are used medici-nally. Their constituents include a couma-rin glycoside (responsible for the hay-like aroma), tannins and bitter compounds. These substances give Woodruff sedative, diuretic, vulnerary and antispasmodic properties. In herbalism it is used in the form of an infusion or decoction to treat nervous irritability, overwork, muscular spasms of various kinds, heart palpitations and insomnia. **Strong doses may cause vertigo, vomiting and headache.** Exter-nally compresses of Woodruff are used to treat slow-healing wounds, skin rashes and ulcerous conditions. The herb is also occasionally used in homeopathy. It is an effective moth repellent.

Flower

Flowering time: April to June

Lady's Bedstraw

Flower

Fruit

A perennial herb with a creeping rhizome and decumbent or erect branched square stems. The linear leaves, which are arranged in whorls of eight to twelve, have turned-under margins, a prominent midrib and are dark green and shiny above, pale and felted below. The small, bright-yellow, honey-scented flowers are arranged in dense terminal panicles. The four pointed lobes of the corolla spread horizontally like a wheel from the top of a very short tube. The fruit is a smooth double achene, green at first and black when dry.

Lady's Bedstraw is common and widespread throughout Europe, including the British Isles. The green parts of the plant contain the enzyme parachymozine, which causes milk to curdle, and the herb was once used in cheese-making, hence one of its common names, Cheese Rennet. The generic name, *Galium* (from the Greek word *gala* = milk), is thought to refer to this milk-curdling property, which is possessed by many other plants in the Rubiaceae (bedstraw) family. According to a Christian legend this was one of the herbs in the hay in the manger at Bethlehem. It was from this belief that the plant was given the name Lady's Bedstraw by which it is mainly known today. The leaves and stems produce a yellow dye, the roots a red dye. The related Goosegrass or Cleavers (*G. aparine*) also has medicinal properties. It can easily be distinguised from Lady's Bedstraw because it has backward-pointing prickles along the angles of the stem, whitish flowers and the green and purplish fruit is covered with white hooked bristles. Lady's Bedstraw and Goosegrass are still used in herbalism.

The flowering stems of Lady's Bedstraw contain glycosides, traces of an essential oil, silicic acid and enzymes. These substances give the plant diuretic, antiseptic and antispasmodic properties. It is used in an infusion for kidney and urinary disorders. Externally it is used in compresses to treat slow-healing wounds, skin rashes and ulcerous conditions.

Flowering time: July onwards

Dyer's Greenweed

A small deciduous spineless shrub with a creeping woody rhizome and erect or ascending smooth, green stems. The alternate, almost sessile leaves are lanceolate. The yellow flowers are arranged in terminal leafy racemes. Like other members of the Leguminosae (pea) family the plant has characteristic flowers with a large upper petal (standard), two side petals (wings) and two lower petals jointed along their edges (keel). The fruit is a long, flat, hairless pod.

Dyer's Greenweed is found throughout most of Europe at the edges of woods and by roadsides, mostly in dry places. It is also grown as a garden plant. In the British Isles it is a widespread but uncommon native plant in England and Wales and southern Scotland; it is rare in northern Scotland and absent in Ireland. The leaves and flowers contain a yellow pigment that was once used to dye cloth and wool. It was combined with the blue dye from Woad (*Isatis tinctoria*) to produce an excellent green. The practice of dyeing cloth in this way was introduced into England by Flemish immigrants in the 14th century. The colour became known as Kendal green after the town in Cumbria where the dyeing of wool was developed. For medicinal purposes Dyer's Greenweed was used as a laxative, to expel uroliths and for gout. It is now only rarely used in herbal medicine.

The flowering stems are the medicinal parts. Their constituents include the alkaloids cytisine and sparteine, the flavonoid genistein and a yellow glycoside (luteolin). These substances give Dyer's Greenweed strong diuretic, weak cardioactive and laxative properties. Besides being a remedy for kidney and urinary disorders, it has also been used to strengthen heart action, to raise blood pressure and to alleviate rheumatic and arthritic pain. It is not a suitable remedy for individuals with hypertension or for pregnant women.

Flower

Dried flowering stems

Flowering time: June to August

Great Yellow Gentian, Gentian

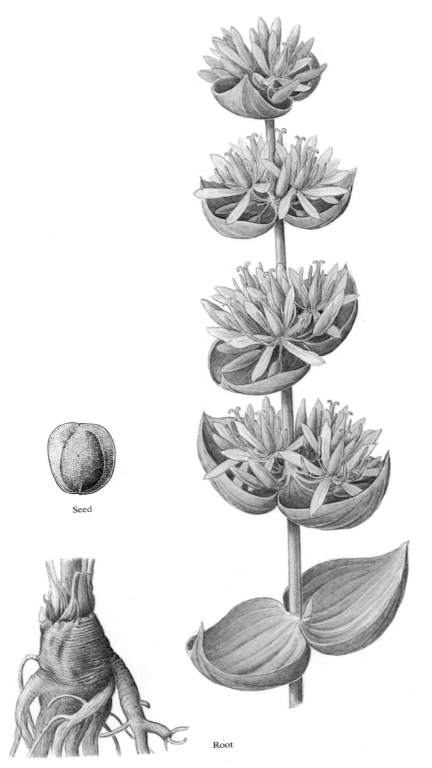

Seed

Root

A perennial herb with a thick rootstock and a basal rosette of large, elliptical, bluish-green leaves with prominent veins on the underside. Not till it is four to eight years old does it bear a tall, unbranched, hollow stem with opposite, sessile, oval leaves. The showy, stalked, golden-yellow flowers grow in tight clusters in the axils of the uppermost leaves. The anthers are almost as long as the corolla. The fruit is a capsule with many winged seeds.

Native to the Carpathians, Great Yellow Gentian occurs rarely in the other mountain ranges of Europe and Asia. In many countries it is now protected having been overcollected in the past for the roots, which are used in the production of gentian brandy and bitter liqueurs. It is not native to the British Isles but it is grown as an ornamental plant in gardens. The plant is now commercially cultivated for the wine and pharmaceutical industries in eastern Europe and America. It is regarded as one of the best herbal tonic medicines available. It may have acquired its name, *Gentiana,* from Gentius, King of Illyria, who is reputedly the first person to have used the plant medicinally.

The roots of old plants are used. Among the constituents are the bitter glycosides (for example, gentiopicrosides), a flavonoid derivative (gentisin), alkaloids, sugars and pectin. These substances give Great Yellow Gentian a markedly bitter taste and it acts as a tonic on the whole digestive system. Taken at least half an hour before meals it stimulates the appetite, and promotes the flow of digestive juices and bile. It is used in conventional and homeopathic medicine as well as in herbalism.

The fermented root is used in the manufacture of bitter foodstuffs and liqueurs. Before fermentation the root is dried slowly until it turns a reddish-brown colour (for medicinal uses the root is dried quickly so that it retains its yellow colour).

Flowering time: July to August

Herb Robert

An annual or biennial herb with thin, reddish, glandular stems that branch stiffly. The long-stemmed alternate leaves are palmately divided into three to five lobes, which in turn are divided twice over. The reddish-violet flowers are long-stalked and usually grow in pairs. The beaked fruit is a schizocarp that splits when ripe into one-seeded parts (merocarps). The merocarps have a network of ridges and a white hair tuft near the apex. The whole plant is densely hairy and smells unpleasantly when rubbed between the fingers.

Herb Robert grows throughout Europe, including the British Isles, in woods, thickets, hedgerows and on rocks and walls. The generic name, *Geranium,* is derived from the Greek word *geranos* (= a crane), a reference to the pointed 'beak' on the fruit. This is why other *Geranium* species have the name cranesbill. The 'robert' of the plant's common name is believed to be a corruption of the Latin word *ruber* (= red) or to refer to Robert, Duke of Normandy, for whom a medieval treatise was written. The plant may also be named after St Robert, an eleventh-century French ecclesiastic. Herb Robert is still used in herbalism.

The flowering stems are used medicinally. Their constituents include an essential oil, tannins and the bitter compound geraniin. These substances give Herb Robert astringent and diuretic properties and it is used in an infusion to check pulmonary haemorrhage and nosebleeding, and to treat severe diarrhoea, kidney and bladder disorders. Externally compresses and ointments are used to treat various skin disorders, boils and septic cuts. A decoction can be used as a gargle for tonsillitis.

Flower

Flowering time: May to September

Wood Avens, Herb Bennet

Fruit cluster

Detail of fruit

Root

A perennial hairy herb with a thickened rhizome and an erect branched stem. The basal leaves are stalked and odd-pinnate, with two or three pairs of unequal-sized leaflets and a large, lobed, terminal leaflet; the smaller alternate stem leaves are trifoliate and have paired, leaf-like stipules. The erect, solitary, terminal flowers have recurved sepals and spreading yellow petals. The fruit consists of a sessile group of achenes with hooked appendages. The hooked fruits are spread by becoming attached to the fur or feathers of passing animals.

Wood Avens grows throughout most of Europe in shady places on damp rich soil. It is common in the British Isles. The generic name, *Geum,* is derived from the Greek word *geyo* (= I stimulate) because the rootstocks of this and related species, when freshly dug up, have a pleasant clove-like aroma. The rootstock was once used as a moth repellent and to flavour ale. They have also long been used to treat chest diseases. The alternative common name, Herb Bennet, may be a corruption of *herba benedicta* (blessed herb) because the plant was believed to be a powerful charm against evil spirits. Or the plant may have once been called 'St Benedict's herb' in memory of the saint who founded the Benedictine order of monks. The plant is still used in herbalism and homeopathy, but rarely if ever in conventional medicine.

The rhizomes are used medicinally. Their constituents include tannins, bitter compounds, an essential oil with gein and eugenol, and organic pigments (leucoanthocyanins). These substances give Wood Avens astringent, antiseptic, tonic, antiinflammatory and antidiarrhoeal properties. It is used as a powder or decoction to treat gastritis and enteritis, intestinal colic, liver disorders and to check internal bleeding. Externally Wood Avens is used in gargles for stomatitis, gingivitis and other mouth inflammations and bad breath (halitosis), and in compresses and bath preparations for skin disorders and haemorrhoids.

Flowering time: June to August

Ground Ivy

A perennial herb with a long creeping, rooting rhizome and ascending or erect flowering stems. The opposite leaves are rounded, cordate to reniform, long-stalked and crenate, and are quite different from those of true Ivy (*Hedera helix*) (Pl. 113). The large blue-violet flowers grow in groups of two to four in loose whorls at the base of the leaves, usually on the same side of the stem. The flower has a straight corolla tube and two notched lips, the lower lip with darker markings. The fruit consists of four one-seeded nutlets.

Ground Ivy grows throughout most of Europe in grassland, thickets, woods and waste places, especially on damp heavy soils. It is common in most parts of the British Isles, but rare in northern Scotland. The generic name, *Glechoma,* is derived from the Greek word *glaukos* (= grey green), a reference to the leaf colour. The specific epithet, *hederacea,* refers to the ivy-like creeping habit of the plant − but on the ground, not on trees. Ground Ivy has long been used as a medicinal herb, primarily for fever, coughs and sore eyes. The faintly mint-scented leaves were also used in brewing to clear and sharpen the flavour of ale, or gill. The plant is still used in herbalism and homeopathic medicine.

The flowering stems are used medicinally. The constituents include the bitter compound glechomine, an essential oil, tannins (6−7 per cent), saponin and potassium salts. These substances give Ground Ivy astringent, anti-inflammatory and tonic properties and an infusion is used for gastritis, enteritis and diarrhoea, for kidney disorders, bronchial catarrhs, coughs and some asthmatic conditions. It also stimulates the appetite and is a general tonic. Homeopathic tinctures are prepared from fresh plant parts. Externally Ground Ivy is used in gargles for mouth infections, and in compresses and bath preparations for skin disorders.

The fresh shoots and leaves can be added to salads and soups or prepared and eaten like spinach.

Flowering time: March to June

Flower

Soybean, Soya Bean

Fruit

Part of flowering stem

Seed

A cultivated annual herb with an erect hairy stem and large trifoliate leaves. The white to violet-tinged flowers grow in clusters from the leaf axils. The fruit is a slightly curved and hairy pod with variously coloured seeds depending on the variety.

Soybean is native to eastern Asia where the wild form still grows. It was not known in Europe until the 17th century but has been cultivated since ancient times in China, Korea and Japan. It is now grown on a large scale in Europe and America for the seeds, which are an important source of edible oil and flour. It ripens with certainty only in warm regions where grapes and maize thrive and for this reason it is not grown on a commercial scale in Britain. The generic name, *Glycine,* is derived from the Greek word *glykys* (= sweet), a reference to the sweet taste of the beans of some species in the genus. The word 'soy' has come to us through Dutch and Japanese words from the Chinese *shi-yu,* from *shi* (= salted beans) and *yu* (= oil).

The seeds (beans) are used medicinally. They contain valuable nutritive substances — proteins (40 per cent), fatty oil (20 per cent), carbohydrates, lecithin (a phospholipid), vitamins and minerals. Soybean is an important constituent of some infant foods and milk substitutes. It is also an ideal food for diabetics because its sugars remain largely unabsorbed. Because foodstuffs made from Soybean flour and Soybean oil are low in cholesterol they are thought to help prevent arteriosclerosis and coronary heart disease. The protein-rich beans are increasingly being mixed with meat products or used on their own as meat substitutes.

The expressed oil from the beans is used to make plastics and many other products. It is an important cooking oil and is used as a major raw material of margerine. Fermented beans are used to make oriental sauces and pastes and the well-known Worcester Sauce in Britain. Blanched Soybean seedlings are a popular salad vegetable.

Flowering time: July to August

Liquorice, Licorice

A perennial herb with a woody, creeping rhizome, an erect, branched stem and alternate, odd-pinnate leaves with 9—17 elliptic to oblong leaflets. The blue-violet flowers are arranged in long-stalked axillary spikes. The fruit is a smooth reddish-brown pod.

Native to southern Europe and western and central Asia, Liquorice is now widely cultivated commercially for the pharmaceutical, tobacco and food industries. The growing of Liquorice in England began in the 16th century in the Pontefract district of Yorkshire. It was once an important crop there but cultivation has progressively declined and none remains. All supplies of Liquorice now have to be imported into Britain. The plant may still grow in some gardens. It was in Pontefract that the confectionery Pontefract or Pomfret cakes were originally made. The medicinal properties of the plant were known to the ancient Assyrians and Egyptians. The herb remains a popular remedy.

The roots and underground stolons of three-year old plants are used medicinally. The constituents include a sweet substance, glycorrhizin (7 per cent), — potassium and calcium salts of glycyrrhizinic acid, a triterpenoid saponin — flavonoid glycosides, traces of essential oil, starch, sugars, a phytosterol (sitosterol), tannins and enzymes. These substances give Liquorice expectorant, laxative and antispasmodic actions. It is used either cut into pieces (in tea mixtures) or ground into a powder (in medicines). The extract is made into sticks that have a pleasant spicy flavour. Liquorice is of value for coughs and bronchitis, peptic and duodenal ulcers, and rheumatoid arthritis. It is also used to sweeten and flavour pharmaceutical preparations and, now rarely, as a binding agent in pills. A mixture of powdered Liquorice, Fennel (*Foeniculum vulgare*) (Pl. 97) and Senna (*Cassia angustifolia*) leaves is a popular natural laxative. **In large doses Liquorice causes side effects,** notably headache, high blood pressure and water retention.

Rhizome with roots

Flowering time: summer, autumn

Hedge Hyssop

Flower

A perennial herb with a tangled rhizome and a clump of ascending hollow stems, square in the upper part. The leaves are opposite, sessile, lanceolate and finely serrate. The small, white to pinkish flowers grow singly from the leaf axils on long stalks. The corolla is slightly two-lipped with a wide tube; the upper lip is two-lobed, the lower lip is slightly larger and three-lobed. The fruit is a many-seeded four-valved capsule. The plant is scentless; **all parts are poisonous.**

Hedge Hyssop grows in central and southern Europe and in Asia by riversides, in fens, wet grassland and other damp places. It does not grow wild in the British Isles but is occasionally grown in gardens. The generic name, *Gratiola,* is derived from the Latin word *gratia* (= gratitude) on account of the plant's useful medicinal properties (Hedge Hyssop was once widely used to treat liver disorders and as a purgative). The common name 'hyssop' comes through Latin and Greek from the Hebrew word *esob* for the plant. However, the hyssop of Classical times and the Bible was probably a species of marjoram (*Origanum*). Hedge Hyssop is now rarely used in folk medicine but it still has a place in homeopathy.

The flowering stems are used medicinally. The constituents include the cardiac glycosides gratiolin, gratiogenin, gratiotoxin and an essential oil (gratiolon). These substances give Hedge Hyssop strong purgative, emetic, cardioactive, diuretic and anthelmintic properties. Tinctures from the fresh plant are used in homeopathy for certain gastrointestinal and liver disorders. Hedge Hyssop is a dangerous plant; **it should never be collected and used for self-medication.** Long-term use may affect the eyesight; in large doses it may be fatal. Milk from cows that have grazed on the plant may also be poisonous.

Flowering time: May

Ivy

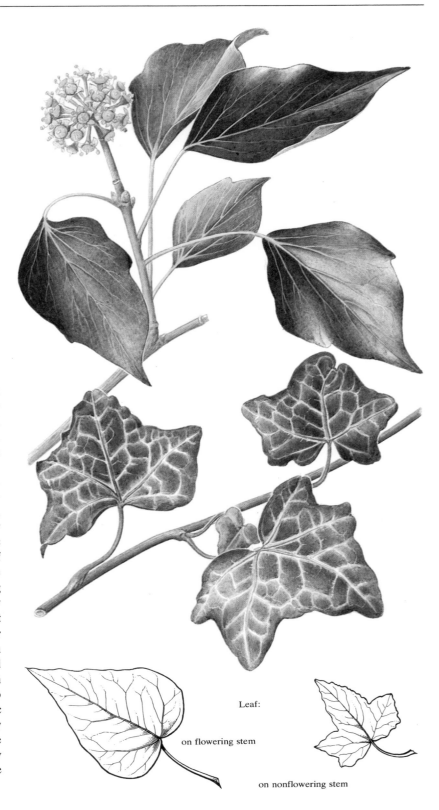

An evergreen woody climber, often carpeting the ground or ascending by means of many tiny, adhesive, fibrous roots on the stems. The leaves are alternate, leathery, shiny, dark green, often with pale veins and are of two kinds: entire, cordate or rhomb-shaped on the flowering branches; palmately three- to five-lobed (ivy-shaped) on the nonflowering branches. The small, greenish-yellow flowers are arranged in small terminal umbels. They secrete abundant nectar. The fruit is a globose, blue-black drupe. **All parts of the plant are poisonous** and children should be warned not to eat the berry-like fruits.

In Europe and Asia Ivy grows wild creeping or climbing in woods, in hedges on rocks and on walls. It is common throughout the British Isles. It is also widely grown as an ornamental plant in gardens and as a covering for buildings. Ivy has long been supposed to have magical powers. It was dedicated to Bacchus, the god of wine, probably because it was supposed to prevent intoxication. The generic name, *Hedera,* is the original Latin word for the plant. The common name, Ivy, comes from the Anglo-Saxon word *ifeg,* of obscure origin.

The young leaves are used medicinally. The constituents include tannins, a saponin (hederin), its aglycone (hederagenin), organic acids and iodine. These give Ivy expectorant, antispasmodic and cardiac actions. Small doses cause dilatation of the blood vessels, larger doses cause constriction of the vessels and the slowing of the heart beat. For these reasons Ivy can be dangerous if taken internally. **It should never be collected and used for self-medication.** In the past Ivy has been used to treat respiratory diseases and rheumatic pain. Externally the fresh leaves can be applied as a compress to slow-healing wounds, bruises and arthritic joints but they are an irritant and may cause dermatitis. If eaten the berries have a mainly purgative action, though if many are consumed the symptoms can be more severe.

Flowering time: September onwards

Leaf:

on flowering stem

on nonflowering stem

Sunflower

A tall annual herb with an erect, sometimes branched hairy stem. The many leaves are large and cordate, opposite below and alternate and long-stalked above. The large, terminal showy flowerheads are composed of yellow ray-florets, which are sterile, and purplish-brown, tubular disc-florets. The fruit is a slightly flattened achene, often streaked with white and black.

Sunflower is a native of western North America where it was first cultivated by American Indians some time before 1000 BC. It was introduced to Europe in the 16th century but did not become a major food plant until it reached Russia, where large-scale cultivation began. Today it is grown commercially in many parts of the world for oil, fodder and ornament. There are many cultivated varieties, some with flowerheads up to 40 cm wide. It is grown as a field crop in southern parts of England. The common name, Sunflower, and the generic name, *Helianthus* (from the Greek words *helios* = sun and *anthos* = flower), were supposedly given to the plant because it follows the sun by day, always turning towards its direct rays. Just as likely an explanation is that the plant was so-named because the flowerheads with disc and ray suggest the sun's appearance. The leaves and flowers were once used to treat malaria.

The expressed fatty oil from the seeds contains glycerides of unsaturated linolenic and oleic acids (about 45 per cent) and saturated palmitic and arachic acids (about 4 per cent). It is used in salves, plasters and liniments for rheumatic pain. It is also widely used in foodstuffs as a salad and margerine oil, in soaps and as a lubricant. In homeopathy a tincture from the seeds is used internally to relieve constipation and externally on cuts and bruises. The seeds are also roasted and eaten, used as a coffee substitute and ground into flour.

The dried flowerheads are also used medicinally in some countries. They have diuretic, carminative, anti-inflammatory and antidiarrhoeal properties.

Flowering time: June to September

Longitudinal section of flowerhead

Fruit

Christmas Rose, Black Hellebore ☠ ☠

A perennial herb with a thick black rhizome and a large clump of roots. Rising from the rhizome are stalked, dark-green, evergreen basal leaves each divided into seven or nine lanceolate segments, which are serrate towards the tip. The flowering stems bear undivided, bract-like leaves and, usually, a solitary, white or pinkish flower with five perianth segments. The flowers appear in late winter and early spring, hence the name, Christmas Rose. The fruit is a follicle. **All parts of the plant are extremely poisonous.**

Christmas Rose is native to southern and central Europe but it is now also established north of the Alps. It grows on lime-rich soils in woods and on rocky slopes but is relatively rare in the wild. It does not grow wild in the British Isles but is often grown as a garden plant. The related Green Hellebore (*H. viridis*) — also poisonous — is, however, native to parts of England and Wales where it has a local distribution in moist woods and scrub, again preferring calcareous soils. Its flowers are yellowish green. Those of Purple Hellebore (*H. purpurascens*) are purplish. The generic name, *Helleborus,* is believed to derive from the Greek word *helleboros* (from *helein* = injure and *bora* = food) and indicates the poisonous qualities of these plants. The specific epithet of *H. niger* and the alternative common name, Black Hellebore, refer to the dark-coloured rhizome. The medicinal properties of hellebores have been known since ancient Greek times.

The rhizomes and roots contain the toxic cardiac glycosides hellebrin, helleborin and helleborein that affect the heart and the central nervous system. They are also strongly purgative and diuretic. Because of the variable concentration and toxicity of these substances Christmas Rose is now contained only in a few proprietary medicines (used on the Continent) and in tinctures used in homeopathy for certain neurological disorders. **Any use of Christmas Rose should be medically supervised. It should never be collected and used for self-medication.**

Flowering time: January to February

Flower of *H. purpurascens*   *H. viridis*

Root

Hepatica, American Liverwort

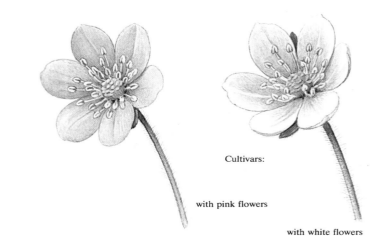

Cultivars:

with pink flowers

with white flowers

A perennial herb with a short scaly rhizome, which bears light-blue, rarely pink or white flowers and, after they have faded, smooth, almost leathery, trifoliate and liver-shaped leaves, green above and reddish-purple below. There is an involucre of three green bracts just below the flowers. The flowers produce a fair quantity of pollen but little nectar. The fruit is an achene.

Hepatica is common in dampish woods, scrub and grassland throughout most of Europe. It does not grow wild in the British Isles but is grown in many varieties as a rock-garden plant. In some countries it is now a protected species. The generic and common names are derived from the Greek word *hepatikos,* meaning 'pertaining to the liver' (*hepar* = liver), an allusion to the shape of the leaves.

The leaves are used medicinally. Their constituents include saponins, tannins and the glycoside hepatilobin. These substances give Hepatica strong diuretic, astringent and vulnerary properties. An infusion or decoction is used in herbalism to treat kidney, gall bladder and liver disorders, and coughs and bronchitis. A tincture is also used in homeopathy. **Large doses can be toxic;** for this reason Hepatica should be used only under the supervision of a qualified medical or herbal practitioner. The herb is used in gargles for stomatitis and for chronic irritations of the throat and pharynx.

Flowering time: March to April

Smooth Rupturewort

An annual or biennial, rarely a perennial herb with a mat-forming, branched, densely leaved, more or less glabrous prostrate stem. From the axils of the small, oval, sessile, yellow-green leaves grow racemes of small, white flowers. The fruit is a nutlet with one shiny black seed.

Smooth Rupturewort grows throughout most of Europe in dry sandy places. In the British Isles it is an extremely rare native plant occurring in a few scattered places, mostly in East Anglia. Another rupturewort, Hairy Rupturewort (*H. hirsuta*), was introduced to Britain and is now naturalized in a few localities. As its name suggests this species is hairy all over and the whole plant appears grey or whitish. The flowers are arranged in distinct roundish axillary clusters. Ruptureworts were once used to treat urinary disorders and hernias, hence the generic name *Herniaria* (from the Latin word *hernia*) and the common name Rupturewort. Both species are still used in herbalism.

The flowering stems are the medicinal parts. Those of Smooth Rupturewort contain a triterpene saponin that decomposes into quillaic acid and simple sugars. Hairy Rupturewort contains saponins that decompose into galactonic acid, glucose and other sugars. Both plants also contain the flavonoid glycoside rutin, the coumarin glycoside herniarin and an essential oil. These substances give the plants mild diuretic, mild antispasmodic and antiseptic properties. They are used in infusions on their own or mixed with other herbs to treat bladder, kidney and gall bladder disorders and they help prevent the formation of kidney stones and gravel.

Seed

Part of flowering stem of *H. hirsuta*

Flowering time: July

Sea Buckthorn

Twigs with flowers:

female

male

A deciduous shrub or small tree with much-branched, thorny grey twigs and alternate, almost sessile, linear to lanceolate leaves, which have inrolled margins and are dark green above and silvery white below. The greenish dioecious flowers appear before the leaves; the male flowers are in axillary clusters, the female flowers in short, few-flowered racemes. The flowers are covered with brownish scaly hairs. The fruit is bright-orange, ovoid and drupe-like. It is considered poisonous in some parts of Europe.

Sea Buckthorn has a scattered distribution in Europe on dry, sunny slopes. In the British Isles it grows on fixed sand dunes and occasionally on sea cliffs, mostly on eastern and southeastern coasts. It is also grown in parks and gardens for ornament. In Greek, *hippophaes* means a spiny plant and this word gave rise to the generic name in Latin, *Hippophae*. The origin of the Greek word is not as straightforward and there have been several explanations for it. It is said that the ancient Greeks fed buckthorn berries to horses, which then acquired a gleaming coat (*hippos* = horse; *phaeithon* = shining). Or the name could refer to the belief that the plant cured blindness in horses ('it gave them light'; the Greek word *phaino* = light). There has also been a suggestion that the suffix '*phaes*' in the Greek name comes from a word meaning 'I kill', but this seems unlikely.

The fruits are used medicinally as a tonic on the Continent. They contain organic acids, tannins, the flavonoid glycoside quercetin, provitamin A, abundant vitamin C and vitamins B complex and E. The freshly pressed juice from the berries is made into syrups and preserves and used both preventively as a protection against possible infection, particularly in late winter and early spring, and as a general tonic during convalescence. The constituents of the berries also strengthen the eyesight and have an antisclerotic effect.

Flowering time: March to April

Hop, Hops

A perennial climbing herb with a branched rhizome, long roots and a long, leafy, angled stem which twins in a clockwise direction. The leaves are opposite, palmately three- to five-lobed and coarsely serrate. The green flowers are dioecious: the male flowers are in drooping, axillary panicles; the tiny female flowers are clustered in stalked, ovoid, cone-like spikes or strobiles (hops) with persistent, large, overlapping bracts. The bracts become papery when the fruiting head is ripe. The fruit is an achene enclosed in the perianth. All parts of the plant are roughly hairy.

Hop grows in hedges and thickets throughout Europe, often as an escape from cultivation. In the British Isles it grows wild in many parts of England and Wales but is introduced in Scotland and Ireland. Hops have been used to clear, preserve and flavour beer since the Middle Ages but it was not until the 16th century that the process was introduced into Britain by Flemish immigrants. Only the female plants are grown commercially; the cones must not be pollinated. The origin of the generic name, *Humulus,* is uncertain; it may come from the Latin word *humus* (= ground), a reference perhaps to the rich soil in which Hop thrives. The plant is still one of the most useful of herbal remedies.

The cones or strobiles are used medicinally. When dried they have a spicy aroma and a bitter taste. The constituents include a resin with bitter compounds (chiefly humulone and lupulone), oestrogenic substances and an essential oil with humulene. These substances give Hop mild sedative, hypnotic, stomachic, diuretic and weak antiseptic properties. An infusion is used in herbalism for digestive disorders, nervous irritability, to induce sleep and as an antiaphrodisiac (in men). An effective way of using hops for insomnia is in pillows. A tincture of the fresh cones is used in homeopathy.

The distilled essential oil is contained in some perfumes. Young shoots and immature leaves can be added to salads.

Male flowers

Flowering time: July to September

Henbane

Seed

Fruit

A biennial or annual herb with an erect stem, woody at the base, and alternate, coarsely toothed, grey-green sticky leaves. The bell-shaped flowers grow from the leaf axils. The sepals are strongly veined and fused to form a pitcher-shaped tube; the petals are greyish-yellow with violet veins. The fruit is a many-seeded capsule, enclosed in the calyx. It opens by a convex lid at the top when ripe. All parts of the plant are downy, fetid-smelling and **extremely poisonous.**

Henbane probably originates from the Mediterranean region but it is now widely distributed throughout Europe and Asia. It grows in waste sandy places, by roadsides and on fallow ground, especially near the sea. It grows wild in the British Isles but is generally uncommon. The origin of the common name, Henbane, is confused, but it may mean 'hen killer'. However, the generic name, which comes from the Greek words *hyos* (= pig) and *kyamos* (= bean), and one of the alternative common names, Hogsbean, refer to the supposition that pigs suffer no ill-effects if they eat the plant. Henbane's narcotic and sedative effects have been known since ancient times. Nowadays the plant is grown in some countries for the pharmaceutical industry. It is now considered too toxic for use in herbalism but it is used in homeopathy and occasionally in conventional medicine.

The leaves, sometimes also the flowering stems, are used medicinally. They contain the toxic alkaloids hyoscyamine, atropine and hyoscine which, as in Deadly Nightshade (*Atropa belladonna*) (Pl. 33), affect the central nervous system. These constituents are included in antispasmodic preparations for the treatment of asthma, nervous disorders, muscular spasms, various forms of tremor (especially in the aged) and other disorders. The distilled essential oil is sometimes included in antirheumatic ointments and liniments. **Henbane should be used only under strict medical supervision; it should never be collected and used for self-medication.**

Flowering time: June to September

Perforate St John's Wort, Common St John's Wort

A perennial herb with a stout creeping rhizome which bears clumps of erect, branched stems. The stems are woody at the base and have two raised longitudinal lines. By contrast the stems of the related Square-stalked St John's Wort (*H. tetrapterum*) have four narrow longitudinal ridges. The opposite, sessile, ovate to oblong leaves have numerous reddish, translucent glandular dots. The showy yellow flowers are arranged in terminal cymes. The sepals and petals are black-dotted, especially at the edges. The fruit is a capsule.

Perforate St John's Wort is common throughout Europe, including the British Isles, on grassland, hedgebanks and in open woods, especially on lime-rich soils. *H. tetrapterum* is also native to Britain. Perforate St John's Wort is associated with many ancient superstitions. For example, in medieval times it was hung in windows and doorways to drive away devils and evil spirits. The glands in the leaves, which look like tiny punctures when held up to the light, have given the plant the first part of its common name and the specific epithet. These dots were thought to look like wounds and the plant was used by the Knights of St John of Jerusalem to heal the wounds of Crusaders. It is still widely used in herbalism.

The flowering stems are used medicinally. Their constituents include tannins (the flowers as much as 16 per cent), a red-pigmented flavonoid glycoside (hypericin), the flavonoid glycosides rutin and hyperin, catechol, an essential oil and resin. These substances give Perforate St John's Wort mild sedative, cholagogic, anti-inflammatory, diuretic, antiseptic and astringent properties. It is used to treat chronic inflammation of the internal organs and for gynaecological disorders. The oil, prepared by macerating the fresh stems in olive or sunflower-seed oil, is used to heal wounds, burns, bruises and haemorrhoids. Excessive use of St John's Wort, however, causes a skin allergy in hypersensitive individuals, which becomes aggravated by exposure to the sun.

Flowering time: July onwards

Stem of
H. perforatum

Stem of
H. tetrapterum

Hyssop

Flower

Segment of fruit (mericarp)

A deciduous subshrub, woody at the base, with square herbaceous branched stems. The leaves are opposite, linear and sessile. The bright-blue, tubular, two-lipped flowers with violet stamens grow in clusters from the upper leaf axils, making a long, one-sided spike, which is often interrupted below. The fruit consists of four one-seeded nutlets. All parts of the plant are pleasantly aromatic and the flowers are attractive to bees.

Hyssop is native to the Mediterranean region where it grows wild on old walls and dry banks. It is found as a garden escape elsewhere in Europe and it has been recorded in the British Isles. It is an attractive plant to grow in the garden or in pots. In some countries it is commercially cultivated for the pharmaceutical industry and for use in the manufacture of liqueurs and perfumes. The plant's names are derived through the Greek word *hyssopos* from the Hebrew word *esob,* but the plant is probably not the hyssop mentioned in the Bible. In the past Hyssop was used to treat stomach and chest disorders and its strong aroma led to its use as a cleansing herb. It remains a popular herbal remedy.

The flowering stems are used medicinally. Their constituents include an essential oil with pinene, limonene and pinecamphene, plus the flavonoid glycoside hesperidin and tannins. These substances give Hyssop tonic, stomachic, expectorant, carminative, astringent, antidiaphoretic and weak diuretic properties. It is used in an infusion mainly for cough, whooping cough, asthma and bronchitis. It is also beneficial for inflammation of the urinary tract, kidneys and gall bladder and it stimulates the appetite and digestive juices. Hyssop should not be used in cases of nervous irritability. Strong doses, particularly of the distilled essential oil on its own, cause muscular spasms.

Flowering time: July to September

Elecampane

A robust perennial herb with a large, branched, tuberous root bearing one or several erect and branched softly hairy stems. The leaves are large and toothed, hairy above and downy below; the basal ones are oval and stalked; those on the stem are oval to cordate with a clasping base. The large terminal yellow flowerheads − 6−8 cm wide − have several rows of involucral bracts, the outer ones leaf-like. The fruit is a hairless, four-ribbed achene with a reddish pappus.

Elecampane is a native of Asia and probably also Europe, including perhaps some parts of southern England. It has become naturalized as a garden escape elsewhere. It grows in fields, open woods and on roadsides but is generally uncommon. It can still be found in some cottage gardens. The origin of the ancient name *Inula* is confused. It may be a corruption of the Greek word *helenion,* from Helenus, son of Priam. This could also be the derivation of the specific epithet *helenium*. The common epithet, Elecampane, comes from the medieval apothecaries' Latin name *enula* (from *inula*) *campana* ('enula of the fields'). In the past the root of Elecampane was used as a tonic and to heal skin disorders and dropsy. It was also candied. Elecampane is still a popular herbal medicine, especially in cough mixtures.

The roots of second- or third-year plants are used medicinally. When dried they have a pungent aroma and a bitter taste. The constituents include abundant inulin (up to 50 per cent), essential oils, bitter compounds, resin and mucilage. The bitter substance helenine has an anthelmintic action and was once used for ridding children of pinworm and roundworm. Elecampane also has expectorant, antitussive, diuretic, cholagogic, antiseptic and tonic properties. Nowadays it is mainly used for cough, bronchitis, lack of appetite and digestive disorders. The essential oil distilled from the fresh roots is used as an insecticide and anthelmintic in some countries.

Flowering time: July to August

Seed

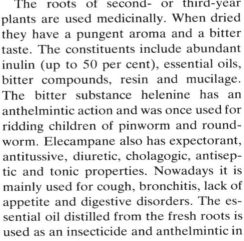

Root

Garden Iris, Common Iris, Flag

Flower of *I. pallida*   *I. florentina*

A perennial herb with a thickened rhizome bearing sword-shaped greyish leaves, which sheath at the base, and a tall, branched stem topped by large, blue-violet, occasionally white, fragrant flowers. The flowers have three broad outer deflexed petals (falls) with yellow beards and yellowish-white and purplish-brown venation; three more or less erect inner petals (standards); and three large petal-like styles with branched tips (crests). The whole flower is enclosed by a green and brown spathe. The fruit is an ovoid, many-seeded capsule.

Garden Iris is native to the Mediterranean region but it has become naturalized throughout Europe. It can sometimes be found growing wild in waste places as a garden escape in the British Isles. There are many cultivated varieties. It is grown commercially for the rhizomes (orris root) which are used in perfumery and pharmaceutical preparations. The finest orris root, however, comes from a related species, Fleur-de-Lis or Florentine Iris (*I. florentina*). This iris has large white flowers tinged with pale blue and a bright-yellow beard on the falls. Pale Iris (*Iris pallida*), with pale-blue flowers, is also grown commercially for its rhizomes. Neither *I. florentina* nor *I. pallida* grows wild in Britain. All irises are named after Iris, the goddess of the rainbow. Orris root has been used since ancient times in perfumery and cosmetics.

The rhizomes of second- to fourth-year plants are used medicinally. During drying they acquire a violet-like scent, caused by the ketone irone; they become yellowish and fragile. The other constituents include an essential oil, glycosides, sugars, resin, starch, mucilage and tannins. These substances give Garden Iris expectorant and diuretic properties but it is rarely used nowadays, even in herbal medicine, because it can cause vomiting and nausea. **The fresh root is strongly purgative.** The dried rhizomes are, however, still used in pharmaceutical preparations to disguise the taste and smell of other medicines.

Flowering time: June

Walnut

A large deciduous tree with a spreading crown and ash-grey smooth, later fissured bark. The alternate leaves are odd-pinnate with seven to nine ovate to elliptic entire leaflets, and are aromatic when bruised. The monoecious flowers appear in spring before the leaves: the male flowers are borne in pendulous catkins; the inconspicuous female flowers grow at the ends of the twigs in groups of two or three. The green, rounded fruit is a drupe with an ovoid crinkled nut (the familiar walnut) inside.

Walnut is native to southeastern Europe and western Asia. It was imported to Italy about 100 BC and reached the British Isles in the 16th century if not before. It is widely planted in gardens and parks for its fruit, for ornament and for its valuable hard wood; in some parts of Britain it has become naturalized. The generic name, *Juglans,* is a corruption of the Latin *Jovis* (Jupiter, the king of the gods) and *glans* (= nut). The Anglo-Saxon name for Walnut was *walh-hnutu,* which is said to come from the German words *walhaz* (= foreign) and *hnut* (= nut). There are many ancient Greek and Roman myths and superstitions about walnuts. Later, in the Middle Ages, walnuts were believed to cure mental disorders because of the resemblance of the shelled nuts to the human brain.

The green outer layer (pericarp) of the fruits and the leaflets are used medicinally. Their constituents include the tannin juglandin, organic acids, an essential oil, the glycoside hydrojuglone and a bitter compound (juglone). These give Walnut astringent, haemostatic, anti-inflammatory, antispasmodic and mild sedative properties. In herbal medicine it is used mainly for stomach and intestinal disorders and as a skin treatment. A tincture prepared from the fresh leaves is used in homeopathy for the same ailments.

The ripe nuts contain a large amount of fatty oil and are widely used in the food industry and in confectionery. The expressed oil is used in cooking, in artists' paints and in soaps.

Flowering time: June

Female flowers   Male flowers

Juniper

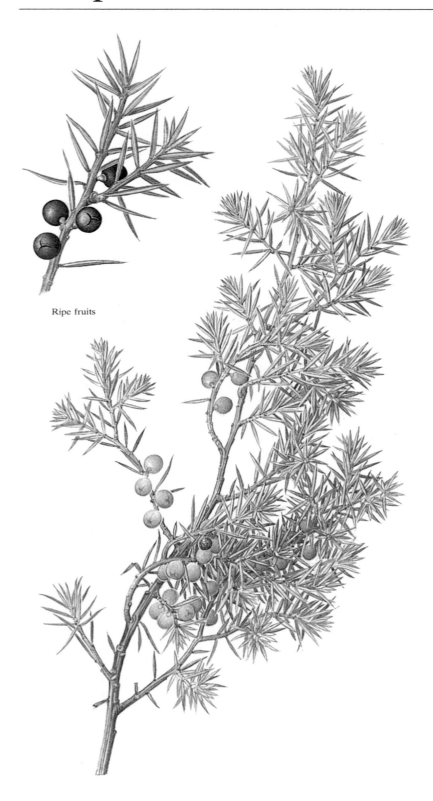

Ripe fruits

A coniferous evergreen shrub or rarely a small tree with flexible reddish-brown twigs thickly covered with needle-like blue-green leaves arranged in whorls of three. Each needle has a broad white band on the upper side and is keeled below. The plant is dioecious; the female cones are green, the male cones yellowish. The three-seeded, berry-like globose fruits are green at first, then blue-black when ripe in the second year.

Juniper is found throughout Europe at the edges of woods, in heath and scrub and on moorland, mostly on lime-rich soils. In some countries it is a protected species. It is one of Britain's native conifers; it has a widespread but local and decreasing distribution. Juniper is, however, often grown in parks and gardens and there are now many cultivated varieties. Juniper berries have long been used for medicinal purposes and as a spice. They were believed to resist the plague and cure the bites of snakes. Nowadays they are mostly used for flavouring certain meats, liqueurs and especially gin. The English word gin is derived from an abbreviation of Hollands Geneva as the spirit was first called, which in turn came from the Dutch word *genever* and from *Juniperus,* the original Latin name for the plant.

The constituents of the berries include a resin (10 per cent), an essential oil (juniper berry oil, 0.5−2 per cent) with pinene and borneol, inositol, a flavonoid glycoside and a bitter compound (juniperin). These give Juniper strong diuretic, tonic, rubefacient, carminative, antiseptic and aromatic properties. The crushed dried berries are used on their own in an infusion or in tea mixtures for dropsy and bladder and kidney disorders, and for rheumatic pain. The wood is used for the same purposes but it is not as potent as the berries. **Juniper must not be taken internaly when the kidneys are inflamed or during pregnancy. Long-term use may also damage the kidneys.** Juniper is also used externally in compresses and bath preparations to relieve rheumatic and arthritic pain, for wounds and as a tonic.

Flowering time: May to June

Laburnum, Golden Rain ☠ ☠

A deciduous shrub or small tree with smooth greyish-green bark and trifoliate, long-stalked leaves, which are dark green and glabrous above and paler and felted below. The yellow flowers are arranged in long, drooping racemes. The fruit is a brown pod with black seeds. **All parts of the plant are extremely poisonous, especially the pods and seeds.**

Laburnum, native to southern Europe, grows on sunny slopes and on rocks, mostly on lime-rich soils. It may have been introduced to the British Isles in the 16th century and has since become naturalized in some waste, bushy places. Laburnum is often planted in gardens, streets and parks and children should be warned never to pick and eat the seeds or to put the twigs or bunches of flowers in their mouths. *Laburnum* is the ancient Latin name. The hard, dark heartwood used to be greatly valued as a substitute for ebony for the manufacture of small turned articles. The plant has occasionally been used as an emetic and as an antitussive and sedative in the treatment of asthma and whooping cough, but because it is so poisonous it is now rarely used in any medical treatment.

The seeds contain the highly toxic alkaloid cytisine, also proteins, tannins, glycosides and choline. Cytisine is isolated and used in pharmaceutical preparations to treat, for example, hypotension. In homeopathy a tincture prepared from the fresh leaves and flowers is sometimes used to treat various neurological and digestive disorders. Laburnum is a dangerous plant; **it should never be collected and used for self-medication.** Symptoms of poisoning include dilatation of the pupils, stomach cramps, vomiting, giddiness, muscular weakness, convulsions and respiratory failure and death. If poisoning is suspected medical aid should be sought immediately.

Fruit

Seed

Flowering time: May to June

Great Lettuce, Greater Prickly Lettuce, Wild Lettuce

Leaves of *L. serriola*

An annual, sometimes biennial herb with an erect leafy, white or reddish stem which branches at the top. The stiff, bluish-green leaves have prickly toothed margins and a prickly midrib beneath. The stalked basal leaves are oval and are arranged in a rosette; the alternate stem leaves may be pinnately divided into broad lobes, they clasp the stem at their base and are held horizontally. The numerous, short-stalked yellow flowerheads are arranged in a panicle. The smooth blackish fruit, an achene, has a white beak and a pappus of white hairs. All parts of the plant secrete a **poisonous latex**.

Great Lettuce, originally native to southern Europe, has since spread to most of the rest of Europe. It is locally common in the British Isles, growing in waste grassy places, especially near the sea. It is absent in Ireland. It used to be grown in gardens as a medicinal plant, as was the related Prickly Lettuce (*L. serriola*). Prickly Lettuce is broadly similar to Great Lettuce, but its stem leaves in full sun are held vertically, not horizontally, and the achene is greyish-green when ripe. The generic name, *Lactuca,* and hence the common name Lettuce, derive from the Latin word *lactus* (= milk), a reference to the milky fluid that flows from the stems when they break or are cut. Great Lettuce is still cultivated on a small scale for the pharmaceutical industry. The related species *L. sativa* is the well-known culti-vated Garden Lettuce.

The latex on its own and the flowering stems are used medicinally. The con-stituents include bitter compounds (mainly lactucin and lactucopircin), alka-loids, caoutchouc, proteins and organic acids. These substances have analgesic and sedative effects and Great Lettuce was used as a narcotic before the discov-ery of opium and later as an adulterant of opium. It is still occasionally used in homeopathy but rarely in conventional medicine. **Great Lettuce should be used only under strict medical supervision; it should never be collected and used for self-medication.**

Flowering time: July to September

White Deadnettle, Archangel

A perennial herb with a creeping rhizome and an erect, square, leafy stem. The opposite, stalked leaves are cordate, long-pointed and sharply serrate, very similar to those of Common Nettle (*Urtica dioica*) (Pl. 242) but they do not sting. The white flowers, arranged in loose whorls, grow from the upper leaf axils. The corolla is distinctly two-lipped; the upper lip forms a hood; the lower lip has two very small lateral lobes each with a small tooth and a notched middle lobe. The anthers are black and tucked under the hooded upper lip. The fruit consists of four nutlets. All parts of the plant are finely hairy.

White Deadnettle grows throughout Europe and is a common weed of waste places, roadsides and hedgebanks in England but is rarer in the west and north Scotland. The 'dead' in White Deadnettle's name refers to its lack of stinging hairs. The generic name, *Lamium,* is derived from the Greek word *lamios* (= throat) and refers to the shape of the corolla. White Deadnettle has been used medicinally probably since the Middle Ages, particularly for menstrual problems. It remains a popular remedy for bladder disorders.

The flowers are used medicinally. When dry they smell of honey and have a bitter taste. The constituents include mucilage, tannins, saponin, flavonoid glycosides, tyramine, methylamine and potassium salts. These substances give White Deadnettle mild astringent, anti-inflammatory, expectorant, diuretic, tonic and hypnotic properties. In herbalism an infusion is used for catarrh of the upper respiratory tract, bronchitis, insomnia and for urinary and gynaecological disorders. In homeopathy a tincture prepared from fresh material is used for the same purposes. Externally a strong infusion is used in healing compresses or bath preparations and as a gargle.

Tea made from the fresh flowers, sweetened with honey, can be drunk as a 'spring cure'. The tender young leaves can be prepared and eaten like spinach.

Flower

Flowering time: March onwards

Garden Lavender, Lavender

An evergreen subshrub with a much-branched woody stem, the square green shoots thickly covered with entire, linear leaves, which at first are white-felted, later green. The small, bluish, two-lipped flowers are arranged in spike-like terminal panicles often interrupted below. The fruit consists of four nutlets. All parts of the plant are aromatic.

Garden Lavender is a native of the west Mediterranean region but it is widely grown in country gardens and it has become naturalized in some warm parts of Europe, but not in the British Isles. Lavender is also cultivated on a large scale for its oil, most of which is contained in special glands on the calyx. Lavender oil is mainly produced in the south of France, but also in minor quantities elsewhere. In Britain it is produced not from *L. angustifolia,* but from a related species, *L. intermedia,* which is a hybrid of *L. angustifolia* and Spike Lavender (*L. latifolia* or *L. spica*). The generic name, *Lavandula,* is thought to derive from the Latin word *lavare* (= to wash), a reference to the Romans' habit of using Lavender to perfume their washing water. The plant remains one of the most popular and well-known of the traditional herbs.

The flowering stems or the flowers alone are used medicinally. Among the constituents are an essential oil (up to 3 per cent) with linalyl acetate, linalool, camphor and borneol as the main components, also tannins (12 per cent). These give Garden Lavender mild sedative, carminative, antispasmodic, rubefacient and tonic properties. In herbalism it is still used internally for headache, nervous disorders and insomnia, as a cough suppressant and for flatulence, but mostly it is used externally as a skin freshener. The essential oil, which is obtained from the fresh plants by steam distillation, is a component of various proprietary preparations.

The oil's chief use, however, is in perfumes, colognes and toilet articles. It is also used to mask unpleasant odours in medicines.

Segment of fruit (mericarp)   Dried herb

Flowering time: July to August

Motherwort

A perennial herb with a stout rhizome and an erect, rough, square, branched and leafy stem. The stalked opposite leaves are oval, palmately three- to five-lobed, irregularly toothed, green above and white-felted below. The white or pink hairy flowers grow in whorls in the upper leaf axils, forming a long, interrupted spike. The calyx is bell-shaped with five equal teeth; the corolla is two-lipped with purplish spots on the lower lip. The fruit consists of four nutlets. All parts of the plant have an unpleasant smell, but the flowers are attractive to bees.

Motherwort is native to Siberia but it has become naturalized in waste places, ditches and in hedges throughout most of Europe. It used to be grown in gardens for medicinal purposes, which is how it came to be introduced to the British Isles. It is, however, rarely found in the wild in Britain. The plant was named Motherwort because it was used to treat female disorders. The reason why this and related species were named *Leonurus* (originally a Greek word) is probably because the plant's tall leafy stems were thought to resemble lions' tails. Motherwort remains a popular herbal remedy for nervous tension and menstrual problems. It is also used in homeopathy.

The flowering stems are used medicinally. Their constituents include a bitter compound (leonurin), an iridoid glycoside (leonuride), tannins, an essential oil and alkaloids (for example, leonurinine). These substances give Motherwort mild sedative, cardiotonic, antispasmodic, hypotensive and astringent properties. An infusion is used for migraine, hysteria, anxiety, diarrhoea and menstrual irregularities. Motherwort is also beneficial for nervous heart disorders, irregular heartbeat and high blood pressure; treatment for these conditions should be **medically supervised.** In homeopathy preparations of the fresh plant are used for the same purposes. Motherwort generally has the same effects as Common Valerian (*Valeriana officinalis*) (Pl. 245).

Flowering time: July to September

Flower

Lovage

Fruit   Flower   Fruit cluster

A perennial herb with a robust, hollow, angled and branched stem and large, long-stalked, bi- or tripinnate leaves with glossy dark-green leaflets. The stem leaves are less divided. The small greenish-yellow flowers are arranged in a compound umbel. The fruit is a yellow-brown, ovoid double achene with winged ribs. All parts of the plant are strongly aromatic.

Lovage is probably a native of the Mediterranean region but it has become naturalized locally in meadows and other grassy places in most parts of Europe, including the British Isles. It is widely grown as a garden herb and is commercially cultivated on a small scale for medicinal purposes in some countries. Lovage was known to the ancient Greeks who chewed the fruit to aid digestion and to relieve flatulence; the plant has remained a popular herbal remedy. It enjoyed a reputation in many European countries as an aphrodisiac, hence possibly its common name. More likely the name Lovage is derived through an old English word *loveache,* from the earlier Latin name *ligusticum,* after Liguria in Italy where the herb grew profusely.

The roots of two- or three-year plants or the flowering stems (collected before flowering) are used medicinally. Their constituents include an essential oil with terpineol and butyl phthalidine as its main components, furanocoumarins, sugars, esters of organic acids and resin. These substances give Lovage stomachic, carminative, cholagogic, diuretic, mild expectorant, antidiaphoretic and antirheumatic properties. In herbalism an infusion is used mainly to relieve flatulence, as an appetizer, for dropsy and urinary disorders, rheumatism and nervous exhaustion. A hot infusion can be used an inhalent and if added to bath water, it has a cleansing and deodorizing effect on the skin. **If taken internally in excess Lovage may cause nausea and vertigo.** In particular, large doses should never be taken by pregnant women or by persons with kidney diseases.

Flowering time: July to August

Common Toadflax

A perennial herb with a creeping rhizome and an erect, leafy, usually branched stem. The alternate leaves are linear, greyish green and entire. The yellow flowers are arranged in a dense elongated spike. The corolla is two-lipped and the tube is extended at the base into a long pointed spur. There is a bright orange spot at the throat of the tube which acts as a honey-guide for nectar-seeking bees. The fruit is an ovoid capsule with winged seeds.

Common Toadflax grows throughout Europe in meadows, cultivated fields and waste places. It is native to the British Isles; it is common in England, Wales and southern Scotland but is less frequent in the far north and in Ireland. The resemblance of toadflaxes to species of flax (*Linum*) in early summer accounts for the second part of the common name. The generic name, *Linaria* (from the Latin word *linum* = flax), also reflects this similarity. Several explanations have been put forward to explain the connection with toads in the common name, the most likely being the resemblance of the un-usual-shaped flower to little toads and of the mouth of the flower when the sides are squeezed (like a Snapdragon, *Antir-rhinum majus*) to the wide mouth of a toad. Or it may just mean a wild, useless flax — one fit for toads. The medicinal properties of Common Toadflax have long been known. It was used to treat liver and spleen disorders and tuberculosis but is generally little used by herbalists today, except on the Continent.

The flowering stems contain flavonoid glycosides (linarin and pectolinarin), pectins, phytosterine, antirrhinic acid, tannic acid and vitamin C. These substances give Common Toadflax diaphoretic, diuretic, mild laxative and anti-inflammatory properties. An infusion is used for consti-pation, dropsy, inflamed kidneys and dis-orders of the liver and spleen. Externally it is used in compresses or bath prepara-tions for skin rashes, varicose veins and haemorrhoids. A tincture is used in homeopathy.

Flower

Flowering time: July to October

Flax, Linseed

Flowers

Seed

An annual herb with a tall, slender, leafy stem, usually branched at the top, and alternate, linear or lanceolate, sessile leaves marked with three veins. The blue or white flowers are arranged in erect terminal panicles. The stamens are united into a tube at the base; the stigmas are club-shaped. The fruit is a globose capsule with shiny, flattened, brown seeds with a short blunt beak.

Flax is now unknown in the wild but originally it may have been a native of Asia. It has been cultivated since at least 5000 BC, probably first by the ancient Mesopotamians and later by the Egyptians who wrapped their mummies in cloth made from it. The Romans spread flax cultivation to northern Europe and now the plant is grown all over the world for the oil extracted from the seeds and for its fibres, which are made into linen and other cloths. It may persist for a year or two as a casual in sunny waste places in countries where it is cultivated. *Linum* is the original Latin name for the plant and comes from the Greek name *linon*. The common name, Flax, has an old and confused derivation — perhaps ultimately from a word meaning 'to plait'.

The seeds are widely used medicinally. Their constituents include 30−40 per cent of a fatty oil (linseed oil) with esters of linoleic acid (60 per cent), linolenic acid (20 per cent), stearic acid (8 per cent) and oleic acid; also mucilage, proteins, a cyanogenic glycoside (linamarin) and enzymes. Whole or crushed, the seeds are a reliable means of relieving constipation. After they have been swallowed the mucilaginous layers of the seed coat swell and, with the oil which acts as a demulcent and laxative, there is a rapid evacuation of the bowels. Externally, crushed seeds mixed to a paste with water are used to make hot poultices to relieve pain and to heal septic wounds, skin rashes and ulcers. The extracted oil is used in the pharmaceutical industry to make liniments for burns and rheumatic pain.

The oil is also important in the manufacture of paints, soap and printer's ink.

Flowering time: June to August

Common Gromwell

A perennial herb with a short, non-stoloniferous rhizome and an erect, much-branched, densely leafy stem. The alternate leaves are sessile and lanceolate with distinct lateral veins beneath. The small creamy-white flowers are arranged in monochasial cymes growing from the upper leaf axils. The corolla tube has five hairy, longitudinal folds in the throat. The fruit consists of four gleaming white, smooth, ovoid nutlets which are very hard. All parts of the plant are roughly hairy.

Common Gromwell grows throughout most of Europe on sunny bushy slopes, in scrub and woodland margins, especially in warmer parts and on lime-rich soils. It is native to the British Isles and is quite common in England and Wales, but rarer in Scotland and Ireland. It is occasionally grown in gardens and is attractive to bees. The generic name, *Lithospermum,* is derived from the Greek words *lithos* (= stone) and *sperma* (= seed) on account of the exceptionally hard seeds. The common name Gromwell comes through an old French word *gromil* from the medieval Latin name *gruinum milium,* which may have meant 'crane's millet'. The allusion to cranes has not been explained but 'millet' again refers to the seeds. Both Common Gromwell and the related Field Gromwell (*Buglossoides arvense,* formerly *Lithospermum arvense*), a common weed of cornfields, were traditional remedies for kidney stones but they are not often used nowadays.

The fruits are the medicinal parts. Their constituents include up to 50 per cent of mineral substances, mainly silicic acid and calcium salts. These compounds give the seeds diuretic properties and they are used, crushed, in an infusion for urinary disorders and uroliths. The dried leaves can be used as a tea substitute. A red colouring agent is obtained from the rhizomes.

Segment of fruit (mericarp)

Flowering time: June to July

Stagshorn Moss, Common Clubmoss

Stem

An evergreen perennial, flowerless, moss-like plant (but related to ferns) with long, branched, creeping stems densely covered with alternate, bright-green linear leaves, which taper to a long, hair-like white tip. Only the fertile stems are ascending. They have appressed scale-like leaves and are terminated by two or three yellow-green, long-stalked, spore-bearing cones (sporophylls). **All parts of the plant, except the spores, are poisonous.**

Stagshorn Moss has been growing in Europe for more than 300 million years – since the Palaeozoic Era. It serves as an indicator of acidic and moist soils and occurs in woodland humus and on heaths and moors. It is native to the British Isles; it is common in mountain grassland but is scarce and decreasing elsewhere. The related Interrupted Clubmoss (*L. annotinum*) is also found in Britain, but only in the mountainous areas of northern England and Scotland where it is rare. Its leaves are not hair-pointed like those of Stagshorn Moss and the fertile branches bear ordinary leaves. The generic name, *Lycopodium,* is derived from the Greek words *lykos* (= wolf) and *podion* (= little foot), an allusion to the appearance of the club-shaped cones. The common name also refers to this characteristic. The whole plant was once used medicinally; the spores do not seem to have been used alone until the 17th century.

The spores contain up to 50 per cent of fatty oils, phytosterin, organic acids, an alkaloid (sporonine) and sugar. They have vulnerary, haemostatic and diuretic properties. Internally the powdered spores are occasionally used to treat chronic kidney, liver, stomach and nervous disorders. Mostly, however, the spores are used only externally – as a soothing dusting powder for wounds, eczema, nappy rash and cracked skin. At one time the powdered spores were used to coat pills to prevent their adhesion. A tincture prepared from the spores is often used in homeopathy. **Only the spores should be taken internally, never the other parts of the plant, which contain toxic alkaloids.**

Gipsywort

A perennial herb with a creeping rhizome and a stiffly erect, unbranched, square stem. The numerous opposite leaves are lanceolate to elliptic, short-stalked and deeply toothed, the lower ones pinnately divided. The small, white flowers are arranged in dense whorls in the axils of the upper pairs of leaves. The corolla is weakly two-lipped with four nearly equal lobes; the lower lip is purple-spotted. The fruit consists of four small nutlets. Gipsywort is broadly similar in appearance to mints (*Mentha*) but is distinguished by its lack of smell, its lobed lower leaves and tight whorls of whitish flowers.

Gipsywort is native to Europe, including the British Isles, and grows in damp places with nitrogen-rich soils, such as ditches, marshes and around buildings. It is common in England and Wales, less so in Scotland and Ireland. It is supposed to have been given its common name, Gipsywort, because itinerant fortune-tellers stained their skin with the strong black dye from the herb in order to pass themselves off as Egyptians or Africans to lend credance to their tales. In the Middle Ages Gipsywort was used to treat malaria and many other healing properties were attributed to this plant. It, and the related North American Bugleweed (*L. virginicus*), are still used in homeopathy, in herbalism and, in some countries, also in conventional medicine.

The flowering stems are used medicinally. Their constituents include an essential oil, tannins, a bitter compound (lycopin) and organic acids. These substances give Gipsywort sedative, astringent and cardioactive properties; they also reduce the activity of iodine in the thyroid gland. It was once prescribed for hyperthyroidism and related disorders such as Basedow's disease. In homeopathy tinctures of the fresh plant are used to treat anxiety and various heart disorders such as angina and spasms. Gipsywort preparations take a long time to take effect and need careful medical supervison. **It is not a suitable herb for self-medication.**

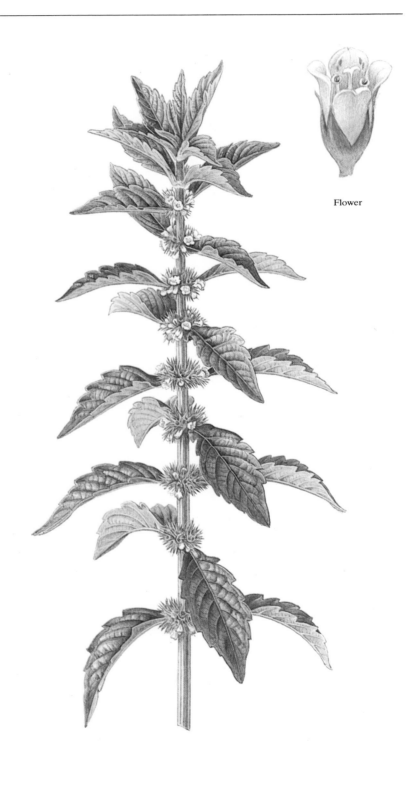

Flower

Flowering time: July to September

Creeping Jenny

Fruit with seeds   Flower

A perennial herb with a prostrate, far-creeping, angled and branched stem. The leaves are opposite, roundish to broadly ovate and short-stalked. The large yellow, bell-shaped flowers grow singly on short stalks in the leaf axils. The leaves and the corolla are dotted with glands. The fruit is a five-valved globose capsule but it is produced only rarely — the plant usually spreads by means of its creeping stems that root at the nodes.

Creeping Jenny is common in damp grassy places throughout most of Europe. It is native to the British Isles but is rare in the north. The common name, Creeping Jenny, clearly alludes to the plant's trailing habit. Another English name is Moneywort and the plant's specific name *nummularia* is from the Latin word *nummulus,* a diminutive of *nummus* (= a coin, money). The reference in this case is to the rounded leaves, which are arranged two by two on the stems and with their faces turned upwards look like rows of pence. In some country areas the herb was called Twopenny Grass or Herb Twopence. Creeping Jenny was a popular herbal remedy in the past. It and related species called loosestrifes in the same genus, *Lysimachia,* are useful ornamental plants, and are still used in herbal medicine, especially on the Continent.

The flowering stems are used medicinally. When dry they are pale green and have a bitter, astringent taste. Their constituents include saponins, tannins and silicic acid. These substances give Creeping Jenny astringent and antiseptic properties. It is used in an infusion for gastroenteritis and severe diarrhoea. The fresh, macerated flowering stems are used in compresses applied externally to slow-healing wounds, ulcers and skin rashes and they also relieve rheumatic pain. The decoction and the fresh juice have a soothing emollient action on the skin.

Flowering time: May onwards

Common Mallow

A biennial or perennial herb with a spindle-shaped taproot and an erect, ascending or decumbent stem. The basal leaves are roundish, shallowly lobed and long-stalked; the alternate stem leaves are shorter-stalked, deeply palmately lobed and toothed. The large, stalked, rose-purple flowers with prominent violet veins grow in clusters in the leaf axils. The five petals, up to four times as long as the calyx, are notched. Both the leaves and stems are softly hairy. The disc-shaped fruit (a schizocarp) splits into one-seeded wrinkled mericarps when ripe. The fruits are popularly called 'cheeses' after their shape.

Common Mallow grows throughout Europe in field edges, woodland margins and clearings, on roadsides and waste ground. It is commonly found all over the British Isles, but is rarer in the far north. Common Mallow was once widely used as a medicinal plant and foodstuff but it has largely been replaced for medicinal purposes by Marshmallow (*Althaea officinalis*) (Pl. 14).

The flowers and leaves, free of mallow rust, are used medicinally. When properly dried the flowers are blue. The constituents include abundant mucilage, tannins, an essential oil, organic pigments (anthocyanins) in the flowers, and provitamin A and vitamins B and C (in the leaves). These substances give Common Mallow emollient, expectorant, anti-inflammatory and astringent properties and it is used in much the same way as Marshmallow — for bronchitis, laryngitis and other respiratory disorders, gastritis and enteritis, and as a mild laxative. It also promotes the healing of internal injuries, damaged mucosa and gastric ulcers. Externally Common Mallow is used in compresses and bath preparations for skin rashes, boils and ulcerous conditions, and in gargles and mouth washes.

The fresh leaves and young shoots can be added to salads and soups and cooked as a vegetable.

Dried herb

Fruit

Flowering time: June onwards

Common Mallow

Flower

A biennial or perennial herb often grown as a garden plant and as food for bees. In appearance it is identical to wild Common Mallow described in the previous plate (Pl. 139), but its flowers are a darker colour and the petals are less notched. It is this mallow that is cultivated commercially in some countries for the pharmaceutical industry. It is originally from the Mediterranean region.

The leaves and flowers have similar constituents to those of wild Common Mallow and they likewise have emollient, expectorant, anti-inflammatory and astringent properties. It is mostly the flowers that are used in herbal tea mixtures.

Dwarf Mallow (*M. neglecta*) and Musk Mallow (*M. moschata*) — both native to the British Isles — have similar medicinal properties. Dwarf Mallow differs from Common Mallow in being an annual, having more or less prostrate stems, leaves with more rounded lobes, whitish or pale-violet, violet-veined petals, which are only twice as long as the calyx, and smooth, brownish-green hairy mericarps.

Musk Mallow is a perennial with erect stems, which are often purple-spotted. It is distinguished from Common Mallow in having reniform basal leaves, deeply and narrowly divided stem leaves, usually solitary rose-pink flowers in the leaf axils, and hairy, blackish mericarps.

Flowering time: June to September

White Horehound

A tufted perennial herb with a short, stout rhizome, erect, square, branched stems and numerous opposite, wrinkled, bluntly toothed, ovate and long-stalked leaves. The small white tubular flowers are arranged in dense whorls in the axils of the uppermost leaves. The calyx tube has ten veins and ten hooked teeth; the corolla is two-lipped with the upper lip nearly flat. The fruit consists of four nutlets. All parts of the plant have an apple-like smell.

White Horehound grows throughout most of Europe in dry waste places and by roadsides, chiefly where it is warm and sunny. It is native to the British Isles but is rather uncommon and does not occur at all in northern Scotland or northern Ireland. It is easily distinguished from Black Horehound (*Ballota nigra*) (Pl. 35) by its downy appearance, by the ten teeth on the calyx, white flowers with the almost flat upper lip and by its sweet smell. The generic name, *Marrubium*, is said to come from the Hebrew word *marrob* (= a bitter juice). White Horehound has been a popular herbal remedy for coughs and other chest complaints since ancient Egyptian times and it is still regarded as one of the most effective herbal expectorants known. It is cultivated commercially on a small scale for the pharmaceutical industry in some countries.

The flowering stems are used medicinally. When dry they have an irritant effect on the mucosa and a bitter taste. Their constituents include the bitter diterpene compound marrubiin (6.5 per cent), tannins, an essential oil and saponin. These substances give White Horehound expectorant, mild sedative, stomachic, cholagogic, antispasmodic and emmenagogic properties. In herbalism it is used in an infusion for respiratory complaints such as coughs, colds, asthma and bronchitis, and for liver and gall bladder disorders. It has also proved beneficial for menstrual pain and menstrual irregularities. Externally White Horehound is used in compresses to treat painful and inflamed wounds.

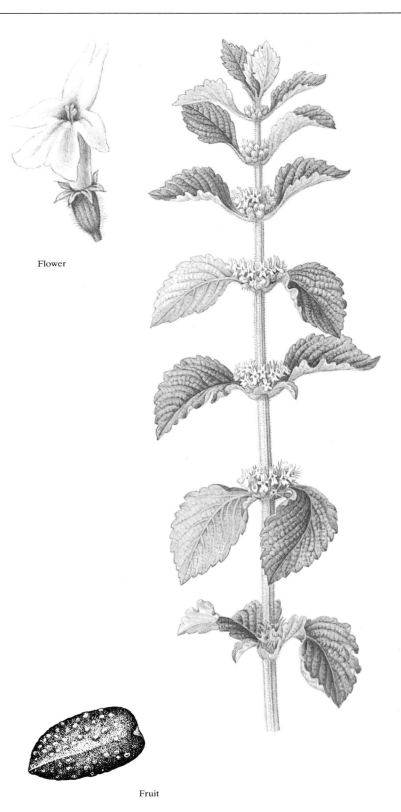

Flower

Fruit

Flowering time: June to September

Ribbed Melilot, Common Melilot, Yellow Sweet Clover

Flower

Seed

A biennial herb with a tall, angled, branched stem. The alternate, stalked leaves are trifoliate with oblong, toothed leaflets and stipules joined to the stem. The yellow flowers are arranged in long slender spikes in the upper leaf axils. The fruit is a hairless ovoid pod with transverse wrinkles and brown when ripe. **All parts of this and other melilot species are slightly poisonous.**

Ribbed Melilot is common in fields, on dry hedgebanks, along railway embankments and on waste ground throughout Europe. It is not native to the British Isles and it and other melilots were introduced from the Continent probably in the 16th century. It is now widely distributed in England and Wales; it is rarer in the north. The generic name, *Melilotus,* comes from the Greek words *meli* (= honey) and *lotos* (= fodder, clover), all the plants in this genus being very attractive to bees. The 'ribbed' in the common name refers to the wrinkled seed. Melilots were popular fodder plants and strewing herbs and they have a long history of medicinal use, mainly in ointments and poultices. Ribbed Melilot is still used by herbalists and it is collected for commercial use by the pharmaceutical industry in some countries.

The flowering stems or just the flowers alone are used medicinally. When dry they have a bitter taste and a hay-like smell due to coumarin. The constituents include melilotin and other coumarin glycosides, tannins, an essential oil and flavonoid pigments. These substances give Ribbed Melilot aromatic, expectorant, antispasmodic, antithrombic, astringent and anti-inflammatory properties. It is contained in some proprietary preparations for use in the treatment of thrombosis and varicose veins and is a component of medicinal cigarettes for bronchial asthma. More often, however, Ribbed Melilot is used in plasters and salves, compresses or bath preparations. **Ribbed Melilot should always be taken internally under professional supervision.** Large doses may cause bleeding, headache, vertigo and vomiting.

Flowering time: June onwards

Balm, Lemon Balm

A perennial herb with a short rhizome and an erect, much-branched square stem. The opposite, stalked leaves are ovate, yellow green and crenate. The small, two-lipped flowers, which grow in whorls in the upper leaf axils, change colour as they mature from a pale yellow through white to pale blue. The fruit consists of four smooth nutlets. All parts of the plant are finely hairy and have a strong lemon scent.

Flower

Balm is native to the eastern Mediterranean region but it has been widely introduced elsewhere. In the British Isles it often occurs as a garden escape and is naturalized in some parts of southern England. It is grown in gardens as food for bees, as a medicinal and culinary plant, and for ornament. In some countries it is commercially cultivated. Balm's connection with bees is reflected in the generic name, *Melissa,* which is from the Greek word for a honeybee. The common name, Balm, is an abbreviation of balsam, after its sweet-smelling aroma when fresh. Balm has been a medicinal herb for a long time. It was thought to be especially beneficial as a tonic in cases of anxiety and depression. It has been included in herbal wines and is still a constituent of liqueurs such as Benedictine.

The leaves are used medicinally. Their constituents include 0.1 to 0.25 per cent of an essential oil with citral, linalool, geraniol and citronellal as its main components, plus tannins, a bitter compound and hydroxyterpenic acid. It is the oil that imparts the lemon scent. Balm has carminative, antispasmodic, stomachic, diaphoretic and sedative properties. It is used in infusions for digestive disorders, nausea, flatulence, nervous anxiety, headache and insomnia. It can be used in pot-pourris, herb pillows and in herb mixtures for aromatic baths and cosmetic waters.

With their delicate lemon flavour the leaves have a variety of uses in cooking and they also make a refreshing addition to salads, cold drinks and wine cups.

Segment of fruit (mericarp)

Flowering time: July to August

Water Mint

Flower

Segment of fruit (mericarp)

A perennial herb with a branched rhizome and erect, square stems, branched in the upper part. The opposite, sessile leaves are ovate, sharply toothed, wrinkled and hairy. The bluish tubular flowers are arranged in slender, terminal, axillary spikes. The calyx and corolla have four equal lobes. The fruit consists of four brown nutlets. All parts of the plant smell aromatically of Caraway seeds.

This variety is a cultivated plant produced by the multiple crossing of several species of mint in garden and field cultivation. The wild Water Mint still grows in wet or damp places throughout Europe, including the British Isles, and many modern hybrid mints, such as Peppermint (*Mentha × piperita*) (Pl. 145), have this species as one of their parents. Water Mint is believed to have been used and grown since at least Roman times. In the Middle Ages it was a popular strewing herb and was called *menastrum*. The original Latin name for mints was *menta* (from the Greek *minthe*) and the common name is derived from this. Water Mint is not as strong medicinally as Peppermint, but it is favoured for large-scale cultivation because it is more frost-resistant, is not subject to mint rust caused by the fungus *Puccinia menthae,* and it thus gives more reliable yields. Unlike Peppermint, however, it contains no menthol.

The flowering stems or the leaves alone are used medicinally. Their constituents include an essential oil with carvone as the main component, tannins and bitter compounds. These substances give Water Mint stomachic, carminative, cholagogic, antispasmodic and slight astringent properties. It is used fresh or dried in an infusion to stimulate the appetite, to treat digestive and gall bladder disorders, flatulence, diarrhoea and abdominal spasms. The essential oil obtained by distillation from the fresh leaves and stems is also used medicinally. **Large doses of Water Mint may cause vomiting.**

Flowering time: July to September

Peppermint

A perennial herb with a tangle of rhizomes bearing numerous erect, square, reddish stems, which are much branched at the top. The opposite, stalked, dark-green or reddish and sometimes hairy leaves are ovate to lanceolate, acute and serrate. The small, reddish-violet flowers are arranged in long and stout terminal spikes. The fruit consists of four nutlets but is rarely produced and the plant normally spreads by means of underground stolons that root at the nodes. All parts of the plant smell and taste of peppermint.

Peppermint is a cultivated form — a hybrid between Water Mint (*M. aquatica*) (Pl. 144) and Spearmint (*M. spicata*). Nowadays it is widely grown commercially for pharmaceutical and culinary purposes. In the British Isles it is grown in the Home Counties. Peppermint also grows wild in Europe in damp waste places, but in Britain it is not a common native plant and if found in the wild it is probably a garden escape.

The leaves are used medicinally but they must be free of mint rust (*Puccinia menthae*). The constituents include an essential oil (peppermint oil) with, as its main components, menthol (up to 50 per cent), 5—10 per cent esters (mainly menthyl acetate) and menthone (15—30 per cent), plus tannins and bitter compounds. These substances give Peppermint stomachic, carminative, cholagogic, mild antispasmodic, expectorant, antiseptic and local anaesthetic properties. It is used in proprietary medicines and in infusions to stimulate the appetite, to treat respiratory infections, digestive and gall bladder disorders, diarrhoea, flatulence and abdominal spasms. Because of the menthol it contains Peppermint is added to aromatic waters, drops and spirits for embrocations and as analgesics to relieve sprains and headaches. The essential oil obtained by steam distillation from the fresh or partially dried herb is used for flavouring toothpastes and mouthwashes, pharmaceutical preparations, liqueurs and confectionery. The fresh leaves make a refreshing tea substitute.

Flowering time: July to September

Flower

Bogbean, Buckbean

Fruit

Seed

A perennial herb with a thick, far-creeping rhizome which bears alternate, long-stalked trifoliate leaves with sheathing bases and an erect, leafless stem (scape) topped by a raceme of numerous five-lobed white or pinkish flowers. The petals are fringed with white cottony hairs. The fruit, an almost globose capsule, is crowned by the style, which persists until the seeds are ripe.

Bogbean grows throughout Europe at the edges of ponds and lakes, in fens and bogs, often in shallow water and usually on acidic substrates. It is still common in the British Isles, but in some countries it has become so rare that either the whole plant or the parts below water are protected in some localities. The generic name, *Menyanthes,* is from two Greek words, *men* (= month) and *anthos* (= flower). It has been suggested that the plant was so named because it remains in flower for a month and because it regulates the menstrual cycle. The preferred common name, Bogbean, refers to the plant's habitat. In the Middle Ages Bogbean was recommended as a cure for scurvy, rheumatism and gout. The bitter-tasting leaves were once used in beer-making and in herbal cigarettes. It is still widely used in herbal medicine for digestive disorders and as a tonic.

The leaves are used medicinally. Their constituents include a glycosidic iridoid bitter compound (loganin), tannins, pectin, flavonoid glycosides and inulin. These substances give Bogbean bitter tonic, stomachic, choleretic and emmenagogic properties. It is used in much the same way as Common Centaury (*Centaurium erythraea*) (Pl. 52) and Great Yellow Gentian (*Gentiana lutea*) (Pl. 106) to stimulate the appetite and the digestive juices. On the Continent it is used in proprietary preparations such as bitter stomach drops and herbal tonic teas. Bogbean is not suitable for treating diarrhoea and **it should not be taken in large doses,** which may cause vomiting and diarrhoea.

Flowering time: May to June

Watercress

A perennial semiaquatic herb with a creeping or ascending, hollow, angled, hairless stem, which roots at the nodes. The alternate leaves are odd-pinnate with one to four pairs of oval, entire or slightly toothed leaflets and a larger terminal leaflet. The lowermost leaves are stalked, the upper ones sessile. The leaves and stems stay green all year. The small white flowers are arranged in tight terminal racemes that become longer as the fruits ripen. The fruit is a stalked, sickle-shaped siliqua with ovoid seeds arranged in two rows.

Watercress is native to western and central Europe but it is now cultivated in all parts of the world as a salad herb. In the British Isles it still grows wild in lowland streams and ditches and other damp places, where there is some moving water. Watercress's pungent taste gave the plant its generic name, *Nasturtium,* which comes from the Latin words *nasi tortium* (= 'convulsion of the nose'). The herb is rich in vitamin C and has long been used as a remedy for scurvy.

The flowering stems, collected before flowering, are used medicinally. Their constituents include a glucosinolate (gluconasturtiin), which decomposes into a pungent essential oil, also provitamin A, vitamins B complex, C, D and E, iodine, and various minerals with iron, manganese and calcium. These substances give Watercress tonic, stomachic, diuretic and irritant properties. It has numerous uses in herbal medicine, for example, as an appetizer, for digestive and gall bladder disorders, and for coughs and asthma. The fresh diluted juice or an infusion of the dried herb can be taken internally but, fresh or dried, **Watercress should always be used with care**; large doses may cause inflammation of the mucosa of the bladder and gastrointestinal tract. Externally the fresh juice is used to treat some skin disorders.

Being rich in vitamin C, fresh Watercress is a useful addition to the diet in winter and early spring; it can be eaten raw in salads or used to flavour soups.

Flowering time: June onwards

Fruit

Seed

Catmint, Catnep, Catnip

Flower

A perennial herb with a tall, hairy, square stem, which branches from the base upwards. The opposite leaves are oval with a cordate base, coarsely dentate, whitish beneath and grey-green above. The flowers are clustered in whorls in the upper leaf axils. The calyx tube has 15 ribs and 5 unequal teeth; the corolla is two-lipped and white, with purplish dots. The fruit consists of four smooth nutlets. All parts of the plant have a penetrating mint-like odour liked by cats, hence the names. Bees find the flowers very attractive.

Catmint is native to parts of Europe and Asia but it has been introduced and become naturalized elsewhere. In the British Isles it grows wild on hedgebanks and roadsides, usually on lime-rich soils in England and Wales, but is generally uncommon. In southern Scotland and Ireland it is introduced. It is still grown for ornament in country gardens even though cats often lie on the plant and damage it. The generic name, *Nepeta,* is derived from the town Nepete in Italy where Catmint was once cultivated. Catmint has an old reputation as a medicinal and seasoning herb. The dried leaves have also been smoked for their mild hallucinogenic effect.

The flowering stems, without the woody parts, are used medicinally. When dry they have a sharp, balsam-like taste and a strong, pungent aroma reminiscent of Balm (*Melissa officinalis*) (Pl. 143). The constituents include 0.5−0.7 per cent of an essential oil with carvacrol and thymol, plus tannins and bitter compounds. These substances give Catmint mild sedative, stomachic, carminative, antidiarrhoeal, diuretic, antipyretic and emmenagogic properties. It is used in tea mixtures in the treatment of nervous disorders, neuroses and migraine and, on its own in infusions, for gastrointestinal disorders, chills, colds, ammenorrhoea and other menstrual complaints. Externally it is used in ointments for haemorrhoids.

Segment of fruit (mericarp)

Flowering time: July to September

Black Cumin, Fennel Flower

An annual herb with an erect, branched stem and alternate, finely divided, feathery, greyish-green leaves. The bluish-white, star-shaped flowers are terminal and solitary. Petals are absent. The fruit is a globose capsule with small black, rough seeds. The flowers produce abundant pollen and are attractive to bees.

Black Cumin is native to southern Europe and western Asia but it has long been cultivated and used as a spice in warm countries and it has become widely naturalized. The peppery seeds are added to curries and other hot dishes. To the Arabs and Indian peoples the seeds are also considered a cure-all for a wide variety of ailments. The generic name, *Nigella,* comes from the Latin word *niger* (= black) and refers to the black seeds. The specific epithet *sativa* means 'cultivated'. The related Love-in-a-Mist (*N. damascena*), from the Mediterranean region, is a common garden plant. Its seeds have been used as a condiment too.

The ripe seeds have a camphor-like scent and a bitter, later aromatic taste. Their constituents include saponin, an essential oil, a bitter compound (nigelline) and tannins. These substances give Black Cumin diuretic, cholagogic, carminative, anthelmintic, antispasmodic, galactagogic and emmenagogic properties. The seeds are mainly used for digestive and menstrual disorders, and for bronchitis. They are, however, slightly poisonous; **large doses should not be taken.**

In cooking the seeds can be used as a substitute for pepper and can be sprinkled on bread and cakes. The distilled essential oil is used as a flavouring in confectionery. In France the seeds are sometimes called *quatre-épices* (four spices). Black Cumin seeds should not be confused with those of true Cumin (*Cuminum cyminum*), which taste quite differently. The two plants are unrelated.

Longitudinal section of fruit   Seed

Flowering time: July

Yellow Waterlily, Brandy Bottle

Fruit

Rhizome

A perennial aquatic herb with a stout creeping rhizome bearing long-stalked, broadly ovate to cordate, tough, leathery leaves that float on the water's surface. The large yellow flowers, which have a smell of alcohol and are pollinated by insects, grow on long stalks above the water. The petals are much shorter than the sepals. The fruit is a fleshy, flask-shaped capsule, which has air bladders in its tissues so that it stays afloat for a while.

Yellow Waterlily grows throughout Europe and Asia in nutrient-rich, still or slowly flowing water. It is protected in many countries, but not in the British Isles where it remains quite common, particularly in the south and east. It is cultivated for the pharmaceutical industry on the Continent. The plant has acquired its alternative name, Brandy Bottle, because of the shape of the seed capsules and the stale-alcohol smell of its flowers. The generic name, *Nuphar,* comes from the medieval Latin word *nenuphar* for a waterlily, and this in turn is a corruption of the Arabic *ninufar* and Sanskrit *nilotpala* for another water plant, the Indian Blue Lotus (*Nelumbo nucifera*).

The rhizomes are used medicinally. They contain alkaloids (nupharine, nupharidine), glycosides, tannins and other substances that are currently being investigated for their physiological effects. In small doses these constituents have a cardiotonic action and they are included in certain pharmaceutical preparations prescribed on the Continent. They affect the central nervous system and in large amounts they may cause paralysis. Yellow Waterlily is not used in herbal medicine but tinctures are used in homeopathy. **It should be used only under medical supervision;** it is not suitable for self-medication.

Flowering time: June to September

White Waterlily

A perennial aquatic herb with a stout creeping rhizome bearing long-stalked, roundish leathery leaves, green above and often reddish below. The white flowers are long-stalked and showy. There may be as many as 25 petals, the innermost ones longer than the sepals. The flowers and all the leaves float on the surface of the water. The flowers open only when the sun is shining. The fruit is a globose fleshy capsule which ripens and splits open under water.

White Waterlily is found throughout Europe north to Siberia in nutrient-rich, still and slow-flowing water. It is protected in many countries, but not in the British Isles where it is a widespread native plant, especially in lowland areas. White Waterlily is also widely grown in gardens for ornament in pools. Breeding and selection have produced a great number of variously coloured varieties, even dwarf forms (*N. pygmaea*), which are frost-resistant. The generic name, *Nymphaea,* has the same derivation as *Nuphar* (see Pl. 150). The specific epithet means 'white' and refers to the flowers. The plant was long thought to be an anaphrodisiac and was used to reduce libido. It does, in fact, seem to have this property.

The rhizomes are used medicinally. When dry they have an astringent taste. The constituents include several little-investigated alkaloids (for example, nupharine and nupharidine), glycosides and tannins. These substances give White Waterlily astringent, cardiotonic and antispasmodic properties. A decoction will check diarrhoea and bleeding but preparations are rarely used in herbal medicine. The constituents are included in proprietary medicines to reduce sexual drive. **White Waterlily should be used only under medical supervision;** it is not suitable for self-medication.

Rhizome

Flowering time: June to August

Basil

Dried flowering stems

An annual herb with a square branched stem and numerous opposite, stalked, ovate, slightly toothed and glabrous leaves, often reddish in colour. The small white, yellowish or pinkish flowers are arranged in whorls in the upper leaf axils. The fruit consists of four nutlets. All parts of the plant are hairy and aromatic.

Basil is native to southern Asia and the Middle East but it has long been grown in Europe as an ornamental, culinary and medicinal herb. It is grown commercially in central and southern Europe. It is a difficult plant to grow in Britain because it needs plenty of warmth and moisture so it often does best if kept indoors on a kitchen window sill. There are several varieties. The specific epithet, *basilicum,* — and the common name — are derived from the Greek word *basilikos* (= royal), perhaps because the pungent smell was regarded as 'fit for a king's house', as the herbalist John Parkinson wrote. In the old days there were strange superstitions linking Basil with scorpions. The plant was for a time recommended for relieving insect stings and for female complaints. Nowadays Basil is little used in herbal medicine but it remains a popular seasoning herb.

The flowering stems are the medicinal parts. Their constituents include an essential oil with linalool as the main component, also tannins, glycosides and saponin. These substances give Basil stomachic, carminative, expectorant, antispasmodic, mild sedative and galactagogic properties. An infusion is sometimes used for chronic gastritis, stomach pains, flatulence; constipation, respiratory disorders such as cough and whooping cough, and for urinary infections. It is an excellent preventive for travel sickness. Externally Basil can be used for invigorating baths, in compresses for slow-healing wounds, and in gargles.

The essential oil, obtained by steam distillation from the fresh herb, is used in perfumery, in making incense, and in the food industry. In cooking Basil leaves can be used, preferably fresh, to flavour soups, salads and meat and fish dishes.

Flowering time: August

Spiny Restharrow

A deciduous subshrub with a woody root and erect or ascending, branched, spiny stems, often woody at the base and with one or two longitudinal rows of hairs. The numerous glandular leaves are trifoliate at the bottom, mostly simple higher up the stems, with conspicuous stipules clasping the stem and serrate margins. The pink flowers with a broad standard and wing, both shorter than the keel, are arranged in long, loose racemes in the upper leaf axils. The fruit is an ovoid hairy pod with one to four seeds.

Spiny Restharrow grows throughout Europe on dry banks, in hedgerows and by roadsides, chiefly on lime-rich soils. It is a native but uncommon species in the British Isles; it is absent from much of Scotland and Wales and also Ireland. The plant is grown commercially in some countries for the pharmaceutical industry. The generic name, *Ononis,* comes from the Greek word *onos* (= an ass) and suggests that donkeys and other grazing animals like eating it. A related species, Common Restharrow (*O. repens*), can cause problems to farmers ploughing or harrowing fields. The common name literally means 'to check the harrow'. Spiny Restharrow is an old remedy for kidney disorders and bladder stones. It is still used in herbal medicine.

The root is used medicinally. Its constituents include an essential oil, tannins, fatty oil and a flavonoid glycoside (ononin). These substances give Spiny Restharrow diuretic, antiseptic, cholagogic, tonic and hypotensive properties. It is used to treat dropsy and inflammations of the bladder and kidneys, to lower high blood pressure and to alleviate rheumatic and arthritic pain. **Restharrow should be used only under supervision of a qualified medical or herbal practitioner;** it should not be taken often, in large doses and preferably not on its own. For these reasons it is generally prescribed in herbal tea mixtures.

Flower

Fruit

Root

Flowering time: July to September

Green-winged Orchid

Flower:

Dactylorhiza majalis   *Orchis morio*

A perennial herb with rounded tubers and an erect leafy stem. The leaves are lanceolate, broadest in the middle and unspotted; the ones at the bottom are arranged in a rosette, those at the top are sheathed and erect. The violet-red flowers are borne in a loose, terminal spike. The side petals are bent upwards to form a helmet-shaped structure with conspicuous green veins; the lower lip is three-lobed. The fruit is a capsule with numerous tiny seeds.

Green-winged Orchid grows patchily throughout Europe in dry meadows and pastures, especially on lime-rich soils. It is fairly abundant in the south of Britain but is rarer elsewhere. Another native British orchid, Broad-leaved Marsh Orchid (*Dactylorhiza majalis*), has a much more scattered and local distribution. It is distinguished from Green-winged Orchid by its divided tubers, usually spotted leaves, pinkish-mauve flowers and the side petals which are spreading and not formed into a helmet. These species and other orchids are declining in numbers in the wild and many are now protected. They are thus collected for medicinal purposes only where they still grow abundantly and, mostly, they have been replaced by other, less-expensive herbal remedies. At one time orchids were used as aphrodisiacs and the generic name, *Orchis,* from a Greek word for testicle, refers to the shape of the tubers. Green-winged Orchid's specific name, *morio,* however, means 'fool'! A nutritious drink called salep is still made from the dried tubers of some orchids, chiefly species of *Orchis.*

The tubers are the medicinal parts. Their constituents include about 50 per cent of mucilage that changes by hydrolysis to mannose and glucose, also 30 per cent of starch and proteins. These substances give Green-winged Orchid emollient, stomachic and antidiarrhoeal properties and it was once used for intestinal and stomach disorders.

Flowering time: May to June

Sweet Marjoram, Knotted Marjoram

An annual, sometimes a biennial herb or subshrub, with an erect, branched, square, slightly hairy stem. The greyish leaves are opposite, oval and short-stalked. The small, white or purplish two-lipped flowers are arranged in roundish clusters ('knots') in the leaf axils. The fruit consists of four smooth nutlets, which ripen only in warm regions. All parts of the plant are pleasantly aromatic.

Sweet Marjoram is native to the Mediterranean region but it has been grown as a culinary and medicinal herb since ancient Egyptian times. It was later used by the ancient Greeks and Romans and was introduced to Britain probably during the Middle Ages. It is now cultivated commercially in many countries. It is not as hardy in Britain as Pot Marjoram (*O. onites*) or Marjoram (*O. vulgare*) (Pl. 156). The names *Majorana* and Marjoram come from the medieval Latin name *maiorana*.

The flowering stems are the medicinal parts. Their constituents include 1—2 per cent of an essential oil with a spicy fragrance containing terpinines and terpineol, plus tannins, bitter compounds, carotenes and vitamin C. These substances give Sweet Marjoram stomachic, carminative, choleretic, antispasmodic and weak sedative properties. In herbalism it is used mainly for various gastrointestinal disorders and to aid digestion. It is also an ingredient of ointments and bath preparations used to alleviate rheumatism.

Mostly, however, Sweet Marjoram is used as a culinary herb. Of all the marjorams it has the best flavouring for cooking and is an excellent addition to soups, sauces and meat dishes.

Flower

Flowering time: June

Marjoram, Wild Marjoram, Oregano

Flower

Seed

A perennial, often bushy herb with an erect, reddish, square stem, branched above. The leaves are oval, opposite and stalked. Both the leaves and stems are hairy and dotted with glands. The two-lipped purplish flowers are arranged in dense cymes, forming terminal panicles, and have conspicuous purplish bracts. The fruit consists of four nutlets. All parts of the plant are pleasantly aromatic.

Marjoram is native to Europe and grows wild on dry sunny slopes, hedgebanks, roadsides and in grassland, usually on lime-rich soils. It is locally common in England and Wales but rarer farther north. It is also cultivated commercially in many countries but most supplies are still collected from the wild in the Mediterranean region. It is grown on a small scale in Britain. The generic name, *Origanum,* comes from the Greek words *oros* (= a mountain) and *ganos* (= joy, splendid), after the attractive appearance and scent of the flowers and leaves and after the natural habitat of the plant in mountains in Greece and other Mediterranean countries. Marjoram used to be considered a remedy for all manner of complaints and was also a strewing herb. The plant is widely used as a culinary herb and remains a favourite herbal remedy.

The flowering stems are used medicinally. The constituents include 0.4 per cent of an essential oil with thymol as its main component, also bitter compounds and tannins (8 per cent). These substances give Marjoram astringent, expectorant, antispasmodic, antiseptic, mild tonic, stomachic and carminative properties. It is used in herbal tea mixtures to treat stomach and gall bladder disorders, diarrhoea, coughs, asthma, nervous headache, general exhaustion and menstrual pain. Externally Marjoram is used in gargles, bath preparations, liniments and inhalents.

Marjoram is a favourite kitchen herb, especially in Italy where it is used to flavour pizzas and spaghetti dishes. It has a stronger taste than Sweet Marjoram (*Origanum majorana*) (Pl. 155).

Flowering time: July to September

Wood Sorrel

A perennial herb with a slender, creeping, scaly rhizome bearing long-stalked leaves (the aerial stem is atrophied). The bright yellow-green, clover-like leaves have three obcordate leaflets that fold along the midrib and droop at night and in bad weather. There are two sorts of flowers. Those on long stalks are solitary with white, rarely purple petals with violet veins. They bloom in spring and are visited by insects for the nectar they produce. The other flowers, which are borne in summer, have short stalks, are self-pollinated and they do not open. They produce most of the seed for the next generation of plants. The fruit is a five-angled capsule that bursts when ripe ejecting the small rough seeds out several metres.

Wood Sorrel forms spreading masses in shaded damp woods, thickets and hedges on light, usually acidic soils throughout Europe. It is native to the British Isles and is found in most parts. The generic name, *Oxalis,* is from the Greek word *oxys* (= sour) and both it and the specific name, *acetosella,* refer to the pungent acid taste of the leaves. The plant was once used to flavour sauces until it was displaced by the similar-tasting but unrelated French Sorrel (*Rumex scutatus*).

The flowering stems are used medicinally. Their constituents include oxalic acid and potassium oxalate, mucilage and vitamin C. These substances give Wood Sorrel diuretic, antiscorbutic and weak antipyretic properties. The fresh herb or juice was once used as a tonic and to treat scurvy but the plant is no longer prescribed for internal use. **Oxalic acid and potassium oxalate are irritants and in large doses they can cause poisoning** with haemorrhaging, diarrhoea and even kidney failure. Compresses made from the macerated leaves are, however, safe to apply to skin infections and swellings.

The fresh leaves improve the flavour of spring salads and soups, but they should always be used sparingly and infrequently and never by those with kidney or urinary disorders.

Flowering time: April; September to October

Fruit

Seed

Peony

A perennial herb with tuberous fleshy roots and a stout, erect, branched, glabrous stem. The ternate or biternate leaves have ovate to lanceolate segments, dark green above and lighter below. The terminal, showy, wine-red or white flowers have eight petals and five petal-like sepals. The fruit is a capsule with shiny black seeds. **All parts of the plant are poisonous, especially the flowers.**

Peony is native to southeastern Europe but it has been widely introduced elsewhere as a garden plant. There are many varieties, the most popular being the double forms with dark-red blooms. Peony has a long history of medicinal use and is named after Paion, a physician of ancient Greece. There are many superstitions connected with the plant. In ancient times it was thought to be of divine origin. Later, the seeds were believed to ward off evil spirits. Peony is now rarely used by Western herbalists but it remains popular in Chinese medicine.

The flowers are the main medicinal parts but the roots and seeds are also effective. Only the petals of double, red varieties are used. The constituents include glycosides, an alkaloid (peregrinine), tannins, sugars and mucilage and, in the flowers, the anthocyanidin pigment paeonidin. These substances give Peony antispasmodic, diuretic, vasoconstrictive, sedative and emmenagogic properties. It was once used internally to relieve spasm of the smooth muscles, asthmatic attacks, epileptic seizures, to treat gout, kidney stones and haemorrhoids, and as an abortifacient. Because of its toxicity **Peony should be used only under strict medical supervision;** it should never be used for self-medication. Herbalists, if they use it at all, would prescribe it only in herbal mixtures, never on its own. In homeopathy a tincture of the fresh plant is used for the relief of haemorrhoids.

Seed

Tubers

Flowering time: May to June

Iranian Poppy

☠ ☠

A perennial herb with a branched taproot. In the first year it forms a basal rosette of pinnately divided and toothed leaves; in the second and ensuing years it produces erect robust stems terminated by large, red, solitary flowers with bracteoles beneath that distinguish this species from the similar Oriental Poppy (*P. orientale*). The fruit is a globose capsule with brown seeds. It opens by pores under a cap-like apex formed by the dry stigmas. All parts of the plant are covered with white hairs and are **poisonous.**

Iranian Poppy is native to south-east Asia but it was introduced in the 18th century to botanical gardens in Europe and it soon became popular as an ornamental plant. It is grown commercially in Iran. *Papaver* is the original Latin name for poppies. The common name, poppy, is derived from the Anglo-Saxon word *popig,* which is a corruption of *papaver.* This poppy is used by the pharmaceutical industry because it has many of the valuable medicinal constituents possessed by Opium Poppy (*P. somniferum*) (Pl. 161).

The roots are used medicinally. Their constituents include the toxic alkaloids thebaine, alpinigenine and oripavine. It is possible to derive codeine and other pain-killing substances from thebaine. Unlike opium alkaloids, thebaine does not have additive narcotic properties, it cannot be used directly and it thus poses no danger of drug addiction: morphine, the precursor of the addictive drug heroin, can be obtained only with great difficulty from it. For pharmaceutical purposes, therefore, there may be considerable social and economic benefits in introducing this poppy into cultivation in place of Opium Poppy. Crop scientists have discovered that Iranian Poppy can provide up to 37 kg of codeine per hectare compared with Opium Poppy's much lower yield of 3 kg per hectare. **Iranian Poppy should never be used for self-medication.**

Seed:

P. bracteatum

P. rhoeas

P. somniferum

Flowering time: May to June

Common Poppy, Corn Poppy

Fruit:

P. rhoeas   P. argemone

An annual herb with a slender, erect or ascending branched stem. The lower leaves are stalked and pinnately lobed with narrow toothed segments tipped with a bristle; the upper leaves are sessile, usually with only three toothed lobes. The flower stalks are long and grow from the leaf axils. They first bear a drooping bud followed by a large, solitary red flower that has four petals, usually with a dark blotch at the base. The fruit is an ovoid hairless capsule, rounded at the base and with a ring of pores near the top when ripe. All green parts of the plant are hairy and they exude latex when cut. **The plant is slightly poisonous.**

Common Poppy, a native of Europe and Asia, grows on embankments and in waste places and is a weed of arable fields and gardens. It can be found in most parts of the British Isles, except the far north. Two other weeds of cultivated ground, especially in southern England, are Long-headed Poppy (*P. dubium*) and Prickly Poppy (*P. argemone*). Both have long, narrow seed capsules; in Long-headed Poppy they are hairless, in Prickly Poppy they are bristly and have thicker ridges (see fig.). Neither species is used medicinally. In the botanical name of Common Poppy, *rhoeas* (from the Greek word *rhoias*) means a kind of poppy.

The red petals are used medicinally. Their constituents include traces of rhoeadane alkaloids (for example, rhoeadine and rhoeagenine), a red anthocyanin pigment, and mucilage. These substances give Common Poppy sedative, hypnotic, demulcent and mild expectorant properties and the dried petals are used in herbal medicine to treat irritable coughs and hoarseness, bronchitis, and to induce sleep. The flowers are also used in the pharmaceutical industry to colour medicines. The dried petals are not poisonous but the plant can poison livestock if they eat it in large quantities.

The seeds, which have a pleasant nutty flavour, are used sprinkled on bread and cakes, especially on the Continent, and they are processed for their oil.

Flowering time: June to August

Opium Poppy

☠ ☠

An annual herb with tall, sometimes slightly hairy, branched stems which bear bluish, glossy, ovate to oblong, pinnately lobed, undulate and toothed leaves, the lowest short-stalked, the upper ones sessile and clasping at the base. The solitary large white, lilac or red flowers are borne terminally. The fruit is a globose hairless capsule. All parts of the plant exude latex and all parts, except the ripe seeds, are **extremely poisonous.**

Opium Poppy is native to the Middle East, southeast Asia and Asia Minor but it has been widely introduced elsewhere and is now naturalized throughout Europe. It is cultivated commercially in many countries for its seeds, for opium (the dried latex of the capsules) and for ornament. It can occasionally be found growing wild as a garden escape all over the British Isles. **It is illegal to grow Opium Poppy as a field crop or in allotments without government permission.** Decorative varieties can, however, be grown in gardens. The word opium comes from the Greek word *opion* meaning poppy-juice (*opos* = plant juice or sap).

The pharmaceutical industry processes the dried latex obtained from the unripe seed capsules to make opium; it also uses the dried ripe capsules and the empty dry ripe capsules. About 25 alkaloids have been isolated from opium but 6 (morphine, thebaine, codeine, narcotine, papaverine and narceine) account for about 98 per cent of the total. Morphine, the most potent constituent, is present in the greatest amount. Although opium is still occasionally used in its crude state, the alkaloids are now mostly used in purified form by the medical profession. These drugs have not yet been superceded by any synthetic product. Morphine is a narcotic, analgesic and antispasmodic. Codeine (about 3 per cent) has similar effects to morphine but is much milder. All opium alkaloids are narcotics and long-term use causes physical deterioration and eventually death. Needless to say **Opium Poppy should never be collected and used for self-medication.**

Flowering time: June to August

Capsule with dried latex

Butterbur

Rhizome

A perennial herb with a creeping horizontal rhizome. First to appear in the early spring are the flowering shoots with erect scaly stems bearing spike-like clusters of reddish-violet flowerheads. The plant is usually dioecious. The male flowers produce abundant pollen and are attractive to bees. The very large, long-stalked, cordate and serrate leaves, green above and grey-woolly beneath, are produced in summer. The fruit is an achene with a pappus of long hairs.

Butterbur grows throughout Europe on damp ground by streams, roadsides, in ditches, copses and wet meadows. The male plants are locally common throughout the British Isles; the female plants have a more restricted distribution. Butterbur is easily confused with the related Winter Heliotrope (*P. fragrans*), which has become a serious weed in Britain. The generic name, *Petasites,* comes from the Greek word *petasos* (= a broad- brimmed hat), a reference to the large leaves. The common name, Butterbur, may indicate that the leaves were once used to wrap up butter during hot weather. In the old days Butterbur was thought to banish the plague; it is now little used in herbal medicine.

The rhizomes and leaves have medicinal action. When dry the rhizomes have an unpleasant smell and a bitter taste. The constituents include an essential oil, a bitter compound, an alkaloid, mucilage, tannins and inulin. These substances give Butterbur antispasmodic, diuretic, diaphoretic and anthelmintic properties. An infusion is used to treat coughs, hoarseness, urinary disorders and to expel intestinal parasites. A poultice of fresh leaves can be applied externally to swellings, rashes, swollen veins and glands and rheumatic joints. In homeopathy a tincture of the fresh plant is used for neuralgia.

Flowering time: March to April

Parsley

A biennial herb with a stout, white, vertical taproot. In the first year it produces a rosette of triangular tripinnate leaves; in the second year, solid, branched stems with alternate, trifoliate, stalked leaves and terminal compound umbels of small yellowish-green flowers. The fruit, an ovoid double achene, splits into sickle-shaped seeds. All parts of the plant are strongly aromatic.

Native to the Mediterranean region, Parsley is now widely cultivated in several varieties, the curly leaved forms being preferred in Britain where Parsley is grown in all market-garden districts for culinary purposes. On the Continent plain-leaved varieties are preferred for garnishes and flavouring. The use of Parsley as a medicinal and sacred plant dates from ancient Greek times; the Romans seem to have been the first to use it as a food. It was introduced to Britain in the 16th century and is now naturalized in many scattered localities in waste places and on old walls. The generic name, *Petroselinum,* and the common name, Parsley, come from the Greek word *petroselinon* (from *petra* = rock and *selinon* = celery).

The fruits, leaves and roots are used medicinally. The constituents include an essential oil (fruits 7 per cent, roots 5 per cent) with apiole, myristicin and pinene as the main components, also the flavonoid glycoside apiin. The medicinal action is due largely to the essential oil, which gives Parsley strong diuretic, stomachic, carminative, irritant and emmenagogic properties. In small doses in infusions Parsley stimulates the appetite, aids digestion, alleviates kidney and bladder disorders and regulates menstrual flow. **Very strong doses can be toxic;** they may cause haemorrhaging and nervous disorders. The essential oil, which is obtained by steam distillation from the ripe fruits (parsley seed oil), should be used only under strict medical supervision. The juice from the fresh roots heals wounds and reduces swellings. The fresh leaves are rich in vitamin C.

Flower

Seed

Root

Flowering time: June to August

Masterwort

Flower

Fruit

A perennial herb with a stout, knotted rhizome, rosette of basal leaves and a tall, furrowed, hollow stem terminated by large compound umbels of whitish or pinkish flowers. The leaves are ternate or biternate, the segments broadly ovate and serrate; those up the stem have inflated membranous sheathing stalks. The fruit is a broadly winged ribbed achene.

Masterwort grows wild in the hills and mountains of central and southern Europe, usually alongside streams, in damp meadows and by springs. It was once often grown as a medicinal plant and pot herb. In the British Isles it is naturalized in a few places, having originally been a garden escape. The common name Masterwort comes through the German *meisterwurz* (master root) from the medieval Latin word *magistrantia*, after the use of the 'hot' pungent rootstock against 'cold' diseases (the plant promotes sweating). It is now rarely used in herbal medicine in Britain.

The rhizomes are the medicinal parts. When dry they have a penetrating aroma and burning taste and cause salivation. The constituents include a large amount of essential oil with limonene, phellandrene and pinene as its main components, plus a coumarin glycoside (imperatorin), bitter compounds and tannins. These substances give Masterwort diuretic, diaphoretic, stomachic and carminative properties. It is used in an infusion or in powder form for anorexia, digestive disorders, flatulence and enteritis. **In large doses it is toxic.** A tincture of the fresh rhizome is used in homeopathy for similar complaints.

Flowering time: July to August

Kidney Bean, French Bean, Haricot Bean

A cultivated annual herb that is either a shrub (bush or dwarf beans) or a vine (pole beans). In the second instance the stem may be up to 3 metres long, it twines spirally upwards anticlockwise, and has alternate trifoliate leaves. The flowers, of various colours, are arranged in scanty racemes growing from the leaf axils. The fruit is a slightly curved pod with usually kidney-shaped seeds of various sizes and colours.

Kidney Bean is native to tropical America and was first cultivated by the American Indians in prehistoric times. The plant is now grown all over the world in a great many forms and varieties as a vegetable and ornamental plant. Some varieties are cultivated for the stringless green or yellow pods and boiled and eaten as a vegetable; some are grown for the large, edible seeds which are dried before sale. Scarlet Runner Bean (*P. coccineus*) and Lima Bean (*P. lunatus*), grown as ornamentals and vegetables, also have medicinal value. The generic name, *Phaseolus,* comes from the Greek word *phaselos* (= a little boat), supposedly because of the pod's appearance. 'Bean' is an Anglo-Saxon word.

The dry ripe pods without the seeds are used medicinally. Their constituents include amino acids, vitamin C, mineral substances and starch. These substances give Kidney Bean diuretic and hypoglycaemic properties. It is included in herbal tea mixtures to treat rheumatism and kidney disorders. The dried seeds, ground into a powder, are used to make hot poultices for application to eczema. **The seeds should never be used internally in whole or in powdered form as a remedy, or eaten raw or partially cooked** because they contain a toxic cyanogenic glycoside (phasine), which can cause damage to the red blood cells and intestinal lining. It is not destroyed by drying. Properly cooked, however, beans are harmless and nutritious.

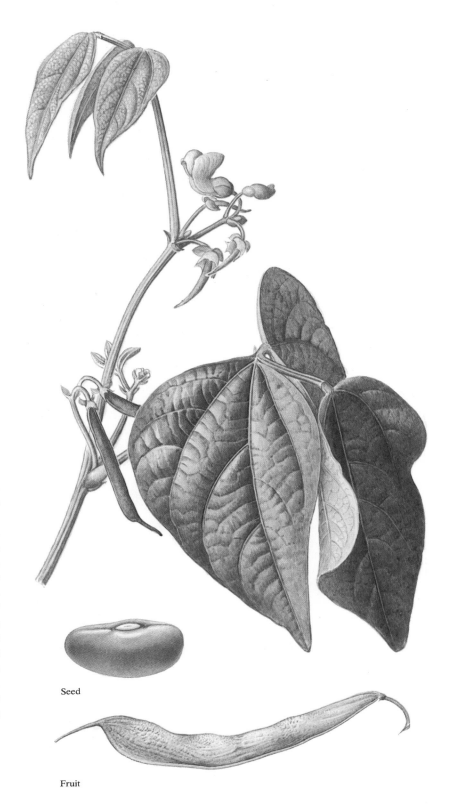

Seed

Fruit

Flowering time: June to September

Cape Gooseberry, Chinese Lantern, Winter Cherry

Fruit with part of calyx

A perennial herb with a creeping rhizome, erect, angled stems and opposite, stalked, triangular to ovate and pointed leaves. The stalked, dirty-white, funnel-shaped flowers grow singly in the upper leaf axils. After flowering the net-veined calyx increases in size, encloses the round fruit (a red or orange berry) and turns orange red (the so-called Chinese lantern).

Cape Gooseberry grows wild in central and eastern Europe and Asia. It is a popular garden ornamental and is sometimes found as a garden escape in other parts of Europe. In the British Isles it has become naturalized in waste places and hedges in a few localities. The generic name, *Physalis,* comes from the Greek word *physa* (= a bladder), a reference to the inflated, paper-thin calyx. The fruits have been used in herbal remedies but mostly they are now eaten whole or in preserves.

The ripe fruits, without the calyx, contain a bitter compound (physalin), alkaloids, organic pigments and vitamin C. They are diuretic and can be used to treat kidney and urinary disorders, gravel, gout, arthritis and rheumatism. Because of their high concentration of vitamin C the fresh berries are also beneficial during convalescence. They can be eaten on their own (in small quantities, otherwise they may cause diarrhoea), in jam or made into a tea.

The dried Chinese lanterns make an attractive winter decoration as they retain their shape and colour for a long time.

Flowering time: July

Anise, Aniseed

An annual herb with an erect, branched, ribbed stem, which bears long-stalked, lobed, cordate and coarsely toothed lower leaves and finely divided, feathery, ternate or pinnate upper leaves. The small white flowers are arranged in compound umbels. The fruit is a ribbed, roundish double achene. All parts of the plant are strongly aromatic.

Anise is native to the eastern Mediterranean region and was first cultivated and used as a spice by the ancient Egyptians and later by the Greeks and Romans. It is now widely grown in warm countries for the pharmaceutical, liqueur and confectionery industries. In the British Isles Anise seeds ripen only in good summers. The common name Anise comes through the Latin word *anisum* from the Greek name *anison* for the plant. Anise has kept its traditional reputation as a digestive tonic and cough medicine. For flavouring it is nowadays often replaced by the less-expensive Star Anise (*Illicium verum*).

The fruits are used medicinally. Their constituents include an essential oil (aniseed oil) with anethole as its main component, plus fatty oil, proteins, sugars and organic acids. The medicinal action is mostly due to the essential oil which gives the fruits aromatic, expectorant, antispasmodic, carminative, diuretic, antiseptic and galactagogic properties. The essential oil, which is obtained by steam distillation, is an ingredient of carminative and expectorant medicines for children and it is used to flavour various proprietary preparations. Alcohol extracts of Anise fruits are also used in the manufacture of various medicines.

The greatest quantities of Anise, however, are used to flavour liqueurs and confectionery and in perfumery.

Fruit

Flowering time: July to August

Burnet Saxifrage

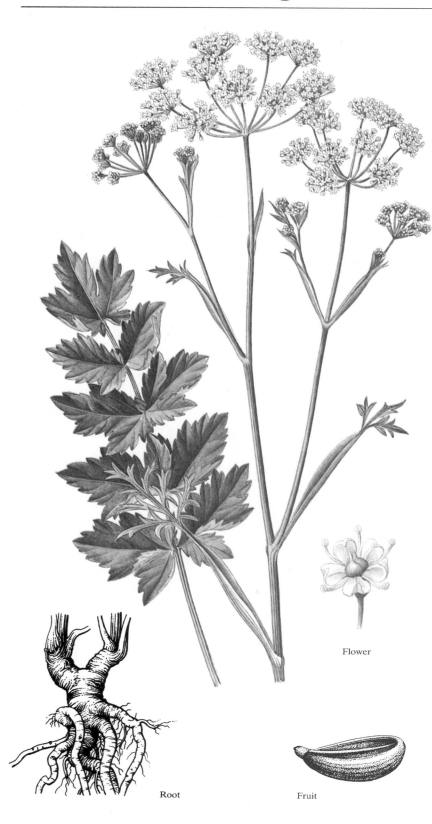

Flower

Root

Fruit

A perennial herb with a spindle-shaped taproot and an erect, finely ribbed and usually downy stem, which is branched above. The basal leaves are odd-pinnate; the stem leaves have sheath-like stalks and more divided, linear leaflets. The small white flowers are arranged in terminal umbels. The fruit is an ovoid, compressed, double achene with five slender ribs.

Burnet Saxifrage grows throughout all of Europe in dry grassy places, usually on lime-rich soils. In the British Isles, where it is native, it is less common in the north. The larger Greater Burnet Saxifrage (*P. major*) also grows wild in Britain – in shady grassy places – but is generally less frequent than *P. saxifraga*. Burnet saxifrages were given the second half of their common names, which come from the Latin word *saxum* (= rock) and *frangere* (= to break), because they were thought to break up and remove kidney and bladder stones. Their leaves resemble those of burnets (*Sanguisorba*) (Pl. 213), which is how the plants came to acquire the first part of their name, but the two genera are not closely related. Burnet Saxifrage and Greater Burnet Saxifrage have similar medicinal properties and both are still used in herbal medicine.

The roots are the medicinally active parts. Whey dry they have a strong aroma – of billy-goat – and absorb moisture easily. The constituents include an essential oil, furanocoumarins and their derivative pimpinellin, tannins, saponins and resin. These substances give Burnet Saxifrage expectorant, antispasmodic, stomachic, diuretic and antiseptic properties. It is used in an infusion or powdered form to treat asthma, infections of the upper respiratory tract, digestive disorders, flatulence and diarrhoea. **Large doses can harm the kidneys.** Externally Burnet Saxifrage is used in compresses and bath preparations to treat slow-healing wounds and in gargles.

Flowering time: July to August

Common Butterwort

A perennial carnivorous herb with a basal rosette of sticky, entire, fleshy, bright yellow-green, ovate leaves. The stickiness is caused by a fluid secreted by warty glands and this catches and digests insects which provide the plant with the nitrogen it needs. The leaves curl up round an insect should one become entrapped. Rising from the centre of the rosette are scapes, which are topped by two-lipped, tubular, bluish-white flowers with a long slender spur. The fruit is an ovoid capsule which splits into two halves.

Common Butterwort grows wild in northern and central Europe in bogs, on damp heaths, moors and damp rocks. It has, however, become rare and is protected in many countries. In the British Isles it is still common, except in the south. Common Butterwort has been used to curdle milk in butter making, particularly in Scandinavian countries, hence its name. The generic name, *Pinguicula,* comes from the Latin word *pinguiculus* (= 'somewhat fat') and refers to the greasiness of the leaves. The leaves were once used to soothe sore and chapped skin and as a skin softener. The plant is nowadays little used in herbal medicine.

The flowering stems are the medicinally active parts. Their constituents include proteolytic enzymes, organic acids and mucilage. These substances give Common Butterwort antispasmodic, demulcent and expectorant properties and it has been used in an infusion for persistent cough, whooping cough, asthma and bronchitis, especially in children. In homeopathy a tincture prepared from fresh material is prescribed for similar disorders. The fresh leaves are effective against slow-healing cuts and sores.

Flower

Flowering time: May to June

Scots Pine

Needles (from left to right):

P. mugo, P. sylvestris,
P. nigra, P. strobus

A tall coniferous tree with a flat crown, when mature, and rusty coloured bark on the upper trunk and branches, greyish-brown and furrowed bark on the older wood. The paired needles are long, stiff, glossy bluish green and usually twisted. (The needles of Mountain Pine (*P. mugo*) are slightly smaller and in long sheaths; those of Black or Austrian Pine (*P. nigra*) long and coarse; and those of Weymouth Pine (*P. strobus*) long, soft and slender and in clusters of five.) Scots Pine is monoecious with the female flowers in small reddish cones in pairs at the end of the shoots and the male flowers in clusters at the base of the shoots. When the sharp-pointed female cones are ripe − after two or three years − the cone scales open to release the winged seeds. All parts of the tree contain resin.

Scots Pine is Britain's only native large conifer. It is still common in the highlands of Scotland but the ancient forests there are now much depleted. It has been widely planted elsewhere. It thrives best on poor sandy soils. The tree was a major source of turpentine, resin and tar in the past.

The young shoots are used medicinally. They contain an essential oil with mainly bornyl acetate, fatty acids, resin and a large amount of vitamin C (in fresh material). These substances give Scots Pine expectorant, antiseptic, irritant and diuretic properties. It is seldom used internally because **it can irritate and harm the kidneys** but externally it is used in inhalent mixtures for coughs, bronchitis, asthma and other respiratory disorders, and in bath preparations and poultices for rheumatism, rashes and ulcerous conditions. The resin extract is a component of liniments and plasters used to treat rheumatic and arthritic pain, strained muscles and frostbite. The pollen has been used in powders to treat chafed skin and in rejuvenating cures. The essential oil, extracted by steam or water distillation from this and other *Pinus* species, is also used medicinally − again mainly for respiratory disorders.

Flowering time: May to June

Ribwort Plantain

A perennial herb with lanceolate, parallel-veined leaves arranged in a basal rosette and long, erect, five-angled, furrowed, leafless flowering stems. The inconspicuous brownish flowers are arranged in a dense cylindrical spike. The long white stamens are very conspicuous. The stems and leaves are silky hairy. The fruit is a two-seeded capsule, which opens by a cap.

Ribwort Plantain grows throughout Europe in dry grassy places such as roadsides, pastures and lawns. It is a common native plant in the British Isles. In some countries it is now commercially cultivated for the pharmaceutical industry. The generic name, *Plantago,* is derived from the Latin word *planta* (= sole of the foot) because the shape of the leaves of some plantain species resembles a footprint. Ribwort Plantain is distinct in having narrow, lance-shaped leaves, hence the specific epithet *lanceolata.* The prominent veins on the leaves gave the plant its common name. This species is just one of several plantains that have long traditional uses as healing herbs for sores and bites. The mucilaginous seeds of two species in particular, Psyllium or Fleaseed (*P. psyllium*) and Ispaghula (*P. ovata*), are also widely used as laxatives.

The leaves and seeds are used medicinally. The most important constituent of the leaves is an iridoid glycoside (aucubin). It is unstable and causes the dried leaves to darken. Other constituents include mucilage, carotenes, tannins, enzymes and silicic acid. These substances give the leaves expectorant, emollient, demulcent, vulnerary and astringent properties. An infusion of them is used for cough, whooping cough, hoarseness, bronchitis and other respiratory disorders. Coughing in children is alleviated by a thickened syrup made from the leaves sweetened with honey. The seeds contain abundant mucilage, fatty oil, aucubin and enzymes. Swallowed whole they are an effective and harmless laxative. Crushed fresh leaves can be applied externally to swellings, bruises and inflamed wounds.

Flowering time: April to August

Dwarf Milkwort, Bitter Milkwort

Flower

A perennial herb with a branched rhizome and a short, erect or ascending stem, woody at the base, which bears small lanceolate leaves. The larger obovate to elliptic basal leaves are arranged in a dense rosette. The blue flowers are arranged in a terminal raceme. The two inner sepals are petal-like and much larger than the three outer ones and they are arranged on either side of the three true petals, which are joined at the base, the largest and lower one keeled and fringed. The stamens are joined to form a tube. The fruit is a two-seeded, heart-shaped capsule.

Dwarf Milkwort is native to Europe where it has a scattered distribution in damp upland pastures or dry stony grassland, mostly in central Europe. It occurs only rarely in the British Isles on lime-rich soils in southeastern and northern England. Common Milkwort (*P. vulgaris*) is encountered more often in Britain. The generic name, *Polygala,* comes from the Greek words *polu-* (= much, many) and *gala* (= milk) for the plant was believed to increase milk flow in nursing mothers and in cows.

The flowering stems, sometimes with the roots, are used medicinally. When dry they have a distinctive bitter taste (the specific epithet *amara* means bitter). The constituents include important triterpenoid saponins (senegins), a bitter compound (polygamarin), the glycoside gaultherin, tannins and an essential oil. These substances give Dwarf Milkwort expectorant, stomachic and diuretic properties. It is used in the form of a decoction or powder to treat coughs, bronchitis and other infections of the upper respiratory tract, and digestive disorders. It is also included in proprietary expectorant medicines. In folk medicine it is still recommended for nursing mothers but it has not yet been etablished whether the plant really is a galactagogue.

Flowering time: May to August

Angular Solomon's Seal

☠

A perennial herb with a thick, white, creeping rhizome and angled, arched stems, which bear numerous alternate, ovate to elliptic leaves in two rows. The white, drooping, tubular fragrant flowers grow singly or in pairs from the leaf axils. The fruit is a dark-blue berry. **All parts of the plant are poisonous** and children should be warned not to eat the berries which may be mistaken for bilberries.

Angular Solomon's Seal has a scattered distribution throughout Europe in woods and copses, usually on lime-rich soils. It is native to the British Isles but it occurs only in northern and western England and Wales, where it is rare. Two other species of Solomon's seal occur in Britain: Solomon's Seal (*P. multiflorum*), which is found in woods in most parts of England and Wales but is common only in the south, has rounded stems and clusters of bell-shaped flowers constricted in the middle. Much rarer is Whorled Solomon's Seal (*P. verticillatum*), which grows in mountain woods in Scotland. It is distinguished by its whorls of lanceolate leaves and flowers and its berry, which is red at first, then dark blue. These two species of Solomon's seal are also poisonous. The generic name, *Polygonatum,* comes from the Greek words meaning 'much jointed' and refers either to the swellings on the roots or to the jointed stems. The common name, Solomon's seal, may allude to the circular scars on the rootstock left by the stems of the previous years.

The roots and rhizomes are the medicinal parts. Their constituents include starch, saponins, mucilage, tannins, sugar and organic pigments. These substances give Angular Solomon's Seal diuretic, hypoglycaemic, astringent and vulnerary properties. It has been used internally as a diuretic but mostly it is used only externally in compresses or bath preparations for treating rheumatism, bruises, eczema and other skin disorders. **All species of Solomon's seal should be taken internally only under the supervision of a qualified medical or herbal practitioner;** large doses can be harmful.

Flowering time: June to July

Fruit

Root

Flower cluster:

P. verticillatum   *P. multiflorum*

Knotgrass

Flower

An annual herb with branched prostrate or erect stems and shortly stalked, alternate, linear to ovate leaves with silvery stipules at their bases. The small white or pinkish flowers grow in clusters in the axils of the upper leaves. The fruit is a three-sided achene surrounded by the persistent perianth.

Knotgrass is a common spreading weed of waste places, roadsides, arable land and rocky seashores throughout the British Isles, where it is native. It is also widespread on the Continent. The generic name, *Polygonum,* has the same origin as *Polygonatum* (Pl. 173) and it and the common name refer to the numerous swollen joints on the stem. The specific epithet, *aviculare,* means a small bird and comes from the fact that small birds often feed on the fruits. Knotgrass was once believed to be effective against cholera and tuberculosis. It is still used by herbalists as a remedy for diarrhoea.

The flowering stems are used medicinally. They are usually collected in autumn when they have the greatest concentration of silicic acid. They also contain tannins, a flavonoid glycoside (avicularin) and perhaps also saponins. Knotgrass, like other members of the dock (Polygonaceae) family, has strong astringent and haemostatic properties and it is used in an infusion to check external and internal bleeding, gastritis and enteritis and severe diarrhoea. The infusion also acts as a tonic. Knotgrass is also a component of diuretic tea mixtures taken for kidney disorders, uroliths and kidney stones.

Flowering time: June to September

Common Bistort, Snakeroot

A perennial herb with a stout, snake-like twisted rhizome and an erect, unbranched stem. The basal ovate to lanceolate leaves with undulate margins and winged petioles are arranged in a rosette; the smaller stem leaves are triangular, sessile and clasp the stem. The pink flowers are arranged in a dense terminal spike. The fruit is a three-sided achene surrounded by the persistent perianth.

Common Bistort grows throughout Europe in damp meadows and other grassy places, often on silica-rich soils. It is widespread and fairly frequent in the British Isles, especially in northern England and southern Scotland; it is rare in Ireland. The common name, Bistort, comes from the Latin word *bistorta* (= twice twisted) and refers to the contorted rootstock, as does the alternative common name, Snakeroot. Common Bistort was traditionally used to treat dysentery and infectious diseases, to stop bleeding and to treat snake bite. A traditional pudding, known as Easter ledges, is still made from the young leaves in Cumbria and Yorkshire and the plant has been known by this name. It remains a popular herbal remedy, especially for diarrhoea and throat and mouth infections.

The rhizomes are used medicinally. Their constituents include abundant tannins (15−20 per cent), starch, a bitter compound (catechin) and silicic acid. These substances (especially the tannins) give Common Bistort strong astringent, antidiarrhoeal, haemostatic and anti-inflammatory properties. The dried rhizome is used in infusions, decoctions or in powder form to check internal and external bleeding, to treat gastritis and enteritis, severe diarrhoea, dysentery and incontinence of urine. The high concentration of starch in the rhizome, which produces mucilage, is also beneficial. Externally Common Bistort is used in gargles, mouthwashes, compresses and bath preparations.

The young leaves can be eaten in salads or cooked like spinach and the root is edible after it has been soaked and roasted.

Flower

Flowering time: June to August

Waterpepper, Smartweed

An annual herb with a semi-erect branched stem and lanceolate leaves with undulate margins and glandular below. The small pink or greenish flowers are arranged in loose terminal, interrupted, often nodding spikes. The perianth segments are dotted with numerous yellow glands. The fruit is a three-sided dull, brownish-black achene.

Waterpepper is native to Europe, including the British Isles, and is common in damp places on rich soils, often near shallow water. It has an acrid and burning taste and was once used as a substitute for pepper (hence the common name). The fresh herb was also used to cure scurvy.

The flowering stems are used medicinally. The most important constituents are tannins. The plant also contains bitter compounds, an essential oil, a glycoside, formic acid, acetic acid, polygonic acid and vitamin C (in fresh material). These substances give Waterpepper strong astringent, haemostatic, diuretic and anti-inflammatory properties. It is used in an infusion or powder form for uterine haemorrhage and menstrual disorders, for dropsy and other urinary complaints, rheumatism, diarrhoea and haemorrhoids. Fresh bruised leaves can be applied to bleeding or slow-healing wounds. Waterpepper is also used in homeopathy and in veterinary medicine. **Large doses of Waterpepper should not be taken** because they may cause gastrointestinal irritation. The fresh juice may also irritate the skin.

Flowering time: July onwards

Pale Persicaria

An annual herb with ascending or prostrate branched stems, which are swollen above the nodes. The alternate, broadly ovate to lanceolate leaves have undulate margins and usually a brown spot shaped like a half moon and whitish dots on the upper surface; they may be slightly cobwebby below. The small pinkish or greenish-white flowers are arranged in longish, dense, terminal, erect spikes. The perianth segments, peduncles and leaves are glandular. The fruit is a three-sided achene.

Pale Persicaria grows throughout Europe on stream banks, in ditches, beside ponds, in waste places and on cultivated ground. It is a common native British plant. Botanically it is an aggregate species with several subspecies and hybrids. The common name is a corruption of the former generic name, *Persicaria,* which comes from the Latin word *persicum* (= a peach). The specific epithet, *lapathifolium,* means 'sorrel-like leaf'. Pale Persicaria is still used in herbal medicine on the Continent where it is a traditional remedy for acute pain caused by kidney stones.

The flowering stems are used medicinally. Their constituents include tannins, an essential oil, organic acids and a large amount of vitamin C (in fresh material). These substances give Pale Persicaria astringent, haemostatic and diuretic properties and it is used to check internal and external bleeding, diarrhoea and various urinary disorders.

Leaf

Flowering time: June onwards

Polypody

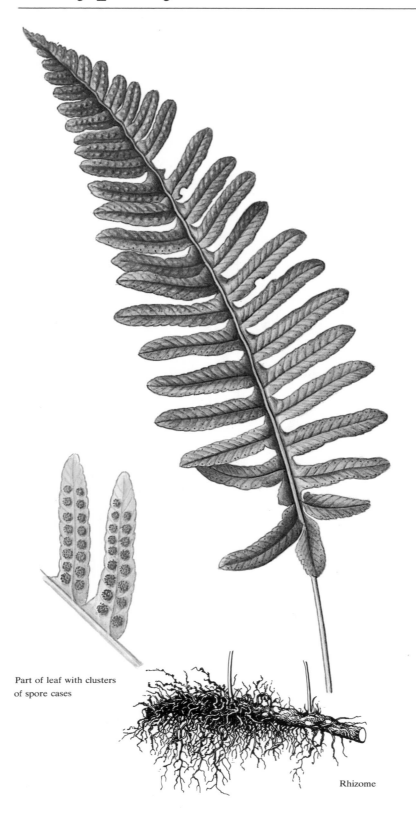

A perennial fern with a creeping, slightly flattened, branched rhizome, which bears numerous red-brown scales. Each year new fronds arise alongside the old, over-wintering ones. The fronds are simple, long-stalked, smooth and pinnately divided with lanceolate segments (pinnae), rounded at the tip. Clusters of spore cases (sori) are arranged in two rows on the undersides of the upper segments. The sori are orange at first, later brown.

Polypody is common throughout Europe, including the British Isles, in damp shady woods and on rocks, especially in wetter districts. The generic and common names come from the Greek words *polu* (= many) and *pous or podos* (= a foot), a reference to the branched and creeping habit of the rhizome. In the past Polypody was principally used as a mild purgative and expectorant. It was known to the ancient Greeks. It remains popular for coughs and chest complaints.

The rhizomes are used medicinally. When dry they break easily, are greenish inside and have a sweet flavour. Their constituents include fatty oil, an essential oil, bitter compounds, a saponin, sugars and mucilage. These substances give Polypody expectorant, diuretic, cholagogic, laxative and anthelmintic properties. It is used in an infusion or in powder form for persistent chest and lung infections, gall bladder disorders, urinary infections such as cystitis, and for worm infestations.

Part of leaf with clusters
of spore cases

Rhizome

Black Poplar

A large deciduous tree with spreading branches that arch downwards and brown, later greyish-black, deeply furrowed bark. The alternate, serrate leaves are triangular-ovate with a wedge-like base and flattened petioles. The reddish-brown axillary buds are long and sticky and curve upwards at the tip. Black Poplar is dioecious, with crimson male and green female flowers in catkins that open early in spring before the leaves appear. The stigmas are greenish. The fruit is a capsule which releases seeds with a white pappus.

Black Poplar is probably native in wet woods and beside streams in eastern and central England; elsewhere it is naturalized. It is a fast-growing tree and is often planted as a screen beside roads and industrial buildings. Introduced hybrids are also planted. Aspen (*P. tremula*) (Pl. 180) and White Poplar (*P. alba*) are closely related trees. White Poplar is not native to Britain but is a popular ornamental tree, often planted as wind-breaks. The generic and common names come from the Latin word *populus* (= people). Poplars were much planted in Roman cities and were 'trees of the people'.

The leaf buds are used medicinally. Their constituents include an essential oil, tannins, the phenolic glycosides salicin and populin, and resin. These substances give Black Poplar pronounced diuretic, anti-inflammatory and antiseptic properties. It is used in an infusion for infections of the upper respiratory tract, for gout (it reduces the amount of uric acid in the blood), and to relieve rheumatic pain. An ointment from the dried or fresh buds — or from the dried or fresh bark of young twigs — is applied externally to treat skin rashes, cuts, haemorrhoids and arthritic and rheumatic joints. White Poplar and Aspen have similar medicinal uses.

Flower cluster

Leaf and twig with buds

Flowering time: April

Aspen

Leaf and twig with buds

A small deciduous tree with smooth bark, which is yellowish at first, blackish later. The alternate, almost circular leaves have bluntly toothed or wavy edges and strongly sideways-flattened petioles, which tremble in the slightest breeze. The slightly sticky buds are stoutly oval. Aspen is dioecious with separate male and female catkins, which have purple hairy bracts. The female flowers have purple stigmas. The flowers open before the leaves appear. The fruit is a capsule which releases seeds with a white pappus.

Aspen grows throughout Europe, including the British Isles, in open woods, especially on poorer soils. It is also often planted in gardens and avenues. Aspen, and the old name Asp, come from the Anglo-Saxon name *aespe* for the tree. The word 'asp' was sometimes used to mean tremulous, after the trembling leaves. The specific epithet also refers to this distinctive feature of the tree. Except on the Continent, Aspen is not widely used in herbal medicine. A better-known resinous product from poplar buds is balm of Gilead, which comes from the tree called Balm of Gilead (*P. gileadensis* or *P. candicans*), from Balsam Poplar (*P. balsamifera*) or American Aspen (*P. tremuloides*). Balm of Gilead is also obtained from a North American fir (*Abies balsamea*). The true balm of Gilead is, however, the resin of tropical shrubs or small trees of the genus *Commiphora*.

The leaf buds, occasionally the young bark and the leaves of Aspen, are used medicinally. Like the buds of Black Poplar (*P. nigra*) (Pl. 179), Aspen buds contain the phenolic glycosides salicin and populin, also an essential oil and bitter compounds. These substances give Aspen strong diuretic, anti-inflammatory and antiseptic properties and the buds are used in an infusion for infections of the urinary tract, enlarged prostate gland, for gout and rheumatism. Externally compresses, bath preparations and ointments are used for haemorrhoids and for the treatment of burns. Preparations from fresh leaves are used in homeopathy.

Flowering time: February to March

Silverweed

A perennial herb with a short rhizome and prostrate rooting stolons. The leaves are odd-pinnate with pairs of larger leaflets alternating with smaller ones. The leaflets are oval to oblong, coarsely serrate and usually silvery silky on both sides or only below. The bright-yellow, long-stalked solitary flowers grow from the leaf axils. The fruit is an achene.

Silverweed grows throughout most of Europe on waste ground, roadsides and in pastures on damp rich soil. It is native to the British Isles and common. Grazing animals seem to find it an attractive food. In the past the starchy rootstock was cooked and eaten as a vegetable or ground to make bread and porridge. The generic name, *Potentilla,* comes from the Latin word *potens* (= powerful), after the medicinal action of some of the species. The specific epithet, *anserina,* from the Latin word *anser* (= a goose), was probably given to the plant because geese are thought to be partial to the leaves. The silvery appearance of the plant gave it its old name of *Argentina* (from *argentum* = silver) and its common name Silverweed. It has long been a traditional treatment for bleeding and for cosmetic purposes. It was once used to remove freckles, spots and other blemishes.

The flowering stems and leaves, and sometimes the rhizomes are used medicinally. The constituents of the aerial parts include tannins, bitter compounds, mucilage, organic pigments and mineral compounds. These substances give Silverweed strong astringent, anti-inflammatory, haemostatic, antiseptic and stomachic properties. An infusion is used for gastritis and enteritis, severe diarrhoea, indigestion, colic, internal haemorrhage, bladder and kidney complaints and excessive menstrual bleeding. Externally Silverweed is used in gargles to relieve painful gums and toothache and in bath preparations and compresses to treat wounds, swellings and skin disorders. In homeopathy a tincture prepared from the fresh plant is used for stomach disorders and for painful menstruation.

Flowering time: June to August

Leaf

Tormentil, Tormentilla

Dried, cut rhizome

A perennial herb with a stout rhizome and ascending or almost erect, non-rooting branched stems. The basal leaves are stalked, coarsely toothed, ternate and are arranged in a rosette; the stem leaves are sessile, also ternate, but they have in addition a pair of palmately lobed leafy stipules. The long-stalked yellow flowers are arranged in loose terminal cymes. Unusually for the rose family (Rosaceae), they mostly have only four (not five) petals and sepals. The fruit is an achene. The fresh rhizome is red-fleshed and has a pleasant rose-like scent.

Tormentil grows throughout Europe, including the British Isles, in grassland, open woods, heaths, bogs and fens, especially on light acid soils. The common name Tormentil is believed to come through a medieval Latin word *tormentilla* from *tormentum* (= pain), supposedly a reference to the use of the herb to relieve griping stomach pains and toothache. The strongly astringent rootstock is still used in herbal medicine but in conventional medicine it has largely been replaced by the equally astringent Rhatany (*Krameria triandra*). A red dye was once extracted from Tormentil rhizomes and the root-stocks were also used to tan hides.

The rhizomes are the medicinally active parts. Their constituents include abundant tannins (up to 20 per cent), the triterpene alcohol tormentol, a glycoside (tormentillin), starch, sugars and a bitter compound (chinovic acid). These substances give Tormentil strong astringent, haemostatic, anti-inflammatory, vulnerary and antiseptic properties. It is used in decoctions or powder form for diarrhoea, dysentery, and internal gastric and intestinal bleeding. **Tormentil must be used internally with care;** strong doses may cause vomiting. Externally Tormentil is used in compresses or ointments for slow-healing wounds, skin rashes, grazes, burns and sunburn. A tincture or decoction is used as a gargle for throat and mouth inflammations.

Flowering time: June to September

Cowslip

A perennial herb with a short, stout rhizome, dense fibrous roots and wrinkled, toothed, finely hairy, ovate to oblong, stalked leaves, which are arranged in a rosette. From the rosette in spring arise one or more scapes each with up to 30 sweet-scented, deep-yellow flowers in a nodding terminal umbel. The corolla has orange spots in the throat. The fruit is a capsule enclosed by the calyx.

Cowslip was once widespread in the British Isles in meadows and pastures, especially on lime-rich soils. It is now much less abundant. In some European countries it is protected. It is often grown in gardens and there are numerous cultivated varieties. Cowslip is often mistaken for Oxslip (*P. elatior*), which is a hybrid between Cowslip and Primrose (*P. vulgaris*) and is distinguished from Cowslip in having larger pale-yellow flowers in a one-sided cluster. The generic name, *Primula*, is from the Latin word *primus* (= first) and refers to the early flowering of some members of the genus. The meaning of the common name, Cowslip, is obscure, but it could be derived from the Anglo-Saxon word *cuslyppe,* meaning cow dung or cowpat, an allusion to the plant's occurrence in cow pastures.

The flowers, with or without the calyx, and occasionally the rootstock, are used medicinally. The constituents of the flowers include a flavonoid (quercetin), saponins (in the calyx) and an essential oil. The rhizomes and roots contain a relatively large amount of saponins, the glycosides primulaveroside and primveroside and glucuronic acid. These substances give Cowslip expectorant, antispasmodic and diuretic properties, the rootstock being stronger than the flowers. An infusion is used for respiratory infections. Cowslip is also included in various proprietary expectorant preparations. The flowers make a tea substitute, which is mildly sedative; they can also be candied for cake decorations and made into wine. Oxlip has similar uses. **Some *Primula* species cause dermatitis in hypersensitive individuals.**

Flower of *P. elatior*

Flowering time: April to May

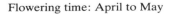

Selfheal

Segment of fruit (mericarp)

A low perennial herb with a creeping rhizome which bears erect or ascending, square, red-tinged stems, branched below. The opposite stalked leaves are ovate and entire or serrate. The blue-violet, two-lipped flowers are arranged in dense, terminal, oblong, spike-like panicles. The corolla has a hooded upper lip. The fruit consists of four smooth brown nutlets, each with a ridge running from the apex to the base. The flowers are attractive to bees.

Selfheal grows throughout Europe in grassland, woodland clearings, hedgerows and waste places. It is a common native plant in the British Isles. It was a traditional remedy for throat infections and the generic name, *Prunella,* is supposed to come through *brunella* from a German word, *die Braûne* for sore throat. Selfheal was also regarded as a valuable healer of wounds, hence the principal common name and many alternatives (for example, Hook Heal, All Heal and Woundwort).

The flowering stems are used medicinally. Their constituents include tannins, bitter compounds, an essential oil, saponins and a glycoside (aucubin). These substances give Selfheal astringent, anti-inflammatory, haemostatic and antiseptic properties. An infusion is sometimes used to check diarrhoea, internal bleeding and in the treatment of peptic and duodenal ulcers. Its most important use nowadays is, however, as a mouthwash or gargle for throat and mouth infections.

The tender young leaves can be added to salads or prepared like spinach.

Flowering time: June to September

Dwarf Cherry, Sour Cherry, Morello Cherry

A deciduous shrub or small tree that sends out suckering shoots and has smooth, shiny, brownish-red bark that peels off in strips around the trunk, and spreading or ascending branches. The alternate leaves are ovate, dark green, glossy above and finely serrate. The small white or pinkish flowers, with bud scales and leaf-like bracts at the base, grow in clusters on shortened twigs. The fruit is an edible dark-red, globose, bitter drupe.

Sour Cherry is native to Asia but it has been introduced to other parts of the world and it is now grown in many cultivated varieties. It is naturalized in hedges in a few localities in England, Wales and Ireland. *Prunus* is the ancient Latin name for a plum tree, but the genus as a whole now includes such trees as Wild Cherry (*P. avium*), Almond (*P. dulcis*) (Pl. 186), Cherry Plum (*P. cerasifera*), Cherry Laurel (*P. laurocerasus*), Bird Cherry (*P. padus*) (Pl. 187), Peach (*Prunus persica*) and Blackthorn or Sloe (*P. spinosa*) (Pl. 188). The word cherry and the specific and former generic names *Cerasus* come from the Greek word *kerasos* for cherry. The wood of Sour Cherry and the similar Wild Cherry is used to make furniture, veneers and ornamental carvings.

The fruit stalks, fruit and leaves are used medicinally. The main constituents of the stalks are tannins, flavonoids and potassium salts. These substances give Sour Cherry astringent and diuretic properties and the stalks are included in tea mixtures used in herbalism to treat bronchitis, diarrhoea and as part of a weight-loss regime. The leaves have similar properties; they also relieve flatulence and have a beneficial effect on anaemia. The fresh juice from the fruits has a large concentration of iron and calcium salts, besides tannins and organic acids, and it is used for digestive disorders, poor liver function and for anaemia. A syrup made from the ripe fruits is also used to improve the taste of various medicines.

The fruits can be eaten stewed or bottled or made into conserves.

Flowering time: May

Twig with fruits

Piece of bark showing gummosis
(production of excessive gum)

Almond

Kernel (almond)

Fruit

A deciduous shrub or small tree with smooth reddish bark, spreading branches and alternate, stalked, oblong to lanceolate, glossy and finely serrate leaves. The white or pink sessile flowers appear in early spring before the leaves. The fruit is an elliptical, light-green, velvety drupe which contains one (rarely two) oval seeds (almonds) in their hard-pitted shell.

Almond is native to the Caucasus region but it was introduced to southern Europe in ancient times and it is now grown in all parts of the world. Many varieties have been developed, among them the Bitter Almond (var. *amara*) and Sweet Almond (var. *dulcis*). **The raw Bitter Almond seed is highly poisonous,** but the extracted oil is edible. Almonds were probably introduced into England by the Romans but the tree may not have been grown in Britain until the 16th century, and then mainly for its blossom. Almond is sensitive to frost and in Britain the fruits rarely ripen fully because the summers are too cold. The common name Almond comes through old French and Latin words from the Greek name *amugdale* for the tree.

From the medical viewpoint bitter almonds are more useful than sweet almonds. They contain up to 50 per cent fatty oil, proteins, enzymes, vitamins, sugar and the cyanogenic glycoside amygdalin, which on hydrolysis produces the poisonous prussic acid. A medicinal water made from bitter almonds is used to treat cough, nausea, vomiting and retching. It was once used to flavour other medicines but has been replaced by other natural substances or by synthetic extracts. More important is the extracted oil, from both bitter and sweet almonds. Sweet almond oil is used to prepare emulsions in which other remedies may be suspended, especially cough medicines, and it is used in massages. The oil from both almonds is widely used in cosmetic and toilet preparations and in the confectionery, perfumery and liqueur industries.

Sweet almonds are the familiar nuts used in sweet and savoury dishes.

Flowering time: March to April

Bird Cherry

A deciduous shrub or small tree with peeling brown bark and alternate, stalked, ovate and finely serrate leaves with flattened red glands on each side of the petioles. The white flowers are arranged in long, loose racemes, which are erect at first, then drooping. The fruit is a globose, shiny black, bitter-sweet drupe. All parts of the plant have a smell of bitter almonds. Bees find the flowers very attractive.

Bird Cherry is native to Europe and Asia and grows at the edges of woods, by streams and in ravines. In the British Isles it is found much farther north than Wild Cherry (*P. avium*); it is widespread and quite common in northern England and Scotland and is probably introduced elsewhere. It is also grown in parks and gardens for ornament and several varieties have been developed. As the tree's common name implies the bitter fruit is taken by birds. Bird Cherry has a long history as a herbal remedy but is little used today. The wood, which is very tough and hard, is used for ornamental carving and to make rifle butts.

The bark from young twigs is the medicinally active part. Its constituents include the cyanogenic glycosides laurocerasin and isoamygdalin, an essential oil and tannins. These substances give Bird Cherry diuretic, sedative and antipyretic properties but it is used only rarely in folk medicine because of the danger of prussic acid poisoning. It has been used to treat rheumatic and arthritic pain and fever. **Bird Cherry should be used internally only under strict medical supervision.** It is also used in homeopathy.

Twig with fruits

Flowering time: May to June

Blackthorn, Sloe

A deciduous, much-branched and very spiny shrub that often forms dense thickets owing to its vigorous production of root suckers. The bark is brownish black. The small alternate leaves are oval, stalked, finely serrate, dull above and hairy below. The pure white flowers are solitary or in pairs and appear before the leaves. The fruits (sloes) are dark-blue, globose drupes with a whitish bloom and astringent green flesh.

Blackthorn is native to Europe and grows in dry sunny hedges, wood margins or scrub on poor stony soils. It occurs throughout the British Isles except the northernmost Scottish islands. Several varieties suitable for growing in gardens have been bred. Fruit stones have been found at Neolithic dwelling sites and so Blackthorn has had a long association with man. It is probably one of the parents of the damson and other domestic plums (*P. domestica*). The alternative common name, Sloe, is a corruption of the Anglo-Saxon word *slah* and may mean 'bluish', a reference to the fruits.

The flowers and ripe fruits are used medicinally. The constituents of the flowers include traces of flavonoid and cyanogenic glycosides (including amygdalin, but this is lost on drying), sugars, tannins and vitamin C (in fresh material). These substances give the flowers diuretic, tonic and mild laxative properties. They are used in an infusion and, in homeopathy, in tincture form. The fruits contain tannins, organic acids, pectin, sugars and vitamin C. When dried they are astringent and are used to treat bladder, kidney and stomach disorders, including diarrhoea.

The fresh fruits can be eaten raw or in a compote, or made into juice, syrup, jam and wine.

Twig with fruits (sloes)

Flowering time: March to May

Lungwort

A perennial herb with a creeping rhizome and a clump of angled, unbranched, erect or ascending stems. The alternate leaves are oval or cordate, mostly white-spotted; the lower ones are stalked, the upper ones sessile and clasping at the base. The bell-shaped flowers are arranged in terminal monochasial cymes. They are pink at first, then blue after fertilization. The fruit consists of four one-seeded nutlets. All parts of the plant are stiffly hairy.

Lungwort grows throughout most of Europe in woods, wood margins, scrub and hedgerows. It is probably not native to the British Isles but it is locally naturalized in some places, especially in the south. It is often grown in gardens for its ornamental spotted leaves, as is the related Bethlehem Sage (*P. saccharata*). The generic and common names of Lungwort refer to the blotchy leaves, which were likened to diseased lungs in the past and the plant was once used to heal various lung disorders. Narrow-leaved Lungwort (*P. angustifolia*) has also been used medicinally. It is native to the British Isles but occurs only in Hampshire, Dorset and the Isle of Wight. These lungworts should not be confused with a lichen (*Lobaria pulmonaria*), which is the lungwort sold by herbalists today and also used for chest complaints.

The leaves and flowering stems are used medicinally. Their constituents include tannins, mucilage, saponins, silicic acid and mineral salts. These substances give Lungwort emollient, expectorant, anti-inflammatory, diuretic, diaphoretic and astringent properties. It is used in herbal medicine in an infusion to soothe bronchitis, cough and whooping cough, and to check diarrhoea. Externally it is used in compresses and bath preparations for wounds and skin disorders.

Leaf: *P. officinalis*   *P. saccharata*   *P. angustifolia*

Flowering time: March to May

Sessile Oak, Durmast Oak

Twig with fruits

Leaf with gall ('oak apple')

A large deciduous tree with a long main trunk, fan-shaped crown and deeply furrowed, brownish-grey bark. The alternate, leathery, dark-green leaves are short-stalked, lobed and wedge-shaped at the base, without the 'ears' (auricles) of Pedunculate Oak (*Q. robur*) (Pl. 191). Oaks are monoecius; the greenish-yellow male flowers are arranged in slim pendulous catkins; the stalkless female flowers are arranged in bud-like spikes in the leaf axils at the tips of the twigs. The flowers are wind-pollinated. The fruit is a stalkless, bluntly conical nut (acorn) resting in a shallow scaly cup (cupule).

Sessile Oak is the dominant native oak tree of woods on wetter soils in northern and western upland regions of the British Isles. The common name Oak is a corruption of the Anglo-Saxon name *ac* for the tree. The word 'sessile' in the name refers to the acorns, which are short-stalked or sessile unlike those of Pedunculate Oak.

The bark and leaves, sometimes the leaves and galls ('oak apples') are used medicinally. The acorns are separated from the cupule, dried, divested of the seed coat and roasted. Roasting converts the starch in them into dextrins and eliminates the bitter tannins. Acorns are then a suitable food in cases of severe diarrhoea and inflammation of the lymph nodes. Roasted acorns can be ground to make a coffee substitute and mixed with cocoa and sugar to make acorn cocoa. These beverages will check diarrhoea and act as a general tonic. With their astringent, antiseptic and anti-inflammatory properties fresh oak leaves will promote the healing of wounds. They contain a flavonoid glycoside (quercitrin) besides tannins. Galls (tumours caused by a gall wasp) are a raw material for the production of pure tannins, which have many uses in medical practice in powders, gargles, ointments and other preparations for checking bleeding.

Flowering time: May

Pedunculate Oak, Common Oak

A large deciduous tree with a short trunk from which large branches arise to form a massive, round-topped crown. The brownish-grey bark is smooth at first, later deeply fissured. The alternate, leathery, dark-green, lobed leaves are almost stalkess and have 'ears' (auricles) at the base. The flowers and leaves appear together; the male flowers are in pendulous catkins; the female flowers are arranged in bud-like stalked spikes in the leaf axils at the tips of the twigs. The oblong brown acorns are on stalks.

Pedunculate Oak is the dominant native oak tree on rich heavy soils in the British Isles and is thus most common in woods and hedges of lowland areas. It has been revered in Britain since at least the times of the Druids. The timber is hard and tough, which made it the best construction material in the old days for ships and for the frames of houses (the specific epithet *robur* means strength). Tall, lightly branched trees are used today for high-class joinery and furniture. The bark was once used to tan leather.

The bark is the main medicinal part. Its constituents include tannins (7−20 per cent), pyrogallic acid and catechins. These substances give oak bark very strong astringent and also antiseptic and anti-inflammatory properties. In herbal medicine a decoction is used to treat gastroenteritis and severe diarrhoea. Externally it is used in compresses and bath preparations to treat chilblains, frostbite, burns, haemorrhoids and skin diseases, including fungal infections. A decoction will also check the sweating of feet.

Bark

Flowering time: April to May

Lesser Celandine, Pilewort

Prostrate form

A perennial herb with club-shaped tubers, branched ascending stems and long-stalked glossy, cordate leaves, which are sheathed at the base. The bright golden-yellow flowers grow singly on long stalks from the leaf axils. Each flower has three sepals and eight to twelve petals. On some plants tiny bulbils form in the leaf axils. The fruit is an achene. **The root, tubers and mature leaves are poisonous.**

Lesser Celandine forms carpeting masses in woods, meadows, scrub, grassy banks and beside streams throughout Europe, including the British Isles. It is one of the earliest of Britain's wild flowers to appear in the spring. It is a very variable plant. Despite its name it is not related to Greater Celandine (*Chelidonium majus*) (Pl. 57). The Latin word *Ranunculus* menas 'little frog' and the plants in this genus were so-named because many of the species in the group grow in marshy places. The specific epithet, *ficaria,* comes from the Latin word *ficus* (= a fig) and refers to the appearance of the tubers. The tubers also gave the plant its alternative common name, Pilewort (the plant has long been a remedy for haemorrhoids.

The flowering stems are used medicinally. Their constituents include the toxic protoanemonin and anemonin, a saponin (ficarin), tannins and abundant vitamin C (in fresh material). These substances give Lesser Celandine astringent and anti-scorbutic properties. In the past it was used internally to treat scurvy, a disease caused by lack of vitamin C in the diet. Nowadays Lesser Celandine is mostly used only externally in ointments and bath preparations for treating haemorrhoids, warts and scab. It has an acrid burning taste and is a severe irritant, especially the fresh flowering plant. Grazing cattle avoid it. **The fresh plant should never be taken internally.** Even handling the plant may cause skin blistering. It is rendered non-toxic by drying and heat-processing. The first leaves and very young top parts are also not toxic. They have been eaten like spinach, but there are safer ways of adding vitamin C to the diet.

Flowering time: March to May

Garden Radish, Radish

An annual or biennial herb with a round to spindle-shaped tuberous taproot of various colours, an erect, branched stem and lyrate, pinnately lobed, toothed leaves. The leaves and stem are stiffly hairy. The white or pinkish flowers have dark veins and are arranged in a longish terminal raceme. The fruit is a siliqua, which is prolonged into a narrow seedless beak; the seeds are brown.

The familiar Garden Radish was grown as a vegetable by the ancient Egyptians and the Greeks and Romans knew several varieties. Its origin is uncertain but it is thought to be a native of western Asia. Nowadays it is cultivated in many forms, the black-rooted variety being the one used for medicinal pruposes. Garden Radish is sometimes found growing wild as a garden escape in the British Isles. The closely related Wild Radish (*R. raphanistrum*) (its flower is pictured on Pl. 222) is a common and troublesome weed throughout Britain. It is poisonous to livestock if they eat it in large quantities. The common name, Radish, is a corruption of the Latin word *radix,* meaning root and also the Romans' name for the plant.

The black roots contain antiseptic thioglucosinolates, vitamins C and B complex and mineral salts. They are generally eaten raw and unpeeled and have antiseptic, tonic, carminative, choleretic and stomachic actions. They are used sliced or grated on bread and butter, or the pressed juice alone is taken for hepatitis and gall bladder disorders (but not for inflammation of the gall bladder), gallstones and digestive disorders. Radish is also used in homeopathy. The popular red, red and white or white radishes (*R. sativus* var. *radicula*) are less potent but are excellent and wholesome salad vegetables. The leaves are also edible.

Flowers

Fruit

Flowering time: June to August

Buckthorn

Twig with flowers

Bark

A deciduous shrub or a small tree with spiny opposite branches that often end in thorns. The bark is smooth at first, later it becomes rough and scaly. The buds are covered by dark scales. The dull-green leaves are opposite, ovate to elliptic, stalked and finely serrate, and have two or three pairs of lateral veins. The small, yellowish-green, usually unisexual flowers grow in axillary clusters on the previous year's short shoots. The fruit, a drupe, is black when ripe and contains two to four seeds. **The fruits and the fresh bark are poisonous.**

Buckthorn grows throughout Europe, including the British Isles, in hedgerows, scrub, woodland and fens, usually on lime-rich soils. It is most common in central and southern England. The purgative nature of Buckthorn has been known to northern peoples since at least Anglo-Saxons times. The specific epithet, *catharticus,* comes from the Greek word *kathartikos* (= a cleanser or purifier). The common name Buckthorn is a translation of *cervi spina* (= buck's thorn), which was an early name for the plant referring to the characteristic spines on the branches.

The ripe fruits are used medicinally. Their constituents include anthraquinone glycosides, flavonols, pectin and vitamin C. Dried or fresh, the fruits are strongly laxative, also diuretic. An infusion of the macerated fruits or a syrup is used (for adults only) for cases of chronic constipation. On the Continent the fruits are still used on medical practice, but in Britain now only in herbal medicine. **Buckthorn fruits must always be taken with great care** because strong doses irritate the gastrointestinal mucosa to the point of bleeding and cause vomiting and severe diarrhoea. The dried bark (at least one-year old) has also been used as a laxative. **Fresh bark should never be used.**

The fruit and bark yield a yellow dye.

Flowering time: May to June

Alder Buckthorn

☠

A deciduous shrub or a small tree with smooth, blackish-grey bark and almost opposite and ascending branches. The buds lack scales. The shiny-green leaves are alternate, oval to obovate and entire, with seven to nine pairs of lateral veins. The small greenish-white, bisexual flowers grow in axillary clusters on young shoots and are followed by drupes that turn from green to red and finally violet-black on ripening. **The fresh bark and the fruits are poisonous.**

Alder Buckthorn grows throughout Europe, including the British Isles, on peaty heaths, stream banks, in damp woods and fens, usually on acidic soils. It is rare in Scotland. It is often seen together with Alder (*Alnus glutinosa*) (Pl. 13) and the modern specific epithet, *alnus,* as well as the common name, reflect this association. The foliage of the two species is also rather similar. Alder Buckthorn has similar medicinal properties to the related Buckthorn (*Rhamnus cartharticus*) (Pl. 194), but the bark, not the poisonous fruit, is used.

The bark from young twigs is used medicinally. After drying it is either heat-treated or stored for at least a year before using to destroy the anthraquinone glycosides and derivatives in the fresh material. These substances cause severe vomiting, diarrhoea and abdominal cramps. Other constituents in the bark include tannins and bitter compounds. The bark or an extract from it is used as a strong laxative for chronic constipation usually in cases where other, milder agents have failed to produce the desired result. Alder Buckthorn bark is also a choleretic and very small doses are used to treat liver, gall bladder and spleen disorders. On the Continent it is still widely used in conventional medicine; in Britain it is now mostly used only in herbal medicine. **Alder Buckthorn should be used only under the supervision of a qualified medical or herbal practitioner; strong doses are toxic. Fresh bark and the fruits should never be used.**

Bark

Twig with flowers

Flowering time: May to June

Medicinal Rhubarb, Chinese Rhubarb

Lower part of plant

A perennial herb with a thick rhizome and a basal rosette of coarsely toothed palmately divided leaves. The tall, robust, hollow, finely furrowed stem is branched towards the top and bears terminal panicles of reddish to greenish-white flowers. The fruit is a triangular achene. The whole plant is reddish.

Medicinal Rhubarb is native to northeast Asia where it still grows wild. In China it has been used as a remedy for more than 4,000 years and is now cultivated there and in other eastern countries for pharmaceutical purposes. *R. palmatum* does not grow well in Britain and another species, *R. officinale,* sometimes called Turkey Rhubarb, is grown on a small scale for medicinal use. The familiar Garden Rhubarb grown for its edible stalks (*R. rhaponticum*) is not normally used medicinally although its stems are laxative. **The leaves of all rhubarbs are poisonous.** The name Rhubarb came originally from the ancient Greek words *rha* (= an old name for the River Volga) and *barbaros* (= foreign), meaning 'a strange plant from beyond the Volga', along which the herb probably came to Europe.

The rhizomes of 5- to 7-year-old plants are used medicinally. When dried they have a bitter taste. The constituents include two types of glycosides: tannin glycosides with free gallic acid, cinnamic acid and glucose; and anthraquinone glycosides based on the aglycones chrysophanol, emodin, aloe-emodin and rhein (up to 10 per cent). The rhizomes also contain starch and calcium oxalate. In small doses Rhubarb is astringent and is used to treat diarrhoea, and to stimulate the appetite. Stronger doses are laxative after 8 to 10 hours and are used to treat chronic constipation. Rhubarb is included in some proprietary preparations and is also a component of herbal tea mixtures and digestive powders. **Medicinal Rhubarb must not be used by individuals with urinary disorders, uroliths, kidney stones, arthritis and rheumatism, or by children or nursing mothers.**

Flowering time: July

Black Currant

A deciduous shrub with erect, spineless twigs and alternate stalked leaves that are three- to five-lobed, the lobes pointed and coarsely toothed. There are yellow glands on the underside of the leaves. The small greenish-white flowers are arranged in loose, pendulous racemes in the leaf axils. The fruit is a globose black berry. All parts of the plant are distinctly aromatic.

Black Currant is native to Asia and north and central Europe. It is also widely cultivated for its fruits and many varieties have been developed. In the British Isles it still grows wild in woods and hedges, especially by streams, but it is not very common. It is introduced in Ireland. *Ribes* is an old Arabic name and the specific epithet, *nigrum* (= black), refers to the colour of the edible fruits in the wild. The medicinal properties of Black Currant have been known since at least the 16th century but today the plant is used more in the food and drink industries than as a herbal remedy.

The leaves and fruits have medicinal action. The leaves contain an essential oil, tannins, vitamin C, sugars and organic acids. They have diuretic and diaphoretic properties and an infusion in used in herbal medicine for urinary infections, rheumatism and diarrhoea. They also act as a tonic and can be used as a substitute for ordinary tea. The fruits contain abundant vitamin C (when fresh), vitamin B complex, organic acids, sugars, pigments and pectin. They are nutritive and act as a general tonic. They are usually processed fresh and made into syrup, jam, cordials and wines, or eaten raw or stewed. An infusion prepared from dried berries can be used as a gargle for throat and mouth infections.

Twig with fruits

Flowering time: April to May

Castor-oil Plant, Castor Bean

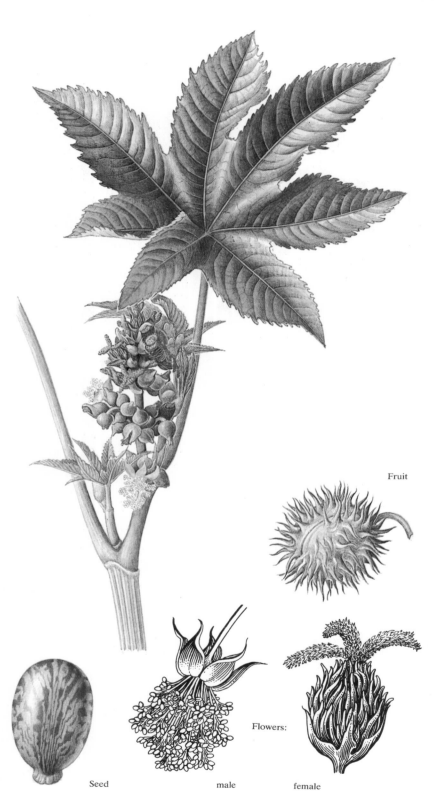

Fruit

Seed

Flowers:

male

female

A very variable plant: an annual herb in northern and central Europe; a two- to three-year shrub in the Mediterranean region; and a perennial tree in the tropics. The large reddish leaves are long-stalked, alternate and palmate with coarsely toothed segments. Terminating the stems are panicle-like inflorescences of green monoecious flowers, the stalked female flowers above and the male flowers below, both without petals. The fruit is a spiny greenish capsule with large, oval, shiny, bean-like seeds with variable brownish mottling on a whitish background. **The seeds are extremely poisonous;** only two or three can be fatal.

Castor-oil Plant is native to India and tropical Africa but it has been cultivated in warm regions for its oily seeds since ancient times. In ancient Egypt and the Orient the seed oil (which is non-toxic) was used as a cosmetic for beautifying the hair and complexion, for treating wounds and for burning in lamps. Nowadays the plant is grown in many forms for the seed oil, which is used in paint and soap products, as a medicine and for ornament. The generic name, *Ricinus,* means 'a tick' because of the form of the markings on the seeds. The common name Castor-oil is derived through the Spanish *agno casto,* by which the plant was known in the West Indies; 'casto' became 'castor' oil.

The seeds (castor beans) are peeled and cold- or heat-processed for medicinal use. They contain up to 50 per cent of fatty oil, extremely toxic albumins (ricins), which are removed from the expressed oil by boiling it in water, and the alkaloid ricinine. In medical practice castor oil is used as a laxative — often given in a warm-flavoured drink — to treat constipation. It also has an anthelmintic action. **Large doses may cause vomiting and severe diarrhoea.** Externally the oil is used to soothe eye irritations and sometimes for skin complaints, such as ringworm. **The seeds should never be eaten whole, or processed for the oil at home.**

Flowering time: August to October

False Acacia, Locust Tree

☠ ☠

A deciduous tree with stout paired spines on the branches. The bark is brown at first, later grey, furrowed and twisted. The alternate leaves are bluish green beneath and odd-pinnate, with 7−15 oval, stalked, entire leaflets with small spines at their tips. The white fragrant flowers are arranged in pendulous racemes, which grow from the leaf axils on young shoots. The flowers are attractive to bees. The fruit is a smooth brown flat pod with black or dark-brown seeds. **The seeds, bark and roots and perhaps other parts too are poisonous.**

False Acacia is native to North America but it was introduced to France in the 17th century and it is now widely grown as an ornamental tree, especially in towns. It spreads aggressively by means of suckers and it is sometimes planted to form thickets. It has become widely naturalized. In Britain, for example, it can be found in milder parts of the country on poor, sandy and stony soils. False Acacia is a fast-growing tree and yields a hard and close-grained wood which was once used in shipbuilding and is now used for turned articles, wheels and floors. The generic name, *Robinia*, honours the French botanist Jean Robin who obtained seeds of the tree from America and grew them in the Jardin des Plantes in Paris. The true acacias (wattles and mimosas) are also in the family Leguminosae but are in a different genus, *Acacia*.

The flowers and bark have medicinal action but they are rarely used therapeutically. The flowers contain flavonoid glycosides and an essential oil. They relax muscular and nervous spasms. The bark contains the toxic albumins robin and fazin, which are emetic and purgative. There have been cases of poisoning from the seeds and bark. Symptoms of poisoning include drying of the throat, vomiting, diarrhoea, dilated pupils, weak and irregular pulse and breathing difficulties. **False Acacia should never be collected and used for self-medication.**

Seed

Fruit

Flowering time: May to June

Dog Rose

Section of hip

Twig with fruits (hips)

A deciduous shrub with arched, downward-curving branches, which are armed with stout hooked prickles. The leaves are odd-pinnate with five to seven ovate to elliptic, serrate leaflets. The petioles and midribs often bear prickles. The stalked, usually sweet-scented flowers have large spreading pink or white petals. The fruit consists of numerous hairy achenes enclosed in the enlarged, fleshy, flask-shaped, bright-red receptacle — the familiar rosehip.

Dog Rose grows throughout Europe in hedges, scrub and woods. It is the commonest of British wild roses; it is rarer in Scotland. The plant is very variable in form. The origin of the common name, Dog Rose, is confused. A popular explanation is that the name is a translation of the medieval Latin *rosa canina,* which in turn came from the ancient Latin (from Greek) word *cynorrhodon,* the belief being that the plant's root cured the bite of mad (rabid) dogs. The ancient Greeks may, however, have just been implying that Dog Rose was of 'little worth' in the garden, 'dog' being a derogatory term. Remains of Dog Rose hips have been found at prehistoric dwelling sites, which suggests that the plant has long been associated with man.

The hips are the medicinally active parts. Their constituents include vitamin C (up to 1 per cent), carotenes, vitamin B complex, sugars, pectin, tannins, and malic and citric acids. The fruits also contain fatty oil. The best-known and widely used medicine is rosehip tea, which has tonic, astringent, mild diuretic and mild laxative effects. When fresh the hips are an excellent source of vitamin C. Fresh or dried, they are beneficial for convalescents, against exhaustion and colds. The tea is best made by macerating the crushed hips (without the hard achenes), not by lengthy boiling. A decoction from the hips can be used as a gargle for bleeding gums and it will relieve toothache.

Fresh hips can also be made into jam, syrup and medicinal wine.

Flowering time: June to July

Cabbage Rose, Pale Rose

A deciduous shrub with thin brown branches armed with numerous greatly flattened, almost straight prickles. The leaves are odd-pinnate with five to seven ovate to elliptic, dark-green, serrate leaflets, softly hairy beneath. The petioles and peduncles are almost thornless, but have glandular bristles. The fragrant flowers are a pink colour, the many petals whitish towards the base. The fruit consists of numerous hairy achenes enclosed in the enlarged, fleshy, flask-shaped, bright-red receptacle — the familiar rosehip.

The origin of Cabbage Rose is confused, but one of its ancestors was probably French Rose (*R. gallica*), which is also the ancestor of many of the 10,000 or so other cultivated roses. There are several garden varieties of Cabbage Rose but it is now usually grown for ornament only by lovers of old-fashioned roses. It and French Rose (which has red petals) are, however, cultivated commercially for rose oil (otto or attar of roses), which is used by the pharmaceutical and perfumery industries. Most rose oil is obtained from the fragrant Damask Rose (*R. damascena*), which is grown on a large scale in Bulgaria. Cabbage Rose is so-named because of its double flowers, which look like small heads of cabbage.

Rose oil is obtained by steam distillation or solvent extraction from the petals. Its main constituent is geraniol. Besides essential oil, rose petals also contain tannins, glycosides and pigments. All these substances give the petals astringent and anti-inflammatory properties and they are used in infusions to treat diarrhoea and externally to bathe wounds. Rose oil is the basis of many perfumes and it is also used to give a pleasant taste and smell to medicines, chiefly ointments, lotions and creams. The familiar rose water, which can be used as a face tonic, is prepared by water distillation from the petals or by impregnation of distilled water with rose oil.

Dried petals

Immature fruit (hip)

Flowering time: June to July

Rosemary

Flower

Segment of fruit (mericarp)

An evergreen subshrub with erect or ascending branches, which are pale green and downy when young, later brown and woody. The opposite leaves are simple, leathery, linear, dark green above and white-felted below. The two-lipped bluish flowers grow in whorls in short axillary or terminal racemes. The fruit consists of four brown nutlets. All parts of the plant are strongly aromatic.

Rosemary is native to the Mediterranean region. It is now widely cultivated for ornamental, culinary, medicinal and perfumery purposes. In Britain it thrives only in dry, warm parts sheltered from the wind. Most of the supplies used commercially in Britain are imported from such countries as Spain, France and Morocco. The common and generic names are derived from the old Latin names *rosmarinus* or *ros maris* ('dew of the sea'). It was so-called because of its habit of growing close to the sea. Rosemary has been used as a culinary and medicinal herb since ancient Greek and Roman times and it is still a popular remedy.

The leaves and young shoots are used medicinally. The constituents include an essential oil (up to 2 per cent) with cineole, camphor and borneol as the main components, plus tannins, saponin and organic acids. These substances give Rosemary a pronounced rubefacient action and the dried herb and rosemary oil, obtained by steam distillation from the fresh parts, are components of anti-rheumatic liniments and ointments. Rosemary also has sedative, diuretic, stomachic, cholagogic, tonic, aromatic, antispasmodic and antiseptic properties. It is especially beneficial for fatigue and neuralgia. **Very strong doses are poisonous. Rosemary oil should never be taken internally.**

Fresh or dried Rosemary leaves have many culinary uses and they can also be used in soothing herbal bath preparations. Infusions and oil extracts are excellent hair tonics. The distilled oil is used in toilet preparations, disinfectants and extensively in perfumery.

Flowering time: May

Madder, Dyer's Madder

A perennial herb with a long, reddish-brown, much-branched rhizome, red fibrous roots and rough, square, ascending prickly stems which branch at the top. The stiff, lanceolate, sessile leaves have prickly margins and grow in whorls up the stem. The small yellow flowers are arranged in axillary and terminal dichasial cymes. The fruit is a globose, fleshy, purple, one-seeded berry.

Madder is native to the Mediterranean region and Near East and was once widely grown as a dye plant. It is still grown as a medicinal plant in some parts of Europe. In the British Isles it was cultivated a little and it still occurs as a casual. The generic name, *Rubia,* means red — the plant has traditionally been the source of a permanent red dye. Wild Madder (*R. peregrina*), which grows wild in southern and western parts of the British Isles, yields a rose-pink dye. The common name Madder comes from the Anglo-Saxon name *maedere* for the plant.

The rootstock of two- to three-year-old plants is used medicinally. It remains red when dried. The constituents include anthraquinone glycosides and derivatives such as alizarin (madder red) and purpurin (madder purple), organic acids, tannins, pectins and sugars. The medicinal action is mainly due to the glycosides, which are isolated and included in proprietary preparations used on the Continent. Madder has diuretic, antispasmodic, antiseptic, choleretic, emmenagogic and laxative properties. It is used in powder form or in an infusion for kidney and bladder disorders, and it has a marked ability to disintegrate kidney stones and uroliths. In homeopathy a tincture of the fresh roots is used for amenorrhoea, spleen disorders and various other complaints. When taken internally the colouring matter in the rootstock gives urine, mucus, sweat and milk a pink tinge.

Twig with fruits

Rootstock

Flowering time: June to August

Blackberry, Bramble

Twig with fruits (blackberries)

A deciduous shrub with sprawling or erect, prickly, woody, arched and biennial stems that often root where they touch the ground. The stalked leaves have three to five oval, serrate leaflets with white or grey hairy undersides. The petioles and veins are also prickly. The white or pink flowers, arranged in terminal racemes, are borne on separate, erect, second-year stems that die after flowering. The fruit is a compound fleshy drupe (the blackberry) which turns red, later a glossy black and comes away with the conical receptacle when ripe.

Blackberry grows abundantly in woods, hedges and scrub throughout the British Isles, where it is native; it is extremely variable with many varieties and hybrids. Blackberries have been picked and eaten in Europe for thousands of years and since at least ancient Greek times the medicinal value of the leaves has been known. They have been used to check bleeding and diarrhoea and in antidiabetic treatments. The alternative common name, Bramble, is a corruption of the Anglo-Saxon word *brom* (= a thorny shrub).

The leaves contain tannins, organic acids, sugars and vitamin C and have mild astringent, antiseptic, antifungal, diuretic and tonic properties. An infusion is used in herbalism to treat stomach disorders, enteritis and diarrhoea. The fragrant tea is also prescribed for flu, colds and coughs and it is a pleasant substitute for ordinary tea. Externally a decoction is used as a gargle for sore throats and pharyngitis, as a component of mouthwashes and in bath preparations for treating skin rashes, wounds, ulcers and fungal infections. The fully ripe fruits contain vitamin C, organic acids, pectins and sugars and can be eaten raw or cooked and made into jam, syrup and medicinal cordial and wine.

Flowering time: May to August

Raspberry

A deciduous shrub with erect, woody, prickly and biennial stems, often with a whitish bloom. It sends up suckers from the roots. The odd-pinnate leaves have three to seven serrate, ovate leaflets, the terminal one the largest. They are glossy above and white-felted below. The white flowers, arranged in dense terminal and axillary drooping racemes, are borne on separate second-year stems that die down after flowering. The fruit is a compound drupe — a red (sometimes yellow) raspberry that separates from the conical receptacle when ripe.

Raspberry grows wild in woods and heaths, especially in hilly districts in most parts of the British Isles. The fruit has been picked and eaten in Europe since prehistoric times. Many varieties have been developed. The generic name, *Rubus,* means 'a thorny shrub'. Raspberry was named *idaeus* after Mount Ida in Asia Minor where the shrub grew abundantly. The fruit and the plant may have been called Raspberry after *raspis,* a sweet red French wine. Raspberry remains a popular herbal remedy for a variety of conditions. Nowadays it is especially recommended for pregnant women in the last two or three months before delivery. Taken in small doses in tea form it is believed to ease and speed childbirth.

The leaves contain tannins, pectin, vitamin C, organic acids and fragarin and other substances that have oxytocic properties (they act on the uterine muscles). Raspberry leaves also have astringent, diuretic, expectorant, stomachic, cholagogic and tonic properties. They are used in infusions on their own or in herbal mixtures to treat diarrhoea and stomach disorders, and for chest complaints. Externally an infusion can be used as a mouthwash and gargle. Fresh or fermented, the leaves make a pleasant substitute for ordinary tea. The fresh fruits contain organic acids, sugars, pectin and vitamin C and with the addition of sugar and wine vinegar and diluted with water they make a gargle for fevers and sore throats and a base for summer drinks.

Flowering time: June to August

Twig with fruits (raspberries)

Rue, Herb of Grace

Flower

Seed

A perennial herb or subshrub with erect, little-branched stems, which are often woody at the base. The alternate, smooth, grey-green, gland-dotted leaves are two or three times pinnately divided, with spathulate or oblong segments. The yellowish-green glandular flowers are arranged in terminal cymes. The four petals have undulate margins. The fruit is a capsule with black, crescent-shaped seeds. All parts of the plant are strongly aromatic and are **poisonous.**

Rue is native to southern Europe and was once extensively grown in gardens as a culinary and medicinal herb. It may have been introduced to Britain as early as Roman times and is still grown in gardens, but nowadays mostly for ornament only. In some countries it is cultivated commercially for the pharmaceutical industry. The generic name, *Ruta,* is thought to come from the Greek word *hrute* – hence Rue. Brushes made from the plant were used in churches to sprinkle holy water on Sundays before High Mass and this supposedly is the reason for the old name Herb of Grace or Herbygrass. Medicinally the herb has been used since ancient times for a wide variety of ailments.

The young shoots with the basal leaves are used medicinally. The constituents include a toxic essential oil with methyl ketones, the flavonoid glycoside rutin, bitter compounds, several alkaloids, coumarins and tannins. Rutin is extracted by the pharmaceutical industry. In whole form Rue has sedative, antispasmodic, stomachic, cholagogic, diaphoretic, anthelmintic and emmenagogic properties. **Strong doses are toxic** and may cause mental derangement. **Rue should thus be taken internally only under strict medical supervision. It should never be taken during pregnancy.** Externally Rue is used as an eyewash, in compresses applied to wounds and skin ulcers and in bath preparations. Handling of the plant may cause dermatitis in hypersensitive individuals. In homeopathy a tincture from the fresh leaves is used for varicose veins, rheumatism, arthritis and neuralgia.

Flowering time: June to September

White Willow

A deciduous shrub or medium-sized tree with greyish fissured bark, ascending branches and flexible yellowish-green twigs. The alternate, finely serrate, lanceolate leaves are white-silky hairy on both sides when young, on the underside when mature. White Willow is dioecious; the stalkless male and female flowers appear with the leaves in erect catkins borne in the axils of scaly bracts. The fruit is a capsule containing seeds with long silky hairs.

White Willow is native to the British Isles and grows beside water and in wet woods throughout most of the region. Other native species of willow include Crack Willow (*S. fragalis*), with glabrous, lanceolate leaves, shiny green above and grey green below; Grey Willow (*S. cinerea*) with obovate, grey-green, serrate or crenate leaves; and Almond Willow (*S. triandra*) with lanceolate, glabrous, dark-green leaves. All willows produce abundant pollen and are attractive to bees. The medicinal properties of willow bark have been known since ancient times. The White Willow's supple young twigs have also long provided material for fences, basketwork and for making wickerwork furniture. The common name Willow comes from the Anglo-Saxon *wileg* for the trees. White Willow is so-named because of its white appearance.

The bark from two- to three-year-old twigs is used medicinally. After drying it has a bitter taste. The constituents include the phenolic glycoside salicin and tannins (up to 14 per cent). Because of the salicylic compounds it contains willow bark has antipyretic, diaphoretic, antirheumatic and analgesic properties. The bark of White Willow and other willow species was once used in medicinal practice but nowadays it has been replaced by synthetic preparations, such as aspirin (acetosalicylic acid); however, it still has a place in herbal medicine for fevers and neuralgia. Externally a decoction is used in bath preparations for rheumatic and arthritic pains and in ointments and compresses for cuts, skin ulcers and burns.

Flowering time: April to May

Leaf: *S. alba*   *S. fragalis*   *S. cinerea*   *S. triandra*

Sage

Segment of fruit (mericarp)

A perennial subshrub with a taproot and a square, hairy stem, which is woody at the base and branches towards the top. The greyish-green stalked leaves are opposite, oblong to oval or lanceolate, wrinkled above, hairy and persistent. The two-lipped, blue-violet, reddish-violet or white flowers are arranged in whorls in terminal spikes. They are attractive to bees. The fruit consists of four nutlets. All parts of the plant are strongly aromatic.

Sage is native to the Mediterranean region but it has long been cultivated elsewhere in Europe for culinary and medicinal purposes and several varieties have been developed. It is commercially grown in central and southern England. It is still collected on a large scale from the wild in northern Mediterranean countries. The generic name, *Salvia,* is from the Latin word *salvere* (= 'to be in good health'); the old French word *saulje* (also from *salvere* through *salvia*) has given us the modern English name. Sage was traditionally used as an aid to conception.

The leaves are used medicinally. Their constituents include an essential oil (up to 2.5 per cent) with thujone (15−35 per cent), borneol, cineole and camphor, also bitter compounds (salvin and picrosalvin), oestrogenic substances, resin and tannins. These substances give Sage antiseptic, antifungal, astringent, diuretic, carminative, antidiarrhoeal, antispasmodic and antidiaphoretic properties. It has a wide variety of medicinal uses. In herbal medicine, for example, it is used in an infusion to reduce sweating and lactation, and to treat colds and coughs, nervous conditions and gastrointestinal disorders. A tincture prepared from the fresh leaves is also used in homeopathy. **Sage should not be taken in large doses for a long period because of the thujone it contains.** The essential oil, obtained by steam distillation of the partially dried leaves, is used by the pharmaceutical, perfumery, liqueur and food industries.

In cooking Sage is usually used with pork, but it is also good with other meat dishes and in salads and spreads.

Flowering time: June to July

Clary

A biennial herb with a square, erect, little-branched stem. The large, almost sessile, opposite leaves are broadly ovate, wrinkled and irregularly shallowly lobed or toothed. The white, violet or pink two-lipped flowers are arranged in whorls in a terminal spike and are interspersed with bracts of the same colour. The fruit consists of four nutlets. All parts of the plant are strongly aromatic and hairy.

Clary is native to the Mediterranean region but it has long been cultivated elsewhere for ornament and as food for bees. It was introduced to England in the 16th century and was sometimes used in brewing instead of hops. In Germany Clary was mixed with elderflowers and used by wine merchants to flavour wine converting it into a form of Muscatel. Nowadays Clary is grown commercially in several countries for its lavender-scented oil. The common name, Clary, comes from the Latin word *sclarea,* a word that may be derived from *clarus* (= clear), after the use of the mucilaginous seeds to clear the eyesight.

The flowers, flowering stems and leaves are used medicinally. When dried all parts are strong-smelling and have a bitter taste. Their constituents include tannins, essential oil with linalool and linalyl acetate as the main components, and bitter compounds. These substances give Clary tonic, astringent, antidiaphoretic, carminative, antispasmodic and emmenagogic properties. In herbal medicine an infusion is used to treat digestive upsets, cramps, flatulence, diarrhoea, as a general tonic, to inhibit perspiration and in the treatment of menstrual disorders. The decoction and Clary vinegar can be applied externally in compresses or bath preparations to wounds and ulcerous conditions. The essential oil, which is known as sage clary or Muscatel oil, is obtained by steam distillation from the fresh or partially dried flowering stems and leaves. It is used in herbal medicine, but more widely in toilet waters, perfumes and soap and to flavour wine vermouths and liqueurs.

Flowering time: August

Flower

Segment of fruit (mericarp)

Dwarf Elder, Danewort

Fruits

Rhizome

A perennial herb with a stout, creeping, white rhizome and numerous erect, leafy, furrowed stems which die down at the end of the growing season. The stalked, opposite, odd-pinnate leaves have seven to nine oblong to lanceolate, finely serrate leaflets and conspicuous stipules. The white or reddish-tinged flowers have red anthers and are arranged in flat-topped terminal cymes. The fruits are small, matt-black, globose inedible drupes. All parts of the plant have an unpleasant fetid smell and are **slightly poisonous**. Children should be warned not to eat the bitter berries.

Dwarf Elder is native to Europe and Asia where it is a weed of woodland clearings, roadsides and waste places. It was probably introduced to the British Isles where it has a scattered distribution. The generic name, *Sambucus*, dates from ancient Greek times and may refer to the *sambuke*, a kind of harp believed to have been made of elder wood. The alternative common name, Danewort, is derived from the *danes* or diarrhoea caused by the plant (the name seems to have nothing to do with the Danish people). Dwarf Elder has long been considered an important medicinal plant. It has a much stronger action than its close relative Elder (*S. nigra*) (Pl. 211) and is nowadays rarely used because of its purgative effects.

The rhizomes, sometimes the flowers and fruits, are used medicinally. Their constituents include a glycoside, a bitter compound, anthocyanins, an essential oil, tannins and a saponin. These substances give Dwarf Elder diuretic, marked diaphoretic and strong laxative properties. It is occasionally prescribed for dropsy, kidney disorders and rheumatism in herbal medicine and in homeopathy. **It should be taken internally only under strict medical supervision**; large doses cause vertigo, vomiting and diarrhoea. **The berries should never be eaten whole or used for self-medication**. The alcohol extract from macerated rhizomes is said to promote hair growth and it is sometimes used to treat dandruff.

Flowering time: July to August

Elder

A deciduous shrub or a small tree with arched branches and greyish-brown, deeply furrowed, corky bark. The pith of the trunk and branches is white. The stalked, opposite, unpleasant-smelling, odd-pinnate leaves have five or seven oval to lanceolate, serrate leaflets and very small or no stipules. The small fragrant creamy-white flowers with yellow anthers are arranged in flat-topped terminal cymes. The fruits are small, glossy black, edible drupes borne on red stalks.

Elder is native to Europe and grows throughout the British Isles in woods, scrub, waste places, near dwellings, and around rabbit warrens, usually on nitrogen-rich soils. It grows vigorously and soon becomes established if planted. The common name Elder is probably derived from the Anglo-Saxon word *ellaern* or *aeld* (= fire, kindle) because the hollowed stems were once used for getting fires going. Elder has been regarded as a most valuable medicinal and cosmetic plant since ancient times and all parts have been used at one time or another. It remains a popular remedy, especially for colds, and it is also a base for excellent beverages.

Nowadays primarily the flowers and fruits are used medicinally. The constituents of the flowers include the flavonoid glycosides rutin and quercitrin, the cyanogenic glycoside sambunigrin, essential oil, mucilage, tannins and organic acids. These substances are principally diaphoretic and an infusion is used to treat colds and other respiratory infections and mild nervous disorders. Cosmetically the flowers are very beneficial and the wine made from them is a safe hypnotic. The fruits contain organic pigments (anthocyanins), amino acids, sugar, rutin and a large amount of vitamin C (when fresh). They are mildly laxative, also diuretic, diaphoretic and mildly sedative. They are used in tea mixtures for colds and weight loss and are also beneficial for nervous disorders such as insomnia and migraine. **The leaves are purgative and should not be used.**

Flowering time: June to July

Fruits (elderberries)

Red-berried Elder

Fruits (elderberries)

A deciduous shrub with brown bark and pale-brown pith and erect, much-branched stems. The stalked, opposite, odd-pinnate leaves have five or seven oval to lanceolate, serrate leaflets, which are pale green on both sides. They appear after the flowers have faded. The stipules are glandular. The flowers are arranged in dense ovoid, terminal panicles. They are yellowish green with cream anthers and so are distinct from those of Elder (*S. nigra*) (Pl. 211). The fruits are also distinct in being red, in drooping clusters.

Red-berried Elder is native to southern and central Europe where it grows as a weed in open woods, woodland clearings and on scrubby banks, usually in mountain districts. It has been introduced to the British Isles and is commonly planted for its ornamental berries. It is naturalized in some places, especially in Scotland. The specific epithet, *racemosa*, refers to the flower clusters.

The fully ripe fruits are used medicinally. They are bitter tasting and are used fresh or dried. Their constituents include vitamin C, essential oil, sugar, pectins, organic pigments (anthocyanins), organic acids and trace amounts of glycosides. These substances give Red-berried Elder diaphoretic, nutritive, and antiseptic properties, which are more pronounced in the fresh fruits. The fruits have been used for constipation and gastrointestinal infections, but **they cause vomiting and diarrhoea in large amounts** and it is best not to use them for medical purposes or in cooking.

Flowering time: April to May

Great Burnet

A perennial herb with a thick branched rhizome, a basal rosette of odd-pinnate leaves with 7 to 15 long-stalked, ovate, toothed leaflets, and an erect, branched stem with only very few leaves. The small crimson flowers are arranged in dense terminal, oblong spikes. The fruit is an achene enclosed in the four-winged receptacle.

Great Burnet is native to Europe and grows in damp meadows and pastures. It is not widespread in the British Isles and is most common in central and northern England. The related Salad Burnet (*S. minor*) also grows wild in Britain, in chalk and limestone grassland northwards to southern Scotland. The crimson-brown (burnet) colour of the flowerheads of Great Burnet and Salad Burnet has given them their common name. The generic name, *Sanguisorba,* from the Latin words *sanguis* (= blood) and *sorbeo* (= I absorb), refers to Great Burnet's traditional use in staunching wounds and as a remedy for internal bleeding.

The rhizomes and sometimes the young shoots and leaves (gathered before flowering) are used medicinally. Their constituents include tannins, saponins, a glycoside (sanguisorbin), flavones and vitamin C (in fresh material). These substances give Great Burnet astringent, haemostatic, mild antiseptic, diaphoretic and anti-inflammatory properties. In herbal medicine a decoction from the rhizomes is used for gastritis, enteritis and diarrhoea, for bleeding gums, nosebleed, strong menstrual flow and for difficulty in urinating. The young shoots and leaves are used in compresses and bath preparations to treat open wounds, rashes and ulcers and in gargles for gum infections and tonsillitis. **Great Burnet should never be taken in large doses.**

Salad Burnet has less potent medicinal actions. Its young leaves and shoots can be added to salads and soups or cooked as a vegetable. They also have several cosmetic applications.

Flowering time: June to September

Sanicle

Fruits

A perennial herb with a thick, brown, fibrous rhizome and a basal rosette of deeply palmately lobed, long-stalked, glossy and toothed leaves. The flowering stems are erect, branched at the top, with a few small, usually sessile leaves. The small white or pale-pink flowers are arranged in a terminal rounded umbel, which is made up of several secondary, few-flowered umbels. The fruit is an ovoid double achene covered with hooked bristles.

Sanicle grows throughout Europe, including the British Isles, in shady woods on lime-rich soils. It is a traditional remedy for checking bleeding and for treating open wounds and this medicinal use is reflected in the generic and common names – the Latin word *sanus* means whole, sound or healthy.

The flowering stems, together with the basal leaves, and the rhizomes are used medicinally. The constituents include tannins, saponins (primarily in the rhizomes), essential oil, mucilage and mineral salts. These substances give Sanicle astringent, haemostatic, expectorant, antispasmodic, carminative and anti-inflammatory properties. An infusion of the stems or the powdered rhizome is used for flatulence, gastritis, enteritis, internal ulcers, internal haemorrhage, urinary infections, liver disorders and for coughs and bronchitis. Externally it is used in gargles, bath preparations or compresses for throat infections, inflamed gums, slow-healing wounds, skin rashes and ulcerous conditions.

Flowering time: May to July

Soapwort

A perennial herb with a branched, orange, creeping rhizome and a tuft of erect or ascending downy stems, which are branched at the top. The opposite leaves are ovate to elliptic, three-veined and sessile and the pinkish tubular flowers are arranged in terminal panicles. The fruit is an ovoid capsule, which opens by means of four or five teeth to release the small black seeds.

Soapwort is native to central and southern Europe where it grows in damp waste places, hedges and by streams. It may originally have been introduced to the British Isles from the Continent in the Middle Ages for growing as a source of a lathery liquid used for washing wool and woollen cloth, but some authorities regard it as native to Britain, at least in some parts. It is now widespread. It is also sometimes found in gardens. The use of this natural cleanser dates back to ancient Greek times, if not before – the generic name, *Saponaria*, comes from the Latin word *sapo* (= soap). It is not an effective substitute for modern soap but it is possible to wash with it and it is occasionally used for cleaning delicate old fabrics and tapestries and for producing a 'head' on beer. Soapwort is also a traditional remedy for skin diseases.

The rhizomes of two- to three-year old plants are used medicinally. Their constituents include triterpenoid saponins (up to 5 per cent), flavonoids and sugars (up to 30 per cent). These substances give Soapwort expectorant, diuretic, diaphoretic, choleretic, cholagogic and laxative properties. In herbalism a decoction is used for coughs and bronchitis and, externally, for various skin conditions. **Soapwort is dangerous if taken in strong doses or over a long period of time** because the saponins can cause haemolysis (breakdown of the red blood cells), which results in severe irritation of the gastrointestinal tract. **It should thus be taken internally only under professional supervision.** The flowering stems have a similar but milder action.

Seed

Rhizome with roots

Flowering time: June to September

Summer Savory

Flower

Segment of fruit (mericarp)

An annual bushy herb with erect, branched, square stems. The opposite greyish leaves are lanceolate to linear, entire and gland-dotted. The small, purplish or almost white, bell-shaped, two-lipped flowers grow on short stalks in small clusters in the upper leaf axils. The flowers are attractive to bees. The fruit consists of four smooth nutlets. All parts of the plant are aromatic.

Summer Savory is native to the Mediterranean region but it has been widely introduced and grown elsewhere as a seasoning herb. It was popular among the ancient Greeks and Romans who used it in sauces. Winter Savory (*S. montana*), from southern Europe and north Africa, was introduced to the British Isles in the Middle Ages as a culinary herb and it is sometimes found naturalized on old walls. It is perennial and more bushy than Summer Savory. The common name Savory reflects the savoury taste of the plants, but originally it came from the old name *Satureia*. Some authorities believe that *Satureia* meant 'satyr', the plant supposedly having aphrodisiac properties.

The nonwoody flowering tops are used medicinally. Their constituents include an essential oil with carvacrol and cymene as the main components, also tannins, mucilage and resin. These substances give Summer Savory astringent, antiseptic, expectorant, antispasmodic, stomachic, carminative, tonic and anthelmintic properties. It is used mainly for stomach and intestinal disorders, flatulence, to stimulate the appetite, to check diarrhoea and to destroy intestinal parasites. It also makes an effective gargle.

The distilled essential oil is used commercially as a flavouring. The fresh or dried leaves can be used on their own or in herbal mixtures to season meats, fish, poultry, eggs and, especially, all kinds of beans. The herb should always be used sparingly. Winter Savory has a stronger and less-pleasant flavour and is best used only in herbal mixtures. Otherwise it has the same medicinal properties and use as Summer Savory.

Flowering time: July to August

Round-leaved Saxifrage

A perennial herb with a basal rosette of long-stalked, roundish, pale-green, deeply toothed and often hairy leaves. The stoutish stems are sparsely leafy and hairy. The flowers, white with yellow spots at the base and characteristic red spots towards the apex of the petals, are arranged in loose narrow panicles. The fruit is a many-seeded capsule.

Round-leaved Saxifrage grows in damp and shady places in mountainous areas in mixed woods, shrub and on stream banks throughout central and southern Europe. It does not grow wild in the British Isles, but there are several other species that do. For example, Meadow Saxifrage (*S. granulata*), which has white, green-veined flowers, can be found growing on sunny banks and dry grassland over much of Britain, but it is becoming less common than it used to be. In Ireland and in the south-west of England it is mostly introduced. Several species of saxifrage are common rock-garden plants. The derivation of Saxifrage (and *Saxifraga*) has been given on Pl. 168. True to their name members of the genus have long been used for kidney and bladder disorders. On the Continent, Round-leaved Saxifrage still has a part to play in herbal medicine.

The flowering stems are used medicinally. Their constituents include tannins, bitter compounds, resin and glycosides, which give Round-leaved Saxifrage primarily a diuretic action. It is used in herbal medicine in an infusion to help disintegrate kidney stones and uroliths. Mostly, however, it is a component of diuretic herbal tea mixtures with Peppermint (*Mentha × piperita*) (Pl. 145), Lesser Celandine (*Ranunculus ficaria*) (Pl. 192), Smooth Rupturewort (*Herniaria glabra*) (Pl. 117) and Milk Thistle (*Silybum marianum*) (Pl. 221).

Flowers:

S. granulata   *S. rotundifolia*

Flowering time: June to August

Common Figwort

Rhizome with roots

A perennial herb with a short, knotted rhizome, a tall, erect, square stem and opposite, short-stalked, pointed ovate or cordate, coarsely serrate leaves. The small, two-lipped, flask-shaped, un-pleasant-smelling, brownish-red flowers are arranged in loose terminal panicles. The flowers are attractive to wasps, which pollinate them. The fruit is an ovoid capsule containing pitted seeds.

Common Figwort is native to Europe and it grows in most parts of the British Isles in damp and wet woods, alongside streams and in other wet places. It was once used to treat scrofula (tuberculosis of the lymphatic glands of the neck) and this is how it acquired its generic name, *Scrophularia*. The plant was also once known as Throatwort. The common name Figwort refers to the supposed resemblance of the root swellings to figs – and to the swellings of piles. Nowadays in herbal medicine it is used mostly for skin complaints.

The rhizomes and the flowering stems, separately or together, are used medicinally. Their constituents include cardiac glycosides, saponins, resin, organic acids and pectin. These substances give Figwort diuretic, mild laxative and vulnerary properties. It has been used internally for glandular and skin disorders but it is now mostly used only externally in compresses to treat swollen glands, ulcers, abscesses, earache, slow-healing wounds, burns, chronic eczema and haemorrhoids. In homeopathy a tincture prepared from fresh material is used for similar conditions. **Figwort should be taken internally only under the supervision of a qualified medical or herbal practitioner;** strong doses may cause blood in the urine (haemoglobinuria) and may also affect the heart.

Flowering time: June to August

Biting Stonecrop, Wall-pepper ☠ ☠

An evergreen mat-forming perennial herb with a creeping branched rhizome and numerous ascending or erect stems, which are of two kinds: non-flowering stems with numerous overlapping, wedge-shaped, fleshy, sessile yellowish leaves; and fewer-leaved flowering stems terminated by bright-yellow, star-shaped flowers arranged in a monochasial cyme. The leaves have a sharp burning taste like pepper. The fruit is a follicle, grouped with others in a cluster. **All parts of the plant are poisonous.**

Biting Stonecrop is native to Europe and grows throughout the British Isles on dry grassland, shingle, dunes, embankments, walls, roofs and screes, mainly on calcium-rich soils. It is the commonest British stonecrop. A white-flowered form, White Stonecrop (*S. album*), is also often found on rocks and walls but it may be native only in western England. Its leaves are bright green, often red-tinged and cylindrical and its flowers are arranged in flat-topped clusters. An explanation of the generic name, *Sedum,* is that it comes from the Latin word *sedere* (= to sit) because the plant appears to be sitting on the rocks on which it grows.

The flowering stems and leaves are used medicinally. Their constituents include several alkaloids (for example, sedamine and sedinine), the flavonoid glycoside rutin, mucilage, tannins, sugar, vitamin C and calcium carbonate. These substances give Biting Stonecrop rubefacient, astringent, irritant, antisclerotic and hypotensive properties. **It should never be taken internally** because it causes headache, listlessness and vomiting. It is a component of liniments and ointments for external use. The fresh macerated aerial parts are also used in herbal medicine to treat skin disorders. They must be applied for only a short while because **they can cause blistering. The fresh plant juice may cause permanent eye damage.** In homeopathy a tincture of the fresh plant is used to treat haemorrhoids. **Biting Stonecrop should never be collected and used for self-medication.**

Flowering time: June to July

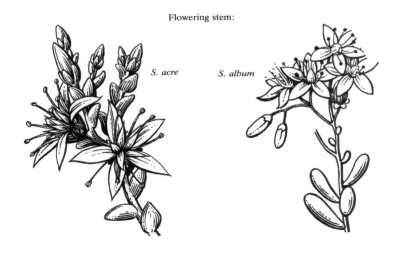

Flowering stem:

S. acre   *S. album*

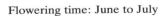

Houseleek

Flower

A perennial herb with a dense basal rosette of fleshy obovate to oblong, sharp-tipped, bluish-green, often reddish leaves that persist for several years. In older plants a long, thick, leafy flowering stem grows from the centre of the rosette in early summer. The numerous dull-red flowers are arranged in terminal cymes. The leaf rosette dies after flowering but the plant spreads vigorously by means of stolons. The fruit is a follicle, grouped with others in a cluster. Bees find the flowers very attractive.

Houseleek grows on weathered rocks and screes and is now often planted out in rock gardens — formerly also on walls and roofs because it was believed to ward off lightning. It is native to central and southern Europe, but not to the British Isles. It was, however, introduced long ago and it is found growing wild on old buildings throughout the country. The plant hybridizes readily and there are many ornamental forms. The generic name, *Sempervivum,* comes from the Latin words *semper* (= always) and *vivus* (= alive) and refers to the vitality of the plant. The specific epithet, *tectorum,* means 'of the roofs'. In the common name the suffix leek is from the Anglo-Saxon word *leac* (= plant).

The leaves are used medicinally. Their constituents include tannins, bitter compounds, sugars and mucilage. These substances give Houseleek astringent and vulnerary properties. A decoction has been used in the past to treat diarrhoea but the plant is nowadays rarely used internally. It has, however, several external applications. The raw macerated leaves or the pressed juice from them is applied in poultices to inflammations caused by insect bites and to itching burning skin. It is particularly recommended for softening the skin and alleviating corns. The pressed juice diluted with water makes a gargle for stomatitis.

Flowering time: July

Milk Thistle

An annual or biennial herb with a tall, erect, furrowed and branched stem. The alternate leaves are large, oblong, white-spotted, prickly and wavy-lobed or pinnately divided, the lower ones sessile, the upper ones clasping. The stems are terminated by solitary, spiny, violet flower-heads composed only of tubular florets. The fruit is a blackish, speckled, obovoid achene with a long white pappus.

Milk Thistle is native to southern Europe but it has been widely introduced elsewhere for ornament and as a medicinal plant. In the British Isles it has become naturalized locally. Milk Thistle is so-named because of the milky veins on the leaves, the milk having come, it was believed, from the Virgin Mary. The specific epithet, *marianum*, has the same derivation. At one time the plant was held to increase the flow of milk in nursing mothers, though there is no modern evidence for this. More certain are its effect on the liver and gall bladder.

The ripe fruits are used medicinally. Their constituents include fatty oil, proteins, an essential oil, bitter compounds, and the important flavones silybin and silymarin. These substances give Milk Thistle bitter tonic, choleretic and cholagogic properties. It is processed by the pharmaceutical industry — especially on the Continent — into tinctures, drops, tablets and other preparations with specific proportions of active constituents. These preparations are used in medical practice for treating gall bladder diseases, to stimulate the flow of bile and for the regeneration of tissue in cases of liver damage. In herbal medicine the fruits are used in the form of a decoction or powder or they are chewed whole for the same complaints. A tincture of the seeds is used in homeopathy. **Treatment with Milk Thistle should be medically supervised.**

The leaves, young shoots, receptacle and root can be cooked and eaten as a vegetable.

Fruit

Flowering time: June to August

White Mustard

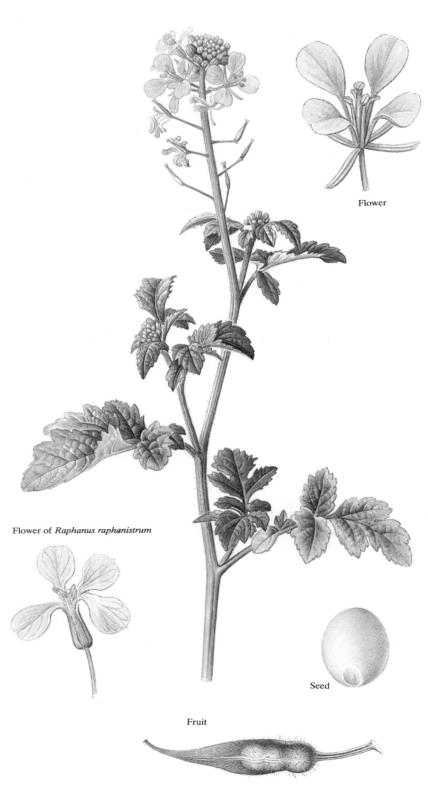

Flower

Flower of *Raphanus raphanistrum*

Seed

Fruit

An annual herb with an erect unbranched stem. The alternate, stalked, toothed leaves are lyrate and deeply pinnately lobed with the terminal lobe the largest. The yellow flowers are arranged in a raceme. The sepals spread out horizontally below the petals, unlike those of the related Black Mustard (*Brassica nigra*) (Pl. 40) and Wild Radish (*Raphanus raphanistrum*). The petals do not have the prominent veining seen in Black Mustard and Wild Radish. The fruit is a siliqua with a flattened sabre-shaped beak and yellow or pale-brown, smooth round seeds. All parts of the plant are roughly hairy. The flowers produce abundant pollen and are attractive to bees.

White Mustard is native to the Mediterranean region but it is widely cultivated elsewhere for its oil, for fodder and for mustard production. It is naturalized as a weed of arable and waste land throughout the British Isles. White Mustard is closely related to Charlock (*S. arvensis*), which is another common weed of arable land. It is not so powerful medicinally as Black Mustard but, even so, it has been used as a medicinal and pungent seasoning herb since ancient Greek and Roman times. The plant is called 'white' (*alba*) because of the light-coloured mustard powder obtained from its seeds.

The ripe seeds are used medicinally. They contain fatty oil (up to 30 per cent), mucilage and the glucosinolate sinalbin (up to 2 per cent), which, in the presence of moisture and the enzyme myrosinase, changes into mustard oil with a high concentration of sulphur. White Mustard has local rubefacient and irritant effects and the ground seeds are used like those of Black Mustard in compresses and plasters applied externally to ease rheumatic pain. A hot mustard plaster (up to 40 °C) is more effective but it may blister the skin. The whole seeds are laxative and antiseptic.

The seeds are preservatives and in the food industry they are used whole in pickling vegetables and ground to make various kinds of prepared mustard.

Flowering time: May onwards

Bittersweet, Woody Nightshade

A perennial subshrub, woody at the base, with long climbing or trailing stems. The alternate leaves are ovate and entire or deeply lobed at the base. They become narrow and more pointed towards the top of the stem. The violet flowers, which have five spreading, later recurved petals and conspicuous yellow anthers, are arranged in long-stalked terminal cymes in the upper leaf axils. The fruits are scarlet-red, ovoid berries. **All parts of the plant are poisonous.** Bittersweet is easily mistaken for the highly poisonous and rarer Deadly Nightshade (*Atropa belladonna*) (Pl. 33), even though its flowers are a different colour and shape and its berries are red, not black. Bittersweet berries are not as poisonous as those of Deadly Nightshade but they can cause serious illness if eaten, particularly in children. The related black-berried Black Nightshade (*S. nigrum*) is also poisonous.

Bittersweet grows in woods, hedges and waste places and on shingle beaches throughout most of Europe, including the British Isles. Black Nightshade is also native to Britain. Bittersweet has been an important medicinal herb since ancient Greek times. It is now little used in conventional medicine but it still has a place in homeopathy.

The green shoot tips are used medicinally. Their constituents include non-glycosidic and glycosidic saponins, steroidal glycosidic alkaloids (such as soladulcine) and tannins. These substances give Bittersweet expectorant, mild diuretic, antiseptic and stimulant properties. It has been used to treat chronic bronchitis, asthma, rheumatism and chronic skin disorders but is rarely prescribed by herbalists today. In homeopathy, however, preparations from the fresh plant are still used. The constituents of Bittersweet have recently been the subject of intensive study because they could be used to make steroid compounds. Bittersweet should be used only under strict medical supervision; it **should never be collected and used for self-medication**.

Flowering time: June to September

Flowers

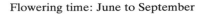

Goldenrod

Flower cluster of *S. virgaurea*   *S. canadensis*

A perennial herb with an erect, often downy stem, which may branch at the top. The leaves are alternate, the basal ones obovate to elliptic, usually toothed and stalked; the upper ones narrower, entire and mostly sessile. The short-stalked yellow flowerheads are arranged around the stem in a terminal raceme or panicle. The ligulate ray-florets are female, the tubular disc-florets bisexual. The fruit is a hairy, brown, ribbed achene with a pappus of white hairs.

Goldenrod is native to Europe and it is common in dry woods and grassland, and on rocks and hedgebanks throughout much of the British Isles. The related Canadian Goldenrod (*S. canadensis*), a native of North America, is often grown in gardens as an ornamental plant. It sometimes escapes and it has consequently become widely naturalized in Europe. It has dense one-sided spikes of yellow flowerheads in branched clusters. The generic name, *Solidago*, is derived from the Latin word *solidare* (= to join or make whole), a reference to the healing properties once attributed to Goldenrod. It was mainly recommended as a wound herb and for kidney disorders and seems to have been used medicinally since the Middle Ages. It remains a popular and safe herbal remedy.

The flowering tops are used medicinally. Their constituents include tannins, saponins, bitter compounds, an essential oil and flavonoids. These substances give Goldenrod diuretic, astringent, vulnerary, anti-inflammatory, expectorant, antispasmodic and carminative properties. In herbal medicine an infusion is used to treat kidney and bladder disorders, to improve kidney and prostate function, for flatulence and indigestion, and for chronic bronchitis, coughs and asthma. Externally Goldenrod is used in poultices, ointments and bath preparations for varicose ulcers, eczema and slow-healing wounds. A tincture prepared from the fresh plant is used in homeopathy.

Canadian Goldenrod also has medicinal properties.

Flowering time: July to September

Japanese Pagoda Tree

A tall deciduous tree with a dense spherical crown and green, later grey bark. The alternate odd-pinnate leaves have 9—17 stalked, oval to lanceolate, prickly tipped leaflets, which are dark green above, greyish and downy below. The creamy-white flowers are arranged in loose terminal panicles. The fruit is a pod, constricted between the three or four black, bean-shaped seeds. **The seeds are poisonous.**

Japanese Pagoda Tree is native to eastern Asia but it is widely grown elsewhere as an ornamental tree in parks and gardens. There are pendant forms and ones with violet flowers. The tree flowers profusely in late summer but does not bear fruits in Europe. The generic name, *Sophora*, comes from the Arabic name *sufayra* for a tree of the bean or pea family (Leguminosae).

The flower buds, the leaves and the bark are used medicinally. When dry they have a bitter taste. Most important of the active constituents is the flavonoid glycoside rutin (up to 20 per cent), which decreases the permeability of the capillaries. It is extracted by the pharmaceutical industry and included in medicines prescribed for circulatory and neurological disorders. Japanese Pagoda Tree is not a suitable plant for self-medication; **it should be used only under strict medical supervision.**

Bud

Flowering time: September

Rowan, Mountain Ash

Flower cluster

A deciduous shrub or small tree with a slender crown, smooth, shiny greyish bark and smooth greyish-brown twigs. The alternate odd-pinnate leaves have 9–19 sessile, lanceolate and sharply serrate leaflets, which are dark green above and paler below. The small, white, unpleasant-smelling flowers are arranged in terminal compound corymbs. The fruits are small, globose, scarlet pomes (rowanberries). They have a sour and astringent taste but are not poisonous.

Rowan is native to Europe where it grows in woods, scrub, on mountain rocks and by mountain streams. It occurs throughout the British Isles, but is rare in lowland areas. It is often planted as an ornamental tree in avenues and gardens. Rowan is not a true ash (*Fraxinus* spp.) but its leaves are ash-like. The specific name, *aucuparia*, means 'bird-catching' – the berries are a favourite food of birds and they were once used by bird-catchers as bait in traps to ensnare birds. Rowan bark has been used for dyeing and tanning; the strong flexible wood for making small carved objects and tool handles. The fruits have been used as a laxative and to make drinks to prevent scurvy.

The ripe fruits are used medicinally. Their constituents include a large amount of organic acids, tannins, sugars, pectin and vitamin C (particularly in fresh fruits). These substances give Rowan mild purgative, diuretic and general tonic properties. The dried fruits or the pressed juice of fresh fruits is used for constipation and kidney disorders. **Large doses of the fruits should not be taken.** The fruits are a raw material for the manufacture of sorbose, a sweetening agent for diabetics. Vitamin C (ascorbic acid) has also been extracted commercially from them.

The berries, particularly those of cultivated sweet-fruited varieties, can be used to make compotes, syrups, conserves and wines. They are also used in liqueur manufacture.

Flowering time: May to June

Betony, Wood Betony, Hedge Nettle

A perennial herb with a short woody rhizome and an erect, square, usually unbranched and furrowed stem. Most of the leaves are arranged in a basal rosette. They are oval to oblong, wrinkled, regularly round-toothed and long-stalked; the few opposite stem leaves are smaller and become sessile near the top. The reddish-purple two-lipped flowers are arranged in dense axillary whorls forming a terminal spike, which is interrupted below. The fruit consists of four smooth, three-cornered nutlets. All parts of the plant are roughly hairy.

Betony is native to southern and western Europe, including the British Isles where it grows in open woods, hedges, heaths and moors, usually on lighter soils. It is common in England and Wales, rare in Scotland. Betony is still used in herbal medicine but it has lost the importance it had in the past when it was considered not only a remedy for all ills but also a magical plant. The Romans called it *vettonica* and this became *betonica*, from which the common name, Betony, is derived. The modern generic name, *Stachys*, means 'spike' and refers to the flower cluster.

The flowering stems with the basal leaves are used medicinally. When dry they have a spicy smell and a bitter taste. Their constituents include abundant tannins, bitter compounds, essential oils and alkaloids (for example, stachydrine). These substances give Betony astringent, tonic, stomachic, vulnerary, antiseptic and sedative properties. In small doses it is antidiarrhoeal; **in large doses it can be purgative and emetic**. In herbal medicine it is used in an infusion or in powder form to treat diarrhoea, cystitis (inflammation of the urinary bladder), asthma and neuralgia. The tea is invigorating, particularly if prepared in a mixture with other herbs. The dried leaves have been used in herbal smoking and snuff mixtures. Fresh leaves, unprepared or parboiled, can be applied to infected wounds and swellings. Betony is also used in homeopathy.

Rhizome with roots

Segment of fruit (mericarp)

Flowering time: June to September

Common Comfrey

Flower cluster: *S. officinale* (white form)

S. tuberosum

Segment of fruit (mericarp)

A perennial herb with a black, turnip-like root and a square stem, which is branched near the top. The lower leaves are alternate, stalked and ovate to lanceolate; those higher up the stem are narrower and their bases continue as wings down the stem to the leaf below. The bell-shaped white, cream, purple or pink flowers are arranged in nodding cymes in the upper leaf axils. The fruit consists of four ovoid, glossy-black nutlets. All parts of the plant are roughly hairy.

Common Comfrey is native to Europe and grows in damp grassy places. It is widespread throughout the British Isles on river banks and in ditches but it is rarer in Scotland. It may have been introduced in the north and in Ireland. Tuberous Comfrey (*S. tuberosum*), another introduced species, now grows throughout Britain, especially in Scotland. It is smaller than Common Comfrey and the leaf bases extend only a little way down the stem. Common Comfrey has long had a medicinal use, primarily for treating wounds and fractures. This traditional use of the plant is reflected in the name Comfrey, which comes from the Latin word *confervere* (= to join together).

The roots and leaves are used medicinally. Their constituents include tannins, abundant mucilage, allantoin, starch, traces of pyrrolizidine alkaloids and an essential oil. These substances give Common Comfrey astringent, scar-healing, vulnerary, anti-inflammatory, emollient and mild sedative properties. Internally it is used in an infusion or in powder form for chronic respiratory infections, stomach and duodenal ulcers, and diarrhoea. Mostly, however, Comfrey is used externally in compresses, plasters, liniments, ointments and bath preparations. Comfrey is also used in homeopathy and it is contained in many proprietary preparations. **Note:** Comfrey has been reported to cause serious liver damage if taken in large amounts over a long period of time. Although this effect is in dispute it would be best to err on the cautious side when taking Comfrey internally.

Flowering time: May to June

Dandelion

A perennial herb with a long taproot and a basal rosette of oblong entire or toothed or deeply pinnately divided leaves. In early spring hollow scapes are produced. These are terminated by solitary heads of numerous yellow ligulate florets surrounded by two rows of involucral bracts, the inner onces erect, the outer ones spreading. When the flowers have faded the head turns into a ball of long, ribbed, spiny achenes, with a pappus of white hairs at the end of a long stem or 'beak'. All parts of the plant contain lactiferous ducts; the latex is non-poisonous.

Dandelion, a native of Europe, is a common weed of grassland, gardens and waste places on nitrogen-rich soils. It is one of the most useful of native British medicinal herbs as all parts of the plant are effective and safe to use; it is regarded as one of the best herbal remedies for kidney and liver complaints. The common name, Dandelion, is a corruption through the French *dent de lion* (= lion's tooth) of the medieval Latin name *dens leonis*, after the jagged edge of the leaves.

The roots, flowering stems, leaves (collected before flowering) and flowerheads are used medicinally. The root is the most active part. The constituents include the terpenoid bitter compounds taraxacin and taraxacerin, a glycoside, sterols, amino acids, tannins, inulin (up to 25 per cent), mineral substances, rubber (caoutchouc) and provitamin A, vitamins B and C (in leaves). These substances give Dandelion bitter tonic, stomachic, cholagogic, nutritive and strong diuretic properties. It is used in an infusion to stimulate the appetite, aid digestion, for biliary and liver disorders, dropsy, rheumatism and arthritis. The pressed juice from the stalks or leaves is an effective cure for warts. The fresh young leaves can be eaten raw as a spring salad. The flowers contain carotenoids and triterpenes. They are used, boiled with sugar, for coughs but honey has greater medicinal value. They can be made into an excellent wine.

The roots, dried, roasted and ground, make a caffein-free coffee substitute.

Dried flowering stems

Detail of fruit

Fruit

Flowering time: April to October

Yew

Twig with male flowers

An evergreen coniferous shrub or tree with a stout trunk, usually a rounded crown and reddish-brown scaly bark. The alternate leaves (needles) are long, narrow and flattened, dark green above, paler below, and have inrolled margins. Yew is dioecious: the male flowers are in globose yellow cones and produce abundant pollen; the tiny green female flowers, resembling buds, are borne singly on short stalks in the leaf axils. The ripe fruit consists of a seed partially enclosed by a bright-red, fleshy cup-like structure (aril). **All parts of the plant, except the red arils, are extremely poisonous, especially the seeds.**

Yew was once common and widespread in Europe but it is becoming rarer and is now protected in many countries. In the British Isles it grows wild on cliffs, in scrub and in woods, usually on lime-rich soils. A few ancient native Yew woods survive in southern England. It is also often planted out for ornament in parks and gardens in several different varieties. Yew wood is close-grained, tough, non-resinous and very flexible. It used to be used to make longbows, hence the name *Taxus*, which comes from the Greek word *taxon* (= bow). The common name Yew is a corruption of the Anglo-Saxon word *iw* or *eow*. Yew was once used to treat snake bite and rabies but because of its extreme toxicity it is no longer used medicinally, except occasionally in homeopathy.

The needles contain the very toxic alkaloid taxine, also glycosides, bitter compounds, resin and vitamin C. In homeopathy a tincture prepared from the fresh needles is used, for example, to treat gout and rheumatism, arthritis, urinary tract infections and heart and liver conditions. The poisonous substances are absorbed within a matter of a few minutes from the gastrointestinal tract after ingestion. In small amounts they slow down the heartbeat and cause collapse and gastroenteritis; in larger doses they can cause sudden death. **Yew should never be collected and used for self-medication.**

Flowering time: March to April

Wall Germander

A perennial subshrub with a woody, creeping rhizome bearing tufts of square, ascending, purplish herbaceous stems. The opposite dark-green leaves are pointed oval and have rounded teeth. The pinkish-purple flowers are arranged in whorls of two to six in the upper leaf axils forming extended terminal spikes. The calyx tube has five teeth; the corolla has one five-lobed lower lip, with a large spreading middle lobe. There is no upper lip so the stamens are exposed. The fruit consists of four smooth nutlets. All parts of the plant are hairy and fragrant.

Wall Germander grows wild in southern and central Europe on dry sunny slopes, rocks and walls, and in woodland, chiefly on lime-rich soils. It is not native to the British Isles but it was introduced as a medicinal herb and as an edging plant in gardens and it can sometimes be found naturalized on old walls. The related Wood Sage (*T. scorodonia*), with greenish-yellow flowers, is, however, a native British species. Wall Germander is said to have been named after Teucer, son of Scamander, first king of Troy, who in Greek mythology used this or related plants as a medicine. The specific epithet, *chamaedrys*, probably also the common name Germander, are derived through the medieval Latin word *gamandrea* from the Greek *khamai* (= on the ground) and *drus* (= oak), an allusion to the shape of the leaves. Wall Germander was once a popular remedy especially for gout; it was also used in powdered form for treating head colds and as snuff. It and Wood Sage are still used by herbalists.

The flowering stems are used medicinally. Their constituents include an essential oil, flavonoids, bitter compounds and tannins. These substances give Wall Germander bitter tonic, astringent, stomachic, choleretic, antiseptic and diuretic properties. It is used to stimulate the appetite and improve digestion, and also for diarrhoea. Externally it is used to treat slow-healing wounds and haemorrhoids.

Flower

Flowering time: July to September

Breckland Thyme, Wild Thyme

Flower

A perennial herb, woody at the base, with mat-forming rooting branches and ascending or erect, square, hairy flowering stems. The opposite leaves are linear to elliptic, glandular and almost sessile. The violet two-lipped flowers are arranged in whorls forming dense terminal rounded spikes or heads. They are attractive to bees. The fruit consists of four small nutlets. All parts of the plant are aromatic.

Breckland Thyme is a very rare native British plant and grows only on the Breckland in East Anglia. It is more common elsewhere in Europe, where it is widespread on dry grassland and heaths on sandy soil and is called Wild Thyme. It is a very variable plant. More familiar in Britain is the cultivated Garden Thyme (*T. vulgaris*) (Pl. 233) and two other wild thymes – Wild Thyme (*T. praecox*) and Large Thyme (*T. pulegioides*). A fragrant cultivated form is Lemon Thyme (*T. × citriodorus*), which is a popular flavouring herb and a good bee plant. The derivation of the name *Thymus* (and Thyme) is confused. The name may come from a Greek word (*thumon*) for a herb used in sacrifices, because the plant was used as incense or as a fumigator.

The flowering stems are used medicinally. Their constituents include an essential oil (up to 0.6 per cent) with thymol and carvacrol as the main components, plus bitter compounds, tannins (3–7 per cent) and mineral substances. Thymol is a strong antiseptic, better than phenol because it does not burn the skin and it acts as a deodorant. The essential oil from this and other species of thyme (especially Garden Thyme), obtained by distillation from the flowering stems of wild or cultivated plants, is used in the manufacture of toothpastes, mouthwashes, gargles and other toilet articles. It is also contained in some proprietary preparations used as expectorants and antispasmodics in the treatment of whooping cough, bronchitis and gastrointestinal disorders. Externally the oil is sometimes used in bath preparations as a nerve tonic and in compresses or ointments for wounds.

Flowering time: May to September

Garden Thyme, Common Thyme

A perennial subshrub with much-branched, square, ascending stems, which are woody below. The opposite, small, linear to elliptic, almost sessile, evergreen leaves have inrolled margins and are white-felted below. The small white or pink two-lipped flowers are arranged in whorls in the upper leaf axils forming dense terminal spikes. The fruit consists of four nutlets. All parts of the plant are aromatic.

Garden Thyme is native to the Mediterranean region but it is widely grown elsewhere as a medicinal and culinary herb. It may have been introduced to the British Isles by the Romans. It is one of Britain's best known and most widely used culinary herbs and is cultivated commercially in market gardens. A variegated variety is sometimes grown for decorative purposes. The antiseptic and preservative properties of thymes were known to the ancient Egyptians who used the oil for embalming.

The flowering tops are used medicinally. Their constituents include an essential oil (up to 2.5 per cent) with thymol and carvacrol as the main components, plus tannins, bitter compounds, saponins and organic acids. The medicinal action is like that of Breckland (Wild)Thyme (*T. serpyllum*) (Pl. 232) but is stronger. Garden Thyme is an effective antiseptic; it also has expectorant, antispasmodic, carminative, deodorant and anthelmintic properties. It is particularly beneficial for gastrointestinal and respiratory disorders and against hookworm. In herbal medicine it is used in infusions, extracts, compresses, bath preparations and gargles. The distilled essential oil is widely used in the pharmaceutical, cosmetic and food industries (for some of the uses see Pl. 232).

Garden Thyme is an essential ingredient of *bouquet garnis;* on its own it can also be added (with care) to sauces, soups, meat and fish dishes. The fresh leaves give flavour to salads. In the liqueur industry Garden Thyme is used to give flavour and aroma to Benedictine.

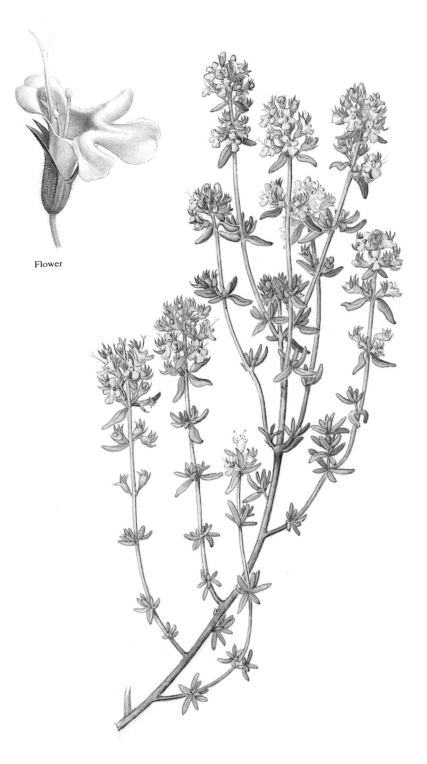

Flower

Flowering time: May to June

Small-leaved Lime

Dried flowers

A tall deciduous tree with a domed crown with downward-curving branches and smooth, grey, later rough and fissured bark. The stalked alternate, cordate leaves are slightly asymmetrical, sharply serrate, dark green and shiny above and greyish green below with rust-coloured hairs in the axils of the veins. The fragrant yellowish-white flowers are arranged in clusters of 3 to 15 in a stalked erect or spreading cyme, half-joined to a large oblong membranous bract, in the leaf axils. The fruit is an ovoid, hairy achene, the bract acting as a wing.

Small-leaved Lime grows wild in Europe in deciduous woods and woodland margins. It is a native tree of some parts of England and Wales, especially on lime-rich soils; elsewhere it is introduced. It is a popular tree for planting in avenues and in gardens. The flowers are a rich source of food for bees; one tree yields up to 10 kg of light-coloured honey. The generic name, *Tilia,* is the original Latin name for this and related species. The common name, Lime, comes from the Anglo-Saxon word *lind* – hence Linden Tree. *Lind* may derive from an Indoeuropean word meaning 'pliable', the reference being to the former use of the inner stringy bark fibres (bast) for making ropes and matts.

The flowers (linden blossoms) are used medicinally. When dry they have a pleasant scent and a mucilaginous taste. Their constituents include an essential oil, mucilage, tannins, flavonoid glycosides, saponins and sugars. These substances give the flowers strong diaphoretic, also antispasmodic, diuretic and mild sedative properties. An infusion – linden tea – is of benefit for feverish chills and flu. The flowers are also used to stimulate the appetite, for digestive disorders, respiratory catarrh and to soothe the nerves. They are often used in diuretic tea mixtures. Charcoal made from dry lime twigs is used to expel gas from the intestines, to counteract stomach acidity, to treat gall bladder and liver disorders and in cases of poisoning. The bark is also used.

Flowering time: July

Large-leaved Lime

A tall deciduous tree with a narrow crown, spreading branches and smooth grey, later fissured bark. The stalked alternate leaves are larger than those of Small-leaved Lime (*T. cordata*) (Pl. 234); they are dark green and hairy above, paler and hairy below, with whitish tufts in the axils of the veins. The leaf stalks are also hairy. The fragrant yellowish-white flowers are arranged in clusters of only three to seven in a stalked pendulous cyme, half-joined to a membranous bract, in the leaf axils. They produce abundant pollen. The fruit is an ovoid, hairy, ribbed achene, the bract acting as a wing.

Large-leaved Lime is probably native to the British Isles but it is not common in the wild. However, it has long been planted in avenues, parks and gardens. The commoner Lime (*T. × vulgaris*), another widely planted ornamental tree in British parks and gardens, originated as a hybrid between Large-leaved Lime and Small-leaved Lime. The specific name of Large-leaved Lime, *platyphyllos,* means 'broad-leaved'.

The flowers act medicinally like those of Small-leaved Lime. They contain a small amount of an essential oil, mucilage, tannins, saponins, flavonoid glycosides and sugars. The glycosides are primarily responsible for the diaphoretic action of lime flowers. The dried flowers are used on their own or in various herbal tea mixtures to stimulate the appetite, alleviate rheumatic pain, for colds and chills, and for urinary disorders. They are also beneficial for insomnia and headaches. A decoction is used as a mouthwash, as a gargle for sore throats and also in cosmetic lotions and creams.

Flowering time: June to July

Red Clover

Seed

A perennial herb with a branched rhizome and erect or ascending, angled and branched stems. The alternate leaves are trifoliate with ovate and entire leaflets patterned with a characteristic white crescentic band on the upper surface. The reddish-purple or rarely whitish flowers are arranged in dense terminal, globose, sessile flowerheads. They are an important source of nectar for bees. The fruit is a pod, which contains one or two seeds and opens by the top falling off.

Red Clover is native to Europe and it is common throughout the British Isles in pastures, meadows and other grassy places. It is also widely cultivated as an animal fodder or for ploughing in to enrich the soil. This and related species were named *Trifolium* after their three-lobed (trefoil) leaves. The common name, Clover, comes from the Anglo-Saxon word *claefre*. In the past Red Clover has mostly been used as a vulnerary. It is still used in herbalism, internally as well as externally.

The flowerheads are the medicinally active parts. Their constituents include tannins, phenolic glycosides, organic acids and organic pigments. These substances give Red Clover astringent, expectorant, antispasmodic and vulnerary properties. An infusion is used to treat bronchitis, coughs, hoarseness, diarrhoea and chronic skin conditions. It is also a component of herbal tea mixtures for treating chest colds and stomach disorders, giving these mixtures, in addition, a pleasant taste and smell. Externally Red Clover is used in compresses and bath preparations to treat rashes, ulcers, burns and sores.

Red Clover flowers make a pleasant tea substitute. The fresh young leaves can be added to salads and soups or cooked and eaten like spinach.

Flowering time: May to September

White Clover, Dutch Clover

A perennial herb with creeping stems that rise at the tip and root at the nodes. The leaves are long-stalked, ovate, trifoliate, finely serrate and patterned with a whitish angled band on the upper surfaces. The white or pinkish flowers are arranged in terminal solitary, dense, globose, long-stalked heads. They are an important source of nectar for bees, yielding up to 100 kg of honey per hectare. After fertilization the flowers fold down over the fruits (pods) and turn brown. In the pods are three to six yellow-brown seeds.

White Clover grows in grassy places everywhere in the British Isles, especially on clay soils. With its rooting stems it is a troublesome weed in gardens. It is also grown as a fodder plant. The leaves of some cultivated strains contain a glycoside which produces prussic acid when eaten by animals and in larger quantities this can cause poisoning. For this reason plant geneticists have produced glycoside-free strains of White Clover. Like other clovers it is an important nitrogen-fixing plant and is grown to enrich the soil.

The flowerheads are the medicinally active parts. When dry they have a honey-like fragrance and a slightly astringent taste. The main constituents are tannins, sugars, mucilage and organic acids. These substances give White Clover astringent, anti-inflammatory and antiseptic properties. An infusion is used to treat gastritis, enteritis, severe diarrhoea and rheumatic pains. It is also used as an inhalent for respiratory infections. The fresh flowers make a pleasant substitute for ordinary tea.

The young leaves are edible like those of Red Clover (*T. pratense*) (Pl. 236).

Seed

Flowering time: June to September

Fenugreek

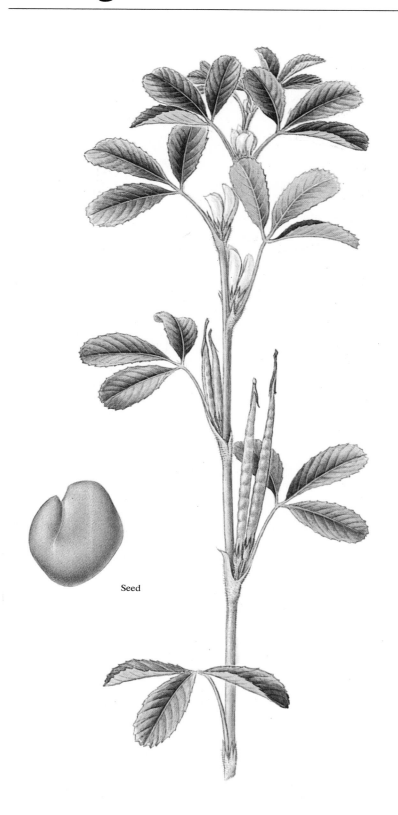

Seed

An annual herb with an erect or prostrate, smooth, little-branched stem and tri-foliate leaves, the leaflets oblanceolate to oblong and slightly toothed. The un-stalked yellowish-white, violet-tinged flowers are solitary or in pairs in the upper leaf axils. The fruit is a hairless, slender, slightly curved pod with an extended tip (beak). The seeds are yellowish brown and a deep furrow divides them into two unequal parts. All parts of the plant are sharply aromatic.

Fenugreek is native to the Mediterranean region but it has been widely cultivated since ancient times as a fodder crop and for medicinal and culinary purposes. The specific epithet, *foenum-graecum* (= 'Greek hay'), and the derived common name, Fenugreek (and also Foenugreek), are reminders of this history. The plant may become increasingly important as a source of a steroid precursor that could be used in sex hormone preparations.

The seeds are used medicinally. They are rich in proteins and mucilage; they also contain the nontoxic alkaloid trigonelline, choline, fatty oil, steroidal saponins (mainly diosgenin and yanogenin) and traces of an essential oil. The seeds have a pungent aroma and rapidly become mucilaginous when chewed. They have tonic, stomachic, demulcent, carminative, hypoglycaemic and galactagogic properties. In the form of a coarsely ground powder they are used to make a tonic herbal tea for convalescents. They also stimulate digestion, ease coughing and simulate milk flow. The unpleasant taste of the decoction or infusion can be disguised by mint or orange oil. Externally the crushed seeds are used to make hot, mushy plasters (which may be mixed with hot milk) applied to bruises, swellings, boils and ulcers. In veterinary medicine too the seeds are used to increase milk production.

Fenugreek is used as a spice especially by Middle Eastern and Indian peoples, and as a coffee substitute. The seeds can also be sprouted and eaten raw in salads.

Flowering time: June to August

Nasturtium, Indian Cress

A perennial or annual herb with a climbing or twining stem. The alternate, long-stalked leaves are reniform to rounded and entire. The large, long-stalked, trumpet-shaped flowers grow from the leaf axils. They are orange, yellow or white, occasionally scarlet or mahogany red and have a prominent spur. They are unscented but produce abundant nectar and are much visited by bees. The fruit is a three-celled capsule.

Nasturtium is a native of South America and was introduced to Spain from Peru in the 16th century and reached other parts of Europe in the 17th century. It soon became a popular garden ornamental. It was not till later that use was made of its medicinal properties. Many varieties have been developed including dwarf forms and some with double flowers. The plant was known from its introduction as *Nasturcium indicum*, later *Nasturtium indicum* or Indian Cress, *nasturcium* being the ancient Latin name for a kind of cress.

The seeds are used medicinally. Their constituents include the glucosinolate glucotropaeolin (up to 1.5 per cent), which hydrolyses to yield antiseptic substances (including a mustard oil); also fatty oil (up to 20 per cent) and proteins. The seeds are effective antiseptic agents against bacteria such as *Staphylococcus, Proteus, Streptococcus* and *Salmonella*. The antiseptic substances are eliminated in the urine and partly also through the lungs and so the seeds are used for acute infections of the urinary tract and for acute bronchitis. They are usually powdered and administered in the form of pills. The fresh juice from the plant has the same antiseptic effect.

The fresh leaves contain vitamin C and iron as well as antiseptic substances and they give a sharp, mustard-like flavour to salads. The open flowers, which can also be added to salads, are stimulants. The flower buds can be preserved in vinegar and used as a substitute for capers to flavour sauces and as a garnish.

Seed

Flowering time: May to October

Coltsfoot

Dried flowerheads

A perennial herb with a much-branched creeping rhizome and erect, purplish, woolly and scaly stems, which bear terminal, solitary, yellow flowerheads in early spring. The long-stalked basal leaves — roundish cordate with black-edged teeth and white-felted below — appear after the flowers have died. The fruit is a smooth achene with a long white pappus.

Coltsfoot is native to Europe, including the British Isles. It grows abundantly on bare and waste ground, arable land, roadsides, banks, screes and dunes, usually on damp soil. It is a long-established remedy for coughs and this traditional use is reflected in the generic name, *Tussilago*, which comes from the Latin word *tussis* (= cough). The common name, Coltsfoot, refers to the leaf shape — it is a translation of the medieval Latin name *pes pulli* (= foal's foot). It remains popular in herbal medicine.

The flowerheads (collected before they are fully open) and the young leaves are used medicinally. Their constituents include abundant mucilage, an essential oil, tannins, mineral salts, sterols, organic pigments (flowers), and a glycosidic bitter compound and inulin (leaves). These substances give Coltsfoot bitter tonic, expectorant, demulcent, astringent and anti-inflammatory properties. Because of the mucilage content it is used mainly in herbal tea mixtures for coughs, catarrh, bronchitis, laryngitis and asthma. It is included in some proprietary cough medicines too. Coltsfoot is also a component of tea mixtures taken to stimulate the flow of bile, to check diarrhoea and as a general tonic. A decoction is used externally in compresses, poultices and bath preparations applied to slow-healing wounds, skin ulcers and rashes. The dried leaves are included in herbal tobaccos to relieve chest troubles. The fresh leaves, after first being washed and crushed, are applied to skin inflammations and rheumatic joints.

The flowerheads can be used to make a pleasant wine.

Flowering time: February to April

Small-leaved Elm, <small>Smooth Elm</small>

A tall deciduous tree with a narrow crown, suckers and brown, smooth, later longitudinally furrowed bark. The alternate stalked leaves are obovate to lanceolate, with pointed tips, doubly serrate margins, smooth and shiny surfaces and asymmetrical bases. Clusters of almost sessile, greenish flowers with tufts of reddish stamens appear in early spring before the leaves. They are pollinated by the wind. The fruit is a broadly winged achene with the seed near the notch at the tip of the wing.

Small-leaved Elm grows in warmer parts of Europe in thickets, hedgerows and wet woods. It was once common in eastern and southern England but has greatly declined in numbers because of the spread of Dutch elm disease. This disease, which is caused by a fungus (*Ceratocystis ulmi*) and is spread by bark beetles, has also destroyed vast numbers of English Elm (*U. procera*). Wych Elm (*U. glabra*) is not only a hardier tree than Small-leaved Elm and English Elm — it grows further north and west than other British elms — it is also more resistant to Dutch elm disease. Elm wood is tough and durable, even in permanently wet conditions and consequently it is used for building boats and for harbour works. *Ulmus* is the original Latin name for the trees and the common name, Elm, is derived from it.

The yellow inner bark from young twigs of Small-leaved Elm and other elm species is used medicinally. As it dries it curls into a cylinder. It has an astringent taste. The constituents include tannins, bitter compounds and mucilage. These substances give the bark astringent, demulcent and anti-inflammatory properties and it is used in a decoction or in powder form to treat digestive disorders and severe diarrhoea. Externally a diluted decoction is used in compresses or bath preparations for inflamed wounds, haemorrhoids and as a mouthwash and gargle. In homeopathy a tincture prepared from fresh bark is given for ezcema and other skin complaints.

Fruit

Twig

Flowering time: March to April

Common Nettle, Stinging Nettle

Leaf:

U. dioica   U. urens

A perennial herb with a tough, creeping, branched rhizome and erect, square, leafy stems. The opposite, stalked leaves are cordate, long-pointed and coarsely serrate. There are four stipules at each node. The small green dioecious flowers are arranged in panicles in the upper leaf axils; the male clusters are spreading, the female ones pendulous. The fruit is an achene enclosed by the persistent perianth. All parts of the plant bristle with stinging hairs, the tips of which break off when touched and release formic acid and other substances that cause blistering, burning and itching of the skin.

Common Nettle is a common weed of hedgerows, woodland margins, wasteland and neglected gardens throughout the British Isles. Generally less common is the related annual Small Nettle (*U. urens*), which is smaller, more easily uprooted and stings less powerfully than Common Nettle. In some countries nettles are grown commercially as a source of chlorophyll. The generic name, *Urtica*, comes from the Latin word *uro* (= I burn). The common name, Nettle, comes from the Anglo-Saxon word *netele*. Originally this word may be derived from a root meaning a needle, referring either to the sharp sting or to the old use of the fibrous nettle stems in cloth-making.

The flowering stems and the leaves are used medicinally. Their constituents include tannins, histamine, 5-hydroxytryptamine, organic acids, vitamin C, provitamin A and mineral salts. These substances give Common Nettle astringent, tonic, diuretic, haemostatic, antirheumatic, galactagogic and blood-purifying properties and the plant has many therapeutic applications in herbalism and homeopathy. For example, it is used to treat urinary, liver and respiratory disorders, gastritis and enteritis, rheumatism and skin disorders.

The young shoots are rich in vitamin C and can be added to salads or cooked like spinach. They make a pleasant beverage, nettle beer. Nettle is also recommended as a hair tonic and face wash.

Flowering time: July to September

Bilberry, Whortleberry, Blaeberry

A low deciduous subshrub with a creeping rhizome and numerous erect, leafy, branched, green and angled stems. The alternate, shortly stalked leaves are oval, finely serrate and bright green; they are easily distinguished from those of Cowberry (*V. vitis-idaea*) (pl. 244). The pitcher-shaped pink or greenish-pink flowers with very short turned-back lobes grow singly or in pairs in the upper leaf axils. The fruit is a globose, edible, blackish berry with a blue-grey bloom.

Bilberry is native to Europe and grows on humus-rich acidic damp soils in woods, heaths and on moors. It is common throughout much of the British Isles; it is rarer in eastern and southern England. *Vaccinium* is the ancient name for this and related plants. The specific epithet refers to the leaves, which are like those of Myrtle (*Myrtus communis*). The derivation of the 'bil' and 'whortle' in the common names is unknown; 'blae' means blue-black. The sweet fruits, which are rich in vitamins, have long been a popular food. They have also been a traditional remedy for diarrhoea.

The leaves of non-flowering twigs and the fruits are used medicinally. The constituents of the leaves include tannins, organic acids, a glycoside (arbutin) and plant insulins. These substances give the leaves astringent, antiseptic, diuretic and weak hypoglycaemic properties and they are used in an infusion for gastritis, enteritis, and diarrhoea. They are also included in herbal tea mixtures with an antisclerotic action. **It is advisable not to take this infusion in strong doses or over a long period of time.** The ripe berries are used fresh or dried. They contain sugars, pectin, organic acids, tannins, mineral salts, vitamins B and C and organic pigments (anthocyanins). Dried berries are chewed to check diarrhoea. Wine and an alcoholic extract from the berries also have a costive action. The pressed juice from the berries and conserves are beneficial for mouth and throat infections.

The wholesome berries can be eaten raw or stewed and made into pies.

Flowering time: April to June

Leaf:

V. vitis-idaea   *V. myrtillus*

Cowberry, Red Whortleberry

Twig and fruits of *Vaccinium oxycoccus*

Flowers of *V. vitis-idaea*

A low evergreen subshrub with a creeping branched rhizome and numerous erect, leafy, arched and rounded stems. The alternate, shortly stalked leaves are obovate, leathery, often notched, dark green and glossy above and gland-dotted below and they have inrolled margins. The leaves are sometimes confused with those of Bearberry (*Arctostaphylos uva-ursi*) (Pl. 22); the leaves of Cranberry (*V. oxycoccus*) and Bilberry (*V. myrtillus*) (Pl. 243) are quite different. The white or pinkish bell-shaped flowers with short turned-back lobes are arranged in short drooping terminal racemes. The fruit is a globose, red, edible berry.

Cowberry is native to Europe and grows on humus-rich acidic soils on rocky moors, heaths and in woods. It is found in upland regions of the British Isles. The berries are more acid than those of Bilberry and are not as popular for eating, though they have long been gathered as food. Cranberries — red, like cowberries — are also edible. The specific epithet, *vitis-idaea,* means 'grapevine of Mount Ida' (in Asia Minor). The common name Cowberry is a translation of the generic name, *Vaccinium.*

The leaves and fruits are used medicinally. The constituents of the leaves include glycosides (mostly arbutin), tannins, organic acids, sugars and vitamin C. These substances give Cowberry leaves astringent, antiseptic, diuretic and hypoglycaemic properties. Their effect is much the same as Bearberry's: they are used in an infusion to treat infections of the urinary tract and bile ducts, kidney stones, rheumatism and diarrhoea. The ripe berries have a high concentration of vitamin C; they also include the glycosides arbutin and vaccinilin, sugars and organic acids. The fresh or dried berries can be eaten raw or stewed as a remedy for diarrhoea, but not by individuals with inflamed kidneys or kidney stones for they contain oxalic acid. Because of the arbutin content **Cowbery should not be taken in strong doses or over a long period of time.**

Flowering time: May to June

Common Valerian, Valerian

A perennial herb with a massive root system and a short rhizome, which bears angular, erect, furrowed, usually unbranched stems. The opposite leaves are odd-pinnate with 7−13 entire, ovate or lanceolate, irregularly toothed leaflets. The lower leaves are usually stalked, the upper ones sessile. The small funnel-shaped white or pinkish flowers are arranged in a dense terminal corymb. The fruit is an ovoid achene with a pappus formed from the calyx.

Common Valerian is native to Europe and it grows in rough grassy and bushy places, often on damp soils. It is found in most parts of the British Isles. It is a very variable species and there are numerous microspecies. In some countries it is grown commercially for the medicinal root. The plant first came to be called *valeriana* in the ninth or tenth centuries. The name may be derived from the Latin word *valere* (= to be healthy), it may have come from an early herbalist, Valerius, who first used it medicinally, or it may derive from the Roman province of Valeria. Valerian was much esteemed in the Middle Ages when it was used as a sedative for treating certain kinds of epilepsy. It has remained a popular and effective herbal remedy for insomnia and 'nerves'.

The rhizome and roots of second-year plants are used medicinally. Among the constituents are an essential oil (0.5 to 1 per cent), valepotriates (epoxy-iridoid esters, such as valtrate), traces of alkaloids, bitter compounds and tannins. In combination these substances are sedative, hypnotic and antispasmodic. They are included in pharmaceutical preparations prescribed for nervous heart disorders, convulsions, nervous dyspepsia, depression, nervous exhaustion, anxiety, headaches and chronic insomnia. In herbal medicine an infusion is used for the same disorders and a tincture from the fresh root is used in homeopathy. **Valerian should not be taken in strong doses for a long period of time** because it can become addictive and may also cause other side-effects.

Lower part of plant

Flowering time: June to August

False Helleborine, White Hellebore, White Veratrum

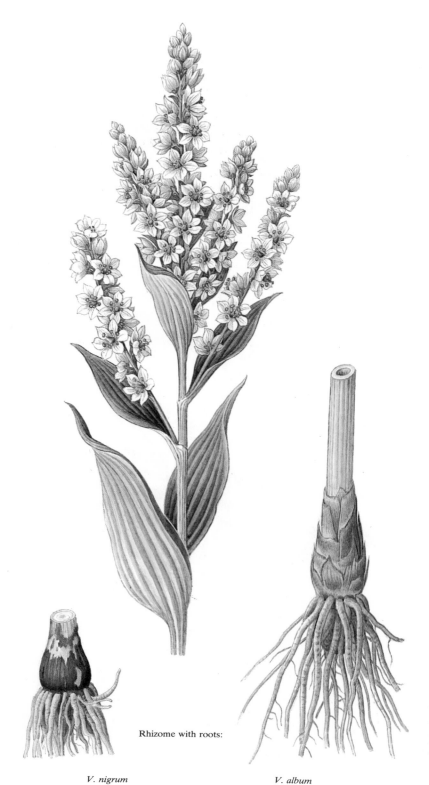

Rhizome with roots:

V. nigrum   *V. album*

A perennial bulbous herb with a massive root system, a short vertical rhizome covered with remnants of old leaf stalks and a robust, unbranched stem. The alternate, broadly ovate to elliptic leaves have sheathing bases, are longitudinally grooved along the prominent veins and are hairy beneath. The numerous yellowish-green, star-shaped flowers are arranged in compound panicles, the lowermost flowers are bisexual, the upper ones usually male. The fruit is a downy capsule. **All parts of the plant are extremely poisonous.**

False Helleborine grows in damp meadows in the hills and mountains of central and southern Europe, often forming spreading masses. It does not grow wild in the British Isles. The generic name, *Veratrum*, comes from the Latin words *vere* (= truly) and *atrum* (= blackish) and refers to the black rootstock of another European species, Black Hellebore (*V. nigrum*). Both these species — and American Hellebore or Green Hellebore (*V. viridis*) — have been used as arrow poisons and for medicinal purposes. These plants are rarely used in medicine today because of their toxicity but extracts are used by the pharmaceutical industry and they are occasionally used in homeopathy.

The rhizome and roots are the medicinally active parts. Their constituents include several toxic alkaloids, (for example, veratrine and protoveratrine A and B), which widen the lumen of blood vessels and lower blood pressure; also bitter compounds, glycosides, resin and organic acids. The alkaloids are processed to make antihypertensive and heart preparations. The plant was once prescribed as an antispasmodic, a diaphoretic, an emetic and a purgative and to treat rheumatic pain and neuralgia. Herbalists cannot now prescribe it in Britain. If taken internally False Helleborine causes collapse, severe vomiting and diarrhoea and breathing difficulties. Only 1 or 2 grams are fatal. **False Helleborine should never be collected and used for self-medication.**

Flowering time: July

Large-flowered Mullein

A biennial herb with a spindle-shaped branched root which bears, in the first year, a basal rosette of large, oblong to elliptic, pointed, entire or crenate leaves and, in the second year, a robust, tall, usually unbranched stem terminated by a dense spike of sessile yellow flowers. The smaller stem leaves are alternate, sessile, ovate to elliptic, and have bases that extend down the stem as a wing to the leaf below. The three upper stamens are white woolly. The fruit is an ovoid capsule with small seeds. All parts of the plant are densely covered with yellowish-grey down.

Large-flowered Mullein grows throughout Europe on sunny dry banks, in woodland clearings and in waste places. It is a rare casual in the British Isles. A related and very similar species, Great Mullein or Aaron's Rod (*V. thapsus*), however, grows wild throughout Britain. Several mullein species are grown as garden ornamentals. **Except for the flowers, the plants are poisonous,** especially to animals, and the downy hairs on them can cause skin irritation. The origin of the names is explained in the next plate (Pl. 248). Several species of *Verbascum* have been used medicinally in the past, particularly as cough and cold remedies.

The flowers – without the calyx – are the medicinally active parts. After drying they are bright-yellow with a honey-like scent and mucilaginous taste. Their constituents include saponins, mucilage, glycosides, yellow pigments and tannins. These substances give Large-flowered Mullein expectorant, emollient, demulcent, antispasmodic, diaphoretic and mild diuretic properties. It is an important ingredient of herbal tea mixtures for treating chest colds and it is also included in some proprietary cough medicines. The extract is used in making emollient ointments. Externally Large-flowered Mullein is used in compresses and bath preparations for varicose ulcers and haemorrhoids. The medicinal properties of Great Mullein and Orange Mullein (*V. phlomoides*) (Pl. 248) are similar.

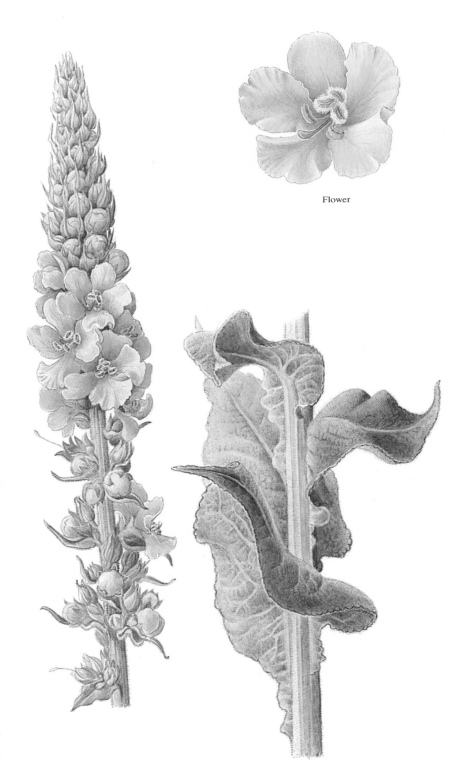

Flower

Flowering time: June to August

Orange Mullein

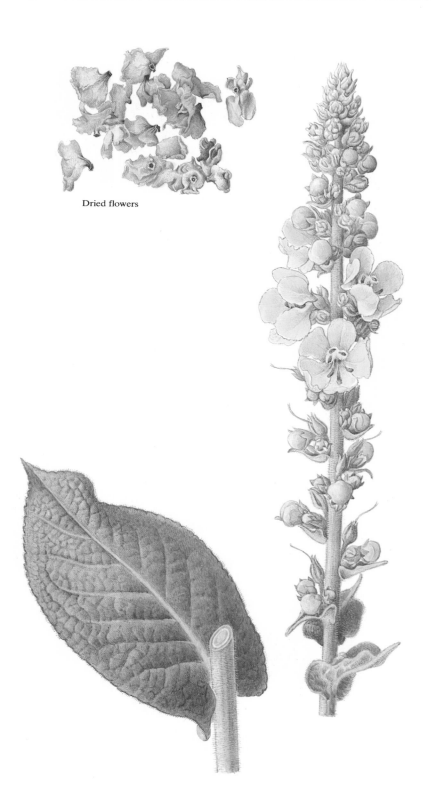

Dried flowers

A biennial herb, very similar to Large-flowered Mullein (*V. densiflorum*) (Pl. 247) but its stem leaves do not — or hardly — run down onto the stem and the flowers are larger, sometimes orange yellow, and are arranged in a looser spike. **The seeds are poisonous** and the plant is avoided by grazing animals as are other wild mullein species. All mulleins are attractive to bees.

Orange Mullein is native to central and southern Europe. It is, however, widely grown as an ornamental plant and it occasionally occurs in the British Isles as a casual. It is only rarely naturalized, however, and then mostly in southern England. The generic name, *Verbascum*, comes from the Latin word *barbascum* (*barba* = beard), after the 'bearded' stamens or downy foliage. The soft, felted leaves also gave rise to the common name Mullein, which comes through French from the Latin word *mollis* (= soft).

The flowers are used, like those of Large-flowered Mullein, in herbal tea mixtures for coughs and colds. The dried leaves are also used in tea mixtures. Fresh and bruised, the leaves are applied to slow-healing wounds. At one time the leaves of several mullein species were included in herbal smoking mixtures too. The root has been used to treat cramps, haemorrhoids and diarrhoea and the vinegar extract from the root was considered beneficial for toothache. In homeopathy tinctures of mulleins prepared from the fresh plants are still used to relieve earache and migraine.

The flowers yield a yellow dye, once used by women of ancient Rome to dye their hair golden yellow. They are still used to give aroma to some liqueurs and are included in cosmetic preparations.

Flowering time: June to September

Vervain

A perennial herb with a square, erect, stiff stem, loosely branched towards the top and sparsely leafy. The opposite, dull-green leaves are pinnately divided into oblong lobes, often with rounded teeth, the terminal lobe the largest; the upper leaves are smaller and less divided. The small, slightly two-lipped, pale-lilac flowers are arranged in long terminal spikes. The corolla tube is almost twice as long as the calyx. The fruit consists of four reddish-brown nutlets. All parts of the plant are roughly hairy.

Vervain grows wild in most parts of Europe in waste places and by waysides, always in a sheltered spot. It is uncommon in the British Isles, where it is native, and is mostly found only in England and Wales. Vervain has long been associated with magic and sorcery as well as with medicine. Roman soldiers carried it in their packs to protect them, and lovers used it in love potions. The common name, Vervain, is derived from *verbena,* which was the classical Roman term for altar plants used in religious ceremonies. Vervain was once believed to ward off plague and if worn round the head it would keep away headaches and prevent poisonous bites. It remains a popular herbal remedy for nervous complaints.

The flowering stems are used medicinally. Their constituents include the glycosides verbenalin and verbenin, tannins, an essential oil, mucilage, saponins and mineral compounds. These substances give Vervain astringent, diuretic, stomachic, tonic, diaphoretic, antispasmodic, vulnerary, mild sedative and hypnotic properties. It is used internally in an infusion for various disorders associated with the stomach, liver and kidneys. It is also excellent for stimulating the metabolism, for treating general nervous exhaustion, insomnia and migraine. Externally Vervain is used in gargles and in compresses and bath preparations for skin disorders. A tincture prepared from the fresh plant is used in homeopathy.

Flower

Flowering time: July to September

Heath Speedwell, Common Speedwell

A perennial herb with creeping, branched, often mat-forming stems which root at the nodes, and ascending flowering shoots. The opposite, short-stalked and sessile leaves are oval and bluntly serrate. The small white or lilac, dark-veined flowers are arranged in dense, slender, erect spike-like racemes that grow from the upper leaf axils. The stamens and style are also lilac. The fruit is a triangular to heart-shaped capsule. All parts of the plant are hairy.

Heath Speedwell is a common native European plant. It is found throughout the British Isles in woods, dry grassland and heaths. The genus *Veronica*, speedwells, may have been dedicated to St Veronica, who is said to have wiped Christ's face on his way to the Crucifixion. The name Speedwell was first applied to *V. officinalis* and refers to the plant's strengthening and healing powers.

The flowering stems are used medicinally. Their constituents include tannins, bitter compounds, an essential oil, organic acids, a glycoside (aucuboside) and vitamin C. These substances give Heath Speedwell astringent, expectorant, stomachic, vulnerary and diuretic properties but these actions are weak. It is still occasionally used in herbalism as a cough medicine and also for stomach complaints, kidney disorders and rheumatism. The decoction is sometimes used as a gargle, in hot compresses and as a bath preparation for rheumatic pain and skin disorders. It makes a pleasant tea substitute.

Flowering time: May to August

Lesser Periwinkle

A perennial herbaceous subshrub with creeping stems that root at the nodes and with short, ascending flowering shoots. The opposite, short-stalked leaves are evergreen, leathery and elliptic. The usually solitary blue, mauve or white flowers grow in the axils of the upper stem leaves. The five petals are slightly unequal in size and there is a white ring around the opening to the corolla tube. The fruit is a follicle with tiny, rough, blackish seeds. **All parts of the plant are poisonous.**

Lesser Periwinkle is native to the Mediterranean region and may also be indigenous in more northerly parts of Europe. It is occasionally found growing wild in the British Isles in woods, copses and on hedgebanks but it is probably not a native plant. Ripe fruits are rarely produced in Britain. It is grown as a ground cover plant in gardens, as is Greater Periwinkle (*V. major*), which is also poisonous. The generic name *Vinca* came originally from the Latin word *vincio* (= I bind), after the plants' long trailing stems, which were once used for tying and binding. Greater Periwinkle and a related plant, Madagascan Periwinkle (*Catharanthus roseus,* formerly *V. rosea*), were traditional remedies for diabetes.

The flowering stems are used medicinally. Their constituents include several alkaloids, tannins, saponins, pectin and organic pigments. These substances give Lesser Periwinkle tonic, astringent, hypotensive, vasodilating and diuretic properties. It is used in some proprietary preparations for cardiovascular disorders and in herbalism for treating bleeding from the nose and gums, for diarrhoea, coughing spasms and stomatitis, and in gynaecology. Greater Periwinkle has similar medicinal actions. **Both species should be used only under strict medical supervision: they should never be collected and used for self-medication.** Madagascan Periwinkle has been found to inhibit the growth of certain cancer-forming cells and two toxic alkaloids, vincristine and vinblastine, isolated from it are used to treat certain cancers.

Flowering time: April to July

Flower:

V. minor (white form)   *V. major*

White Swallow-wort, Vincetoxicum

Rhizome with roots

Fruit

A perennial herb with a rhizome, fibrous roots and a tall, erect, hollow stem. The opposite short-stalked leaves are oval to lanceolate with a heart-shaped base, sharply pointed, smooth and dark green. The yellowish-white flowers are arranged in loose terminal and axillary cymes. The fruit is an elongate capsule with downy seeds. All parts of the plant contain a milky juice (latex) and are **poisonous.**

White Swallow-wort is native to the eastern Mediterranean region but it has spread through cultivation elsewhere. It prefers warm, rather dry, lime-rich soils. The generic name, *Vincetoxicum,* comes from the Latin words *vinco* (= I conquer) and *toxicum* (= poison) for the plant causes vomiting.

The rhizomes and roots are the medicinally active parts but they are rarely used today. Their constituents include toxic glycosides (mostly vincetoxin), an essential oil, saponins, mucilage and sugars. These substances give White Swallowwort diaphoretic, diuretic, tonic and laxative properties. Strong doses cause retching and vomiting. **It should thus be used only under medical supervision.** A decoction is used externally in compresses for swellings and bruises.

Flowering time: May

Sweet Violet

A perennial herb with a short thick rhizome and creeping above-ground stolons that root at their tips. The cordate, crenate or toothed leaves are arranged in a basal rosette from which arise the solitary long-stalked, fragrant, violet or white, rarely pink flowers with two erect upper petals, two spreading lateral petals and a lower spurred petal. The fruit is a globose hairy capsule.

Sweet Violet grows in hedges, planted woodland and scrub throughout Europe, including most of the British Isles. It is introduced in Scotland. There are several garden varieties and in some countries Sweet Violet is cultivated commercially for the perfumery industry. *Viola* is the original Latin name for the plant and probably comes from the Greek word *ion* (= violet). From *Viola* has come the common name, Violet (through the French word *violette*). The specific epithet, *odorata,* means 'fragrant'; Sweet Violet is the only British wild violet to have scented flowers. It has been used medicinally since ancient Greek times and it remains a popular herbal remedy.

The leaves and flowers together or separately and the rhizome are used medicinally. The constituents of all parts include an aromatic essential oil, saponins, mucilage, a glycoside (violarutin), methyl salicylate and organic acids; the flowers also contain anthocyanin pigments. These substances give Sweet Violet expectorant and diuretic properties and the plant is used for bronchitis, whooping cough, coughs and head colds. It is also a component of diuretic tea mixtures that alleviate rheumatic pain. Externally Sweet Violet is included in compresses applied to swellings, slow-healing wounds, ulcers and rashes, and in mouthwashes or gargles. **In strong doses the rhizome is emetic and purgative.**

The fragrant essential oil, distilled from the fresh flowers, is used in perfumery and to colour medicines. The many garden varieties of violet with large, unscented flowers are not used medicinally.

Flower

Flowering time: February to April

Wild Pansy, Heartsease

Flower

An annual or perennial herb with tufts of creeping or erect angled, hollow, usually branched leafy stems. The stalked alternate leaves are cordate to elliptic, blunt-toothed or crenate, and have leafy palmately lobed stipules at the base of the petiole. From the leaf axils grow leafless flowering stems bearing the solitary flowers, which are yellow, white or violet, or a combination of these colours. The flowers have five unequal petals, the lower and largest one spurred. The fruit is a capsule which opens by three valves.

Wild Pansy is native to the British Isles and the rest of Europe and can often be found growing wild on cultivated and waste ground, in mountain pastures and on coastal dunes. It is a very variable plant and there are many subspecies which differ mainly in the colour of the flowers and the shape of the leaves. It hybridizes readily with related species and is one of the parents of the familiar large-flowered cultivated pansies. The common name Pansy is from the French word *pensée* (= a thought or remembrance). The plant is also associated with love and 'easing of the heart', hence one of its alternative common names, Heartsease. Wild Pansy has similar medicinal properties to Sweet Violet (*V. odorata*) (Pl. 253); it has long been used for skin disorders.

The flowering stems are used medicinally. Their constituents include saponins, mucilage, an essential oil, a bitter compound (violin), salicylic compounds, tannins, flavonoid glycosides and organic pigments (flowers). These substances give Wild Pansy expectorant, diuretic, diaphoretic, tonic, anti-inflammatory and blood-purifying properties. In herbal medicine an infusion is used for respiratory and urinary disorders, feverish conditions, rheumatic pain and chronic skin diseases, such as ezcema. **Strong doses may cause vomiting and allergic skin reactions.** Wild Pansy is also used as a cosmetic preparation for cleansing the skin and shampooing thinning hair, as a gargle, and it is applied in compresses or bath preparations to wounds and sores.

Flowering time: April to September

Mistletoe

A slightly woody evergreen perennial subshrub, which is semiparasitic (deriving mineral salts and water from the host plant) on branches of deciduous trees, often apple (*Mallus*), less commonly conifers. The sessile, opposite, yellow-green leaves — narrowly obovate and leathery — grow at the ends of the regularly branched stems. Mistletoe is dioecious: the small sessile male and female flowers grow in whorls of three to five at the fork between the axils of the branches. The fruit is a **poisonous** one-seeded, white, translucent berry.

Mistletoe is native to Europe and is generally widespread although in the British Isles it is absent from Scotland and Ireland. *Viscum* is the old Latin name for the plant and comes from the word *viscum* (= birdlime) after the sticky juice of the berries. The common name, Mistletoe, comes through the Anglo-Saxon word *misteltan,* perhaps from *mistel* or *mist* (= birdlime) and *tan* (= twig), a reference to the way the plant is spread by birds eating the berries and then depositing the seeds on tree branches in their droppings or wiping the sticky seeds off their beaks.

The young twigs, without the berries, and the leaves are used medicinally. Their constituents include a toxic substance (viscotoxin), choline, acetylcholine, alkaloids and proteins. These substances give Mistletoe hypotonic, vasodilating, cardiotonic, diuretic, sedative and antitumour properties. In medical practice preparations of Mistletoe are used to lower blood pressure, to stimulate heart action and to treat arteriosclerosis. Mistletoe leaves and stems (but not the berries) can be prescribed by herbalists. **In large doses Mistletoe is toxic and it should thus be used only under professional supervision.** The proteins responsible for the antitumour activities of Mistletoe have been the subject of recent research but they are unlikely to be incorporated in cancer drugs although one supposedly anticancer preparation made from Mistletoe extracts is used by homeopathic doctors.

Flowering time: March to April

Dried twigs and leaves

Flowers:

male   female

Maize, Indian Corn

Ripe cob

An annual cereal grass with solid furrowed stems and alternate, broadly linear leaves. It is monoecious: the male flowers are arranged in terminal panicles ('tassels'); the female flowers are clustered in a spike in an axillary spadix (cob) enclosed by modified leaves (the husk) with the yellowish styles (corn silk) hanging out of the husk in a tuft of threads. The one-seeded fruit is usually yellow in colour but it may range from white to black.

Maize is native to tropical Central America and was first grown there thousands of years ago. It is now cultivated throughout the world in many varieties, the familiar Sweet Corn being *Z. mays* var. *saccharata*. It is second to wheat (*Triticum* spp.) in world food production, being a staple food in many countries. Maize is also used in the food industry in the manufacture of edible oil, corn starch, glucose and some whiskies. The generic name, *Zea,* comes from a Greek word *zea* for a kind of grain. The common name, Maize, comes through the Spanish word *maiz* from an American Indian word *mahiz.*

The stigmas and styles of the female flowers, collected before pollination, are used medicinally. Their constituents include saponins, fatty oil, tannins, sugars, essential oil, resin, bitter compounds and mineral compounds. These substances give Maize diuretic (in fresh state), cholagogic, cardiotonic and hypertensive properties. It is occasionally used in herbal medicine for kidney and bladder disorders, arthritis and rheumatism and for the same disorders in homeopathy, when a tincture would be prescribed. From the germinating grains maize oil is extracted for many products. When refined it can be used for cooking. It is rich in unsaturated fatty acids and is also a source of vitamin E. Defatted cornmeal is a nourishing and easily digested food recommended for convalescents and individuals allergic to wheat gluten.

Flowering time: July to August

Glossary of botanical terms

Main parts of a flowering plant

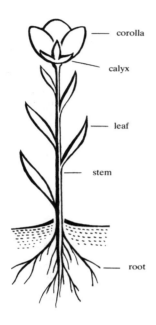

corolla

calyx

leaf

stem

root

Flower

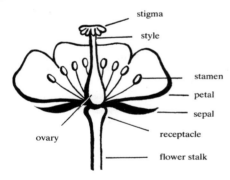

stigma

style

stamen

petal

sepal

ovary

receptacle

flower stalk

Achene   a small, dry, nutlike, one-seeded fruit that does not split open when ripe to release the seed; it may be winged (a *samara*).

Acute   (of leaves) sharply pointed.

Aerial   above ground.

Alternate   (of leaves) arranged successively on opposite sides of the stem.

Annual   a plant that completes its life cycle within one year from germination to death (cf. *biennial*).

Anther   the terminal part of one of the male organs (*stamens*) in a flower that contains the *pollen* grains.

Apex, apical   the growing point of a stem, the tip of an organ; hence apical bud or flower.

Appressed   flattened against but not joined to the stem.

Aromatic   having a distinctive, usually fragrant smell; applied to parts other than the flowers.

Ascending   curving upwards.

Axil, axillary   the upper angle between a *bract* or leaf and the stem on which it grows; hence axillary flower or bud.

Bark   the outer covering of a woody stem.

Basal   (of leaves) at the base of the stem.

Berry   a soft, fleshy or pulpy fruit, usually many-seeded.

Biennial   a plant that completes its life cycle within two years, growing in the first year and flowering and fruiting in the second year.

Bipinnate   (of leaves) when the divisions of a *pinnate* leaf are themselves pinnate.

Blade   the flat, expanded part of a leaf or petal; also the long, narrow leaf of a grass.

Bract   a small leaf or scalelike structure from the *axil* of which a flower or flower cluster often arises.

Bud   an immature shoot, leaves or flowers; also a partially opened leaf or flower.

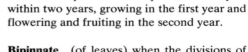

Bulb an underground storage organ with fleshy leaves and shortened stem, the whole enclosing next year's bud.

 Bulbil a small bulb or bulblike structure growing in a leaf axil or among the florets of a flower cluster, which falls to the ground and takes root there.

 Calyx (pl. **calyces**) the outer circle or whorl of the parts of a flower, whole or divided into separate green *sepals* and often joined together in a tube, the **calyx tube.**

 Capsule a dry fruit with one or more seeds, which splits open when ripe by pores or slits, but not down one side (a *follicle*) nor down two sides (a *pod* or *siliqua*).

Carpel a part of the female organ (*pistil*) of a flower, consisting of the *stigma, style* and *ovary* with ovules; there may be more than one carpel, either joined, which results in a partitioned ovary, or separate.

Casual an alien or introduced plant that occasionally grows wild in places but cannot maintain itself for long.

 Catkin a dense *spike* of small male or female flowers, usually long and tassel-like.

Cell (of fruits) the cavity containing the seeds.

 Compound applied to a leaf or flower cluster with a branched main axis.

Cone the flower, and usually the fruit, of a cone-bearing (coniferous) tree, consisting of numerous overlapping spirally arranged *scales*.

 Cordate (of leaves) heart-shaped with the point at the tip.

 Corm the short, underground, bulblike base of a stem that lasts one year, that of the next year growing at the top of the old one (cf. *tuber*).

 Corolla the circle of the parts of a flower immediately within the *calyx*, usually a whorl of coloured *petals,* which may be separate or joined into a tube, the **corolla tube.**

 Corymb, corymbose a flat-topped or convex *racemose inflorescence* with flower stalks of unequal length arising from different points on the main stem, the flowers on the outer (lower) stalks opening first; hence corymbose, in a corymb.

Crenate (diminutive: **crenulate**) (of leaves) with a shallow, rounded, scalloped edge.

Crown (1) a corolla-like ring of appendages (a corona) inside the perianth; (2) that part of the stem or stems that is at the surface of the ground; (3) the branches and upper part of the trunk of a tree.

Cultivar a variety of a plant that was produced from a natural species and is maintained by cultivation.

 Cyme a flower cluster (**cymose inflorescence**) in which the main stem does not continue to grow but forms a flower (cf. *racemose inflorescence*), which opens first; growth continues on new side branches, which in turn form flowers, and so on. There are two main types: a monochasial cyme or *monochasium* and a dichasial cyme or *dichasium*.

Deciduous applied to a tree or shrub that produces a new set of leaves for each growing season, dropping them in the autumn and regrowing them in the spring (cf. *evergreen*).

Decumbent lying on the ground but tending to turn upwards and become erect at the end.

Dentate (diminutive: **denticulate**) (of leaves) shallowly but sharply notched (toothed) at the edge, the teeth directed outwards.

Dichasium a *cyme* with side branches approximately opposite and equal, always longer than the main stem.

Dioecious with male and female flowers on different plants (cf. *monoecious*).

Disc-florets the small, usually tubular central florets of a compound *flowerhead,* typical of the daisy family (Compositae).

Divided (of leaves) separated towards the midrib or base.

Downy covered by fine, downlike hairs.

Drupe a fleshy fruit with one or more seeds enclosed by a stony layer.

Drupelet one drupe in a compound of drupes.

Elliptic(al) (of leaves) oval, but pointed at each end.

Entire (of leaves) not *toothed, lobed* or *divided.*

Erect upright.

Escape an alien or introduced plant now growing wild in an area.

Evergreen a tree or shrub that bears leaves all year, continually shedding and replacing them (cf. *deciduous*).

Family a group of related *genera.*

Feathery (of leaves) cut into many fine segments.

Female flower a flower with a *pistil* but no *stamens.*

Filament the stalk below the *anther* in a *stamen.*

Floret a small flower in a *flowerhead.*

Follicle a dry fruit that contains one or more seeds and splits down only one side when ripe.

Flowerhead (Capitulum) a compact, terminal, compound *racemose inflorescence* with stalkless flowers borne on a shortened main axis, typical of the daisy family (Compositae).

Free not joined to other organs.

Fruit the ripe seeds and their surrounding structures, which can be fleshy or dry.

Furrowed with longitudinal channels, or grooves

Genus (pl. **genera**) a unit of biological classification made up of closely related but distinct *species* and given a common name; genera are grouped into families. The genus is denoted by the first word in the scientific name.

Glabrous not hairy.

Gland, glandular an organ of secretion on the surface, either embedded or protruding, often on the tips of hairs; hence **glandular hairs.**

Globose spherical, usually applied to fruit.

Hermaphrodite with both male and female reproductive organs in the same flower.

Herb, herbaceous any non-woody, soft and leafy plant, hence a herbaceous perennial; also a plant used in medicine and cooking.

Hooded hood-shaped at the end.

Hybrid a plant produced by the fertilization of one species by another.

Indigenous a plant native to the area where it grows.

Inflorescence the arrangement of the flowers and their stalks on a stem or branch. An inflorescence is classified according to its mode of branching, which may be *racemose* (indefinite and not terminating in a flower) or *cymose* (definite and terminating in a flower).

Inrolled the edge of a leaf rolled in towards the centre.

Interrupted not continuous.

Introduced a plant not native to an area but brought in accidentally or deliberately by man.

Involucre a whorl of bracts that forms a structure like a *calyx* around or just below a flower or flower cluster, typical of the daisy family (Compositae).

Keel the lower petal(s) resembling the keel of a boat, typical of flowers of peas (Leguminosae).

Lanceolate (of leaves) narrow with the base broadest, tapering at each end like a lance or spear.

Lateral situated at the side.

Latex milky fluid exuded from some plants when injured.

Leaf axil angle between the leaf and stem.

Leaflet a subdivision of a compound leaf.

Ligulate (of florets) strap-shaped.

Linear (of leaves) long and narrow, almost parallel-sided.

Linear-lanceolate (of leaves) long and narrow, but tapering to a point at the tip.

Lip the lower part of an unsymmetric flower.

Lobed (of leaves) divided towards the midrib, but not into separate leaflets, each division rounded at the apex; some leaves have an enlarged terminal lobe.

Lyrate (of leaves) lyre-shaped.

Male flower a flower with *stamens* but no *pistil*.

Mericarp a one-seeded part of a multiseeded dry fruit (*schizocarp*).

Midrib the central vein of a leaf, usually thickened and conspicuous.

Monochasium a *cyme* with the branches spirally arranged or alternate or with one more strongly developed than the others.

Monoecious with separate male and female flowers on the same plant (cf. *dioecious*).

Native a plant naturally occurring in an area and not introduced from elsewhere.

Nectar a sugary liquid secreted by many flowers attractive to bees and other pollinating insects.

Nectary the nectar-secreting organ, usually at the base of the flowers of many plants.

Needle a long and very narrow leaf of a coniferous tree.

Node a point on the stem where a leaf or leaves arise(s).

Nut (diminutive: **nutlet**) a dry, one-seeded fruit that does not split open when ripe; like an achene but usually larger with a hard, woody outer covering.

 Ob- a prefix meaning inverted or opposite; hence **obovate** (of leaves), invertedly egg-shaped in outline with the widest part above the middle (cf. *ovate*).

 Odd-pinnate (Imparipinnate) (of leaves) *pinnate* with a terminal leaflet, that is, with an odd number of leaflets.

 Opposite (of leaves) growing in pairs at the same level on opposite sides of the stem.

 Oval (of leaves) broadly *elliptic*.

 Ovary the seedbox — the part of the *pistil* containing the ovules and later the seeds.

 Ovate (of leaves) egg-shaped in outline, with the widest part at or below the middle.

Ovoid an egg-shaped solid, usually applied to fruit.

Ovule the egg-containing structure in a flower, which develops into the seed after fertilization.

 Palmate (of *compound* leaves) comprising more than three leaflets arising from the same point.

 Palmately lobed (of leaves) deeply *lobed*, with the axes of the lobes converging on the same basal point.

 Panicle a branched *racemose inflorescence* with stalked flowers, the oldest of which is towards the base; may also be applied to any branched flower cluster.

 Pappus a tuft of hairs or bristles — a modified *calyx* — on some fruits, especially of some members of the daisy family (Compositae), enabling them to be carried away on the wind.

Parasite a plant living in or on another plant and obtaining its food from it.

Pedicel the stalk of a single flower.

 Pendulous drooping.

Perennial a plant that lives for more than two years and usually flowers each year; some herbaceous perennials grow from the root-stock each year, dying down to ground level for the winter.

 Perianth the outer, nonsexual parts of a flower, the *sepals* (*calyx*) and/or *petals* (*corolla*) as a whole. The term **perianth segment** is used to describe an individual sepal or petal when the sepals and petals are indistinguishable as either, as in many monocotyledonous plants.

Petal an inner flower leaf, usually brightly coloured and showy; the petals collectively form the *corolla*.

 Petiole a leaf stalk.

 Pinnate (of compound leaves) with three or more pairs of *leaflets* arranged in two opposite rows along a common stalk; there may be an unpaired terminal leaflet (*odd-pinnate*). Pinnate leaves may themselves be similarly divided — two (bi-) or three (tri-) times pinnate.

 Pinnately lobed (of *lobed* leaves) with opposite pairs of lobes, not separate leaflets.

Pistil the female organ of a flower, consisting of the *ovary* or seedbox, the *style* and the *stigma* which develop into the *fruit* after fertilization.

Pod a dry, many-seeded *fruit,* usually long and cylindrical and splitting open down both sides.

Pollen the powdery substance produced by the *anthers* of a flowering plant and by the male *cones* of coniferous plants, consisting of numerous fine grains — the male fertilizing agents.

Pollination the transfer of pollen by wind or insects from *anther* to *stigma* in flowering plants or from male *cone* to female *cone* in coniferous plants to start the process of fertilizing the *ovules.*

Pome a fruit of some members of the rose family (Rosaceae) with the seeds, surrounded by a tough but not woody or stony layer (the 'core'), embedded in the enlarged fleshy receptacle.

Procumbent trailing, lying loosely on the ground.

Prostrate lying flat close to the ground.

Raceme an unbranched flower cluster, usually conical in outline, with stalked flowers borne on an elongated axis, often without a terminal flower.

Racemose inflorescence a flower cluster, either conical or flattened in outline, in which the main stem continues growing at the tip and there is usually no terminal flower (cf. *cyme*); the flowers open in succession with the oldest flowers at the base and the youngest and smallest at the top. Types of racemose inflorescences include the *catkin, corymb, flowerhead* or capitulum, *panicle, raceme, spadix, spike* and *umbel.*

Ray the spoke or stalk of a small *umbel* in a compound umbel.

Ray-floret the usually strap-shaped (*ligulate*) marginal *floret* of a compound *flowerhead,* typical of the daisy family (Compositae).

Receptacle the cup-shaped, conical or flat uppermost part of the stem bearing the flower parts.

Reniform (of leaves) kidney-shaped.

Rhizome a creeping, usually horizontal underground storage stem, which sends up leafy shoots each season.

Rootstock the erect underground stem and roots of a perennial plant; also used as a general term for any root system.

Rosette a flattened, circular cluster of leaves usually at the base of the stem.

Runner a slender, creeping stem that grows along the surface of the ground and takes root at the tip to form a new plant that eventually becomes detached.

Sagittate (of leaves) shaped like an arrowhead.

Samara a winged *achene* ('key').

Scale a thin, dry structure, usually a modified or degenerate leaf.

Scape a leafless flowering stem that arises directly from the root.

Schizocarp a dry, many-seeded fruit that splits when ripe into one-seeded parts (*mericarps*).

Sepal an outer flower leaf, usually green but may be petal-like; the sepals collectively form the *calyx.*

Serrate (of leaves) saw-toothed at the edge, the teeth directed forwards.

Sessile stalkless; (of leaves) lacking a *petiole*; (of flowers) lacking a *pedicel*.

Sheath an enclosing or protective structure.

Shrub (diminutive: **shrublet**) a woody plant that produces its main growth from the base and does not reach a very large size.

Simple (of leaves) not divided into *leaflets;* (of stems) unbranched.

Silicula a pod, less than three times as long as broad, found in the crucifer family (Cruciferae).

Siliqua a pod, more than three times as long as broad, found in the crucifer family (Cruciferae).

Solitary borne singly.

Spadix a *spike* with a thick, fleshy stem usually enclosed in a *spathe*.

Spathe a *bract-* or petal-like sheath enclosing one or more flowers, usually a *spadix*.

Spathulate (of leaves) spoon- or paddle-shaped.

Species (abbreviation: **sp.,** pl. **spp.**) the basic unit of biological classification, a group of individual organisms with similar characteristics that can interbreed and usually cannot, or do not, breed with other species; species are grouped into *genera*. The species is denoted by the second word(s) in the scientific name.

Spike a compact *racemose inflorescence* with *sessile* flowers borne on an elongated axis.

Spikelet a secondary *spike* or part of a compound spike; in grasses a group of one or more flowers.

Spore the small reproductive body, usually one-celled, found in primitive plants such as mosses, fungi and ferns.

Spreading standing out horizontally or at a wide angle from the stem.

Spur the slender, usually *nectar*-secreting projection from the base of a petal or sepal.

anther —
filament — **Stamen** the male organ of a flower comprising a thin stalk (*filament*) with the *pollen*-producing *anther* at its tip.

Standard the large, often erect upper petal in flowers of, for example, the pea family (Leguminosae).

Stem the main axis of a woody or *herbaceous* plant, bearing the leaves, axillary buds and flowers.

Sterile lacking functional sex organs.

 Stigma the sticky or feathery tip of the *pistil* which receives the pollen.

 Stipule a small leaf- or *scale*-like appendage, usually paired, at the base of a leaf stalk.

Stolon, stoloniferous a slender, short-lived creeping stem that grows along the surface or below ground and takes root at the *nodes* to form new plants; hence a stoloniferous plant, one that produces stolons.

 Style the part of the *pistil* that connects the *ovary* and *stigma*.

Subshrub almost a shrub.

Subspecies (abbreviation **ssp.**) a subdivision of a *species;* subspecies are distinct in structure or colour but can interbreed and are therefore included in the same species. The characteristics separating subspecies are more marked than those separating varieties.

Synonym (abbreviation: **syn.**) a scientific name that has been superseded or rejected.

Taproot the main root, which grows vertically downwards and bears smaller lateral

Tendril a slender, clasping, twining organ, often formed from the whole or part of a stem or leaf or leaf stalk.

Terminal at the end of a stem or branch and limiting its growth.

Ternate (of compound leaves) comprising three leaflets, which may themselves be similarly divided — two (bi-) or three (tri-) times ternate.

Thallus a plant body that is not differentiated into roots, stems and leaves, and characteristic of lower plants (algae, fungi and lichens).

Thorn a sharp-tipped woody structure formed from a modified branch.

Throat the opening of a tubular or funnel-shaped *corolla* or *calyx.*

Toothed (of leaves) shallowly but sharply notched, with the teeth directed outwards.

Trifoliate (of leaves) with three leaflets or lobes.

Tripinnate (of leaves) three times divided in a *pinnate* manner.

Tube, tubular the united parts of a *corolla* or *calyx;* hence tubular *floret.*

Tuber, tuberous a swollen part of an underground stem or root; it lasts only one year, those of the next year not arising from the old ones (cf. *corm*); hence tuberous — producing, bearing or resembling a tuber or tubers.

Umbel an umbrella-shaped *racemose inflorescence* in which all the flowers or the secondary umbels in a compound umbel are borne on stalks (*rays*) which are of equal length and arise from a common point, typical of the carrot family (Umbelliferae).

Undulate (of leaves) wavy in a plane perpendicular to the surface.

Unisexual with separate male and female flowers.

Valve one of the parts into which a *capsule* splits.

Variety (abbreviation: **var.**) a subdivision of a *species,* that can arise naturally but is usually a cultivated form of a plant produced by vegetative (nonsexual) propagation.

net

parallel

Vein a strand of strengthening and conducting tissue running through a leaf or modified leaf, such as a petal. The arrangement of the veins (venation) takes one of several forms; for example, the veins may form a network (net venation) or be in a parallel (parallel venation).

Waste places uncultivated areas but much disturbed by man.

Wavy (of leaves) with curved indentations in the same plane as the surface.

Whorl a ring of several leaves of flowers around a stem (cf. *opposite*).

1

2

Wing (1) the lateral petals in certain flowers, for example those of the pea family (Leguminosae); (2) the membranous outgrowth on the side of certain seeds and stems.

Woolly with long, soft, more or less tangled hairs.

Glossary of medical terms

Abortifacient a substance that causes abortion.

Active constituent (principle) a medicinally effective chemical substance.

Acute (of a disease) of rapid onset, intense severity and brief duration (cf. *chronic*).

Adjuvant a substance that enhances the effect of another.

Alkaloid one of a diverse group of nitrogen-containing basic substances found in plants, usually with a strong medicinal action.

Allopathy a method of treating a disease by the use of drugs that induce in the body effects different from those of the disease (cf. *homeopathy*).

Amenorrhoea delayed menstruation.

Anaemia a deficiency in the number of red blood cells or in the quantity of oxygen-carrying haemoglobin in these cells.

Anaesthetic a substance that reduces or abolishes sensation.

Analgesic (Anodyne) a substance that relieves pain.

Anaphrodisiac a substance that reduces sexual desire.

Angina pectoris a sudden intense pain in the centre of the chest caused by momentary lack of adequate blood supply to the heart muscles.

Anhydrotic an *antidiaphoretic*.

Anodyne an *analgesic*.

Anthelmintic (Vermifuge) a substance that causes the death and elimination of intestinal worms.

Anorexia loss of appetite.

Antibiotic a substance produced by or derived from a microorganism that kills or inhibits the growth of other microorganisms.

Antidiabetic a substance that prevents or relieves *diabetes*.

Antidiaphoretic a substance that checks excessive perspiration.

Antidiarrhoeal a substance that combats diarrhoea.

Antidote a substance that counteracts a poison.

Anti-inflammatory a substance that counteracts inflammation.

Antineuralgia a substance that counteracts *neuralgia*.

Antipyretic (Febrifuge) a substance that reduces fever by lowering the body temperature.

Antirheumatic a substance that relieves *rheumatism*.

Antisclerotic a substance that reduces the amount of fat in the blood and helps prevent hardening (sclerosis) of the arteries.

Antiscorbutic a substance that counteracts *scurvy*.

Antispasmodic a substance or treatment that relieves or cures spasms of the smooth muscles.

Antiseptic a substance that kills or inhibits the growth of disease-causing bacteria and other microorganisms.

Antithrombotic a substance that prevents or interferes with the formation of a blood clot (thrombus).

Antitussive a substance that relieves or prevents coughing.

Aperient (Aperitive) a *laxative*.

Aperitif a substance that stimulates the appetite.

Aphrodisiac a sexual stimulant.

Aromatic a substance with a fragrant smell and usually a pleasant taste.

Arrhythmia any deviation from the normal rhythm of the heart.

Arteriosclerosis hardening and constriction of the arteries.

Arthritis inflammation of the joints, characterized by swelling, stiffness, pain and restricted mobility.

Asthma a condition characterized by difficulty in breathing and exhalation.

Astringent a substance that causes contraction of the tissues and stops bleeding.

Autonomic nervous system that part of the nervous system that controls the involuntary actions of the smooth muscles, heart, blood vessels and glands; the sympathetic and parasympathetic nervous systems are part of the autonomic nervous system.

Bacteriostatic   a substance that stops or retards the growth or multiplication of bacteria (cf. *antibiotic, antiseptic, disinfectant*).

Bitter   a bitter-tasting substance that stimulates the appetite by affecting the secretion of digestive juices.

Bronchitis   inflammation of the air passages characterized by coughing and the production of *mucus.*

Cardiac   any substance that affects the heart.

Cardiotonic   a substance that strengthens the heart's actions.

Carminative   a substance that relieves *flatulence* and griping pain in the stomach and intestines.

Catarrh   the excessive secretion of thick mucus by mucous membranes, especially of the nose and throat.

Cathartic   a substance that stimulates bowel action more forcefully than a laxative; a purgative.

Central nervous system   the part of the nervous system consisting of the brain and spinal cord.

Cholagogue   a substance that stimulates the release of bile from the gall bladder and bile ducts into the duodenum.

Choleretic   a substance that stimulates the production of bile in the liver.

Chronic   (of a disease) of long duration involving very slow changes (cf. *acute*).

Colic   sharp, convulsive abdominal pain.

Coma   a state of unrousable deep unconsciousness.

Compress   a wet or dry, hot or cold pad of material with or without medication applied with pressure to the affected part of the body.

Conjunctivitis   inflammation of the mucous membrane (conjunctiva) that covers the front of the eye and lines the inside of the eyelids.

Convulsions   a violent voluntary contraction of the muscles.

Costive   a substance with a constipating action.

Cramp   a painful spasmodic contraction of the muscles.

Decoction   the extraction of water-soluble constituents of a medicinal plant by boiling; a medicinal preparation obtained in this way.

Delirium   disordered state of mind with great excitement and often hallucinations.

Demulcent   a soothing substance that protects the *mucous membranes* and relieves irritation.

Diabetes (Diabetes mellitus)   a disorder of carbohyrate metabolism in which sugars in the body are not oxidized to produce energy because of the lack of the pancreatic hormone insulin.

Diaphoretic (Sudorific)   a substance that induces or increases perspiration.

Diarrhoea   the passage of liquid stools.

Digestive   a substance that aids digestion.

Disinfectant   a substance that kills bacteria and other microorganisms.

Diuretic   a substance that stimulates the elimination of water by increasing the production and flow of urine.

Dropsy   *oedema.*

Duodenal ulcer   a break in the lining (mucosa) of the duodenum caused by the action of acid digestive juices.

Dysmenorrhoea   painful menstruation.

Dyspepsia   indigestion.

Eczema   inflammation of the skin accompanied by itching, redness and weeping.

Emetic   a substance that causes vomiting.

Emmenagogue   a substance that stimulates menstruation; was often used as a euphemism for an *abortifacient.*

Emollient   a substance that soothes and softens the skin.

Enteritis   inflammation of the small intestine, usually causing diarrhoea.

Essence   a solution of an *essential oil* in alcohol.

Essential oil   a volatile oil present in aromatic plants, usually containing terpenoid substances.

Expectorant   substances that stimulate the formation and expulsion of phlegm (*sputum*) from the respiratory tract.

Extract   a concentrated preparation of the active constituents of a plant or animal drug obtained by evaporating a solution of the drug in water, alcohol or ether.

Fatty (Fixed) oil   a natural vegetable or animal oil that is not volatile (cf. *essential oil*); a mixture of esters of fatty acids, usually triglycerides.

Febrifuge   an *antipyretic*.

Fetid (Foetid)   having a malodorous, stinking smell.

Flatulence   generation of gas in the stomach and intestines.

Flavonoid   any of a group of organic pigments found in plants derived from flavones and related substances, often associated with glycosides.

Galactagogue   a substance that stimulates milk production.

Galenical   a standard medicinal preparation made from crude material of plant or animal origin.

Gallstone   a hard mass formed of cholesterol, bile pigments and calcium salts in the gallbladder or bile duct.

Gastritis   inflammation of the lining of the stomach.

Gastroenteritis   inflammation of the stomach and small intestine, usually causing vomiting and diarrhoea.

Germicide   a substance that kills bacteria and other microorganisms.

Glycoside   one of a group of substances in plants containing a carbohydrate molecule (sugar), convertible by hydrolysis into sugar and a nonsugar component.

Gout   a metabolic disease characterized by painful inflammation of certain joints caused by deposits of salts of uric acid (urates) in them.

Gravel   small stones formed in the urinary tract which are passed with the urine.

Haemolysis   the destruction of red blood cells.

Haemorrhage   profuse internal or external bleeding.

Haemorrhoids (Piles)   enlarged (varicose) veins in the wall of the anus.

Haemostatic (Styptic)   a substance that checks or stops bleeding.

Hallucination   a false perception of something that is not present.

Hallucinogen   a substance that produces hallucinations.

Hepatitis   inflammation of the liver.

Homeopathy   a method of medical treatment where very small amounts of drugs are administered producing in the body symptoms similar to those of the disease (cf. *allopathy*).

Hormone   a substance produced in the body by an organ or cells of an organ and transported to another organ where it has a specific regulatory effect.

Hypertensive   a substance that increases blood pressure.

Hypoglycaemic   a substance that reduces the level of blood sugar.

Hypotensive   a substance that reduces blood pressure.

Hypnotic (Soporific)   a substance that induces sleep.

Influenza (Flu)   a virus infection involving the respiratory tract.

Infusion   the extraction of water-soluble constituents of a medicinal plant by steeping in water that has been brought to the boil; a medicinal preparation that has been obtained in this way.

Insecticide   a substance that kills insects.

Insomnia   the chronic inability to fall asleep or to remain asleep for an adequate amount of time.

Irritant   a substance that causes irritation of a tissue.

Laxative (Aperient)   a substance that loosens the bowels and eases constipation.

Lotion   a medicinal solution for external application to the body.

Maceration   the softening of a hard substance by soaking.

Metabolism   the sum of all the physical and chemical processes that take place in the body and enable its continued growth and functioning.

Migraine   a recurrent throbbing headache usually affecting only one side of the head an often accompanied by nausea and visual disturbances.

Mucilage   a complex gelatinous carbohydrate secreted by certain plants.

Mucous membrane (Mucosa)   the moist membrane lining many body cavities and passages, including the respiratory and digestive tracts.

Mucus   a slimy protective secretion of the mucous membranes consisting chiefly of glycoproteins.

Narcotic   a substance that induces stupor and insensibility and relieves pain.

Nausea   a feeling of sickness.

Nephritis   inflammation of the kidneys.

Neuralgia   a stabbing pain along the course of one or more nerves.

Oedema (Dropsy)   the excessive build-up of fluid in the body tissues.

Parkinson's disease (Parkinsonism)   a neurological disorder characterized by impaired muscular co-ordination, rigidity and tremor.

Pectin   one of a group of acid polysaccharides found in plants; they form gels with sugar in the right conditions.

Peptic ulcer   a break in the lining (mucosa) of the digestive tract caused by the action of acid digestive juices.

Peristalsis   a succession of waves of involuntary muscular contractions of various hollow tubes of the body, especially of the digestive tract, where it affects the transport of food and waste products.

Pharmacist   a person qualified by examination and registration to prepare and dispense drugs.

Pharmacopoeia   an authoritative publication containing a list of drugs and details of the formulae, preparation, standards of production, dosages and uses of medicines.

Phlegm   *sputum.*

Piles   *haemorrhoids.*

Plaster   a paste-like medicinal mixture which can be applied to the affected part of the body and is adhesive at body temperature.

Pleurisy   inflammation of the covering of the lungs (pleura) so that there is pain on breathing and coughing.

Poultice   a pad of hot moist material applied to the affected part of the body.

Purgative   a substance that causes bowel evacuation but more quickly and forcefully than a laxative.

Rheumatism   any of a variety of disorders marked by aches and pains in the joints and muscles.

Rubefacient   a local irritant causing reddening and warming of the skin.

Salivation   the secretion of saliva by the salivary glands of the mouth, especially in excessive amounts.

Saponin   any of a group of plant *glycosides* that produce a soapy foam in water.

Sciatica   intense pain and tenderness felt down the back and outer side of the thigh, leg and foot along the course of the body's longest (sciatic) nerve.

Scurvy   a disease caused by a deficiency of vitamin C.

Sedative   a substance that has a calming effect, relieving anxiety and tension; it may cause drowsiness.

Sputum   saliva mixed with mucus coughed up from the respiratory tract.

Stimulant   a substance that increases physiological activity, especially of an organ.

Stomachic   a substance that stimulates the secretory activity of the stomach and is used as a tonic to improve the appetite.

Stomatitis   inflammation of the mucous lining (mucosa) of the mouth.

Styptic   a *haemostatic.*

Sudorific   a *diaphoretic.*

Tannin   one of a group of complex compounds found in many plants containing acids, phenols and glycosides.

Therapeutics   the branch of medicine concerned with methods of treating diseases.

Thrombosis   the formation or presence of a blood clot (thrombus) in a blood vessel or in the heart.

Tincture   a medicinal extract in a solution of alcohol or alcohol and water.

Tonic   a substance that stimulates and invigorates the body or an organ.

Toxic   poisonous.

Tranquillizer   a substance that has a calming effect, relieving anxiety and tension; less likely to cause drowsiness than a sedative.

Tremor   an involuntary trembling, shivering or shaking.

Urolith   a stone (calculus) in the urinary tract.

Varicose veins   a condition in which the superficial veins, especially of the legs, become distended, lengthened and tortuous.

Vasoconstrictor   a substance that constricts the blood vessels so causing a decrease in blood flow and an increase in blood pressure.

Vasodilator   a substance that dilates the blood vessels so causing an increase in blood flow and a decrease in blood pressure.

Vitamin   one of a group of unrelated substances that are essential in trace amounts for healthy growth and development; they cannot be synthesized in the body but occur naturally in certain plant and animal foods.

Volatile oil   an *essential oil.*

Vulnerary   a substance that counteracts inflammation and promotes the healing of wounds.

Reading list

Anderson, F.J. *An illustrated history of the herbals.* Columbia University Press: New York, 1977.

Blunt, W. & Raphael, S. *The illustrated herbal.* Frances Lincoln/Weidenfeld & Nicolson: London, 1979.

Boxer, A. & Back, P. *The herb book.* Octopus Books: London, 1980.

British Herbal Pharmacopoeia, Parts 1–3. British Herbal Medicine Association: London, 1976–81.

Dyer, S. *A pocket book on herbs.* Octopus Books: London, 1982.

Eagle, R. *Herbs, useful plants.* BBC Publications: London, 1981.

Fitter, R., Fitter, A. & Blamey, M. *The wild flowers of Britain and northern Europe,* 3rd edn. Collins: London, 1974.

Grieve, M. *A modern herbal* (ed. & introd. by C.F. Leyel). Penguin Books: London, 1976.

Griggs, B. *Green pharmacy: a history of herbal medicine.* Jill Norman & Hobhouse: London, 1981.

Griggs, B. *The home herbal: a handbook of simple remedies.* Jill Norman & Hobhouse: London, 1982.

Grigson, G. *The Englishman's flora.* Paladin Books: St Albans, Herts, 1975.

Groves, E. *Growing herbs.* The Herb Society: London, 1977.

Growing herbs. The Herb Society: London, 1977.

Hepper, F. N. *Bible plants at Kew.* HMSO: London, 1981.

Hlava, B. & Lánská, D. *A guide in colour to kitchen herbs and spices.* Octopus Books: London, 1980.

Inglis, B. *Natural medicine.* Collins: London, 1979.

Launert, E. *The Hamlyn guide to edible and medicinal plants of Britain and northern Europe.* Hamlyn: London, 1981.

Law, D. *The concise herbal encyclopedia,* 2nd edn. John Bartholomew: Edinburgh, 1982.

Le Strange, R. *A history of herbal plants.* Angus & Robertson: London, 1977.

Leung, A.Y. *Encyclopedia of common natural ingredients used in food, drugs and cosmetics.* John Wiley: Chichester and New York, 1980.

Loewenfeld, C. & Back, P. *The complete book of herbs and spices,* 2nd edn. David & Charles: Newton Abbot, 1978.

Loewenfeld, C. & Back, P. *Herbs for health and cookery.* Pan Books: London, 1965.

Martindale's extra pharmacopoeia, 27th edn. Pharmaceutical Press: London, 1977.

Masefield, G.B., Wallis, M., Harrison, S.G. & Nicholson, B.E. *The Oxford book of food plants.* Oxford University Press: London, 1979.

Ministry of Agriculture, Fisheries and Food. *British poisonous plants,* 2nd edn. Reference book 161. HMSO: London, 1968. *Culinary and medicinal herbs,* 4th edn. Reference book 325. HMSO: London, 1980.

Mitton, F. & Mitton, V. *Mitton's practical modern herbal.* Foulsham: London, 1982.

Page, M. & Stearn, W.T. *Culinary herbs.* Wisley handbook 16. The Royal Horticultural Society: London, 1979.

Polunin, O. *Flowers of Europe.* Oxford University Press: London, 1979.

Reader's Digest nature lover's library. Field guide to the wild flowers of Britain; Field guide to the trees and shrubs of Britain. Reader's Digest: London, 1981.

Schauer, T. *A field guide to the wild flowers of Britain and Europe.* Collins: London, 1982.

Stobart, T. *Herbs, spices and flavourings.* Penguin Books: London, 1977.

Stuart, M. (ed.) *Encyclopedia of herbs and herbalism.* Orbis Books: London, 1979 (also published in an abbreviated form as *The colour dictionary of herbs and herbalism,* 1982).

Thomson, W.A.R. (ed.) *Healing plants: a modern herbal.* Macmillan: London, 1980.

Trease, G.E. & Evans, W.C. *Pharmacognosy,* 12th edn. Baillière Tindall: London, 1983.

Useful addresses

British Herbal Medicine Association
Lane House, Cowling, Keighley, W. Yorks BD22 0 LX. Tel. 0535 34487

The Herb Society
34 Boscobel Place, London SW1W 9PE. Tel. 01-235 1530

Botanical Society of the British Isles
c/o Department of Botany, British Museum (Natural History), Cromwell Road, London SW7 5BD

National Institute of Medical Herbalists
148 Forest Road, Tunbridge Wells, Kent TN2 5EY. Tel. 0892 30400

Index of scientific names

Numbers in bold type refer to main entries

Index of common names

Numbers in bold type refer to main entries

320